D1521231

The Role of Sisters in Women's Development

The Role of Sisters in Women's Development

SUE A. KUBA

OXFORD
UNIVERSITY PRESS

OXFORD
UNIVERSITY PRESS

Oxford University Press, Inc., publishes works that further
Oxford University's objective of excellence
in research, scholarship, and education.

Oxford New York
Auckland   Cape Town   Dar es Salaam   Hong Kong   Karachi
Kuala Lumpur   Madrid   Melbourne   Mexico City   Nairobi
New Delhi   Shanghai   Taipei   Toronto

With offices in
Argentina   Austria   Brazil   Chile   Czech Republic   France Greece
Guatemala   Hungary   Italy   Japan   Poland   Portugal   Singapore
South Korea   Switzerland   Thailand   Turkey   Ukraine   Vietnam

Published by Oxford University Press, Inc.
198 Madison Avenue, New York, New York 10016
www.oup.com

Oxford is a registered trademark of Oxford University Press

Library of Congress Cataloging-in-Publication Data

Kuba, Sue A.
   The role of sisters in women's development / Sue A. Kuba.
      p. cm.
   Includes bibliographical references.
   ISBN 978-0-19-539334-7
1.   Sisters—Psychology. 2.   Women—Psychology. 3.   Families—Psychological aspects.   I. Title.
   HQ759.96.K82 2011
   155.9'24—dc22
                                                      2010025248

Printed in the United States of America
on acid-free paper

In the still silence of my days during the writing of these pages, I have been sustained by my sisters' support and love. I have written this book because of them.

To Sally, whose life and growth have inspired me
To Barb, whose wit and wisdom have kept me humble

ACKNOWLEDGEMENTS

In the end, a book—especially one about relationships—is a story told with the unimaginable aid of others. It provides a window on a world in time—the time of the author's life and of those who surround her. The context for this book is the early 21st century—a time of turmoil and change perhaps leading to better growth and mutual understanding. That is the hope. At this time it seems even more important to begin to understand the close nature of our connections with others, the potential they have to make us better human beings and the contributions they make to who and what we have become. Without blame for my shortcomings, I would like to thank many people for their assistance, but even more I would like to thank them for their relationships with me and the way those have inspired this book.

The women whom I interviewed shared their life stories in ways that were more candid than I dared hope. They were expressive, kind, and generous in their support of this project. I will always remember the warmth of their faces as they invited me into their homes to discuss the joys and sorrows of the connection they felt with their sisters. Some offered me tea or coffee—one had fresh baked cookies. They genuinely wanted to tell their story, and I was deeply moved by their thoughts and words.

During the development of this research, its implementation, and the writing of the book I have enjoyed the generous support of Alliant International University and the California School of Professional Psychology. They have provided me with a strongly supportive network of psychology colleagues and a group of research assistants. Diane Lassman assisted in the development of the research project, helped to interview the women for the study, and completed some initial data analysis. Christine Szostak and Kristin Shelesky provided initial reading of some chapter drafts and gave a student perspective on the material presented. Bianca Cota provided editorial and referencing assistance in the final stages including a monumental effort at tracking all of the reference material by chapter for the final edition of the book. My professional colleagues at CSPP asked frequently about the progress of the book, encouraged my completion of it, and provided me with sabbatical time that proved essential in the final draft of the manuscript. Special thanks to Drs. Sue Ammen, Siobhan O'Toole, Rhoda Olkin, and Diane Zelman for their encouragement and support in completing the project as we worked together on other developments. Louise Colbert-Mar and the library staff under her super- vision were unbelievably helpful and generous in finding documents and texts I requested. Debbie Wendt and Donna Osborne gave me continuous encourage- ment as they helped with the daily administrative tasks surrounding this work. Dr. Debra Bekerian was especially instrumental in linking me to Oxford University Press and encouraging me toward completion.

Several colleagues and friends agreed to take time from their very hectic lives to read my manuscript and provide feedback to me and to my publisher. Much appreciation for this generous donation of time to Drs. Oliva Espin, Sheila Henderson, Mary Beth Kenkel, Elizabeth Davis-Russell, Robert-Jay Green, and Kumea Shorter-Gooden for your willingness to read the final manuscript. Dr. Audrey Punnett was my kind encourager. We shared a passion for writing and a desire to continue the process over several years of writing and editing together. Dr. Terry Wissler, always a remarkable friend, shared her insights about the ongoing project for twenty years while keeping me grounded in the reality of the world of my sisters and of hers.

The editorial assistance and support of many people created the book that you are reading. My first editorial contact, Dr. Arthur Pomponio, made me believe the manuscript was worth publishing and that others would find my work interesting to read. His support was followed by the extremely professional staff at Oxford, who took up the manuscript when my first contract fell through. Abby Gross, my first OUP editor, helped me to understand the important steps in publishing and managed the initial development of the contract, shepherding my ideas through the initial acceptance by the publisher. My final editor, Sarah L. Harrington, gave structured support and a quick response to all of my questions. Jodi Narde was the face of Oxford providing day to day assistance and communication during the final stages and Wendy Walker provided the painstaking detail as my copyeditor. Each of these individuals provided an important link to the publishing world and helped to bring my ideas to print.

The most important people, who influenced this work, are the family members who tendered their ideas, provided their insight and, by their very lives, created my desire to complete this task. I have dedicated this work to my sisters, Sally Kuba Bonner and Barbara Ellen Charles, whose influence in my life informs every page of this manuscript. My mother, Dorothy McFarland Kuba, was the first to read the entire work. Her love, informed by her intelligent insight, has created a depth that would not otherwise exist. My father, Dr. Robert Joseph Kuba, shared his love of literature and the model of his lifelong achievement. He was with me in every step of this task even though he left us before the final manuscript could be read. I thought of my brothers, Bob and Don Kuba, as I wrote this book, wanting them to understand the strong influence they have exerted in my life even though the focus in this text was not on our relationship with each other. The section on diversity would not have been the same without the influence of Bob's remarkable life and the suggestion by my Aunt, Louella McFarland, that I pay close attention to the relationship between abled and disabled sisters.

It is my California family whom has sacrificed the most during the writing of this book. I have been absent or distracted from our daily living for so many evenings and days. At times, so consumed with this project and my other work, I have neglected them. Yet, they are among my strongest supporters. Louise Ninkovich, my mother-in-law, and Suzy Fortier, my sister-in-law, have provided me with incisive understanding of human relationships and the importance of tending those close to home. They have tolerated my absence from family gatherings and made peace with my love of work. No one has supported me more, understood me better, or been more patient with this work than my partner, Donna Ninkovich. In addition to her love and support, she is my best critic and was my most significant editor. It is hard to imagine understanding relationships between women without the emotional intelligence she brings to my life. She has encouraged me to savor every day, as I move ahead with my intellectual work. To Barrett and Kinsey, who bring pure exuberant energy to my life, "There will be more walks and play now."

CONTENTS

INTRODUCTION

How did my sisters come into my consciousness? That is the essence of what I asked women to share with me in the interviews. Their thoughts and feelings in response have created the foundation of this book. Fundamentally, I cannot remember. Sally was with me in the womb. Did we touch? Certainly. Did we know of each other's presence in a conscious way? I am sure we did not do so in the way that one is conscious as an adult or even as a young child. Yet her presence has altered my life since before we were born. That presence has certainly informed and inspired my sense of self throughout my life. I don't know the moment I became aware of my older sister, Barb, but her awareness of me and of us—Sally and me—is the foundation of a story that my mother tells repeatedly. When my mother came home from the hospital with us, Barb, her first-born, was 18 months old. My older sister ran to greet our mother with outstretched arms, and my mother could not pick her up; with one twin in each arm, she had none left for Barb. It is a tribute to my older sister's grace and my mother's skill that all three sisters became strongly bonded throughout our lives. It could have gone so differently.

As a psychologist and during my training I have often been surprised at the lack of recognition given to the role of sisters. My sisters and I are so deeply embedded in each others' consciousness that I do not know who I would be or how I would view my world had they not been a part of my childhood and adolescence. As a researcher, I wanted to know if other women experienced their sisters' importance as I did. I also hoped to make a difference in the way that sisters are understood by therapists who work with women. I thought it important to understand the ways that sisters help co-create us. Sometimes, I theorized, we become some portion of who we are in order to be different from our sisters. Sometimes we want to emulate them and look up to them. Sometimes they make us laugh or help us not to take ourselves too seriously. They seem to do these things differently than parents do. So my theories, my research, and my therapeutic voice have merged into this book about sisters and their influence on whom we become.

The book is organized into three sections, each written in a different voice. Section I gives the history of our ignorance about the sister role and then tells the story of the research. As much as possible, this section preserves the meaning in the narratives of my participants' lives. Chapter 1 alerts the reader to some psychohistory. It begins with the reasons why sister relationships might have been ignored or minimized, even by authors like Freud, Klein, and Bowen, who discussed the sibling relationship in some detail. The psychological theories that do exist seem to miss the importance of the same-gender bond. These "Misunderstandings and Missed Understandings" are the topic of the first chapter. The title refers to the ways that many psychological theories have failed to distinguish sisters from brothers or to consider siblings very much at all. To fully gauge the reasons for this, I had to delve into the lives of those who theorize. I tried to evaluate the sister or sibling relationships of these theorists as an unconscious explanation for their lack of attention to sisters, or their focus on only certain aspects of the relationship. This first chapter gives a preview of the third section of the book, which explores the theories themselves in more detail and integrates findings from my research into suggested ways that therapists might fully include and understand the importance of sisters.

I am not the first to write about or conduct research into the lives of sisters. Several excellent books have been written based upon interviews with women (e.g., Fishel, 1979; McNaron, 1985). I think what might be different about this work is the use of a method that preserves all of the words of the women who agreed to be interviewed—shaping them into an overall understanding with vast variety and detail. The essence of sister relationships and their importance over the entire lifespan is told in the narrative stories of these women. The extracted themes become part of a larger structure. In other words, the women themselves created the outcome. I paid attention to everything they said, not only those parts that fit my theory of sisters or those of other theorists. This method and the ways in which it is different from other kinds of research exploration are the focus of Chapter 2, "The Voices of Sisters."

Themes begat categories, categories begat clusters, and then clusters formed the structure of experience, which found its own way into the development of a comprehensive view of the relationship. The research approach is fundamentally subjective and intersubjective—a dialogue between the participant and the researcher. Phenomenology purports that the participant is the best author of her own experience. However, the individual woman must reflect upon her experience to become consciously aware, and when that reflection is done in the context of an interview, the researcher becomes part of the developing understanding. I did not stand outside of the interview and measure what these women said. Instead, the meaning was co-constructed between us as I listened to their stories.

This research process required a conscious intentionality about listening to their stories and trying to minimize my influence, while recognizing the

influence is always there. The role of the researcher, from the phenomenological perspective, is that of a co-constructor of meaning. Every attempt was made to let the women be the guide in this process of discovery. The reflection that brought women's awareness of their sisters to light involves a specific intentionality, a desire to understand the relationship, as one recounts it.

During the interview process, women commented upon their conscious reflection. Their ways of coming to understand the sister relationship are described in Chapter 3, "Ways of Perceiving and Knowing." The women told me about this process of consciousness spontaneously. I never asked them to let me know how they knew; it was just a part of the telling. Frequently this awareness was presented at the follow-up interview, when women had more time to reflect on the things they had said about the sister connection in the first interview.

Chapters 4 through 7 provide the detail of the narratives and the essence of the sister experience. The organizing principle for many of the narratives was the detail shared from the sisters' herstory. Since women from teenagers to octogenarians were interviewed, the stories of their relationships were frequently told through the lens of time. It is important to remember that women were initially only asked one question: "Tell me about your relationship with_____(name of sister)." All of the detail emerged from that question and the follow-up questions that encouraged a woman to expand upon what she had just said. The women seemed to use the changes in the relationship with their sister across time as an organizing principle in telling their stories. Those changes are embedded in the family context: the other sisters, mothers, brothers, fathers, and stepfamilies that helped to define why the sisters were important to each other. The family history forms the background for the other organizing principles that emerged from the narratives. These "herstories"[1] are recounted in Chapter 4.

Chapter 5 is an extension and it is named that: "Sister Extensions." It engages the reader in the extended families and relationships of the women who were interviewed. Going beyond the birth family, the chapter covers what women said about their partners and children. It explains the importance of aunts, cousins, and grandfathers. It describes the ways in which friendships are important to the sister connection. The women talked a lot about their relationships with their sisters' partners and children. Nieces were mentioned a great deal and with great variety—they seemed to form a link to the next generation of sisters. Likewise, aunts formed a connection to the generation before.

Some authors have suggested that women form intimacy before identity (Gilligan, 1982) rather than the other way around. In this book, the chapter on intimacy precedes the one on identity. Intimacy and connection seem to define and redefine identity rather than being created by identity in a linear fashion.

---

[1] Throughout the book I use the term "herstory" in place of "history," as a feminist form of the noun and a reference to the woman's self-definition of her story.

Referred to as the intensity of the connection, this dialogue between closeness and distance is the central core of the current relationship with the sister. This intensity included an understanding of how support was given or when it was withheld. It was also described as a part of how the relationship changed over time. Many women expressed regret that their sister connection was not what they had hoped, while others said they felt their sisters were the most important connections in their lives.

While intimacy helped to define it, the development of identity was closely linked to the irrevocable role of sisters. So many aspects of this connection to identity emerged during the research that the sense of identity became another central part of the sister connection. The values, careers, family choices, and presence or absence of children were all a part of this discussion. Many times women discussed the ways they were similar and different from their sister. When there were more than two girls in a family, they attempted to explain the reasons for the unique identity each had formed. It was interesting to see the way these identities changed over time and how the sister connection formed a part of those shifts. The need to define oneself as different from the sister was a theme in early life. Women often found they became more similar as they aged, but some became estranged because of too many differences in values. Included in this sense of identity were the facts of sisters' lives. If they had children, how many? Did they have grandchildren or great-grandchildren? Were they ever married or partnered? Did they share religious traditions? Where did they reside, and did they have contact with others? What type of work did they do? How important was it to their self-definition? All of these factors contributed to a sense of identification with or identification opposing the sister.

Even though the essence of the relationship was discovered during the interview process, I became increasingly uncomfortable after it was finished with the degree to which some elements of identity were not discussed by the participants. I didn't think they were hiding anything; I just knew that certain things about a woman are definitive—her race, her ability and disability, her sexual orientation, the country of her ancestry, the nation to which she belongs. Many of my participants were too similar to one another—these diversity themes rarely emerged. These elements form fundamental differences between women and may create differences or similarities between sisters. To expand the material, I decided to investigate what others had discovered about sisters whose identities were partly formed based upon difference.

Section II begins with the chapter titled "Sisters of Difference." In it, I explore the connections and themes related to disabled and non-disabled sisters and the interesting twists created when one sister is lesbian and the others are not. This chapter focuses on more traditional research created by other authors and extracts themes related to the experience of sisters. The voice of the book shifts to accommodate this shift in material—I am no longer dealing in narratives, but in the extrapolated meaning of sisters based on the little information I could find.

In Chapter 8, a behemoth chapter, I attempt to extrapolate some themes related to identities of sisters that are formed by ethnicity, race, and national origin. Of course this chapter is not complete, as it would take several volumes to understand sister relationships throughout all countries in the world. My decisions about whom to include were based on some foundational literature about sister relationships in specific countries and knowledge related to women who have migrated to the United States. The material is extrapolated from knowledge about family structure and gender issues in various countries and cultures of the world. Hence, much of what I say about potential sister relationships within those contexts is based on conjecture. A fair amount is based on clinical insight gleaned from 25 years as a psychologist in private practice and a professor of multicultural courses in a doctoral program. I have also had some personal experiences with sisters from some of the cultural groups who are represented. Within the chapter I worked to understand how the surrounding political, social, religious, and economic context might influence a sister connection in various countries around the world.

When possible, I found stories about sisters that provide some information or insight. For example, as I write, women are being gunned down in the streets of Iran for protesting an election in which one candidate would have given them more equity of opportunity. Imagine being sisters who are part of that protest— the courage, the fear, the witness to tragedy all being shared. Those are the kinds of relationships that I tried to understand. It is only one person's understanding, mingled with narratives that can be found about specific sisters. Organized by region of the world and related to sisters who take refuge in or immigrate to the United States, the stories of these women and their potential sister connection are presented under the title "Cross Cultural, Racial, and Ethnic Perspectives on Sisters."

To blend my research findings with those of the cross-cultural literature, I then attempted a first-stage integration in Chapter 10. The foundation of this chapter is the narrative of similarity within difference and difference within similarity. The narrative begins with an attempt to understand the differences between sisters. Within that difference, how does identity form? Within that difference, what similarities still emerge? Discrimination, bias, and misogyny are an unfortunate theme. Many sisters, from cultures in the United States and around the world, have to engage in that dialogue.

Likewise, sisters who share an ethnic or cultural background have differences constructed within that similarity. Some are based on the experience of discrimination or assault. Others are based on different experiences as refugees. For instance, I discuss two sisters who fled Cambodia during Pol Pot's regime; one stayed in Southeast Asia and the other immigrated to Vermont. Their lives are intricately interwoven, but their opportunities and experiences are vastly different. Other differences are related to violence experienced at the hands of men. Some sisters have been raped, others molested, and some beaten. Identity can also vary based upon physical characteristics, including the lightness or darkness of skin color and the family valuing of those traits. Similarities are present for these sisters that share ethnicity, but they may differ based on religious values or social class.

As the comparison of themes in my research and the existing cross-cultural literature continues, these individual differences in identity are also related to differences in family history experienced by much younger or much older sisters. Some sisters are caregivers and others are not. Some have careers and others are full-time mothers. As these themes emerged in the cross-cultural descriptions of sisters they were compared to the findings from my research project. Where are the similarities? What new themes are added from a deeper exploration of sisters in the cross-cultural world? Many themes were present from the research, but new ones were added, and those are all described in Chapter 10.

The third section of the book is written in a third voice. It also contributes a unique aspect to the existing work on sisters. Rather than integrate these ideas into only one school of psychological thought, I wanted to provide some information about sisters for several major theories that are used by therapists. I chose theories based on my use of them in my clinical work and, not surprising, their attention to relationships between women in families. There is no attempt to be comprehensive—that would be the subject of another full-length book, I am afraid. Four major theoretical schools are considered. Traditional psychoanalysis is considered based on the works of Freud and Melanie Klein, among others. Object relations approaches are evaluated based on their focus on the first 5 years of life. From those early years come all of the abilities and limitations for forming healthy adult relationships. I have also included the theories created by the authors of relational cultural theory (RCT), which began as a deconstruction of object relations and an attempt to more fully understand women's lives but does not adequately address the importance of the sister connection. RCT also provides an important understanding of cultural integration.

Diverging from these more psychodynamically oriented approaches, the final chapter evaluates the attention to the sister relationship in three schools of modern family therapy: narrative, feminist, and attachment-based family therapy. All three of these focus on the importance of women's roles in the family, and each also considers the ability of the family member to tell her own story. As I discussed each theory, I found it helpful to present the themes related to sisters and offer therapeutic interventions related to sisters that are suggested by the research.

This process has consumed me at various times. I have walked away from it for months, sometimes years, and then returned to take it up again. The importance of the sister connection has always been a factor in my clinical work. At present, several of my clients are actively struggling with sister relationships. Others are being supported by the strength of their sister connection. In the final stages and while on deadline, my sister Barb's husband was hospitalized with conditions that we feared might take his life. Across the country, my twin and mother came to provide practical support and comfort. My support was primarily emotional and was provided at a distance; one of the things that kept me from being there was finishing this book. It seems ironic and somehow wrong that that would be so. I have felt saddened by my absence from my sister's process and guilty about it, yet those actions and reactions are a part of how we have come to be present in each others' lives and, at times, absent from them. I find them defining again our individual identities in the strength of a lifelong series of sister connections.

The Role of Sisters in
Women's Development

PART ONE

THE LIFELONG RELATIONSHIP

1

Misunderstandings and Missed Understandings

"In human intercourse the tragedy begins, not when there is misunderstanding about words, but when silence is not understood. Then there can never be an explanation."
Henry David Thoreau (1906, v. 1, p. 295)

In the history of psychological theory, sisters have been silenced for too long. The importance of this lifelong sibling bond between women has been ignored or misunderstood for many reasons. Some of those reasons are related to the sister and sister–brother relationships of the authors; some are related to the sexism in Western culture. Other reasons are related to the suppression of female thinkers and writers in psychology. For those theorists who considered sibling relationships, these personal and cultural themes resulted in the absence of a detailed explanation about the role of sisters. Several of the major authors of psychoanalytic, object relations, relational-cultural, and family theory are considered here, along with the personal and cultural factors that defined their avoidance of or ignorance about the sister relationship.

For Sigmund Freud and Melanie Klein there was a clearly defined line between reactions to the birth of siblings before the oedipal resolution and after it. As a result, their considerations of sibling influence are couched in terms of male psychosexual development. Object relations theorists such as Winnicott, Margaret Mahler, and D. W. Fairbairn seem to focus exclusively on the threesome of child–mother–father. They, too, placed extraordinary emphasis on the primary attachment to the mother between the ages of zero and four. Much of object relations theory parenthesizes the sibling or sister role. Historically, the women's movement spawned a number of theories that evaluated women's roles and their development more uniquely. Jean Baker Miller, Irene Stiver, and Judith Jordan, among others, wanted to understand different contributors to female development. And in doing so, they paid more attention to female–female relationships. Yet even these authors focus more clearly on the mother–daughter connection, with few references to sisters. Family theorists have been much more consistently aware of sibling influence—yet sisters are not often considered as having a different influence than brothers. The reasons for the lack of attention to sisters may lie in the family connections and disconnections of the theorists themselves. They also lie in the context surrounding theorists, the continuing diminishment of women, and the resultant lack of understanding about how girls play a role in the development of their peers. To understand these missed opportunities, I wanted to explore the history and context of some of the premier psychological theorists and their relationships with sisters, including their own sisters and other sisters who surrounded them.

Psychoanalysis and Sisters

Sigmund Freud: His Family as the Source of his Theory

Recent debates in the literature have suggested that Freud either paid too little attention to siblings, or that subsequent authors have ignored the dense consideration Freud gave to siblings in analysis. When examining his words and the words of others, it is clear that both may be true. Freud's primary focus was on the oedipal complex: the triad of father–mother and son certainly overshadowed his consideration of siblings. Yet, as Susan Sherwin-White suggests in her excellent review of Freud's work on siblings, he spent many pages describing the importance of sibling rivalry, betrayal, the importance of primitive aggression toward a newborn sister or brother, and the lifelong effects of unresolved sibling attachment on the object choices of later life (2007). Freud's focus on the negative relationship between siblings may have occurred in reaction to "a 19th-century cultural assumption that brother-sister relationships were simply comprised of love and were straightforward" (p. 8). Was there more to it than this cultural imperative? It seems worthwhile to explore Freud's own very interesting family connections in an effort to understand his formulations. These family connections and understanding of sisters occurred in three ways for Freud: his own sisters and their role in his life, his wife's sister and her role in his life, and his sisters' daughters and their relationships with each other.

Freud was the first-born child in a family that ultimately totaled seven siblings. Julius was born when Freud was a toddler. Freud felt hostile to him and expressed this directly and indirectly. When Julius died in infancy, Freud's guilt about that loss may have eventually fueled his theory of male development, specifically the oedipal complex, in which other rivals for the mother's attention must be slain, but then the resulting guilt at such a victory overshadows later more mature development. Freud's next sibling was Anna, the object of intense ambivalence throughout Freud's life due to her birth when he was 3. Sigmund and Anna had four other sisters; in succession, they were Rosa, Pauline (Pauli), Marie (Mitzi), and Adolphine (Dolfi). These five sisters were followed by another brother, Alexander, when Freud was 10. It has been suggested that Freud was overjoyed with this brother's birth and that it appeased some of his guilt about Julius' death. Thus, Freud's five sisters became secondary to the brother relationships in his life. The importance of men, reflecting the Victorian patriarchy, was carried over into Freud's family, yet it was the oldest male child—Freud himself—who held his mother's attention, much more than her own husband did. She placed Sigmund's needs above those of her other children, as evidenced by her willingness to make all of her daughters give up the piano because their practicing disturbed the young Sigmund's studies. The following quote tells the story:

> When the noise of his sisters' practicing the piano interrupted his stud-
> ies, "the piano disappeared," Anna Freud recalled years later, "and with it
> all opportunities for his sisters to become musicians." Freud did not see
> this attitude as a problem, or cause for any problem, in women. It was
> woman's nature to be ruled by man and her sickness to envy him.
> (Friedan, 1974, p. 100)

Elsa First (2000) speculates on the relationship between Freud and his sisters based upon a cultural and photographic analysis of the family in the 1870s. When evaluating the photo, First saw the ambivalence Freud's sisters felt, the peripheral place his father held, and the closeness of Freud and his mother. His sisters were described as dependent upon Freud. Deprived of their ability to become musicians, and with a father who could not make appropriate matches for them, "The girls [had] nowhere to go except marriage to men whom they may [have] come to know through their brother" (p. 314). First bases her analysis partly on knowledge that the Freud sisters held menial jobs until they were married. Those jobs were considered beneath their middle-class family status. Lack of economic support from their father made the young women dependent upon their older brother's success. Thus, it is possible they were willing to sacrifice for their brother. The family was really headed by him, starting at a very young age, even with his father present.

Freud's relationship with each of his sisters was unique. His close relationship with Rosa throughout their lives suggested a strong sister–brother bond. For a time, Rosa and her husband lived above the flat where Freud and his wife, Martha, resided. Another sister, Dolfi, was considered unstable. Dolfi correctly predicted the rise of the Nazis against the Jews, but the family ignored her, assuming she was paranoid about the anti-Semitism in Austria during the 1930s (Billig, 1999). Because of the family beliefs about Dolfi's madness, her expressions of concern about the dangers to the Freuds during the rise of Nazi Germany were ignored. This family repression resulted in Freud's last-minute escape to England. Four of his five elderly sisters—all except Anna—were killed in deportation or concentration camps by the Nazis. Anna had moved to the United States with her husband many years earlier and thus escaped the Nazi peril in Europe.

First supports the conclusion of other authors, suggesting that Freud may have molested one of his sisters (e.g., Anzieu, 1986; Krull, 1986). Freud himself reported memories that have been interpreted as symbols of molestation. One such memory depicted him and another boy tearing apart a multilayered colored travel book that belonged to his sister. This symbol has been interpreted as a representation of incest. A different memory depicted Sigmund and another boy throwing one of the Freud sisters down on the ground and taking a bouquet of flowers from her. Interpretations of this as an incestuous scene seem more easily understandable. First suggests these memories could have represented repressed childhood sexual exploration or actual sexual experiences with his younger sisters. Freud's father figured prominently in the first memory—as the one who had given Freud and his friend the book they tore apart. First declares, "the uncanny radiant colors, the complexity and the symmetry of the design of composite flowers symbolizing the labia" was present in both memories (p. 318). Whether Freud learned about women's genitals from sex play with his sisters or these were merely metaphors for other childhood experiences is difficult to determine. In either case, the way these representations of femaleness were remembered suggests that they were Freud's playthings, and women—specifically his sisters—were present to serve his ego and his own development.

Sigmund Freud's wife, Martha, also had a sister who figured prominently in their married life. Minna Bernays lived with the Freuds for 30 years. She was a close confidant of Sigmund's and occasionally the two traveled alone. Many writers have speculated the two had an affair. At one point they shared a hotel room alone, but there is no proof they had sex, at least according to some analysts (Lothane, 2007). On the other hand, Jung reportedly confirmed the affair saying that Minna had confided their romantic and sexual relationship to him. Jung said the proof existed in a dream reported by Freud. In it, both Freud's wife, Minna, and her sister, Martha, were present. According to Jung, the dream left Freud very shaken. Of course, Jung may have had his own reasons for drawing attention to this potential affair; his interpretations may have been tainted by his difficult interactions with Freud. The truth about Freud and Minna's relationship is not known for certain. In his married life, as in his early life, the significance of two or more sisters seems focused on their presence for him rather than their relationship with each other.

This theme replays in a third segment of Freud's family life—his relationship with his own daughters and his nieces. Sigmund and Martha Freud had five children, three of them daughters. The most famous of these, Anna, was not named after his sister or Anna O., his famous patient, but was named after a family friend (another patient of Freud's named Anna). Freud's daughter, Anna, had two older sisters. She was the result of an unwanted pregnancy and was born when Freud was despondent over his medical need to give up cigars. His daughter Anna became the representative of his developing ideas about childhood. It has even been suggested that Freud's successful book publications coincided with Anna's developmental benchmarks (Cupelloni, 2000).

The relationship between Sigmund and Anna seemed to overshadow the significance of any sister–sister or husband–wife bond in the family. In this sense it was the mirror image of Freud's relationship with his mother, where he assumed more importance than his father or female siblings. Freud fought an early marriage between his daughter, Anna, and Ernest Jones. As a result, she did not have a romantic relationship with Jones and neglected her romantic life. Instead she focused on her career as a form of compensation. Her early involvement in the psychoanalytic society made up for her sense of inferiority in relationship to her sisters. "She had neither Sophie's beauty nor Mathilde's elegance and felt inferior for not having succeeded in her studies" (Cupelloni, 2000, p. 114).

During her analytic training, Anna was the subject of analysis by her father—commencing at 10 p.m., 6 nights a week for several years. She never married or had children but developed a close relationship with a female friend, Dorothy, whose children she tended. This relationship seemed to fuel her final separation from her father's ideas near the end of her life (Cupelloni, 2000). Perhaps this friendship/relationship with Dorothy replaced the ones Anna could have shared with her sisters. She felt separated from them; certainly Dorothy filled the role of an emotional partner in Anna's life.

Anna was not the only young woman in the Freud family who struggled to find her place among female siblings. Freud was also concerned with the emotional adjustment of his niece, Martha, one of Marie Freud's daughters. Concerned about the young woman's health, Freud advised Fliess, his friend and Martha's analyst, about treating the family. From that letter and others we learn that Martha was the youngest of three daughters. When Martha was 12 her mother gave birth to twin boys, only one of whom survived. Thereafter, Freud's niece renamed herself Tom. "Tom" became a very successful artist of children's books and, after her renaming, was basically ignored by Freud, who had studied her/him as a child. There is the suggestion that Freud's brother-in-law may have committed incest with this daughter during an extended trip to Europe. This relationship may have revived the seduction theory for Freud, if only momentarily. Very little was said about Tom's relationship to her two older sisters. Tom seems to have been a young, gifted woman whose difficulties Freud blamed upon her father's "half-Asian [meaning Eastern European] heritage." Tom married and had a child, Angela. Tom's older sister later raised the girl following the suicide of Tom and her husband within 7 months of each other (Ginsburg, 2003). This niece, transgendered by modern standards, was the middle child in a family that originally contained two other girls and two boys. The gender identity of Tom became the subject of much speculation in relation to his brothers, especially in relation to one brother's death. However, his relationship with his sisters was unexamined.

Surrounded as he was by female siblings of his own and in his extended family for all of his life, it seems surprising that Freud did not become more aware of the influence of sisters upon one another. He was not completely silent on the matter of siblings, but his theory does lack a significant depth and specificity in understanding the lifelong sister connection.

Freudian Understanding of Sibling Relationships

The importance of the transition from the oedipal to the family complex, brought on by the birth of siblings, is documented in the *New Introductory Lectures on Psychoanalysis* (1933/1964). Most of these relationships are between brother and sister or brother and brother, with little focus on relationships between female siblings. Freud introduced these family constellations and adjustments through clinical examples and case studies, deriving theory from them in the process. To preserve some anonymity he labeled his cases with symbolic names, such as Little Hans, Ratman, Wolfman, etc. Such descriptions provide a deeper understanding of how he might have missed the sister connection.

The first example of sibling rivalry emerged from a brother–sister pair in the case of Little Hans. Freud suggested that:

> The most important influence upon the course of Hans' psychosexual development was the birth of a baby sister when he was 3-½ years old. That event accentuated his relations to his parents and gave him some insoluble problems to think about. (1909/1975, p. 113)

Despite this reference, Freud does not refer to Hans' sister when describing the oedipally driven outcome of this case. He seemed to toy with the idea of sibling importance, acknowledging its significance, but did not fully develop his ideas along these lines.

Two other cases provide evidence that Freud took the sibling relationship seriously. Ratman had incestuous relations and fantasies about his next younger sister, Julie (3 years younger). These fantasies were restrained by the Ratman's father until his death, when Ratman was 21. Same-sex games or homosexual encounters with his younger brother were also described in this case. In another case the Wolfman and his older, more-clever sister also provided Freud with documentation of poor instinctual control between siblings. Freud felt the sister's torment of Wolfman may have included seduction. She later committed suicide. Evidence from Wolfman's analysis also suggested that this sister was molested by her father. So the sins of the father were levied against the son, in a rather ironic twist, with a sister at the core. Because the clients were boys or men, the issue of sister relationship may have been overshadowed by the focus on male development. It is interesting to question why Wolfman—not his sister—was the patient of Freud, since she clearly had symptoms as well.

As in all aspects of Freud's work female development was overshadowed by that of the male. There were, however, quite a few significant statements that provide a window into Freud's thoughts on the matter of female siblings. He paid more attention to sisters when considering the primary relationship between a child and mother and the ways subsequent births of other children affected that relationship.

Freud's statements about the importance of these births include these two:

> A small child does not necessarily love his brothers and sisters; often he obviously does not. There is no doubt that he hates them as his competitors, and it is a familiar fact that this attitude often persists for long years, till maturity is reached or even later, without interruption. (Freud, 1933/1977, p. 253)

And the appearance of the sibling is further complicated by the nurturance provided to the next-born:

> But what the child grudges the unwanted intruder and rival is not only the suckling but all the other signs of maternal care. It feels that it has been dethroned, despoiled, prejudiced in its rights; it casts a jealous hatred upon the new baby and develops a grievance against the faithless mother which often finds expression in a disagreeable change in its behavior. It becomes naughty, perhaps, irritable and disobedient and goes back on the advances it has made towards controlling its excretions. All of this has been very long familiar and is accepted as self-evident; but we rarely form a correct idea of the strength of these jealous impulses, of the tenacity with which they persist and of the magnitude of their influence on later development. Especially as this jealousy is constantly receiving fresh nourishment in the later years of childhood and the whole shock is repeated with the birth of each new brother or sister. (Freud, 1933/1964, p. 123)

Freud's own sibling relationships are very important in understanding these strong feelings of sibling rivalry. Julius' death precipitated Freud's guilt and idealization of his much younger brother, Alexander, and the birth of Anna led to a lifelong grievance against her as his least-liked sibling.

Houzel (2001) suggests that Freud's sexism was apparent in his analysis of sibling rivalry:

> Only little girls are said to bear a grudge against the mother because of a series of disappointments she inflicts upon them, including that involving the conception of new babies. Freud continues to pretend that boys feel no ambivalence in their love for the mother, and vice versa. (p. 130)

Freud's work on sexual development makes some mention of the sibling role, particularly in what he considered stunted sexual development. In the work *Three Essays on the Theory of Sexuality*, translated by Strachey (1905/1962), Freud attempts to extend his work on male sexual development to the female. He describes female sexual excitement as essentially masculine, meaning instrumental. While he contributed much to the understanding of female sexual excitement in masturbation or through stimulation of the clitoris, he did not understand vaginal sexuality in women, which led to the erroneous conclusion that clitoral stimulation was an immature form of sexual excitement leading to the potential for sexual intercourse. In regard to female sexuality, Freud mentions the immature woman, who is sexually unable to fulfill her sexual relationship with her male partner. He describes the sibling connection to this immature development as:

> Girls with an exaggerated need for affection and an equally exaggerated horror of the real demands made by sexual life have an irresistible temptation on the one hand to realize the ideal of asexual love in their lives and on the other hand to conceal their libido behind an affection which they can express without self-reproaches, by holding fast throughout their lives to their infantile fondness, revived at puberty, for their parents or brothers and sisters. (p. 94)

For the female child, according to Freud, a strong interest in affection—presumably in lieu of sexuality—was partly created by strong sibling bonds. Perhaps this reference was related to the developing gender issues for his niece and his daughter Anna, whose parental attachments remained predominant throughout their lives.

One famous case of Freud's did evaluate the strength of the sister–sister bond. The relationship is understood in light of the attraction between Elisabeth von R. and her sister's husband. Elisabeth was one of Freud's first patients. She had a conversion disorder with symptoms of unexplained leg pain and weakness. The story of Elisabeth, who was the youngest of three sisters, was similar to the story of Freud's daughter Anna. Elisabeth's intellectual companionship with her father lasted until his premature death. Wanting that kind of companionship again, Elisabeth tried to transfer the relationship she had with her father to her mother during her protracted illness and death. She also tried to form the same bond with her sister, who died in pregnancy at a young age. Elisabeth was the family caregiver, providing practical and emotional support to each of these family members, yet was absent from her sister's deathbed. When her sister died, Elisabeth's repressed lifelong attraction to her brother-in-law was revealed to her:

> At that moment of dreadful certainty that her beloved sister was dead without bidding them farewell and without her having eased her last days with her care—at that very moment another thought had shot through Elisabeth's mind, and now forced itself irresistibly upon her once more, like a flash of lightning in the dark: "Now he is free again and I can be his wife." (Breuer & Freud, 1957, p. 156)

In this account, the sister relationship is very important but is compromised by the presence of a male whom both find attractive. In comparing this case to others he analyzed with similar themes, Freud's focus is on the conversion hysteria rather than the family constellation; her repressed sexuality became the primary interest for his theory. Billig (1999) suggests that Freud's own repression appeared in his discussion of many of his patients. In the case of Elisabeth, Freud's supposed affair with his own sister-in-law is an interesting parallel to this sister story of repression and unacceptable love between a patient and her sister's husband.

Attempts to reconcile the female developmental trajectory resulted in the development of the Elektra complex—a companion to Freud's oedipal myth. The now-familiar myth describes Elektra as the daughter of Agamemnon and Clytemnestra and sister of Iphigenia. As the story unfolds, Agamemnon, a Trojan War hero, sacrifices his marriage and his family to wage a war that will return Helen, his brother's wife and his wife's sister, to the family fold. Helen has run away or been abducted by Paris of Troy. Agamemnon follows Paris and Helen to Troy and the Trojan War begins. During his prolonged absence, Agamemnon's wife and Elektra's mother, Clytemnestra, develops a new relationship. Upon his return, Agamemnon is murdered by his wife's lover.

Most of Freud's interpretation of the development of women's role in the family is related to the fact that Elektra feels compelled to assist her brother in the murder of her mother—a way of avenging her father's death. However, Elektra's sister was also murdered in the process. Her father sacrificed his oldest daughter, Iphigenia, to the gods in exchange for a fair wind to sail to Troy and the hope of victory against Paris. The story and Freud's interpretation of it ignore the importance of the loss of this sister and the father's role in destroying her. This story suggests that a woman must ignore the murder of her sister by her father and take revenge upon the mother who has slain him—a clear message about the patriarchal family and the small importance allocated to the sister bond or the feminine principle. Phyllis Chesler in *Woman's Inhumanity to Woman* (2001) notes this: "Electra remains indifferent to her sister's murder. For both mother and daughter; sisterly rivalry (Clytemnestra and Helen, Electra and Iphigenia) may also have a determining, though unexamined, role here" (p. 202). Sibling rivalry is not the focus of this tale as it has been applied to women's development. The message is that a girl must revoke the feminine influence, in often violent ways, in order to find her rightful place among the patriarchy and become a mature woman. Interpreted very differently, this myth is a story of the failure of sister connection and the loss that is multigenerational when a sister is removed from the family by violence—Helen by Paris and Iphigenia by Agamemnon.

Freud understood the depth of anger, hostility, and affection that may ignite a sibling relationship from birth onward, and this understanding is present in his cases and theory. His own sibling conflicts are a part of his analysis but never figure prominently in it. Freud does give consideration to some aspects of sibling development and influence. However, bound by his patriarchal Victorian context and his complicated sibling interactions, he all but ignores the unique nature of the sister bond.

Melanie Klein: Speaking of Siblings

Melanie Klein addressed the role of siblings in development more thoroughly than most theorists. Perhaps this is because she analyzed children and could not ignore the presence of siblings in their lives; perhaps she was reflecting the important role of her siblings in her own development. Klein was born the youngest of four children to economically beleaguered parents. Her father was a doctor whose lack of success led him to a career in dentistry. Her mother, forced to work because he was a poor provider, resented his failures. Melanie was tutored in arithmetic and reading by a sister who was 4 years older. Her sister died at age 8, when Melanie was 4. She acknowledged the important role this sister played in her own development as an intellectual (Hughes, 1989). After her sister's death, Klein's oldest brother became her confidant and helped her gain entrance to the Lyceum. It is reported that he stimulated her intelligence and taught her the classics. He died when Melanie was 20. In a household replete with failed hopes and dreams, her siblings strengthened and fed hers.

Klein was affected by her gender and social standing. When she attempted to enter the profession of medicine and psychiatry, she was prevented from doing so. Her role as the famous child analyst depended upon a series of unfortunate events. Tending toward melancholy, she found marriage and child-rearing difficult and surrendered her household responsibilities to her mother upon her father's death. Klein's marriage did not survive this intrusion. When her mother died, Klein joined the psychoanalytic society and began analysis with Ferenczi. He encouraged her toward the analysis of children. Since she lacked child patients, she analyzed her own son, Hans. She was subsequently embraced by the British school of analysts and thereafter had many child patients. One of her most tightly held tenets was that parents should be excluded from child therapy.

An interesting rivalry, which resembled that found between siblings, arose in the British Psycho-Analytical Society when Freud and his daughter Anna took refuge in London during World War II. Anna Freud and Melanie Klein become renowned rivals; each wanted to be the primary theorist for pediatric psychoanalytic theory. Klein's daughter, Melitta, had begun attending the Psychoanalytic Society with her mother at the age of 15. Interestingly, the girl grew up to become an analyst herself, but in classic defiance of her mother, joined the pediatric psychoanalytic camp of Anna Freud. This betrayal, following the death of Klein's son, Hans, in a climbing accident, brought about a resurgence of Melanie's melancholia.

Klein's physical and emotional loss of her children mirrored the childhood loss of her siblings. The resultant melancholia may have been the reason she was the first major thinker to describe sibling relationships in detail. She grounded her theory in the presentation of her analytic cases, just as Freud had done. The birth of siblings became a developmental milestone for children and a cornerstone of Kleinian theory. Perhaps its importance reflects the need to compensate for lost siblings whose promise was cut short by early death. Houzel (2001) summarizes Klein's theory about siblings. Fathers are believed to have good and bad penises; the child believes he or she comes from the good penis, but rival babies are seen as products of bad penises. Aggression expressed toward the mother, who is pregnant, are attacks on these bad babies. This stage of development is completed when good babies are born of the mother. Children who are last babies or only children perceive that they have prevented the parental intercourse and succeeded in stopping the development of bad babies, perhaps creating a sense of control and omnipotence. This complicates the oedipal picture.

Chesler (2001) interprets Kleinian understanding as it relates to the mother–daughter relationship. The child, angry at the mother for being pregnant, attacks her, but is aware the mother is bigger and stronger. Terrified of retaliation and aware that the father and sons are preferred, the female child learns to diminish herself to protect her safety. She also learns to fear any relationship with a woman "in which one woman is dependent upon another for love and sustenance in any sense—physically, psychologically, economically, socially, or sexually" (p. 210). According to Klein, the girl also comes to fear being easily depleted like her mother. Clearly these aspects of Klein's theory can be viewed in parallel with her own mother's life: the loss of two children at young ages, the forced employment, economic struggles, and eventually the responsibility for Melanie's own adult household until her death.

Klein's Cases Reflecting Sister Relationships

Several of Klein's cases provide a distinct view of her approach to sibling or sister relationships. In *The Psychoanalysis of Children* (1932/1975) Klein describes cases involving four small girls. Rita was a child of 2 years and 9 months who was in treatment related to the birth of her brother. Her symptoms included night terrors and anxiety, as well as rage and guilt. She was able to manage these feelings through obsessive rituals and exaggerated goodness. However, she was depressed and totally unable to tolerate frustration of any kind. Klein intervened to have Rita removed from the parental bedroom where, the analyst believed, Rita had witnessed the primal sexual experience between her parents. The birth of her brother was tied to this knowledge and he became the focus of her frustration and rage.

Another young patient named Ruth suffered from anxiety and night terrors, which arose in anticipation of the birth of her sister. In analysis she drew containers and insisted on keeping them closed up so nothing would come out. Klein reports her interpretation:

> I showed her in every detail how she envied and hated her mother because the latter had incorporated her father's penis during coitus and how she wanted to steal his penis and the children out of her mother's inside and kill her mother. (1932/1975, p. 28)

Ruth also feared abandonment by her mother and had, therefore, divided women into two groups. With one group she was friendly; with the other she screamed and cried. This behavior caused Klein to treat Ruth with her sister during the initial analysis. Even with both girls in the treatment room, though, Klein's primary focus was on the parent–child relationship, not the sister connection.

A third patient, Erna, was an only child who wanted siblings tremendously. Klein outlines four components of her desire for a sibling:

1. To give her a "child of her own"
2. Reassure her that she had not "damaged" the child or her mother when attacking the mother's womb
3. Provide "sexual gratification"
4. Be her "confederates" against the parents (1932/1975, p. 74–5).

All of these desires had one aim: the eventual joining together of a sibling horde. "They and she together would kill her mother and capture her father's penis" (1932/1975, p. 75). In a footnote, Klein suggests that siblings help diminish the guilt that such fantasies bring through an imaginary collective act. The complex motivations for wanting a sister or brother seemed to be echoed in this footnote.

Klein worked with sibling issues in the case of Inge. She was a fairly normal child, except for a fear of school, an emerging masculine identification, and homosexual interests (which Klein purports to have changed to a more feminine interest and maternal attitudes). As the youngest, Inge had difficulty with the accomplishments and perceived superiority of her older siblings. This carried over into the school environment and led to a sense of inferiority and an attitude of control towards other children and the analyst (1932/1975, p. 98).

In addition to her consideration of siblings in these four cases, Klein made several other statements about sibling relationships. She describes incest in several cases. Such relationships always included a male sibling. Same-gendered incest was reported between brothers but not between sisters.

More than most other analytic thinkers, Klein provides a thorough understanding of sibling connections. She suggests their importance:

> It is well known that a child's development is helped by his having brothers and sisters. His growing up with them allows him to detach himself more from his parents and to build up a new type of relationship with brothers and sisters. We know, however, that he not only loves them, but has strong feelings of rivalry, hate and jealousy towards them. For this reason, relationships to cousins, playmates and other children still further removed from the nearest family situation, allow divergences from the relationships to brothers and sisters—divergences which again are of great importance as a foundation for later social relationships. (Klein, 1937/1984a, pp. 327–28)

Indeed, Klein moves into the extended family with this statement and provides a picture of the importance of sibling substitutes.

Pathological adaptation may also be related to the sibling connection. Klein suggests that depression (with which she suffered much of her adult life) could be created by weaning and the loss of the maternal breast. Of course this loss was sometimes due to the birth of the next child. This depression was always linked to the loss of the mother in Klein's writings:

> The aggression against phantasied brothers and sisters, who are attacked inside the mother's body, also gives rise to feelings of guilt and loss. The sorrow and concern about the feared loss of the "good" objects, that is to say, the depressive position, is, in my experience, the deepest source of the painful conflicts in the Oedipus situation, as well as in the child's relations to people in general. (1940/1984b, p. 345)

Harkening back to Klein's own feelings of loss, the death of her siblings, and the important role of her mother into Klein's midlife, it seems likely that some repression may have occurred about the source of her depression. She did not lose her mother until much later in life, but the death of her sister when she was 4 and her brother when she was a teen were very significant losses of emotional and intellectual partners in the family. The importance of mother and sisters is explored in other parts of her work.

In another volume Klein suggests that the etiology of lesbian relationships resides in the relationship a girl has with her mother and sisters. Suggesting that these female bonds are emotionally fulfilling, Klein asserts that female homosexual relationships may emerge from the desire to maintain such a close connection and may be based upon fantasized sexual relationships which "recede into the background, become deflected and sublimated, and the attraction towards the other sex predominates" (1937/1984a, p. 310). Likewise, Klein suggests that a mother's attitudes toward her adult daughters can be negatively affected by unresolved sibling issues of her own. This is most likely to emerge during the teen years, when the daughter or daughters begin to sexually mature. Jealousy and rivalry that have not been resolved with her sisters emerge in the relationship with her daughters. In such cases, the woman ceases to be a mother and becomes a competitor with her children. On occasion, the relationship with her daughter may give her the chance to heal a sister conflict from childhood or adolescence.

This rare glimpse into the adult significance of sister relationships is echoed in a case illustrating a different theme. In the case of a neurotic adult female patient, Klein traced this woman's conflicts to an incident in the sister relationship during childhood. The patient was the younger sister and envied permission given her older sister to date young men. Her guilt about this envy led Klein's patient to project the envy onto her sister. Klein's interpretation of a dream about the sister and the emergence of compassion toward her allowed for the resolution of the conflict. Klein reported that "the fact that her sister also represented the mad part of herself turned out to be partly a projection of her own schizoid and paranoid feelings on to her sister" (1957/1984b, p. 210). When the client understood this through the interpretation of her dreams, she was able to feel compassionate toward her sister. Her compassion, therefore, helped to release her own schizoid and paranoid feelings.

Klein's work in understanding the multiplicity of the connections between siblings has laid the groundwork for the interpretation of many child analysts. Did other thinkers expand upon this call? The answer to that is mixed, as sibling relationships recede to footnote status in the development of object relations theory. To summarize Klein's list, siblings help girls to mature. These family peers help a child become a parent, reassure her about the limits of her own aggression, assist in the development of a sexual being, and join with her against the larger parents.

Fairbairn: Acknowledgment to Klein

Fairbairn, an only child, was born in Edinburgh in 1898 to a prosperous Protestant couple. His mother apparently dominated him and fostered his ambition. This dependence was broken during his stint as a soldier in World War I. During the war he was said to observe the losses experienced by those who were separated, like he was, from a person upon whom they were emotionally dependent. Over the course of his life he completed a medical degree, was married twice, and had many children. He was voted into the British Psycho-Analytical Society because of the advocacy of one of his analysands.

Fairbairn's treatment of sibling relationships seems limited to his critical analysis of Klein's work and some case material. In these evaluations he did not evaluate the sister relationship separately; indeed, he seemed to minimize it even when it seemed significant. When reviewing Klein in his book *Psychoanalytic Studies of the Personality* (1952), he acknowledged her contribution, namely that many objects may become the focus of introjection (not just the primary parent or parents). He felt that her work on sibling as object was the most developed among analytic thinkers. Still, he suggested the theory was incomplete, as it did not establish the structure for these introjections or explain the desire of a child to orally incorporate the siblings (as he believed they did the mother). His own evaluation of the object-seeking child displaced Freud and Klein's use of the pleasure and death instincts, providing a different mechanism for incorporation and the eventual development of the personality.

Fairbairn suggested that children experience their parents as objects—there to satisfy their material and physical needs. If the object is not constantly present to provide for those needs, the child learns to repress them. In its extreme, the continuing frustration of the child's needs may lead to shame and the disintegration of the personality. This occurs partly because the inconstant object becomes a bad object and the child identifies with it, making herself or himself a bad child.

It does not seem too far afield to suggest that an immature sister in the role of primary caretaker might represent such an object and create shame related to the drive for relationship and constancy. Although Fairbairn did not make this leap, he did recognize the inability of the child to develop a mutually satisfying affective exchange with an unsatisfying object.

Like Freud and Klein before him, Fairbairn provides us with insight into sibling relationships primarily through case material. One such case includes many sisters and one brother in an unusual family. The patient was a woman with "male pseudo-hermaphroditism" (1952, p. 198). She had essential masculinity with female secondary sexual and genital characteristics. The woman had many sisters, more than one of whom suffered the same syndrome. Their syndromes were never explored, since they never required surgery. In pages of her analysis, Fairbairn mentions those sisters only briefly, but describes in detail the effect of the trauma of the one brother's death shortly after the client had a dream of aggressive oral sadism toward him. Following the brother's death, his wife and daughter came to live with the patient. His daughter, the patient's niece, is described by Fairbairn as an expression of the brother's penis, rather than a complete female towards whom the patient had jealous feelings. One incident suggests hostility between the two women based upon the niece's behavior (trampling the flowers of her aunt). Most of the focus in the case is on the relationship between the patient, her brother, and her brother's family. Given the unusual nature of the family and the prolifera- tion of intersexed "sisters," the focus on the brother and sister does not seem to make sense. The gender confusion, the shared features of this confusion with more than one of her sisters, and the lack of consideration of their relationships to each other is quite astounding.

Fairbairn's lack of siblings and his dependent relationship with his mother may have influenced his formulations in this case and others. Without brothers or sisters, he may have had little knowledge of the role they can play in the develop- ment of identity. Clearly, this example shows his ability to consider the role of the brother as touchstone for sexual identity when the patient is confused. Yet the ability of the other intersexed sisters to model adaptation for the patient was not considered, nor was there an awareness of how such an identity might cause an altered form of gender identity in the family. Such clear negligence of the impor- tance of sisters is often caused by lack of personal empathy for such a bond. In Fairbairn's case it might have been difficult to imagine a brother–sister relation- ship in all of its manifestations—a female sibling bond being nearly impossible for this only child.

Winnicott: Avoiding the Conflict of Rivalrous Sisters

Winnicott was an interesting example of a theorist greatly influenced by female siblings, yet he avoided one of the biggest "sisterly" rivalries in the analytic move- ment: he remained uncommitted in the ideological struggle between Anna Freud and Melanie Klein. When considering his family history, it seemed clear why he might have chosen this path. Born the youngest child and only son in a family of five, he was left to the devices of his mother and two older sisters (5 and 6 years his senior) by a politically ambitious if uneducated father. Winnicott suggested that his father "left him to all of his mothers" (Hughes, 1989, p. 1). Little wonder that he might consider siblings and absent parents as important in child development.

Winnicott believed that the primary object for an infant need not be its mother. He suggested that mothers had two functions: one function was an object mother who satisfies the child's needs; the other was an environmental mother who protects the child from harm. According to his theory, good-enough mothering was natural and could be provided by someone other than the biological mother. Thus a sibling fulfilling the mother role might provide a good-enough object. Unfortunately this theme was not the focus of his published cases. The case of Gabrielle may be the worst clinical example of minimizing the obvious importance of sisters in young female development.

Gabrielle's consultations with Winnicott are summarized in the book *The Piggle: An Account of the Psychoanalytic Treatment of a Little Girl* (published after Winnicott's death, with Gabrielle's permission, in 1977). The consultations began when Gabrielle was 21 months old and continued for 2.5 years, with 17 reported consultations. In this rich record, the important understanding of the birth of her sibling, Susan, and the sister's importance in the analytic hour can be evaluated.

Gabrielle was a toddler who suffered from childhood depression. Her symptoms were listlessness, inability to play, insistence that she was someone else (usually her mother or sister), speaking in an artificial voice, scratching of her face at night, references to the black mummy, and insomnia. These symptoms began at Susan's birth and persisted for several years. Winnicott initially described his patient's symptoms as a disruption of the natural progression toward the achievement of emotional ambivalence. The birth of her sister and its emotional effects upon Gabrielle were described in an initial letter by Gabrielle's mother:

> She had a little sister (now seven months old) when she was twenty-one months old, which I considered far too early for her. And both this and (I would think also) our anxiety about it seemed to bring about a great change in her. (Winnicott, 1977, p. 6)

Winnicott added this comment in a footnote: "I did not know until much later that the mother herself had experienced the birth of a sibling at this very age" (p. 6). His analysis of the situation at the end of the initial consultation suggested:

> Trouble started with the arrival of the new baby, which forced the Piggle [family name for Gabrielle] into premature ego development. She was not ready for simple ambivalence. (p. 17)

Winnicott traced the development of ambivalence for the sister, as well as for the parents, showing evidence that the resolution of splitting may occur through the use of the sister as an object. It was clearly not Winnicott's primary focus in the analysis, but Gabrielle's symptoms would, at times, lead him back to this sister relationship during the consultations and play sessions he had with her. Gabrielle also assumed her sister's identity at many times during the course of her young life—in an attempt to win back her mother's love or regress to being an infant. Winnicott focused on the dynamic interrelationship between mother, father, and Gabrielle. The little girl believed she was her father's favorite and Susan, her sister, was her mother's.

In other attempts to draw attention to the sister relationship, young Gabrielle frequently began her sessions with a reference to her sister. At the ninth consultation, she walked into the session, commented on two toys, and then said:

> Susan does get excited in the mornings. I called to the grownups: "Susan is excited!" She says: "My big sister's up." She wakes mummy and daddy in the night; a little monster. "Mama! Dada!" She has to have a bottle in the night! (p. 111)

Throughout the analysis Gabrielle used her sister's name, as did her mother. They seemed to suggest that the dynamics in the sister relationship were primary. At one point Gabrielle—beginning to feel some guilt about not bringing Susan to therapy—indicated Susan needed it because she woke her parents at night, and yet Gabrielle wanted to keep the doctor for herself. The Piggle began to reflect on Susan's growth and their connection in the eleventh consultation, when she opened the session with these words, "The udder evening I woke and I had a dream about a train. I called Susan next door. Susan seemed to understand. She has had her birthday and she is now two. . . Susan understands better" (p. 135). Susan became less central in the next session, but there was a theme identified by Winnicott related to her. Gabrielle always came with her father alone to see Winnicott. Often, Gabrielle expressed fear that her sister would be angry at being left out of the trip. There was also a play theme Winnicott identified. Gabrielle suggests there was not room for Susan in the car. Susan became the excluded fourth party in the family. In Winnicott's writings about the case it became clear that the integration of the good and bad mother was parallel to the integration of the good and bad sister (in session 13, when she is 4 and Susan is 2). This exchange, as Winnicott neared termination with Gabrielle, suggested her growing understanding of her younger sister and the continuity of the relationship.

> Gabrielle: When we were coming to you, we were a bit early, so we walked around, so I must buy something for Susan and mummy. I like Susan and mummy.
>
> [Winnicott]: Here there is just Gabrielle and me. Is Susan cross when you come and see me?

Gabrielle: Do you know Susan . . . she likes to watch me dance. How old is she? She is two. I am four. Next birthday I will be five and Susan will be three. (p. 170)

Gabrielle's case was successfully concluded and she matured to become successful at making friends and with aspirations to become a teacher. In the parents' comments provided in the *Afterword*, no mention is made of Susan. Winnicott's theoretical work did not seem to reflect the relationship either, although this case did come within a decade of his death.

Winnicott did consider the relationship between Gabrielle's mother and her sister in formulating his theories about Gabrielle. In doing so, he made the mother side of the mother–child relationship come alive (Hughes, 1989). Unlike Klein, who had referred to the mother as an empty box for the child, Winnicott gave her substance and form. He suggested that the mother can have empathy for the child, as Gabrielle's mother had empathy for her at the birth of Susan. Here are Winnicott's words about this issue in the book *Babies and their Mothers*:

The mother has of course herself been a baby. It is all in her somewhere, the experiential conglomerate, with herself dependent and gradually achieving autonomy. Further she has played at being a baby, as well as at mothers and fathers; she has regressed to baby ways during illnesses; she has perhaps watched her mother caring for younger siblings. (Winnicott, 1987, p. 94)

Like Gabrielle, her mother had watched a younger sister cared for by her mother and learned empathy for the experience of being replaced in the mother's arms, "far too early." Winnicott presents us with enough raw materials to speculate about the importance of the sister relationship. In this case, Gabrielle and Susan, their mother, and her sister may have had a significant effect on the development of Winnicott's understanding. Still, the primary focus remains on the relationship between Gabrielle and her parents—Susan and the mother's sister become an unreconciled afterword.

Can the Sister be a Primary Object?

Masterson and Ralph Klein

The importance of siblings for the development of personality disorders is missing from much of Masterson's theoretical discussion. But, like many of the authors who consider early childhood development, he discusses siblings in the context of his cases. The most specific application may be in his analysis of the famous artist, Edward Munch. He analyzed Munch theoretically and suggested that he suffered from borderline personality disorder—a disorder Munch managed through creative expression. In this description, Masterson discusses Munch's relationship with his sister, who helped to parent him after the early death of their mother. When Munch's sister died at age 15, Masterson suggested:

> These early childhood events made an indelible impression on his charac-
> ter, his perceptions and feelings about women, and his need to create
> through his art the real self that was unable to emerge when he was a child.
> From his graphic portrayals of separation anxiety and abandonment
> depression and the difficulties he had in personal relationships in his life, I
> hypothesize that he was a borderline personality and therefore was unable
> to mourn the deaths of his mother and sister. (Masterson, 1988, p. 212)

Here, Masterson seems to suggest that Munch's sister became the primary object. Yet, his thorough description of the stages of pre-oedipal development in the same work did not address the advent of siblings, their role in development, or the potential for introjection Klein and others had suggested earlier. Indeed, Masterson felt that the adolescent or adult individual with a personality disorder was best treated in individual therapy. He recommends against family therapy for the borderline or narcissistic patient, even in adolescence, since the presence of others divests the therapist role as primary object for the patient. He says, "It is not possible to work through the abandonment depression in front of other people" (1988, p. 206). He felt the abandonment depression was the primary key to improvement in the individual with borderline character structure. Without that focus, according to Masterson, the borderline does not invest in treatment. He did suggest that a person with schizoid personality disorder may best be treated in a group context, but did not mention family or sibling involvement.

In another edited book, by Masterson and Ralph Klein (1989), several thera-pists discuss clinical work with sibling or sister issues. Grubb (1989) reported on the case of Ms. C. He described her relationship with six much older siblings, all of whom used her as a go-between and manipulated her. Grubb uses this case to illustrate the boundary between the development of personality disorders and bipolar disorders. In the same book, Richard Fischer (1989) discusses group ther-apy with the personality-disordered patient using Masterson's approach. He drew a parallel between three types of group functioning and cultural/racial and warring factions within the world. He does not make the link to the family con-stellation, perhaps because he thinks Yalom erred in making the group therapy process about the interpersonal rather than the intrapsychic.

Ralph Klein, writing with Masterson about the individual with schizoid person-ality disorder, makes some comments about the inner world of patients with that disorder and, again, all but ignores the sibling role. He suggests that the child has an internal representation of itself and the parent. That representation is known as an internal object. The child needs the parent, as represented by the internal object, to function in a certain way. Likewise, a developmentally arrested parent needs the child to satisfy his or her own immature internal object. If the child does not satisfy this need, he or she is ignored until the need within the parent arises again. By the age of 9 or 10, the child recognizes that the parent/caretaker supplies will never be available; the child also realizes that he or she will never be recognized as satisfying the parental needs for relationship. Thus a distancing occurs with all other potential objects in the child's world. Nothing is expected, and when emotional supplies are offered, no one is trusted. There is no mention of siblings in this discussion. However, Klein does comment upon the family experience of the patient in this way:

> The experience of schizoid patients is that they are not living, dynamic parts of the family systems in which they grew up. They experienced themselves as being treated as objects without unique feelings, used and manipulated for whatever shifting purposes they were called on to serve. (Masterson & Klein, 1989, p. 48)

In tracing the developmental history further, he notes:

> The crucial problem for the future schizoid patient is that the other person is not available to provide the kind of cues or responses that the child needs at those critical moments in life when decisions cannot be made by the child alone. (p. 47)

But cannot an older sibling provide those cues and responses? Indeed, one of the cases within this edited volume describes an oldest daughter of a family and her role as a caretaker for the younger ones. Ralph Klein uses this to illustrate her schizoid development —her role is appropriated for the parents' use. But does she then pass on this schizoid relational style to those siblings for whom she cares? The case descriptions seem to stop just shy of providing implications for younger siblings and sisters or for understanding their effect on the developing child.

Chatham: Applications to Therapy

Chatham (1985), another object relations author, describes the sister or sibling role in more detail when discussing the issues related to multiple caretakers. She reviews the theories of several object relations authors who discuss the assumption of the parental role by children within the family. According to Mandelbaum (1980), this creates poor family boundaries and is especially likely to occur in families containing children who have been diagnosed as borderline or narcissistic later in life. Of the three cases described in detail in Chatham's book, one has no siblings, one has distant relationships with her sister and brother, and the third has a family split. She is the bad child; her sister is the good one. In contrast to Masterson, Chatham advocates family work in such circumstances, and the application is described.

As a whole, object relations theorists have ignored the potential for the sister to be both the good and the bad object. For this approach, the greatest developmental achievement is the understanding of ambivalence—that one can feel both positive and negative feelings toward another. The developmental maturity results in an understanding that needs are sometimes met by others and sometimes they are not. I think siblings, especially sisters, provide ample opportunity for the development of such ambivalence, yet there is little developmental work within object relations theory that considers how this might occur. Much of the work of the object relations theorists focuses on the first four pre-oedipal years of life. Failure to examine the importance of sibling and peer interactions throughout childhood gave rise to missed understandings within object relations theory.

Kernberg: Internal Structure as a Foundation for Relationship

The criticisms leveled at Melanie Klein by Winnicott are partly answered in the self psychology of Otto Kernberg. His theories attempt to explain the integration of internal objects into the ego, id, and superego structures of Freud. Kernberg's developmental trajectories move further into childhood and provide an opportunity to evaluate partial objects (both good and bad) from many sources. The notion that normal development includes the integration of partial objects into an ego identity is described in his work *Object Relations Theory and Clinical Psychoanalysis* (1976). Other partial objects continue to be absorbed as the individual grows and develops, suggesting that sibling or sister relationships may be integrated into the ego ideal. Kernberg suggested that "the enrichment of one's personal life by the internal presence of such selective, partial identifications representing people who are loved and admired in a realistic way without indiscriminate internalization constitutes a major source of emotional depth and well-being" (p. 33–4).

The inclusion of this positive well-being is dependent upon seeing the other as a whole person and achieving ambivalence toward her. The parent who refused to satisfy some needs and was willing to set limits is a necessary component of the internal other that leads to superego development. The comparison of the ideal self to the real self as seen through the prohibitive or frustrating parents' eyes gives rise to a process of guilt and the development of an internal observing mechanism. Perhaps an application of sibling conflict could be integrated here as well.

Kernberg includes sisters or siblings not in a footnote, but in parentheses. His developmental trajectory follows these four steps:

1. Splitting emerges in the third month and comes to full fruition over the next several months.
2. Splitting disappears during the second or third year.
3. Superego functioning is developed during the second to fifth years.
4. There is further development of the superego through the seventh year.

When discussing stage 3 in the development of the ego, Kernberg suggests that there is a period of differentiation of the good and bad self and the good and bad object. He notes a potential role for sisters, but only in parentheses, stating that partial objects are formed "(at first representing mother, and then also father, siblings, etc.)" (p. 67). Thus siblings are recognized as potential internal objects in Kernberg's theory. He does not give details about how this might occur for sisters; indeed, there is little mention of the potential for mutual influence by sisters.

However, a group of women theorists has addressed the issue of women's development in a clearer and more profound way. Their efforts have led to a newly integrated understanding of relationships between mothers and daughters, as well as female friends.

Feminist Therapists and the Foundation for a Sister Connection

Jean Baker Miller

Jean Baker Miller was "one of three children in a poor family, and the girls in her neighborhood didn't go to college." She suffered from polio from 10 months of age and had multiple surgeries before age 10. It is not clear, even in Miller's obituary, if these siblings were sisters or brothers. On the other hand, two sisters, unrelated to Miller, had an important effect on her life and career. When she had polio, she was cared for by women who were twin sisters and worked as nurses. These women recognized Miller's intellectual gifts and advocated higher education for her. They also encouraged Miller's mother to enroll her daughter in a special school for girls, Hunter College High School. The young Miller had to ride an hour on public transportation to attend Hunter; no doubt the effort to get to the school reflected how strongly she wanted an education. Attending an all-girls' academy may have allowed Miller to develop a questioning attitude toward existing patriarchal structures and could have led to the development of a woman-centered psychology. Thus, her nurses played a profound role in her life and the development of her thinking (Backman, 1988).

According to Jordan, a colleague and co-author who knew Miller for 30 years, the experience of being a woman in a male-dominated field helped lead Miller to a paradigm shift in the psychological understanding of women (Woo, 2006). Once Miller entered psychiatry, she became convinced that "a lot of what was written about women was just completely wrong" (p. B8), Jordan said. In an interview following Miller's death, Jordan suggested that Miller was the first to recognize that psychology failed to consider women's voices.

Miller's history included participation in women's consciousness-raising groups of the 1960s. In those groups she was heard by other women and had intimate emotional conversations with others who questioned the ways in which women's emotional connections had been understood. As an analyst, she reinterpreted the words of women to reflect their own rather than a pathological understanding of those connections. Thus, words like "caring" and "connection" became a clear part of the way she described women's relationships with each other. These reflected a sister-like bond, even though the existence of sisters in Miller's life is not mentioned.

Miller lived her adult life with three men—her husband and two sons. In the introduction to her first book, *Psychoanalysis and Women*, she said, "I consider myself luckier than most in being able to engage in my own personal struggle for equality with three fine and rare men, my husband, Mike, and my sons Jon and Ned" (1973, p. xv). Miller described the emotional growth of her husband and sons, which paralleled her own ability to find and express her understanding of women, and felt grateful for their influence.

The Stone Center for Human Development

It was a sisterhood of thinkers, working with Miller, who developed relational-cultural theory. Miller, along with Judith Jordan, Janet Surrey, Alexandra Kaplan, and Irene Stiver, crafted relational-cultural theory at least partly from their own relationships with each other. These relationships were born of the emotional need for support in the male-dominated world of psychiatry and psychology in the 1980s. The women's sense of exclusion from an all-boys' club helped establish a weekly women's circle—the rival of the early psychoanalytic circle. Their combined intellectual efforts re-evaluated existing psychological theory and led to the publication of several books, including *Women's Growth In Connection* (Jordan, Kaplan, Miller, Stiver, & Surrey, 1991), *Women's Growth in Diversity* (Jordan, 1997a, b), and *The Healing Connection* (Miller & Stiver, 1997).

Little is known of the sister relationships of the other women in this group. All are still living, save Alexandra Kaplan and Irene Stiver. Dr. Stiver's obituary lists only her husband as surviving her. Together she and Miller were mentors for the younger women in the group, helping them to find entry into the male-dominated field. Since their works focus on women's development and redefining the mother–daughter connection, very little is written by them about sister relationships. The themes from their work and the likely applications to sister relationships are covered in detail in a subsequent chapter.

McGoldrick and Feminist Family Therapy

Another group of female authors have examined sibling and sister relationships in some detail. Following the established tradition of family therapy, these women evaluate the role of siblings and sometimes sisters in much more detail. McGoldrick, Anderson, and Walsh described their own work together as the product of a sisterhood of theorists (McGoldrick, 1989; McGoldrick, Anderson, & Walsh, 1989).

This 20-year collaboration is described by them in one of their books. In fact, that introductory section is titled "Personal Connections: The Importance of Sisterhood." They have provided us with a clear description of their sister relationships and how those relationships influenced their feminist approach to family therapy. None of the three authors had brothers, but two had multiple sisters. Those sibling constellations contributed to their levels of achievement. According to their own self-analysis, the fact that none of the women had brothers led to an expectation of higher achievement. Had their families had sons, perhaps those expectations would have been less intense for women growing up in a culture that was still emerging from a feminist revolution. Their ability to work together and their sibling positions contributed to their willingness to pen a theoretical reconstruction of family therapy from a woman's viewpoint. Their ideas, along with those of other family therapists, are also covered in detail in a subsequent chapter.

Conclusions

The nature of the sister relationship and its importance in the history of psychological theory development seems tied directly to the context of the theories, their historical time period, and the authors' own experience of having sisters. Not surprisingly, male theorists have been historically less likely to distinguish the sister relationship from that of siblings in general. Many have minimized the importance of siblings altogether. Theories that are based upon universally held principles, like psychoanalysis, have been traditionally related to male development and understanding, generalizing that experience to women.

Three changes have helped to create theoretical understanding of the sister relationship. One of those changes was the advent of modern feminism and its influence on the shaping of psychological theory. A second change, related to the first, was the engagement of women authors as developers of theories that take a uniquely female perspective into account. The third change has been the presence of sister relationships among those authors—women who understood the importance those sisters held for their own development. Contextual and deconstructionist theories like narrative family theories and relational-cultural theory provide more insight into female–female relationships and, therefore, more understanding of the sister connection. Yet these remain theories without research that explores the voices of sisters. It seemed to me there was much to be gained from a project that really listened intently to the voices of a larger, more varied group of women who had sisters. The results of such a project are the subject of the next five chapters of this work.

2

The Voices of Sisters

"[W]omen often feel unheard even when they believe that they
have something important to say."
                    Belenky, Clinchy, Goldberger, and Tarule (1986, p. 5)

Several authors have conducted interviews with sisters and have attempted to
understand what they said (e.g., Fishel, 1979; Stark, 2007). These studies have
yielded important information about women's subjective view of sisters and
have—like many narrative approaches—been based in the authors' own experience of being a sister. This chapter presents the differences between such methods
and the methods used in my research on sisters. It also presents an overview
of the findings from the study and provides an essential description of the experience of sisters.

The method I used to gather and analyze interview material in this project differed from other narrative approaches. My research used phenomenology as a
method (Giorgi, 1985). This method made it possible to understand and bracket
my own experience of being a sister during the research. The process of bracketing
works by limiting the effects of the researcher's experience on the interview
process. It is similar to the methods used by therapists to limit the role of countertransference in therapy. When using the bracketing technique, my own assumptions based upon my relationships with my sisters, my research assistant's
experiences based upon her experience of not having sisters, and our experiences
of other sisters were set aside through individual processes of reflective writing.
These reflections were then reconsidered and compared to the findings of the
research study toward the end. It was expected that similarities would emerge, as
would differences. In this manner, our own presuppositions were prevented from
guiding the findings.

Another significant difference in the completion of this project was the atheo-
retical approach to the research. Some studies of sister relationships have used a
psychological theory as the starting point for understanding the sister relationship. Toni McNaron (1985) did this when she considered the complementary roles
sisters develop in reaction to each other and in order to fulfill family needs. Terri
Apter (2007) did this as well when she organized her work using the theory of
Carol Gilligan (1993) and others. In phenomenological approaches, theory may

be generated or integrated later, but it is not imposed from the start. Instead, the women's experiences create understanding and help develop theory.

The women who participated in the study were, therefore, allowed to speak for themselves. The essence of their experience was preserved, without removal of unique and important differences, even if these were idiosyncratic. This essence created a landscape of the potential within every sister relationship.

The Approach

After bracketing our experience and expectations for the research through a written description, we began to approach women who were willing to talk with us[1] about their sisters and be recorded. The women were recruited through a snowball technique, with one woman who participated nominating another one. Individuals who we knew to have sisters were approached. These included colleagues, students, and acquaintances, but not clients. If the individual had a close emotional connection or professional conflict (student–teacher) relationship with the researcher, that woman was interviewed by the research assistant, and vice versa. The only requirements for these participants were that they had a full biological sister, with whom they were raised, and that they could speak clearly about their experience. Sisters in every decade of life participated. They ranged from teenagers (17) to women in their eighties. Four were African American, one was Japanese American, 19 were white, and the rest declined to state. The average number of sisters was 1.64. Eleven were oldest sisters, eight were youngest, six were middle sisters, and the birth order of the others is unknown. Each woman completed an initial interview and a follow-up interview. Initially, two women from each decade were interviewed; others were added until the phenomenological requirement of saturation was reached. Saturation was defined as the point at which new themes did not emerge from the interviews. In all, 29 women participated.

Some demographics have been described here, but when using phenomenological methods, the representative nature of the sample is not considered; it is the essence of the phenomenon that is significant: has it been fully described and does it encompass the primary elements of the sister relationship? The participants were, therefore, described by the nature of their lives rather than by a summary of their defining characteristics. Each sister filled out a brief demographic questionnaire and then completed the interview. The women were asked one simple question: Please describe as completely as possible your relationship with _____ (fill in sister's name). When a woman had more than one sister, she was asked this question about each of them, starting with the oldest. We used

---

[1] The interviews were conducted by me and research assistant Diane Lassman, PhD.

the following prompts to encourage additional expression and to clarify the women's thoughts: (a) Please tell me more about _____; (b) I am not sure I understood what you meant when you said _____; (c) Say more about that; and (d) Is there anything else you would like to say about your sister? The importance of deepening but not leading the women's expression also mimics a good therapeutic relationship. The women's own words were used to fill in the blanks. The time to complete the interviews ranged from 30 minutes to 2.5 hours.

After the initial interview, the women's interviews were transcribed and read for clarity. At times the audio recordings were difficult to hear or understand. These clarifications and another simple question formed the basis for the second interview. The women were asked: Please describe any thoughts, feelings, or images you have had about _____ (sister's name) since our last interview. This first question was followed with the same prompts used in the initial interview. After completion of that segment of the interview, clarifying questions were asked about the first interview. The woman's words were read to her and she was asked to say more about that specific expression. The follow-up interview was transcribed and added to the original transcript for each woman so that the analysis could begin.

The Analysis

A most important part of phenomenological research is the preservation of every word of the participant. To remain true to the words of these women, we began each data analysis segment with a brief period of self-reflection and relaxation. The purpose of these reflections was to clear the mind of the expectations and ideas we had about the sister relationship. Once this additional bracketing process occurred, we began to break the woman's ideas into meaning units.

These units included phrases, sentences, paragraphs, or stories that are naturally separated in meaning from the words that proceed or follow them. An example of a meaning unit is demonstrated in this quotation:

> And um, ever since that time we've just grown into being friends—best friends. And it's real interesting to talk to my sister because she. . . she's one of my best friends, but she's also the only person that shares my parents. (Andrea-6)[2]

Each meaning unit is translated into psychological language, without loss of the woman's original detail. For example, the meaning unit above was translated

---

[2] The names following any meaning unit or referring to any individual person are fictional. Permission to quote the participants was obtained at the time of the interviews. The number refers to the place this meaning unit holds in the sequence of the meaning units derived from this woman's interview.

to: The woman emphasized that it was a unique circumstance that her sister has become one of her best friends and the only person who shared her parents (19-6). This process of translating meaning units was repeated for each portion of every transcribed interview.

Once we had transcribed all of the meaning units, they formed the basis for the creation of the structure of experience across all women. For the rest of the analysis I worked alone. I took the entire list of meaning units and sorted them into categories. Next, I created themes within each category, and combined all meaning units within a category to create these themes. Thus a list of themes combining information from all participants was generated. These themes formed the basis for a combination of categories into clusters. The clusters were presented in a final structure of the women's experience.

Table 2.1 presents a sample of this process of analysis from meaning unit through cluster.

All of these combinations were done through a process of conscious intention, reflective self-awareness, and a consideration of the possible and essential

Table 2.1 **Two examples of the phenomenological analysis used in this research from quotation through theme**

Quotation	Meaning Unit	Category	Theme
Well, to be together, to talk and to touch and just look at each other. . . .I'll go over there and stay maybe and she'll lay there and half sleep. But she'll wake up and see Elizabeth, and. . . She knows I'm there. (Lynetta-50)	During one sister's dying days, she emphasizes that the three sisters need one another's comfort, presence, and care. (Lynetta-50)	Supportive Interactions Between Sisters	There is an enduring quality to the support felt from the sister, whether functional or emotional: a sense that she will be there when others are not.
Gina and I had a lot more respect for each other's privacy because we never really had anything together, but Brooke and I basically come and go as we please between each other's rooms because we stayed in a room together, but it's not like we're invading each other's privacy or anything. (Hillary-6)	Sharing a room as children lowers current boundaries with her sister when she compares the sense of privacy between her and her two sisters. (Hillary-6)	Perceptions of Closeness/ Distance	Closeness to an individual sister is compared to closeness to and between other siblings.

relationships between the ideas expressed. This method of analysis has been described in more detail by Giorgi (1985), Colaizzi (1978), and Moustakas (1994). Their psychological adaptation of Husserl's phenomenological method provided a basis for analysis that made it much more difficult for me to simply recreate my own experience using these women's words.

The Structure of Experience

The overall experience of having a sister was captured in a visual representation of the women's words (Fig. 2.1). Each portion of the diagram represents a cluster of categories. Basic information about each cluster is presented here. They are described in detail, with accompanying quotes in Chapters 3 through 7.

Ways of Perceiving and Knowing

The most basic element of the sister experience is the way that it becomes conscious. The women described how they came to understand the relationship with their sisters. This understanding was based upon five distinct types of perceiving and knowing. *Frozen images* of sisters persisted in the women's memories. These images gave them a basis for remembering certain events and stories about their sisters. Family photographs and memories of younger sisters as children

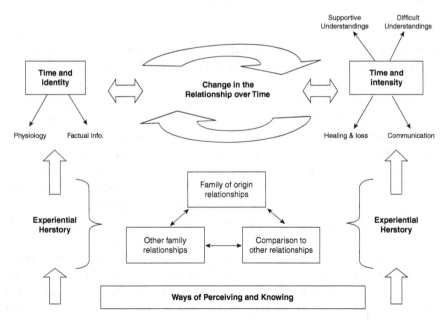

Figure 2.1 The Structure of the Sister Relationship over Time.

were two types of images described. *Oral history* was also an important way of knowing the sister and describing the relationship. Most often, this type of knowing came from repeated stories told by older family members. Sometimes, mothers provided *secondhand information* about the sister, which was a crucial part of understanding the relationship. As participants in the research, the women expressed awareness that the *interview had affected their experience* with their sisters by causing them to compare themselves to others, creating an awareness of memories that were long forgotten, providing an emotional release for pent-up feelings, and, in some cases, resulting in a re-evaluation of their relationship with their sister(s). They also wondered how their interviews might help or affect the *interviewer*, whose presence and relationship with them created a fifth way of knowing.

The Changing Relationship over Time

Time represented another dimension of knowing. Sisters tracked their experiences based upon many indicators of time. There was awareness that sisters pass through developmental stages that change the relationship. These stages were defined by the balance of instrumental and expressive needs. They expressed the knowledge that the sister's importance remained throughout these stages. The sister may have been more important during periods of change in other relationships and less important during periods where achievement was the primary focus. With these life stages came differing expectations and judgments toward the sister. So, time became a primary means of expressing the ways the sister relationship was stagnant or was altered.

The women were sometimes uncertain about how they were presenting the experience. On many occasions they questioned their own veracity and wondered if their judgments were accurate representations of the relationship. Some women felt the sister never fulfilled the expectations they had. At times their judgments of their sisters were harsh. Some women described others' judgments in an attempt to bolster their own position. They said their negative opinions were shared by other sisters in the family. Some women recognized the growth in sister relationships over time. Women who did not experience such growth longed for it; those who had it wondered if it was universal. There was also an expression of hopefulness for the sister and for the self. All of these reactions to one's own remembering formed a part of how the experience changed over time.

With the passage of time came maturation and separation from the sister. These were expected to affect how the relationship was experienced over time. Time was also expected to change memory. For these women, maturation referred to the change in the individual as well as the resulting change in the relationship. Women who were older found that the some of the difficulties with their sisters disappeared as a younger sister matured. Late in life there was often a role reversal, with younger sisters becoming caretakers for ill or dying older sisters.

These changes over time were experienced as a natural progression, but sometimes women attempted to intentionally create a change in a relationship with a sister. Some women expressed a desire to have a more authentic relationship and described ways they had tried to abandon their prescribed family role to facilitate this change.

With time, memories were altered, sometimes softened and sometimes hardened. For some women, time seemed to transform memories about sisterhood and included a healing and forgetting aspect. In some cases, the women worked with their sisters to try to heal a breach between them. For others, pain from the past festered and growth seemed impossible. Another group of women described the importance of the regret and the inability to change the relationship when a sister had died. The loss of a sister could spark new attempts to create more authentic relationships with remaining sisters. In all of these instances there was an attunement to the quality and nature of the relationship and an observation of its changing nature.

Separation from the sister had an effect on this changing nature of the relationship. Closeness in the sister relationship was balanced with an increasing sense of separation and self-definition. In their early years such separation was expressed as new privacy from the child or adolescent sister; in adulthood it was experienced as an ability to remain separate from a sister's emotions. A woman's sense of herself was often in response to this physical or emotional movement away from the sister.

Another dimension of time in the relationship was expressed as hope for the future. Mature women were able to understand the lack of closeness in their relationship and yet still hope for it. The desire was tied to the maturation of each woman and her sister. Sometimes the woman described her own maturation as important for potential growth in the relationship; sometimes she felt the growth depending upon her sister's maturation. The hopefulness emerged in the woman's understanding of her later years. Often she pictured finishing life with a sister— perhaps living together. They expected to do so with humor, candor, and support, having outlived other relatives and primary partners.

The women also expressed hope and concern for their sister's happiness, sometimes criticizing the sister's inability to achieve it. Others were blamed for the sister's failure to achieve happiness. The sisters themselves were sometimes blamed for failing to move toward their own dreams and goals. However, most women wanted their sisters to be happy, and expressed a sense that sisters should have what they desire most. They wished that the sister's actions would be more consistent with her dreams. The hopes for the sister, for her dreams, and for her happiness were an expression of the women's optimism and an overall belief in the sister's ability to move forward.

Hopefulness, maturation, the passage of time, and the change in memory were all dimensions of growth between sisters. These dimensions formed a background as the women told about the history of the relationship—an experience I call "herstory." It is this dimension of the past that formed the next component of the women's experience.

Herstory

This sister–sister bond was understood in light of other close and intimate connections in the women's lives. These formed the women's herstory.[3] The sister relationship was compared to three other categories of relationship: (a) family of origin relationships, (b) family relationships, extended and created, and (c) relationships outside the family. Mothers, fathers, other siblings, and those residing within the family home created a topographical map upon which the sister relationship is located. This map reflected depth, as well as distance. It provided landmarks against which the sister relationship was judged. Among other issues, this map plotted the dimensions of the sister relationship and answered the questions: (a) How close was the relationship with the sister compared to the relationship with the mother? (b) How was the relationship influenced by experiences with the sister and father? (c) How did the sisters form a bond in childhood? and (d)What elements of that relationship persist into adult life? These and many other issues emerged from the findings as a woman described her sister relationship and compared it to other relationships from the past.

Family of Origin Relationships

First women considered the childhood relationship with her sisters. Sisters acted out their childhood dramas with each other, often resulting in residual guilt or jealousy. Sometimes these difficult emotions were caused by differing expectations of other people. These expectations may have been based upon one sister's previous accomplishments or her talents, as occurred when one sister was more artistic or intellectual. The resulting jealousy may have led to violence and even persistent fear. Sometimes this fear became a hypervigilance with respect to the next generation of sisters. Women described watching their daughters' relationship with each other and attempting to prevent viciousness between the next generation of sisters. As suggested by these themes, the effects of these childhood sister interactions were sometimes described as persistent and harmful in later life. In addition to their relationships with each other in childhood, the relationship between two sisters and a third member of the family were often described as significant for the women.

Frequently the women mentioned mother–daughter–sister interactions as a determining factor in their current relationships with their sisters. As I listened to these women speak about their mothers and sisters, it became clear that the

---

[3] The term *herstory* is used throughout the book to describe the woman's personal history.

triadic relationship created the emotional center of the family. Brothers and fathers—when present—may have influenced the alignment within the triad but were rarely a part of its substance. The alignment between the woman interviewed, her sister, and her mother was understood on many dimensions. Among them were closeness, distance, similarity, and difference. Sisters and mothers compensated for each other; one offset the other's absence or lack of skills. Sometimes a sister interfered between the other sister and her mother; sometimes a mother interfered between the two daughters. Often a sister was judged for failing to participate fully in the triad. The relationship was often multigenerational: the next generation of sisters was sometimes included in this analysis and comparison.

Another triad was formed by the father–daughter–sister relationship group. This relationship group was usually defined by intensity of interaction. The father's relationship with one sister may have created jealousy or distance between sisters. In families with traditional gender role assignment, the joyful entrance of the father at the end of his workday was remembered happily by some women. When fathers distanced themselves emotionally, the sisters may have bonded to overcome the sense of emotional loss. They were sometimes kept from creating such closeness by the father's interference. In extreme cases, the women described a strong desire to shelter each other from an abusive father's anger or sexual molestation.

Some women recognized the way a father had been excluded from the center of the family by the women. A few of them described growth in their ability to see and understand this dynamic. Regret about this was sometimes expressed. These views of the father–daughter–sister experience were described much less frequently by the women than their perspectives on the triad with the mother, but the intense emotional feelings about both triads were strongly stated.

Differing expectations by parents led to complexity in the relationship between sisters and siblings. How much did they fit with their sisters and brothers? Some siblings were identified with their mother's family; some were identified with their fathers. This labeling as being a part of mom's family or dad's led to different groups within the family. Groups of siblings and parental expectations also occurred by gender. In families with all female children, one of the girls may have been treated like a son, with expectations for traditionally male activities and interests. A brother's birth may have altered all of these expectations and led to a greater alliance among sisters or a realignment with younger brothers. In addition, parental favoritism could lead to fierce competitiveness and even lifelong estrangement from a sister. Yet some sister bonds formed the basis for emotional closeness of the entire family. The complex dynamics of the family were partially determined by the sister relationship, and in some cases these dynamics helped to create a stronger or more conflicted relationship.

Strong relationships with some family members may have interfered. If the woman was aligned with her mother and sister, this may have created conflict with another grouping in the family. Sometimes sisters aligned with each other against a parent; sometimes they aligned with the parents against a sister's criticism. When the family itself was not close, the lack of closeness required that the sisters work harder to have a strong emotional bond. Thus, family allegiances affected the woman's sister connections.

The women's herstory was also shaped by the lifespan changes in each sister. The women describe a shifting of feelings toward the sister from birth through older adulthood; these feelings include anticipation, jealousy about parental attention, clashes with male siblings, and honest communication with the sister as an adult. In the beginning, the birth of a sister was anticipated with hope, but the outcome was often quite different from those expectations. Sometimes the sisters did develop a close bond immediately. At other times ambivalent feelings or even homicidal rage might erupt based partially upon loss of the parents' affection. The subsequent relationship with the sister was a result of the parental reactions at birth and the ripple effect created by those reactions within the family.

As the sisters grew older their reactions to the relationship were marked by changes at various life stages. In adolescence, protectiveness emerged within some relationships. This might take the form of one sister minimizing her own gifts and abilities in order to divert attention from a less talented and often criticized sister. In young to middle adulthood, sisters exposed each other and their families to new opportunities and adventures. As they grew older, the sisters felt a growing connection with the entire family. Some sisters combined resources to care for ill family members. These life stages contributed to a growing maturity and a depth of understanding for some women; others became more estranged and distant over time.

Some specific conflicts were also described by the women. These included experiences of trauma. For example, some sisters bonded in attempting to understand why one was molested by the father and one was not. Chemical dependency was a specific concern. Some women felt isolated from one sister due to differences in substance use. Some women felt they needed to compensate for a chemically dependent sister. Often these traumas were discussed in light of a family history of chemical dependency.

Another specific circumstance that altered some sister relationships was the mutual operation of a family business. Some women felt the family business created the potential for adult dependency. Others felt the responsibility and decision making was not evenly distributed among sisters and brothers. One woman described how her family excluded one sister from significant decisions. These family business interactions also influenced the sister bond. They may have enhanced this bond or created obstacles that had to be managed or overcome.

Families: Extended and Created

Sisters described being part of a network of extended family members including aunts, cousins, and grandparents who played important roles in the development of attitudes toward the sister. Sometimes these extended family members were preferred company; sometimes they were critical of the sisters' interactions with each other. The mother's relationship with her own sisters was often presented as a role model for the sister relationship. Many women found those model relationships lacking. Another group of extended kin, sisters-in-law, was seldom mentioned. When these adult "sisters" were mentioned, most of the women expressed preference for the biological sister. Likewise, sister bonds between mothers and aunts or among a group of daughters in the extended family were examined. These were less significant than the primary sister bonds. It seemed that extended family members could have an effect on the sister relationship but were generally seen as less central. The circumstances were quite different when it came to families of creation—the primary partner and children of the woman.

The women wanted a resonance between their original family and the one they created with their husbands or partners. They wanted their family of creation to accept and respect their family of origin. These interconnections also had a developmental track. Sisters' families of creation tended to interact during young adult years, sharing activities on holidays or special occasions related to their children. They described buying gifts for their nieces and nephews. There was a desire to be present to support the sister pragmatically and emotionally during times of transition in the sister's family of creation. This was true during the intense experiences of childbirth or partner death. Women also expressed an increased desire for interaction between their sisters and their own families as they grew older. They were particularly attuned to the relationship between couples.

The women talked at length about the relationship between their sisters and their husbands or partners. The description was often presented as a comparison between the two relationships. Some women felt closer to their intimate partner; some felt closer to their sisters. The amount of information divulged to the sister ranged widely, from complete privacy about the primary relationship to detailed openness about it. Two dimensions seemed important in their influence on the sister relationship: (a) the sister's relationship with the brother-in-law or sister's partner and (b) the closeness of the partners or husbands to each other. This closeness between partners made it more likely that the couples would spend time together and that the time would be of higher quality.

The relationship between a husband and sister-in law often created interesting and diverse dynamics. In some cases the two families responsibly shared childcare responsibilities. In others the sister and brother-in-law's relationship violated family norms, creating a sense of betrayal and abandonment. The sister and brother-in-law or partner relationship seemed to change with emotional maturity and time. Often brother-in-laws or partners provided pragmatic help to widowed sisters or mothers. The health needs of husbands, partners, sisters, and parents during older years also created a shifting of responsibilities, bonds, and even living arrangements. The women said they cherished the love between their intimate partner and their family of origin—when it was present.

The women also talked at length about their relationship with their sister's children. The bond between a woman and her sister's children was a unique one that often included surrogate mothering, protectiveness, and a willingness to take over as the parent if the mother was unable to continue her responsibilities. Sometimes young children were confused about which woman was their mother, but generally there was a clear distinction between the mother and aunt role. Women shared a different bond when both were mothers. For example, if a woman had her own children, she was more likely to judge the quality of her sister's parenting. Parenting responsibilities and shared experiences with each others' children was an especially important part of the extended family herstory.

The relationship between women and their nieces was mentioned as a special bond. The story of a niece's birth included a tremendous new connection between sisters. This experience expanded the sister bond into a threesome, with the niece–aunt relationship also being significant. Sometimes this bond was deepened by family perceptions of shared similarity between an aunt and a niece. Their similarity may have created special opportunities for shared adventures and experiences. There was also a hope that the niece would have a sister, in order to recreate the sister bond for the next generation. If a sister died, the relationship between aunt and niece was expected to last past the death of the mother; often such a loss deepened the relationship between an aunt and niece. Nieces, as the potential heirs of the sister connection, had a special and important role to play in an understanding of the sisters' shared herstory.

Relationships Outside the Family

The women who participated knew a lot about their sisters' relationships with other people. These included the relationship with husbands, partners and children. The sisters' ability to have time together was influenced by these relationships. Comparisons were made and the difference in primary affection was noted, as women compared the sister relationship to relationships with intimate partners, extended family, church members, children, and friends. Many feelings accompanied the awareness of the sister's connection to others. These feelings included jealousy, envy, and judgment. Sometimes a bond with a third female family member, such as mother or daughter, created a greater sense of intimacy between sisters. One set of comparisons was made between the sisters' closeness and the emotional feelings for other significant family relationships. Women also compared the relationship they had with their sister to relationships outside the family.

The primary comparison was with other sisters within the family. Closeness between any two sisters was referenced by frequency of contact, history, age difference, similarity of interests, and similarity of current life circumstances. Sometimes a mother was used to form a quadratic relationship in which one woman was closer to her mother, while two other sisters formed a more significant bond. For these women, all other family relationships seemed to be understood in light of the sister bond.

Multiple dimensions of closeness and distance were considered. The other family members may have been more or less significant than the sister, but she seemed to have a special importance in times of crisis. Specific dimensions of a relationship may have made it more or less significant. Similarity of gender, having a twin, birth order, age spacing, and similarity of interests were all important. Sometimes fictional comparisons were even used. The extent to which the family was a "traditional one" was also considered in evaluating the sister–sister bond. Such multiple dimensions gave the relationship a sense of depth when compared to other relationships.

When a woman examined her relationship to her sister, she often compared it to other women's sister relationships. Most of the time, she viewed her own sister relationship as superior to others. The reasons given for this were often contradictory. Some women claimed to be close because of closeness in age, others because of a great difference in age. When the bond was not close, the woman longed to have the same sister connection that she saw in other women's lives.

While not mentioned frequently, the bond with a sister-in-law was sometimes compared to the sister–sister bond. For a few women the sister-in-law played an important role. Sisters-in-law were described as filling a day-to-day void left by a sister's absence: sharing life events and activities, talking about children, exchanging social news. But the importance of a sister-in-law did not diminish the perceived importance of a sister who was present and available.

Likewise, sister and friend relationships were often compared. The way the relationship with sister and the relationship with friend were described, the sister and friend relationship could be symbolized by overlapping circles. Each type of relationship had shared and unique elements. There was a concurrent recognition that neither relationship could totally replace the other, except in rare cases where the sister was the best friend. This instance was more likely when the family of origin moved frequently during childhood. It was also more likely to be true in the later stages of life as the friendship between sisters intensified and deepened. When such a close friendship developed between sisters, the sense of personal privacy shifted. The sister as friend knew more about the woman, and she shared more of herself. This seemed to be true regardless of life stage. There was an experience of enduring friendship, complete knowledge, and unconditional acceptance when sisters became close friends. Despite this trust in the sister relationship, other people had a huge influence on the way the relationship was perceived.

Friends, other sisters, and family members all influenced the woman's opinion about her relationship with her sister. This influence also had a developmental chronology. Relationships with friends during the adolescent years created competitiveness or cooperation between sisters, with resulting consequences for self-esteem. The sister's choice of intimate partners was described as important during adult years. Commitments to others could interfere in the relationships between sisters. There was a sense, however, that nothing would have been allowed to permanently endanger the sisters' relationship.

When sisters had a relationship with a third person, a whole constellation of results could follow. Others may have intruded and disrupted the relationship with the sister. One sister's wisdom in her choice of partners was compared to the other sister's poor choice. Some women attempted to moderate these effects by sheltering the sister from them. At other times, women described their sister's relationships with others in negative or judgmental terms. Thus the sister relationship—sometimes altered and always present—moved through an experiential herstory of her life and formed the basis for evaluating the rest of her relational world.

Time and Intensity

In the final structure, there are two clusters that affected the changing experience of the relationship over time. The most complex of these clusters was the evaluation of closeness or distance in the sister relationship. It included major themes related to communication, affirmative understandings, difficult understandings, and healing and loss.

The perception of closeness or distance was a primary defining characteristic for the experience of the relationship with sisters. Lack of closeness, whether permanent or temporary, was felt as hurtful or painful. The evaluation of closeness was based partly on the emotional closeness in other relationships, such as friendships. There may have been a physical closeness between sisters created by shared physical experiences (e.g., birth of a child) and physical caretaking responsibilities for a parent or sister. This shared physicality differentiated the relationship from a friendship. Emotional intimacy within the relationship was sometimes present and sometimes not. Some women believed the relationship could be described as close without this; others felt it was a defining characteristic. Some women said the love between the sisters was unconditional. The closeness of twin sisters was described as a unique kind of closeness. For twins the boundaries between self-identity and the sister's identity sometimes blurred, creating a sense that the two were one; conflict or a sense of deep intimacy could result from this blurred boundary. The closeness of twin relationships often superseded the closeness of other siblings whether the twin was a man or woman. For all sister relationships a disruption in closeness was considered a very important loss. Some stated the loss of the emotional depth would be unfathomable.

Closeness—or lack of it—was attributed to many diverse sources, including common interests and activities, similar lifestyles or tolerance for differences, proximity in adulthood and childhood (e.g., sharing a bedroom), common residence as adults, birth order, availability of other long-term friendships in childhood, specific events, preference for intimacy with men, parental role by one sister, and openness. The compatibility that developed during childhood was often a contributor to a sense of closeness. Occasionally, a specific event led to a sense of increased closeness between sisters (e.g., one sister leaving the family home). There was a sense that the depth of closeness and love differed during different stages of adult life but generally deepened as the sisters grew older, perhaps a reflection of the return to similar family values. This experience was enhanced by increasing honesty over time. The resolution of conflict made the relationship even closer.

Other relationships affected this sense of closeness. Compatibility of partners was mentioned, as was the assignment of gender roles by the father. Sometimes the women questioned their perceptions about the relationship, attributing the view of closeness to an unwarranted honesty.

There was a sense of presence with the sister that developed in connection with life-altering events such as the birth of children or the emergence of terminal illness. Such presence was expected to continue during future times of crisis. This presence was often a source of joy. Many described it as a necessity. However, at times the sister's presence was experienced with a sense of dread. All manners of being present to the relationship were reported, and the women suggested this presence did not depend upon physical proximity. For some women it continued after death.

The women were acutely aware of times when the relationship was superficial. This superficiality was unfulfilling. The need to keep information about a family member confidential was sometimes the cause for such superficiality. This confidentiality was one instance that created a barrier to a closer emotional interaction with the sister.

Communication

The communication between sisters was often intimate, with topics ranging from relationships with men to discrimination against women. Some sisters talked to each other about their relationship with each other. This interaction could enhance the relationship or make it more difficult. The women were aware of these consequences. Perhaps talking honestly created disconnection in the relationship. Giving feedback to a sister sometimes led to a serious breach, so such emotional outcomes were anticipated and feared.

Personal factors also affected the ability to communicate with a sister. Some women suggested that age differences made honest communication more difficult. Differences in temperament or a lack of mutual connection may have hampered their ability to talk. Variations occurred in the desire for contact, the inability to control anger, and the suppression of feelings in order to maintain peace. Sisters compared the closeness that was possible with some sisters to the distance in other sibling relationships. Strong communication skills made some women the mediator between family members and may have put them in a role to negotiate with their sisters.

Communication occurred in many ways. For example, the women described different degrees of symbolic or nonverbal communication. A special word signaled a need for help or support. During a close empathic moment, the woman may have anticipated what her sister was about to say. The ability to communicate without contact was also described. Some women could sense when their sister was in trouble or hurt with no direct communication whatsoever; this awareness could occur across great distances and was described as spontaneous.

Growth often came from honest communication between sisters. Sisters may have come to a mutual understanding of their parents and early childhood through extended conversations and the sharing of insight. Painful interactions were understood and could be viewed as humorous when sisters communicated openly about them. The intimacy in these interactions was shaped by the frequency of contact and uninterrupted time together. Frequently a new stage of life moved the communication to a deeper level. Sisters who had such communication throughout life were better able to discuss the difficulty of approaching death.

These sister–sister communications were highly valued and changeable. Some women suggested that the relationship brought them contentment and happiness. Others acknowledged that their attitudes may have distorted the value of the sister relationship, making it seem more positive or negative than it actually was. As a woman matured and shared life experiences broadened, she appreciated her relationship with her sister(s) more deeply.

Supportive Understandings

Supportive interactions between sisters integrated admiration, trust, protectiveness, and mutuality. Admiration was given to sisters because of who they were and what they had endured. Some women described admiring a sister's talents and abilities; others felt they respected their sister for the hardship she was able to bear, brought about by a difficult partner or occupational stress. When an older sister was idolized, maturity often brought a clearer picture of her. Trust was also a significant part of the sister relationship. The strong trust shared by some sisters was described as total and exclusive, with emphasis on sharing life's troubling circumstances.

Supportive interactions also took the form of protecting a sister from harm. Certain transitions stimulated protectiveness in the sister relationship. Protectiveness may have taken the form of defending the sister to others, diminishing negative feelings about the relationship, protecting the sister from the truth about herself, or placing oneself in danger to shield the sister from harm. A sister who entered high school after her sibling could stimulate these types of feelings and behaviors. Protectiveness toward an ill sister in childhood often resulted in a persistent attitude of protection that was no longer necessary. Sometimes a woman became protective to shelter her sister from a threatening parent, such as an incestuous father or alcoholic mother. A sister's sensitivity to this protective attitude may have diminished it. Protective attitudes were also expressed in reaction to the interview process. Some women acknowledged a desire to minimize their negative feelings during the interview. All of these forms of protection were considered positive and supportive—at times essential.

Women expected their relationship with their sisters to be mutual, each confiding in the other and expecting support. The safety and trust this created meant sisters shared difficult emotions and traumatic experiences. Such mutuality—when it existed—defined the sister relationship as exquisitely unique. The absence of reciprocal mutuality—often based upon experiences of hurtfulness—was painful. A mutual relationship characterized by trust, admiration, and protectiveness created a sense of affirmation for the individual sisters who crafted it.

With or without mutuality, sisters had a strong influence on one another. Sometimes the women felt drawn to the sister's experience and choices; sometimes they were pushed in the opposite direction. Watching a sister during childbirth was one such experience. Similarly, the sisters' choices of vocation, avocation, and interests led sisters in similar or opposing directions. Also, a sister's experience in relationships with parents, partners, and friends may have enhanced a woman's awareness of the difficulties and care required for those relationships. Sometimes a deliberate choice was made to have a primary relationship that differed substantially from the sister's. These influences were derived from observation, communication, and the emotional force of the sister's behavior and choices.

Women spoke at length about the important role their sisters played in determining their own vocational choices. During formative years, difficulty for one sister may have led to a career choice by another. Parental perceptions of the differing abilities between siblings may have led to competition, increased motivation, or resentment of the sister. The mother's role in this was particularly clear. If she valued the sisters in a similar way, cooperative learning replaced competitive strivings. Sometimes these competitive strivings—when not extreme—were helpful to the women. Current career stressors, including the possibility of sexual harassment in the workplace, were topics of discussion for sisters. Sisters retained their influence on vocational choices throughout childhood, adolescence, and adulthood.

Positive affirmations of sisterhood also included a description of relationship qualities. Playful teasing was suggested, as was intense emotionality. Through these positive affirmations, sisterhood came to be defined as the positive expression of a loving, caring relationship, but these affirmations were not the only interactions that emerged from strong sister relationships.

Difficult Understandings

In contrast to such affirmative understandings of the relationship, women also described coming to know their sisters through difficult understandings.

Sisters have clear memories of arguments and fights that occurred throughout life, becoming less physical as the women matured. Arguments and conflicts were often about unspoken issues of greater concern than the issue that was openly discussed. The sisters might have been fighting about two nieces' inappropriate behavior when the real issue was the rivalry for their own parents' affection. Such disagreements brought discomfort, and attempts were made to justify the position held by the woman describing it. Arguments between sisters may have caused disruption in other relationships. Sometimes a woman found herself at the center of a triangle between two conflicted sisters. She suffered pain when observing their rift and wanted to mend it. Thus the negative interactions created difficulties for the individual woman and often left her feeling impotent to change the circumstances.

In the context of a close sister relationship, conflict was understood as inevitable and insignificant to the total fabric of the relationship. Much like an unusual thread in a tapestry, the conflict and rivalry could enhance or blemish the relationship. This discord occurred on a continuum, ranging from minor irritations to physical altercations. Most sister relationships did not span the entire continuum, hovering at one extreme or the other. One sister may have been the target of another's misplaced aggressive feelings and frustrations. Sometimes the basis of the conflict was due to different levels of competition. Whatever the reason, the conflicts in a sister relationship provided a continual source of anguish and strong need for resolution.

Conflict and sister rivalry were present throughout life. Childhood conflicts arose due to rivalry for the parents' attention but were also based on a desire to gain other resources and benefits. When very difficult, these disputes festered, possibly based upon displacement by a younger sister. Parents encouraged some sister conflicts by comparing one sister to another. In extreme cases, the conflicts between sisters included physical fighting.

The dynamic interaction between sisters during childhood was also influenced by the perceived relationships of other sibling dyads, external friendships, and the relationship to the parents. Sisters were also the target of practical jokes in adolescent or childhood years. Such difficulties were altered when the two become adults and were often accompanied by regret, loss, and awareness of difference. With maturity, these conflicts could be understood with perspective and were often managed with humor.

Conflicts that created rivalry tended to be continuous, but sometimes specific events also led to an increased likelihood of discord. Some women described the birth of their sister as a time of intense animosity. Trauma and the loss of parental affection were given as justification for physical assault and meanness during childhood. In one instance this was accompanied by homicidal impulses. Questionable "accidents" with an infant sister were described. Sisters who moved away provided another opportunity for rivalry. The return of the geographically distant sister was often given undue significance by the parents. Envy erupted when one sister chose a more carefree life (e.g., by not having children). A sister's untimely death during times of conflict led to a diminishment of the relationship in order to assuage feelings of guilt. Such major life events intensified an already conflicted relationship between sisters.

Competition for parental attention or sibling rivalry played a major role in the women's description of conflicts between sisters. Awareness of that rivalry developed when one sister's value was suddenly elevated by parents or siblings. The resulting jealousy created attempts at mediation by some parents. The parents also worked extra hard to treat each child the same. These attempts at correcting the favoritism for one daughter were sometimes successful in decreasing competition and jealousy between sisters. Although this conflict was resolved by the parents, sisters also felt a need to resolve conflicts themselves.

Resolution of conflict in the relationship was sometimes accomplished by allowing time to pass, confronting the problem directly, or just ignoring the conflict. Sisters who learned to handle their conflict in childhood felt this paved the way for their positive relationship in adult life. As a result, resolution with maturity was often more congenial. Other breaches in the relationship between sisters were perceived as irreconcilable due to triangulation within the family. The woman in a conflicted threesome with her sister and another family member may have been required to maintain the conflict in service of the triadic relationship. They may have believed conflicts were woven into the relationship in such a way that it would be unraveled without them. Despite the drive for conflict resolution, some women felt their difficulties with their sisters would never be reconciled.

Among the most conflicted feelings about the sister relationshipwere those associated with guilt. The women described guilt connected to childhood rivalry. Sometimes another person was favored over the sister and that fueled the development of guilt. When guilt from childhood was discussed and understood with the sister, it often led to greater closeness and joy in the connection. If a woman supported her parents' favoritism for one sister over another, this defense led to continuing emotional distance from the less-favored sister. All of these elements contributed to difficult understandings expressed during the interviews. Sometimes these understandings enhanced the relationship; sometimes they distracted from it.

Healing and Loss

Historical causes of distance usually resulted in a desire to heal the relationship. With time, the understanding of jealousy or competition for the affection of parents and friends in childhood was integrated into a closer or more detached relationship between sisters. One sister's success could make the process of reconciliation more difficult. In contrast, the development of personal insight often led to a greater desire for closeness and a greater desire to understand the relationship. Psychotherapy was used by some women to heal themselves and create the possibility for healing the relationship or managing it better. Occasionally a family's inability to relate emotionally resulted in emotional immaturity for one sister. The healing of one woman's losses or grief meant she had to reach out to the less mature sister. When sisters were able to communicate about some of these difficult feelings, greater emotional closeness emerged.

Healing and loss entered the sister relationship in several ways: the loss associated with geographic distance between sisters, the decline of a sister's physical or mental health, and the experience of traumatic family events, including death. The women described the effects of geographic distance as ambiguous. They expressed awareness that high-quality contact minimized the effects of distance. Often the first experience of distance was prompted by occupational choices such as the separation necessary to attend college or to take a job. The women described being acutely aware of this distance during family celebrations or important events—for instance, the birth of a child. Often ambiguous feelings were expressed when the women considered the other life circumstances that keep them apart, such as the time involved in raising children. Yet distance seemed to be crucial to a feeling of ambivalence and a desire to replace the sister with close female friends who were more available. The sister herself served as a replacement for the primary relationship when older women decided to live with their sisters to eliminate the effects of distance. Geographic distance seemed to present an obstacle of mixed difficulty that did not have to affect the quality of the relationship, but did limit its frequency and the ability to rely on the sister for day-to-day support.

Like geography, health issues also influenced the contact between sisters. Sisters were aware of each other's physical health and illness. This awareness could serve as a catalyst for greater contact. The women also responded similarly when a partner or husband's health was at stake. A woman's health crisis often mobilized her sister into a new caregiving role with daily responsibilities. Women whose sisters were ill in childhood described assuming increased responsibility and protectiveness. Sometimes elderly sisters decided to live together for this reason. The women also expressed concern about preventive health and a desire for sisters to comply with health-promoting medical care and medications. This importance of health and illness reflected the women's desire for healing of the sister.

The mental illness of one sister formed a unique demand on the sister relationship. Some sisters lived with mental illness in silence. Sadness emerged when the condition was finally shared with a healthy sister. Illness, partner illness, mental illness, and concerns about preventive health care all formed a unique kind of crisis within the relationship that demanded a specific response from sisters.

Other types of crises also influenced the relationship. The women suggested that traumatic experiences could lead to greater closeness or distance in the relationship. If the traumatic event was shared it could produce either result. The difference between their reactions created the increased sense of closeness or distance. Traumatic events that were not shared enhanced a sense of distance.

Many examples of traumatic events were discussed. Some women told me about the death of a parent in childhood and the consequences for the young sister relationship. The difficult adjustments included assuming a parental role or adjusting to a new blended family. During these adjustments, one sister's role was seen as the primary element in holding the family together. Some women married at a young age to reduce the burden for the single surviving parent. The movement of one sister out of the family home in late adolescence prompted a sense of loss. A sister's decline in health created a sense of impending disconnection. The death of a sister produced two responses. Some sisters described compensating by putting more energy into the relationship with their remaining sister; others negated the importance of the loss and admitted that their denial led to continuing unresolved pain. The loss of a primary partner could either create an opportunity for more contact with the sister or prevent such contact from occurring. Likewise, the woman's own declining health might limit travel and prevent contact with a sister. The response to the crisis sometimes included others.

A family's response to crises did not involve just the sister but a team composed of sisters, mothers, and extended family members. Husbands or partners were often members of this team. All worked together to deal with the physical, emotional, and financial fallout. Likewise, emotional eruptions of anger and frustration could be managed by the sisters if they worked together to understand the deeper meanings of these emotions. Often secondhand sources of information were used to manage such a crisis, with word being passed from one relative to others. Many different crises within the family were described by the women, but a specific crisis occurred during the physical decline of a parent.

This anticipated decline and loss was usually described in relation to the mother's aging and death. Sisters usually worked together to provide the practical and emotional support necessary to the mother. Sometimes disagreements occurred related to the amount of practical support each was able to give. This amount depended upon geographic distance. When a close sister relationship existed, the sister who provided the most practical support often felt emotionally supported by her sisters. Occasionally, a sister disrupted her life to move closer to the mother and provide the necessary aid.

A death of a parent or sister prompted a number of responses. A parental death during childhood meant one sister often assumed parental responsibility. This could occur without regard to expected family roles. As they matured the women wanted to be present with a dying family member. Sometimes, gifts were given to the sisters by the dying person. Younger generations were taught how to manage death through the example of older family members. This example became a template for subsequent death experiences.

When a sister was dying, her sister wanted to prevent it and feared the loss. A fear of survival also emerged: the surviving sister anticipated feeling alone. When the death was unexpected, regrets for recent interactions were considered.

If a sister's life became too painful due to illness, the woman wished for her death to relieve suffering, but she still experienced great pain at the anticipated loss. Sometimes an ill sister was cared for by her sister's children. Death was managed by the sisters and by their families in a process that replicated itself over time.

Time and Identity

The cluster labeled identity issues, interacting with the changing relationship over time and the closeness or distance in the relationship, formed the central core of current understanding in the relationships. Identity was complex, containing many dimensions. Birth order and the experience of the sister's birth formed an early component of identity. The impact of birth order remained somewhat constant over time and affected their expectations of each other, their sense of closeness, their role expectations, and perceived leadership. These expectations may have been altered when a younger sister lost her admiration for an older one. However, birth order alone did not tell the whole story; several factors interacted with it to create a sense of identity. Gender and birth order interacted to create specific expectations for a particular sister. Twins formed an exception to birth-order rules and formed a different bond regardless of gender.

Specific attributes and expectations accompanied birth order. The oldest was often viewed or viewed herself as domineering, organized, and, perhaps, exploitive. She was required to be the leader, and the other sisters may have been jealous of that role. Parents who had trouble fulfilling their obligations may have supported this leadership role for the eldest sister. The sheer number of younger siblings might have required it. Often other siblings tried to be like this oldest sister, and she became the focus of much competition. The oldest girl was sometimes discounted because she was "supposed to be a boy," demonstrating a unique interactive effect of birth order and gender expectations.

Second-born or middle sisters were somehow disadvantaged. Their competitiveness arose from not knowing where they fit in the family. Youngest sisters had a special role: they were expected to be dependent, deeply loved, cute, and perhaps manipulative of older sisters. Being supplanted from this role was described as traumatic. With twin sisters, one was often dominant despite the lack of age difference. The sisters' birth order and resulting role expectations were compared to the mother's role, birth order, and role with her sisters. Some women suggested that, over time, the effects of birth order diminished.

Like birth order, age spacing had a prominent impact upon early childhood and adolescent relationships due in part to different interests and activities. This impact diminished with time. Large differences in age created a sense of "belonging to a different family" with different parents. These differences made it difficult to feel connected to a much younger or much older sister. They also made it difficult to share friends, although some women were able to do so through a shared activity like attending church.

Sometimes the age differences created emotional closeness. The competition for parental attention and the dissimilar role demands were lessened between the sisters. This paved the way for improved connection and the ability to see the sister as a role model. Sometimes an older sister filled a maternal role, which prevented a more peer-like bond. When a much older sister left the family home, this had a significant effect on the family roles and relationships.

A sister's identity was related to her characteristics and the things that influenced their development. A cluster of traits was described as a personality type (e.g., cheerleader). Sometimes the lack of family characteristics in one sister was seen as auspicious. The role of a sister in a family may have been determined by her characteristics (e.g., a peacemaker); her position in the family may have allowed certain characteristics to emerge (e.g., a late child who received less attention may be more independent). Often the understood characteristics of the sister affected the woman's approach to her. For instance, she might never be aggressive with a sensitive sister. Her response to a sister's behavior might be a reaction to one of the sister's characteristics. Her sister's competitiveness may have resulted in a lack of empathy. With time, changes in a sister's characteristics were noted: a temper may have become more controlled, or independence strengthened.

Gender identity and sexual orientation influenced the different identities of sisters. Traditionally feminine and traditionally masculine role expectations were often created for different sisters, and these identities created a difference in interest and activities. When parents wanted a boy and had not had one, a lasting stigma was created. This stigma was not apparent for sisters who were born after the birth of the favored male child. Gender issues also appeared in a different form. As the sisters grew up, discussions of relationships with men and bias against women provided bonds between them. Sometimes these discussions changed sisters' views of men. Likewise, some women described feeling distant from their sister because they preferred emotional closeness with men. Differences in sexual orientation created a unique sense of identity difference. This difference formed the basis for discussions between sisters and an appreciation across different perspectives and lives.

Other differences between sisters provided an appreciation for uniqueness and an opportunity for closer bonding. Some were seen as more academically gifted, others as more creative or practical. The women recognized their parents' role in valuing these differences. Some women suggested that the differences minimized conflict between the sisters.

While birth order and personality characteristics provided some clues to individual sisters' identities, family roles and contexts also helped to define each sister as unique. The women I interviewed placed their sisters within a family context. Sisters were described as caretakers, airheads, leaders, drunks, playmates, aunts, mothers, travel guides, moderators, family trophies, hubs of communication, and adolescent rebels. They were labeled with attributes like compulsive, depressed, artistic or intellectual. The women criticized the limitations on their sisters created by these perceived roles and attributes. They describe the unfairness of the way these roles were attributed persistently throughout life.

In describing a sister's identity the women also considered herstory, location, occupation, health, age, and relational status. Sometimes role limitations were linked to limited opportunity for one sister compared to another. For example, one sister became her mother's primary companion in later life.

In addition, sisters sometimes compensated for a failed or absent parental role. A sister may have replaced a mother or a father in the family. This was often tied to birth order, but sometimes it was not: an emotionally mature younger sister may have filled an emotional parental role in the family. As sisters grew up, the assumed parental role often gave way to a more satisfying peer relationship. Parental roles were a unique form of the roles that helped to define the sister relationship, and like the other roles described, they were a significant factor in sisters' unique identities.

Comparison to the sister also helped women to differentiate themselves. In an attempt to understand the relationship, women often compared themselves to their sisters. Other people made similar comparisons. Similarities in interests, values, perspectives, characteristics, tastes, energy, adventurousness, or activities created the basis for the development of closeness between sisters. Differences may have enhanced the relationship or made it difficult. Some difference was necessary to define identity. Relative talents and intelligence created strength in the relationships. Traits established in childhood were considered enduring and often marked adult choices. These choices were described as existing on different continuums. One continuum was the commitment to career; another embodied a commitment to family. Importance placed upon parenting or primary partner relationships was similarly evaluated.

When sisters were far apart on any of these continuums, this produced a difference in activities and interests that affected their closeness. If one was more invested in the relationship with the parents, this could have a similar effect. Sisters might have envied each other's accomplishments and talents based upon parental response in childhood. This envy may have given way to appreciation of the difference or led to stagnation in the relationship. The balance of similarity and difference seemed important in creating the opportunity for a flourishing relationship between sisters.

Factual Information

Identity issues for sisters were also influenced by facts about the sisters. Facts about sisters' level of activity, qualities, marriage, birth of children, occupation, health, history, location in relation to her sisters, birth of grandchildren, and other major life transitions were given as background for the description of events, feelings, and connection with the sister. These facts emerged in two categories: physiology and religious commitments.

Physiology affected identity in two ways. The nature of the bond was based upon the blood relationship between sisters. This bond existed whether emotional closeness was a part of it or not. This bond might be stronger or weaker than other bonds. It usually survived most other bonds and was sometimes the reason for cooperation in caring for parents or other family members. Yet some women suggested that their blood sister would be a true friend regardless of the genetic connection.

The other dimension of physiology was related to similar biology. Being female, the sisters were able to relate to changes in hormonal mood. They compared themselves physically and considered similarities and differences in physical attributes. These were attributed to differences in parental genetic composition and biological inheritance.

Another aspect of identity was shared religious belief. The religious preference could represent a source of strength and comfort to sisters on a daily basis and in times of crisis. These shared or unshared life circumstances helped women to evaluate the relationship with their sister and give some explanation for its significance.

Conclusions

The sister relationship, based upon a particular way of perceiving, came into consciousness through a variety of methods. Some of these were specific to the research itself. Through this perceptive lens, the women of this study described a structure of their experience of the sister relationship. This description considered elements of time's passage. The closeness or distance of the relationship was evaluated on multiple dimensions. The relationship was always compared to the relationships with others. The differences and similarities between sisters were described and their connection to developing identity was interwoven throughout. From the research came a rich understanding of the thick experience of the sister relationship and its importance throughout a woman's life. Subsequent chapters amplify each of the primary clusters of the research, and the women's own words help to describe the fullness of the sister experience.

3

Ways of Perceiving and Knowing

"It is only with the heart that one can see rightly; what is essential is invisible to the eye."

Antoine de Saint- Exupéry (1943/2000; p. 63)

How do we know what we know? This is one of the fundamental questions that phenomenology hopes to answer. Several women authors have illuminated this process and the ways it may be different for women and men. Carol Gilligan (1982/1993) attempted to understand this process for women who were considering abortion and for teenage girls. Mary Field Belenky with her co-authors (1986) made it the subject of her book *Women's Ways of Knowing*. To really understand the women in my research, it was necessary to bracket that knowledge and to let the women tell me themselves. Their experiences with their sisters were grounded in the methods they used to explore their own understanding. These methods helped them to interpret and evaluate their lives with their sisters. They talked about the importance of those ways of knowing and the people who influenced that knowledge. These expressions were significant, since they may tell us something about how women know what they know. In this case the knowing is about relationships, particularly the relationships with sisters, but perhaps it extends to the way women come to understand all of their relationships. In the final structure created to describe the women's experience (see Fig. 2.1), this element forms the floor upon which the remainder of the experience rests. It seemed important to me to address this way of knowing in some detail before moving on to the other elements of the women's narratives about the relationships with their sisters. Even so, it was not easy to separate the ways of knowing from the knowledge itself.

Frozen Images

Frozen images are those caught in time. The women described images preserved in photographs and images preserved in memory. These images were the source of impressions and ideas about the sister and the family.

[W]e had a photo taken when, oh I don't know, I was probably 4, and we had matching little sailor dresses and so when anyone asks me about my sister I always show. . . them that one first and show them our senior picture, or her senior picture, because I always remember us in those dresses, because I loved to dress like her when I was little. Sometimes I still do. (Eve-39)

The importance of these photographs was apparent from the way the woman described her nostalgia about them. Some of the family photographs were incomplete: one member was left out because of history or birth. For example, one woman described how her much younger sister was left out of a family photograph:

So, in our old family albums, there is just the three of us or with the family photo would be my parents and the three of us and my sister was an afterthought. I mean there are pictures of her, but stuff afterwards. Really, I don't even have a lot of pictures of me with my sister. We just stopped taking pictures. (Tracy-35)

Some families stop taking photographs of the children after the newness of having children fades; others become preoccupied with caring for multiple children and don't have as much time to capture the moments on film or video.

Persistent memories also form the basis of these frozen images. Sometimes emotional experiences keep the memory vivid. The separation from an older sibling was often deeply embedded in memory. One woman described her older sister's preparation for departure on one of her many adventures:

[B]eing in her room and she's packing to. . . you know, go off to Switzerland or going back to college, or just doing various things. And just sitting in her room and talking to her, and the good, good feelings that were associated with those times. (Vicki-17)

The return of an absent sibling could also create a permanent image for the younger girl. The same participant described her sister's return from college at the end of each semester. The return was associated with positive feelings and a ritual that her sister had created to help the younger sister realize that she had been missed.

[W]hen she would come back from being away at college and, this is like I'm six or seven and, my brother's three years older than me, so he'd be nine or ten or whatever. She'd always bring back treats or you know something. And so, we'd have to turn our backs, put our arms, you know, hands behind our backs and then she'd put something in our hands and then we'd try to have to guess what it was. And she would do this for. . . many years. . ., probably throughout college. (Vicki-18)

Some rituals, developed by the sisters together, form the basis for a lifetime of shared experiences. One woman described a cost-saving way to stay in touch using voice mail instead of long telephone calls. She also talked about the cards and letters she received from her sister. These too formed images: the visual image of cards and letters reminded her of her sister during her sister's absences.

Strong emotion led many women to vividly remember specific interactions with their sisters. Sometimes these strong emotions were positive, such as when the sisters would laugh until they cried.

> I remember us laughing so hard that, you know, tears would come down our faces and usually at inappropriate times. Like, we're at a really fancy restaurant cause we love French restaurants and any time we're together we go to French restaurants and of course, chocolate desserts would follow. And, um, something would happen cause we're so in tuned to each other. It's almost like I know what she's gonna say or she knows what I'm gonna say and so we're one ahead, one step ahead of each other and then we start laughing. . . just laughing so hard (Vicki-28).

Images frozen in time did not mature, and several women described the negative consequences of that type of frozen image. One suggested that her protectiveness toward her sister persisted based upon the sister's childhood dependency. One talked about the expectation that her sister would still try to manipulate her as she did when they were younger. She still sees that cute little helpless child when viewing her sister's face: "So, when she says things like that,. . . hey,. . . she's no kid. She's an adult. She's just using this little kid angle because she's got a real cute face and things like that" (Brooke-F87).

At times the woman is aware of this impact; at other times she is not. The women felt that the inability to move beyond such childhood roles had been created mutually. An older sister may be protective and be unable to recognize her sister's growing competence. A younger sister may play dumb or flounder in order to get her older sister to step in and rescue her. One woman said, "She's still. . . floundering around trying to figure things out, and she kinda plays. . . the dumb role to her advantage, I think" (Brooke-F86).

Frozen images were also formed when perceptions differed between the sisters. They remembered and sometimes experienced things differently. One woman contrasted her outgoing behavior during childhood with her sister's more cautious and insecure stance.

> I do think she was a very insecure child growing up, you can always see it in pictures, you know, you can see kind of this, I mean, if we're feeding

the ducks I'm out there with my arm out there feeding the ducks and she's standing back in the back kind of holding onto her bread. (Janice-55)

The same person commented about the qualities she and her sister developed as children. She assumed these qualities have endured into adulthood and continue to affect their life choices today.

You know, those kinds of things manifest themselves later in life—how you grow up and how you respond to new environments and new experiences a little differently affects you as you grow older. And Leslie wanted security and she's always wanted the best and she's always worked towards that. Her first marriage she married a fellow that was quite well-to-do and from a well-to-do family and she had the security but she wasn't happy. (Janice-56)

Memories of the sister that are frozen in this way had an incredible persistence. Some women were surprised by how detailed such memories were when they appeared. One woman exclaimed:

Do you believe I remember stuff from that long ago? I mean we were probably eight or nine years old at the most, [be]cause I remember we were in Hollywood. I remember exactly where the piano was, the whole thing, just like it was yesterday. (Janice-51)

At times, these images conflicted with reality. One young woman joked that her feelings of protectiveness related to her sister and the sister's sexuality will continue when her sister becomes 40 and has been married. It was unclear to the woman whose reality was actually true. Many of the women were aware that the sister sometimes remembered the events differently:

[S]he'd probably say, you know, my dad was picking on her. You know, and so it would be just her perception of how it really happened. And I look at it and say well gee, why isn't she smart enough to quit playing and get over to the table and eat. (Janice-50)

Often, these images created the basis for a comparison between sisters. The sister may have been aware of how events and interactions affected the two differently. One woman recalled taking advantage of her younger sister when they were children. She was also aware this might have frustrated her sister. She describes eating quickly while her younger sister ate slowly. This created the opportunity to take some of her sister's portion. She remembers that when she and her sister would look through the catalog for paper doll clothes, she, as the older sister, would sit on the side where she could see the page first to claim the best outfit.

One woman recognized that the image of her sister was outdated. While her sense of the sister remained that of a dependent younger child, she paradoxically saw the sister as a strong individual. She told a story of when they were young and their mother was ill. The woman had to attend to her sister and couldn't wait to go play on her own, but her younger sister actually stayed with and cared for the ill mother. In retrospect, the woman can see that strength as independence. At a very young age, the sister was taking care of herself in ways the woman had previously overlooked.

> [S]he's strong; I guess that's the word I could use for her. For being a baby and thinking everything's going to turn out alright, she does have an inner strength that's marvelous. And, uh, even though you've had some-body you think taking care of you, I think she's taken care of herself more than she ever knew. When she was three she washed her own hair. (Rebecca-46)

Such comparisons existed in the mind of the woman reporting the experience; the interviewee had often not confirmed them with her sister. Like the other frozen images, the image of the sister that is frozen and comparative provides the women with a foundation for remembering and understanding their relationships with their sisters. If images are indelibly linked to an early memory, voices of others also inform the way that sisters come to know each other. In some families this telling of family tales becomes an oral herstory. This herstory was another way of coming to knowledge about the sister relationship.

Oral Herstory

Oral herstory was also an important way of knowing the sister and describing the relationship. Most often, this type of knowing came from stories told by older family members. The women did not speak at great length about the oral history of their families, but a few did mention it directly. One woman described her fam-ily's report that she had been cared for by her older sister when the woman was a small child. She has no memory of this care but trusted that it did happen. Another woman stated that her family reported extreme conflict between her and her sister when they were children. Another remembers a story told by her grandpar-ents about her own jealousy:

> I hear the story (but I don't actually remember about that), but my grand-parents tell me that they would all come to see the new baby, and it was like I would stand out on the front porch and try not to let them in and

be like, "Oh you don't want to see her, all she does is sleep. She's so stupid." (Hillary-30)

These stories formed the basis for some impressions of the sister that remained important to the women in the study throughout their life with their sister.

Learning Secondhand from the Mother

Sometimes, mothers provided secondhand information about the sister that was a crucial part of understanding the relationship. In each case when this round-about communication was mentioned, the mother was the source. Three examples of this were relayed by the women. The mother's veracity was questioned by one woman: her mother insisted that the two sisters fought often as children, yet the woman had no memory of it. In another instance, the mother relayed emotional reactions of the woman's sister and niece:

> Anita [niece] just graduated from eighth grade a couple of weeks ago and the same night I had my high school graduation. I tried to get out of it and I couldn't, so I called her before hand and got a card and wrote her a note and sent it with my mother. Anyway, my sister never said anything to me, but my mom let me know that Anita was very disappointed that I wasn't there and that made me feel bad. (Tammy-F14)

Sometimes, secondhand information is merely an affirmation of what the woman already knows about her sister. The woman who described the picture of the sailor dresses also said her mother confirmed that those were favorite outfits for both girls. Secondhand information seemed to include methods for confirmation, doubt, and transmission of emotionally difficult material for the women in this research. Family voices and images provided a backdrop for the remembered sister story, but the research process itself also affected the way sisters were understood.

Reactions to Interview

As participants in the research, the women expressed awareness that the interview had affected their experience by causing them to compare themselves to others, creating an awareness of memories that were long forgotten, providing an emotional release for pent-up feelings, and, in some cases, resulting in a re-evaluation of their relationship with their sister(s). Such responses have been common in phenomenological research, where the interview process is assumed to interact with the experience that it describes. The women had much to say about this process, often at the end of the interviews or the beginning of the follow-up interview.

The women commented upon their preparation for the interview. Some asked the purpose of the research and many indicated that they had not participated in research before. One stated that she had retraced her memories so she could share them with me.

The women were frequently surprised by the nature of the interviews and commented upon the structure. One felt the narrative nature of the interview has caused her to think more than a survey-style interview might. Another compared the process to counseling. One said the interview was easy; others frequently asked for clarification. This expression was typical of those who expressed uncertainty about their performance: "I guess I kind of go off on tangents. Is that what you wanted?" (Janice-57). Some clearly wanted more direction from the interview process, as indicated by this comment: "I don't know what else you need to know" (Eve-6).

Quite a few women suggested they were confused by the lack of structure in the interview. They expressed feeling uncertain about what to say. Comment about their confusion often occurred during the follow-up interview. Several women said, "I don't know what else to tell you." Even though many women said they had no additional thoughts, feelings, or images to report since the first interview, they often discussed additional details at length.

Women also described re-evaluating their sister relationships as a result of the research. One woman said that she would not have thought in depth about the relationship otherwise. She stated:

> I guess after talking with you it made me stop and re-evaluate, it's something you don't on a normal basis think about: what your relationship is with your sister. It really made me kinda re-evaluate what that relationship was. (Tammy-F1)

Another woman reflected on the lack of closeness with her sisters while she was growing up. She wishes it could have been different, or that she had a chance to do it over. A third woman suggested that details of the relationship returned when the interview stimulated her memory. This was true even though her sister had suggested the details before.

The interview also gave many women a chance to vent their feelings about their sisters. One woman said she vented more dislikes about her sister during the interview than she had at any other time. Others merely expressed awareness that this venting had occurred during the interview process.

The women commented often on the things they had said during the interviews and evaluated their statements. Sometimes they were concerned about whether they had provided enough information of the right kind. One woman was concerned about her brevity:

I thought about how much I left out, that it was so short. I think it was my expectation that you were going to ask me specific questions and so, I didn't want to ramble on for 15 minutes on the first question. But then it ended up being, you know, the only question. So, I thought it was my expectations that were in error. (Vicki-15)

The same woman suggested that she forgot to mention her childhood experience with her sister. During the follow-up interview some women had difficulty remembering what they had already said and wanted to say more, but without repeating themselves. Another said that she would remember more after the interview, but that the intention to remember it during the interview had interfered with remembering. These general appraisals were sometimes accompanied by a specific analysis of their emotional feelings about what they had said.

The interviewed women wished they had said more positive things about their sisters, feeling they had focused too often on the difficulties. In the initial interview, one young woman said she had focused on recent tension-filled years. That focus represented her desire to confront her sister as she grew older and wiser. She said, "Because I feel like, as I become an adult, I'm not just nodding my head and letting everything go by, as I would when I was a younger kid" (Vicki-23). Another said she felt disloyal when describing her feelings about her sister's relationship with her husband. She compared her concern for her sister to her concern for her children and felt the need to intervene between the husband and wife when her sister was sick:

I feel like I'm telling tales. Her husband's supposed to go get her some pain pills. He's watching [an interview on TV] or something, and is so engrossed he wouldn't go. So, I'm getting mad. And I said, "Tom, could you tape the darn thing and leave?" I said, "I'd go get the medicine but I don't know where the drugstore is; I don't know my way around here." So he finally, finally went. So, I'm just like a parent in this regard. You get mad for your child or for your sister, and he's a nice guy but just thoughtless in this regard. (Rebecca-29)

Despite the desire to convey more positive feelings, some women felt that doing otherwise would be a lie. One even said that all of her feelings about her sister were negative.

Some of the women were ambivalent about what they had expressed. One woman who described interfering with her sister's marital relationship when her sister was sick also said she was ambivalent about disclosing her sister's family difficulties. She recovered by saying, "But they are a wonderful family and I can't say enough good about them" (Rebecca-31). During the follow-up interview, one woman wanted to correct misperceptions she might have created by saying, "I felt that maybe that we were a little bit closer than I really realized we were, in terms of support, and basically that I realize. . . if I ever needed her for anything that she was there" (Tammy-F2).

Some of the women suggested that their portrayal caused them to rethink how close they were to their sisters. In summary, one described her relationship with her sister as nice but superficial, stating: "I would say, you know, that we have a nice relationship but it's not a deep relationship. Oh, I could go on for 10 years" (Janice-14). Another woman suggested that growing older had matured the relationship in a positive way.

At times, uncertainty about her portrayal caused a woman to ask for the evaluation of the interviewer. One woman wanted to know if her answers had been adequate; another wanted to know if the situation seemed crazy to the researcher. Thus, women had much to say about their responses to the interview and the ways that they had portrayed the relationships. When the women re-evaluated their relationships with their sisters as a result of the interviews, the new evaluation was positive. One woman said that she felt more positive because the interview caused her to survey the entire relationship instead of scrutinizing the past few relatively conflicted years.

> But from this little thing that we're doing, it's really made me reflect on the entire scope of it, and how really wonderful it is. And I need to focus on the wonderful times, and if she does have peculiarities or. . . [is] just too sensitive about some things in my opinion. . ., I need just let that go. That's her. . . let that go and then just focus on the positive things. (Vicki-30)

Several other women also expressed their sense that the relationship was better appreciated after the interview than it had been before. Another wanted to use the transcript from the interview to create a greater closeness with her sister:

> [A]nd I don't know what your time line is, but as I'm sitting here thinking, I thought, you know, that would be really fun to have a copy of that. If that's even possible before Christmas, so I may want to share that with her. It's, I mean I see that as just more connection with her. It's like I really want to be connected with her. (Jean-47)

In contrast, one woman suggested that nothing in the relationship had changed as a result of the interview process. These differing reactions to the interview created a continuum of effects, suggesting that the interview process differed in its influence on the recollections of the sister.

The research also had the effect of creating a desire for more information. Some women wanted more information about this particular research project; others expressed a desire to know more about sister relationships in general. Still other women became curious about research as a whole.

One unique effect of the research was a comment upon its privacy. If they preferred, the women were interviewed in their own homes, and one interview was disrupted by the entrance of an adult son who lived with the interviewee. She commented upon this disruption, acknowledging the importance of privacy in research.

The research process had a number of effects on the sister relationship. Women experienced it differently. Their perceptions were altered. Insight was discovered. They were inspired to try to change the relationship. They were aware of and tried to change the perceptions of the interviewer. They shared these reflections honestly and with grace. These interactive effects were a reflection of the co-creative process of meaning characteristic of phenomenological research.

Reactions to the Interviewer

The women also wondered how their interviews might help or affect the interviewer, whose presence and relationship with them created a fifth way of knowing. The expressed themes included some curiosity about the researcher, some assumptions about the meaning of their words to the researcher, and the influence the researcher had on them during the interview. Some women asked directly if the researcher or research assistant had sisters. Others questioned if the researchers shared the same knowledge and values. These questions covered issues that were both superficial and profound, as can be seen from the following two quotes:

> Because she was a cheerleader in high school, you know that type. (Chris-25)

> [W]e're Christian people. I don't know if she mentioned that to you or not. We were Christians, and we marched to a different drummer, I mean, they just do. Are you a Christian? (Stacey-40)

These types of questions signified the importance of the researcher's human qualities for the women. They also suggested that the researcher's presence was a significant factor in their descriptions. One woman became self-conscious talking so personally about her sister with the interviewer, but justified it on the basis of research:

> It's kind of weird talking about this, you know. Yeah.
>   [Interviewer: What do you mean?]
> Um, just talking about something, I guess, so personal. And, you know, we just first met. But, I mean, I don't mind at all [be]cause this is a good project and everything, but I don't know. (Vicki-11)

Several of those interviewed expressed a desire to be helpful to the researchers. Often the women asked them for direction in order to be more helpful.

A special kind of presence was noted in the perception of the researcher as a confidant. Family photos were shared.

> [I've] got a picture I'll show you. . . if you'd like. It's kind of old, but it's not real old, it's a few years old. This is my sister Leslie. . . Then see, this is Sybil. And they're really a lot alike. . . in their looks even, they're very much alike. She's 10 years younger than I. (Janice-33)

This woman also disclosed fear about an upcoming visit with her sister and acknowledged, "I know I'm telling you a lot of private stuff right now" (Janice-34). A young woman asked for confidential handling of the material, stating that she did not want the researcher to disclose information to her parents (Eve-8). In all of these ways, the interviewer served as a witness for the women, and her presence affected the experience of the relationship the women had with their sisters.

Conclusions

The foundation of the sister experience, as described by the women participating in this research, included a number of ways they understood and came to know their relationships with their sisters. Frozen images, presented as photos or timeless memories, guided the sisters in their descriptions. They were also aware of family interpretations as reflected in oral history and secondhand information. Comparisons were an important element: women came to evaluate their relationships based upon other relationships they had or those they had witnessed. They were also affected by the process of the research itself, which increased their awareness of the relationship and sometimes changed their evaluation of it. They appraised their own performance and sometimes felt ambivalent about their expressions. The women considered the importance of the researcher, her values, her use of the research material, and her role as confidant in the expression of the thoughts, feelings, and images connected to the sisters in their lives. All of these ways of knowing formed the basis for the woman's description of the relationship's herstory and her sense of connection or disconnection with her sister(s).

4

Herstory

"Being so wrong about her makes me wonder now how often I am utterly wrong about myself. And how wrong she might have been about her mother, how wrong he might have been about his father, how much of family life is a vast web of misunderstandings, a tinted and touched-up family portrait, an accurate representation of fact that leaves out only the essential truth.

Anna Quindlen (1994, p. 286)

Sisters give each other depth and breadth through a shared history or, in the feminist form, herstory. In my research this herstory was an important part of the experience described by each woman interviewed. Even though they were not asked directly to chronicle the past relationship with their sisters, each woman did. All of them described a complex interplay between their relationships with their sisters and other household family relationships. They discussed the importance of extended family members (e.g., aunts, cousins, and grandparents). Relationships with friends and work associates were somehow woven into the subtle understanding of this herstory. They made comparisons. How did other women get along with their sisters when they had more than one? When were friendships superior to sister relationships? Who would they turn to in a crisis or when someone in the family died? Perhaps more than any other chapter this one describes the women's perspective on how the sister relationship developed. Stories about growing up together, coming to understand the relationships, and watching them change over time were all a part of this herstory.

Effects of Childhood Sister Interactions

Sisters acted out their childhood dramas with each other, leaving an aftermath of optimism, guilt, or jealousy. Sometimes these dramas occurred because other people expect them to. Jealousy formed because a sister was believed to be a better orchestra member or soccer player. These differing accomplishments or talents were supported by other people and became assumed differences between sisters. Valued or neglected, such talents became part of the family story about the sisters. Sometimes fear of failure, loss, or invisibility persisted. Sometimes this fear was transferred to the next generation, as an aunt and mother became acutely aware of the potential that their drama might continue between their children. They tried to stop this from happening, especially if the women had been vicious with each other and did not want to see their daughters perpetuate that hostility. The effects of these childhood sister interactions were sometimes described as persistent and harmful to the women in later life; at other times, the positive nature of the sister relationship formed the basis for humor, candor, and optimism in relationships with other women.

Natural Differences

Natural talents created differences that affected sisters in childhood. Self-esteem, honesty, attractiveness, and sensitivity were used as a basis for women to compare themselves to their sisters. One woman said:

> [B]ut my sister is a very different person. . . she was always a little shy, reluctant—lacked self-confidence, and I had tons of self-confidence. And why that is. . . being brought up in the same family. . . it's sort of fascinating. And I think the older you get, the more you think about it and reflect back on your childhood and think, "Why did I turn out this way?" and "Why did she turn out that way?". . . [I]n later years, now, she has a lot of self-esteem and self-confidence and so forth. (Janice-2)

The same woman described her process of learning to be sensitive to her sister's insecurity:

> And at the time I sure didn't know it. But she was feeling so insecure about herself and about. . . I feel like I don't want to do anything to kind of hurt her or anything. So I feel like I'm always treading a little bit lightly—like I don't want to offend her or say something that she might take in a negative way. (Janice-30)

Such differences were often highlighted by parents and teachers. During adolescence, a teacher of one woman and her sister noted that the woman had the motivation to excel but not the talent, whereas her sister had the talent but lacked the motivation. This feedback further motivated the woman to enjoy the activity throughout life:

> I love playing the piano and my sister and I were both taking piano lessons from our high school band teacher. . . And he'd looked at me one day and he shook his head and we were good friends, but he said: "It's too bad about you." And I said: "What?" And he said: "You have the desire but you don't have the hands for the piano, and you don't really have the inborn talent." He said: "Now, your sister has the hands and the talent but

doesn't have the desire." So, I mean, I laughed because it was true. I don't. (Rebecca-32)

Another woman described her mother's favoritism based upon the differences in the sisters' personalities and abilities:

[Debbie] always felt that my parents were pointing out that I was never in trouble, and I was always a good student, and she never did really well in school and didn't like it. So that is something she felt separated us—that I was more intelligent than she was—and she didn't have those academic aspirations that I did. I felt different from her in that sense, too. (Tracy-31)

The opinions and judgments of other important people became a barometer for comparisons between sisters. Personal worth and self-esteem seemed tied to these parents', teachers', friends', and family members' opinions.

Difficult Emotions

The memories from childhood almost always included an emotional component. Sometimes the emotions were difficult to manage and they were frequently hurtful. The women talked about fear, guilt, jealousy, conflict, and alienation as they described these childhood experiences. Guilt and jealousy were by far the most common difficult emotions associated with these periods. Competition and childhood teasing were also recalled. Fear emerged in the sister relationship for many reasons, some intentional and some inadvertent. In this instance one sister intentionally tried to trick the other into being afraid:

One thing that has become a family joke now, my sister and I have talked about it and she's forgiven me for doing it, is that when she was like in fifth grade. . . this is like the ultimate nasty thing to do. But, there was like one of these. . . men's service clubs and what this particular service club did was choose. . . a girl of the year, ask the teachers to choose one. And [my sister] got chosen as the girl of the year. Well. . . she didn't know this, but her teachers knew it and my parents, and my parents told the rest of us. And. . . this man from the service club was going to come and present her with this award at home. And then they would go to the ceremony the following week where she would get, you know, get applause and everything. Well, she knew. She found out that somebody was going to come see her; well, that something special was happening to her. And the night. . . before the guy came. . . I told her that the guy who was coming was her long-lost father and that she was adopted. And she, poor little Megan, she was. . . absolutely gripped with fear. And I was like, "Don't worry, Megan. He's very, very nice and he's going to take you home." I'm sure I embellished it some more, but I just put the fear into her. I mean, it was horrible to do that! But I got so much satisfaction out of it. (Jean-14)

Guilt formed a backdrop for incidents like the one Jean described. The guilt emerged from every life stage: childhood, teenage, and adult. One woman described wanting to kill her infant sister because of the new arrival's demand on her mother's time and the disappointed desire for a sister-ally against her two brothers. These feelings shocked and surprised the woman when she had them as a young girl. Another woman reported sneaking away from her sister to play with others and the accompanying guilt from such actions:

> [W]e lived on a farm and being the middle child, my brother was expected to be out working; I helped mother. But the minute I could, [I'd] get away... and I would go out and play and make playhouses and this kind of stuff. Once in awhile I'd let her join me. And when my cousins would come, they always thought she was cute and they wanted her around. And I [was] just itching to get away [be]cause when you live on a farm you don't have a lot of playmates. So, when you have somebody your age, you want them to yourself. So, supposedly, I should have some real regrets about how we used to sneak away from Kimberly. (Rebecca-10)

Rebecca was surprised by the difference in how she and her sister recall that incident. Her own recollection was tied to the feelings she had about her behavior, but her sister did not remember the incident or negative feelings about it. Another woman said she refused to take the blame her adult sisters attempted to foist on her. It was difficult for her to maintain that stance. Even though she thought such blame was unfounded, she felt guilty about the possibility that it might be true. Guilt and its validity seemed tied to differential recall by the women and their sisters. They judged their guilt partly based upon these differences in memory.

Other guilt-laden memories were related to jealousy between sisters. Childhood jealousy often led to actions that were designed to hurt the sister. Some women recalled these attempts as creating concern for their parents. In other instances, parents excused the behaviors because they understood the jealousy. Guilt about the behavior was usually present, as described by this woman:

> One time I remember carrying her as an infant and laying her down on the bed, and she rolled off the bed... This was... six months after she was born or something. She was still really little and she rolled off the bed and onto the floor and started crying... I felt so guilty about that. It was almost like I felt like I had, like I'd done that on purpose. You know, because I didn't like her.
>
> And... another time... we were at the ocean. We were there for vacation. I remember holding her and going into the water and dropping her, and...

trying to pick her up and I think my Mom came out, or my Dad came out
and helped me pick her up. . . And I don't remember either of them going,
you know, "Look what you've done" or blaming it on me. (Jean-8)

If the jealousy and hurtful behavior connected to an incident persisted into later
childhood or adolescence, it was often based on continuing closeness between the
younger sister and the mother. The guilt seemed strongest when the older sister
thought she should be punished and was not. In some cases this resulted in an adult
resolution of the incident; in others the jealousy and accompanying guilt continued.

Alienation was reported by one woman. She felt that the relationship with her
sister in childhood and the way their mother favored her sister led to lifelong
alienation from her siblings and family. When she and her sister finally talked
about the experiences of their early years, she cried:

[O]ur discussion that we had. . . made me feel like I had a much deeper connection to her. It's still hard for me to talk about. When we left Indianapolis
we were driving up to see my uncle and aunt in Milwaukee, and on our way
up there we talked, and we both just cried at different times about our relationship with my mom, particularly. And we talked about how. . . I was very
open with her about how I felt like I was. . . being pushed out of the family
by my mom. . . But she wasn't pushing. . . she wasn't trying to push me out.
But. . . I felt like I was being pushed out and. . . that I felt like I was the black
sheep of the family and that I caused the most trouble. (Jean-31)

Although alienation was seldom mentioned, conflicted relationships between
the sisters and other family members were. Parental reactions were often at the
center of these conflicts. Some women felt their parents should have intervened
more directly to stop the conflict between sisters; others felt their parents had
intervened constantly. Occasionally, one sister's defiance pulled the woman into
conflict with her parents. Another type of conflict emerged when the sisters were
collectively blamed for something they had not done. Here is an example:

And we were playing hide-and-seek one day and somehow, even though
Felicia and I swore we weren't in there, the whole shelf fell over. And all
of [mom's] jars broke and we got in so much trouble. And neither of us
had done anything. (Eve-37)

The memory of such conflicts seemed to persist throughout life. For these
women, they represented a host of other incidents with similar themes.

Competition was also present within the childhood relationship. One woman
described feeling shadowed by a much younger sister who wanted to do everything that she did. Another mentioned adolescent competition for male affection:
she and her sister would compete for the same boyfriends. While she often won

that competition, the woman reporting this incident had some remorse about the effect losing may have had on her sister's self-esteem.

Teasing within the sister relationship usually involved at least one third party. The teasing seemed to create ambivalence: feelings of fondness were accompanied by a sense of ridicule. One woman says that the childhood teasing she received from her sister about being gullible persists to this day. She gave this example from their childhood:

> There were times [be]cause Cindy and I both—since [Tabatha] was two years younger, we thought a lot faster and talked a lot faster and of course. . . we were already school-wise and our intelligence was still form-ing faster and maturing a tiny bit faster than [Tabatha], so we kind of were always a step ahead of her, and I would. . . tease her a lot. . . not the good big sister, I would [play] devil's advocate or teased her a lot, that kind of stuff. Like I felt, when I got older I had to sort of make amends to her. I really did goad her. (Morgan-19)

Sometimes when the teasing was very good-natured the woman expressed a fondness about those memories. During visits, the mother and sisters reminded each other of fun and silly incidents that had occurred in childhood, sometimes including teasing. One such incident included recollection of the "jobs" each had when looking for a new home; another included the imitation of a wild animal and a pet name associated with that imitation. While teasing could lead to strong neg-ative feelings in the moment, time made those memories more positive.

Supportive Interactions

Many of these difficult or negative feelings were balanced by positive feelings about early childhood interactions. Most women had some ambivalence; others remained entirely positive or negative. There were many descriptions of the good feeling and memories. The closeness and sharing of their early years bonded some sisters for their entire lives. Sharing was enforced by parents and often meant having to use the same things or spaces. At least two of the women felt they learned compatibility from having the same bedroom with their sisters when they were growing up. This specific experience affected their sense of boundaries. As one teenager explained:

> Sydney and I had a lot more respect for each other's privacy, because we never really had anything together, but Victoria and I basically come and go as we please between each other's rooms because we stayed in a room together. But it's not like we're invading each other's privacy or anything. (Diane-6)

Sharing could be emotional, arising from fond memories of childhood activi-ties or conversations. For example, one woman described joy in dressing like her sister in childhood and kept a photograph of them dressed alike in her wallet. Compatibility from shared experiences may have provided a way to avoid conflict in the present.

Regardless of the emotional valence in a sister relationship, the passage of time often led to greater understanding and growth. Sometimes this growth occurred accidentally; often it occurred by conscious intention. Therapy was sometimes a part of this insight, as was separation from the sister for a period of time in early adulthood. This was especially true when the sister comparisons had been fraught with conflict, or one sister was perceived as being the perfect daughter in the family. One woman reflected on her change in perception when visiting her sister at college for the first time. Another talked about her sister's persistent bitterness and anger, as well as the ways she has learned to adjust to it. She says:

> And I think sometimes the anger just pours out. At least that's the way I've looked at it and so I can get by it. And I have, in my older age, learned to just try to take it as a watershed and just let it go by. . . . (Janice-35)

Whatever insight has come, there was an attempt to understand the sister's perspective—different from her own but just as valid. For example, "she'd probably say, `Dad was picking on me' and so it would be just her perception of how it really happened" (Janice-50). In the process of understanding the sister's feelings, the woman had a reluctance to abandon her parents' perspective on the conflicts. Thus the relationships between sisters were understood through a process of growth and development—an intentional struggle.

Childhood sister interactions were also apparent in attempts to continue family traditions. The women described a desire to maintain such traditions and recognized the importance of the current experience as it related to the historical one. The sister–sister interactions during their youngest years helped to mold the current relationship and formed the central core of the sister relationship. This central core was based in part on the desire to know and understand the relationship, the sister, and the self through the family lens. A more specific view was provided by the mother's interactions with multiple daughters.

Mother–Daughter–Sister Interactions

Descriptions of mother–daughter–sister interactions consumed a great deal of time during the interviews, and the themes emerging from this category were extensive. The women described their mothers' treatment of the daughters and compared that treatment. They discussed the shared caretaking experiences that occurred in childhood. Sometimes the daughter took over the mother's role with her sister; sometimes the two sisters cared together for the mother. This caretaking role was also described in the context of illness or death. The relationships within this mother–daughter–sister threesome were also examined individually and compared to each other. Frequently two members of the group formed an alliance against the third. Such alliances could lead to violations or betrayals by one member of the three. More often than not, the women, using a mature lens, described a sense of supportive mutuality in the relationship between the three. The understandings within the relationship were complex and often merged with the insight into other family connections.

Comparing Mother's Treatment of the Sisters

Not surprisingly, the women compared the treatment received from their mother with her treatment of their sister(s). The focus of these comparisons was not about similarity; that occurred only when women talked about being dressed like their sisters by their mother as young children. The women talked much more about times they felt their mothers treated them differently. These differences centered on the fostering of independence in one girl more than the other and the fairness of punishments or gifts. In an extreme example, one woman described being physically abused by her mother, when her sister was not.

> [B]ut I told [my sister] why I felt the way I did, because I had been abused by my mother and didn't feel particularly close to her. . . . And my sister sort of thought that I was making that up or something. She kind of invalidated it. . . by saying that she just couldn't see that happening. . . . [She thought] I was exaggerating or making these things up, and I told her then, "No, that wasn't true." But she talked to my mother about it; she told her what I had said or maybe just asked about it. I didn't really find out about that conversation. . . My mother got really upset about it and wrote me a letter asking me. . . if she had ever done anything to me, because I guess she's in complete denial of these episodes. (Tracy-4f to 8f)

That woman's sister had a hard time accepting that her mother had been abusive. By contrast, another woman suggested that her sister's perception of unfairness by their parents was unfounded, as illustrated by the following story:

> [Ingrid] always felt that I had—was born with—more good qualities, and that I was the favorite child of our parents. Uh, she was the first born and she felt she got all the ugly side of both parents and that I got all of the good qualities, and she's always resented that. She always felt that I was favored in every way by our parents. Um, I don't agree with that, but there's a lot of things she doesn't know that I didn't get [because of her], but would have been nice if I had. (Caroline-2)

Even though these two stories present opposite sides of the issue, each is concerned with the perception that one sister was treated quite differently from the other. The differing perceptions of fair treatment often led to conflict between the sisters. There was also conflict surrounding the mother's excuse for a sister's lack of responsibility. A middle-aged participant suggested:

> We have a lot of differences. Like, I'm the kind that when I go back to mother's, I feel like I should be in the kitchen all the time, especially when you've taken six kids with you through the years. Even now that I don't have the six kids that travel with me, then I figure I should be the one to be helping mother. My sister can sit in and watch a movie or football game, and it doesn't bother her one whip, but my mother will always say, "Let her go, she's tired." I go, "Okay." (Rebecca-6)

One woman gave a report of her mother's concern that she had not been fair with the daughters. When her mother suggested this she and her sister jumped to the mother's defense. In those cases, the women justified the differing treatment, suggesting that treatment had a different purpose with each daughter. One woman reported this conversation between her mother and sister:

> But my mother has regrets in that she wasn't. . . has never really been able to go help my sister out when she had the babies or when she was sick—like she did me. . . So, my sister looked at her one time and said, "Mother. . . you raised me to take care of myself. . . . You did a good job. What do you have regrets for, I handled it, didn't I?" Mother said, "I just feel so terrible because I wasn't there." [Kimberly] said, "Don't worry about it, you did your job." (Rebecca-41)

The women seemed to come to terms with these differences over time and tried to understand the necessity of a mother's differential treatment. Even the report of abuse against one daughter and not the other was excused based upon the difference in their ages and the circumstances surrounding the mother when the girls were young.

Another theme related to the mother–daughter–sister interaction was the influence the mother had on their interactions. The women reported that their mothers intervened in their childhood conflicts, often punishing them until they were able to get along. One woman said her mother used time-outs, not physical discipline. Several women were concerned that their mothers had used them as examples for their sisters; most often this centered on academic excellence. One woman reported that her mother excused her own drinking during adolescence because of her academic achievement, but her mother did not excuse her sister's acting-out behaviors:

> [A]nd my mother—although I used to go out and drink beer in the country when I was in high school with a friend—my mother never ask me what I did, because she trusted me. I guess it's because I did well in school. And my sister [did not] and unfortunately it was always [my mother saying], "Oh, why can't she be more like her sister?". . . so I think my

sister always thought that I was such a wonderful person who did well in school and, um, she wasn't as smart as I was and caused more trouble for mom and dad than I did. (Tracy-54)

Universally, the women reported strong feelings about being used as an example for their sisters. They did not like it when that occurred. None reported feeling their sisters had been used as an example for them. Feelings about fairness, differences, and intervention by the mother were a profound part of the women's experience.

Caretaking Between Mothers and Daughters

Another dimension of this experience was the nature of caretaking in the mother –daughter–sister triad. Mothers and sisters cared for each other when the need arose because of illness, pregnancy, emotional distress, or impending death. In addition, women discussed the ways they assisted their mothers in caring for a younger sister in childhood. Many components of this experience were explored during the interviews. Mothering by a sister was sometimes voluntary and sometimes required by an overburdened or negligent mother. Usually the role was delegated to the oldest daughter. In this case, parental divorce was the reason:

> [My relationship with Gina] is very different than my relationship with Brooke. Um, a lot of it I think has to do with the age difference between [Gina and me], which is almost 10 years, and the fact that, in a lot of ways, I was pretty involved in her childrearing from about the age of five—her being five when my parents separated—and then my mom started working outside the home. (Hillary-47)

The tasks required of the older sister also varied, with one woman describing her sister's role as a sex educator:

> But my mother never was much to talk and tell you. . . things that really were necessary. And so, I would go to Mandy with it. . . . And she would tell me, you know—as near as she could—what was going on. [Be]cause [there are] things a girl getting up in teens should know. Our mother never told us these things. . . . [Mandy] said, "This is what I know, I ain't sure this is the way it is," but it usually was. (Gretchen-39f to 41f)

At times the sister's assumption of a mothering role was welcomed; at other times it was resented. Divorce or death of a father could also precipitate the need for a "second mother" in the family. This role often was complicated by intense emotional reactions to the loss of the stable family unit, as well as the feelings that the mother was negligent of the younger daughter. Resentment and anger emerged in relation to these circumstances. In one case, the younger sister was a half-sibling who intruded on an established sister trio:

> [My mother] married this man that was 20 years her senior. . . and so that was the real total change. All of a sudden we had this person that was supposedly our father in the house, and he built us a house, [be]cause we'd always lived in apartments. So, that was good. But it was just as stressful because they fought a lot. Then the baby came along, which we were all really happy about, but that was an adjustment. . . say I was 11 and Cindy was 9. And it was kind of weird, when you're a kid, to have your mom pregnant again and have the baby, and so Cindy and I used to fight about who was going to take care of Tabatha, [be]cause we all took a real big role in [her] upbringing. (Morgan-36 to 37)

Sometimes, other family dynamics caused the need for a parent-like intervention by the sister. One woman described her family's loud and conflicted interactions. During them, her mother expected her to protect her younger sister from her older brother. Protection of a sister, in this context, was understood as part of the maternal role. (Other forms of protection are discussed in a later chapter.) The sister's own characteristics sometimes caused a girl to model her mother's behavior in managing the sister. This was described in relation to a sister's passivity or defiance.

Occasionally, the mother role became permanent. In such cases, a mother's immaturity might lead to a permanent assumption of the parenting role by the sister, even in adult life. In this description one woman related how she mothered her sister and her mother:

> Someone or somebody is going to have to take charge and start swallowing pride and I feel like, as the oldest, I might as well be the one to do it. No one else is. And with my mother being the way she is. . . I hate to use the word "immature," but. . . kind of the innocent type that never really matured past a certain point. So, it was like I had to be the mother when we were growing up. Alright, I think I'm going to have to take that role anyway. (Chris-13f)

Caretaking, as a substitute mother, was a common experience. The role might be primary or just a part of the way the sisters were managed by a competent mother.

Sometimes, the mother and daughter worked together to care for an ailing or emotionally troubled sister. In childhood, some women shepherded their distressed sister to their mother for the care she needed. The source of the distress varied, including emotional incidents or bullying peers. During the adult years, this cooperative action was reversed: the mother would direct the distressed sister to the woman and her family for help. One woman described a particularly disturbing time when she was called upon to help her sister:

> I got a phone call from my mom one night, not quite 11 o'clock, and Mother says, "Martha's in trouble, can you get over to the house right away?" So, needless to say, Frances and I literally flew over there. The paramedics had gotten there just before we did and broken a dining room window to get in and my sister was huddled in a corner on the floor with the paramedics trying to talk to her and she just, she was holding her head with both hands, because I guess the pain was just excruciating, and paramedics were trying to help her and get her onto a gurney to get her to the hospital and she was, which I didn't know at the time, she was panicked because she thought she was going to be gang-raped. That was going through her head because here were all these men who had broken through a window and she had no idea that mom had called the paramedics. She had called my mother and told her that her head was killing her and mother called, that's all she could say, and mother called and that's why I got there. But as soon as she heard my voice, and I kept saying, "Martha, it's okay, it's okay," she could relax. Just like that. And then they were able to get her on a gurney and get her to the hospital. (Opal-15)

Opal also described her sister as a user, only calling "when she needed something" from her or her mother. Thus the mother–daughter team called upon each other to respond to a sister in need, sometimes with a resentful afterthought.

When two or more sisters banded together to care for their mother, it was usually because she had become ill or was dying. Often this end stage nurturing was a cooperative effort. Some women described the different roles that each filled for the mother. Many women expressed appreciation for what a sister—geographically closer to their mother—did for her. One woman was aware of the closeness and reciprocal nature of such mother–daughter relationships:

> And I'm really grateful at how she. . . works with my mother. My mother just lives a few miles from them, you know. I've mentioned that before. My mother came through with a kind of a bad scare with some cancer. . . but my sister's just right there. . . And my mom spends a lot of time with my sister and helps her with the kids. . . my mom's like part of their family. (Janice-44)

The mother's illness and the required caretaking created an opportunity for some sisters to get to know each other better. The time spent together, planning the care and administering it, allowed each to observe the other as adults. Difficulties in the sister relationship were often forgotten during this experience:

[W]e were all right there on the scene, and we were all together, and we
forgot all of our past problems with each other and just pulled together
for our mom. (Chris -11f)

Women who lived further away from an ailing mother experienced regret at
being less available. Sometimes they altered their lives to be near the mother and
assist more in the time of her illness. One woman and her husband moved so they
could live with the sister and mother, assuming all would help with the mother's
death. After the mother's death, the husband died and the sisters continued to
reside together:

We all lived here; in fact that's why we came—to move to a larger house.
Elizabeth and Jeremy [sister and brother-in-law] lived in Denver. Mother
and I lived here. Mother was not able to take care. . . I took care of her and
had for a number of years, and then Jeremy, Elizabeth's husband, became
ill, so we just said, look, there was only the two of us left in our immediate family, so why don't we do something so that we can help each other,
because if we can't. . . so we debated whether to move my mother to
Denver or whether to move them here. So we decided it would be better
for them to come here, so each of us sold our homes, and we came out to
this area and bought a larger house so that we could care for my mother
and her husband without having to put them in a rest home or custodial
care or whatever. (Lynetta-39)

The move was difficult for the sister who came from Denver: she had sacrificed
her social and spiritual network in order to care for the mother with her sister.
This type of sacrifice was unusual, but the commitment to work together to care
for the dying mother was not.
There were, however, exceptions, and some women complained about their sisters' lack of involvement in caretaking for the mother. This situation provoked
comparisons between the sisters: who filled the caretaker role in the best manner
over their mother's lifetime? One woman reported that her sister did more, staying inside to help her mother with chores during childhood. Another described
her sister's failure to take appropriate responsibility for cleaning up after a visit to
the mother's home. A third mentioned her sister's failure to participate at all when
her mother returned from hospitalizations.

When my mom was in the hospital, which Mother was frequently, Martha
would come every day religiously to see her and always send a big bouquet, but as soon as Mom came home. . . it was always to my house that
she came home to recuperate because Martha said she couldn't handle it.
I thought it was fair—one time her, one time me—but she always said
she couldn't handle it. So mother always came here. From the day that

she'd get home from the hospital, we'd never see Martha again. She'd never bother showing up. I can remember Mother, who was quite the jokester, she'd say, "If I die, you will send Martha a notice?" Or she'd say, "Send her a copy of the obit." You'd have to know my mom, [be]cause she was hurt because Martha didn't pay any attention. She'd go three or four weeks without ever calling Mother. Here again, Mom was maybe two miles away from us. The only time that she ever called either Mother or me on her own was when she needed something. (Opal-27 to 28)

Unlike the mother's failure to perform her caretaking role, the sister's failure is not forgiven or excused. One sister's failure was perceived to increase another sister's burden. As one woman said, "Well, I just have to clean everything up. Well, I get tired of it, but I guess someone's got to do it so I'm the one" (Diane-22). When sisters didn't share the burden of an elderly mother's illness equally, resentment could build. Conversely, if they came together, past differences were forgotten.

Individual Relationships and Alliances

When discussing the individual relationships within the mother–daughter–sister threesome, the women often compared the quality or closeness of the relationships; sometimes they described the alliance between two of the women against the third. These allies were apparent in all varieties: two sisters against their mother, mother and sister against the woman being interviewed, or the woman and her mother against the sister. The closeness in the relationship was defined partly by the parental role. Some women reported feeling closer to their sister, since they did not see their mother as intruding:

And my mother's the kind of person that always wants to know everything, and if something is the matter with you she always has to know. She always wants to fix it and, you know, sometimes you're like, "It's my problem. Go away!" And whenever I had a problem about anything, I'd tell Ashley, and she's really good about giving me advice. So, when I needed advice I either. . . used to go to her, and we'd spend up to 3 o'clock in the morning sitting in my room. (Eve-19)

Some felt closer to their mothers due to similarity. Some reported a closer connection between their sisters and their mother. These preferences within the threesome occasionally persisted into adulthood but were often altered by changes in the parental role. There was a clear attempt to understand the connection between the three women and to tell the story of the reasons for those differences in connection.

When women felt closer to their sister, they often described the importance of age and role. Older mothers were unlikely to feel like confidants. One woman wanted her mother to be aware of only her good behaviors and confided her conflicts to her sister. Another described her sister's natural empathy, compared to her ill-equipped mother:

> [Be]cause Barb's always even and fair and soothing and comforting to me, and she's that way with everybody. That's the image she projects. So, my mother was always so. . . out in left field. You know, it was a big source of. . . shame attached with it. She was just very strange. [Mom] really never had any business having kids in the first place. Probably didn't want to, but didn't have any choices back then. . . She's just a very different person. . . very strange. (Chris-33)

Balancing the relationships with the mother and with the sister was sometimes a challenge. This was especially true when the woman felt her relationship with each of the other two was stronger than theirs were with each other. One young adult reported competition between her mother and sister when she visited their hometown. In this scenario, the mother and sister eliminated the competition by arranging exclusive time, but the sense of jealousy still prevailed:

> [M]y mom and dad [were] picking me up at the airport, and they wanted to go out to dinner with me. And, I told my mother, "Well, invite Jane and her husband, if you'd like. . ." [Jane] and I are throwing a party on Sunday for all of the friends [be]cause I'm going to be home for such a short time, and we never see each others' friends anymore. We decided to throw a big party, so we'd see everybody at once. . . I asked her, I said, "If you want to invite Mom or Dad, go ahead, and if you don't, that's fine. And she said, "No, I'd rather just have it be our friends.". . . I guess my sister asked my mom and dad if she could go out to dinner with us and my mom said, "No!" (Andrea-32)

In another case, the woman described her role of mediator between her mother and sister based upon a stronger bond with each of them. She felt her sister needed more attention and approval from her mother. As she had matured, she provided a bridge of understanding between them.

There were times when a woman clearly felt closer or more special to her mother than her sister did. This favored status was often attributed to personality characteristics. Some women felt closer to their mothers if they were similar to her. Some felt they were favored because they were different from their mother. In a few cases the women did not allow this favoritism to blossom into a close relationship. As this woman described, she felt more inclined to push her mother away and turn toward her sister:

> I think out of all five kids, I was my mother's favorite. I don't know why, but I was the one that pushed away from her the most. I was real

independent and had a lot of responsibility early on. My mother and I never got close. I think she would like to have been closer, but I never allowed it. For whatever reasons, you know, being a teenager, being a mother, whatever, uh, I always turned to Barb. (Chris-32)

Other individual relationships within the female family group were also compared. A woman with more than one sister sometimes felt two of the sisters had a stronger relationship than she did with either one. This relationship might be based upon common interests, activities, or even bad habits. A third sister describes the closeness of the other two:

[B]ecause the two of them lived together for about four years as adults—Sally was almost an adult—their relationship changed and became more friends, as opposed to myself and my relationship with them. . . . I never was with both of them. . . And I guess that because they were adults now and their relationship was different. (Brooke-26)

One woman described the high energy level she shared with her mother, while her sisters joined forces in eating high-calorie foods and being sedentary. She attributed this difference to the temperaments and physiology that each duo shared:

Physically, we were quite different. I've always taken after my mother's side of the family. My mother was always rather slim and wiry and lots of energy, and my sister, Leslie, took after my father's side of the family. My father's side of the family always sort of had a little bit of a weight problem, and she was always kind of the plump side. So, physically we were quite extreme. (Janice-3)

Another woman seemed to sense that her mother and sister had become primary partners. She compared their relationship to the one between her and her husband.

The closer bond between one mother and a daughter, or two sisters, led to a clear sense of conflict. These conflicts resulted in a sense of alliance between two women against the third. One type of alliance was created when a woman allied with her mother against her sister. Sometimes the woman and her mother kept secrets from the sister. In one case this meant accepting clothing offered by the mother to the sister, who had refused it; in another case it meant comparing notes about visiting a difficult sister who lived far away. In taking her mother's side and bonding more closely with her, some women minimized their sister's pain about childhood and excused the mother's actions. A different woman said her sister had not been prepared for life by their mother and described how the strength of the sister bond outweighed the mother–daughter connection. Lack of knowledge about sexuality was specifically mentioned as a disservice. In all of these cases, the woman took the side of her mother or her sister and formed an allegiance, which left the other one out. When sisters bonded together, often a driving influence was the need to understand a difficult or puzzling mother. Working together they were able to understand the mother better as they matured:

> My mom can be really, really critical. And my sister always says, "If you want to know the bad side of something, call my Mom." She'll give you all the bad reasons. I think that's coming up for [Jane] a lot more, and I'm noticing it. (Andrea-19)

Understanding developed silently for some women and their sisters. The shared experience of a difficult mother may have created that understanding, and it led to a desire to defend the sister when the mother complained. One woman emphasized her sister's optimism even in the face of multiple responsibilities and difficulties, and described the sister's loss of composure at the mother's advice:

> Mother tried to tell me something about her the other day—that Kimberly got a little upset because she'd gone. . . to get their son out of college and close up the. . . apartment or. . . dorm room. [Kimberly had to] clean up after him. . . and mother's trying to quote scripture at her about consider the lilies. . . and. . . Kimberly said, "Well, does [that scripture] work for food, too?" I don't quite understand what she was getting at, if she was just at her wit's end trying to. . . cook, trying to clean, trying to run [everything]. . . . She never complains. It doesn't come out complaining—ever. She'll tell you a story, and I would complain. But she's not telling it in a complaining manner. (Rebecca-66f)

Other women described the need to ally with the sister against the mother's desire to intrude. Sometimes similar defenses were needed to stop intrusion by the mother into the woman's own life. In exasperation, one woman exclaimed to her mother: "It's my problem. Go away!" (Eve-19). Such alliances with the sister were often defensive in nature, providing for each other what the mother had failed to provide.

When a woman felt her mother and sister had joined forces against her, it was particularly painful. This may be the reason the sister–mother alliance was mentioned most often in the interviews. Such alliances began in early childhood or infancy and were sometimes attributed to the sister's younger age. One woman, who had expressed homicidal rage toward her sister during infancy, described acting out against her brothers in an attempt to get her mother's attention away from the sister. These recollections stimulated guilt and ambivalence about her behavior. Attempts to gain closeness to a mother, who was allied with the sister, proved futile leaving the woman feeling hurt and alone.

Violations

Painful feelings could emerge from an alliance of two women within the triad, but women felt much more strongly about violations of privacy, intrusion, and judgment by two against the third. Violations of privacy were mentioned most often, as when a sister or mother would divulge a confidence. In the research, such breaches were described only when the injured party was the woman completing the interview. The attempts to confide in a sister about the mother were particularly difficult. In confidence a woman told her sister she felt she had been abused by their mother. When the sister shared that with the mother and she denied it, the discrepancy created a wedge between the sisters that was difficult to heal. These violations led to a breach of trust in the sister–sister relationship and a lack of willingness to share intimate information. Sometimes, one sister violated the confidence of the mother by providing gossip about family events and relationships. The reverse was also true, with the mother as the offending party. In addition, the mother sometimes violated trust by judging both sisters or by trying to intrude in their relationship with each other. In childhood, this intrusion may have occurred in order to mediate conflict. In adulthood, it is just described as meddlesome:

> [A]nd my mother always tried to come to me and say, "What's wrong with Ashley? She won't tell me what's wrong." [She was] expecting me to tell her, because usually I knew. . . She always tries to get information out of either one of us. (Eve-17)

The women also mentioned their mother's judgmental attitude toward the sisters. These judgments could be based upon similarity, as when both women picked male partners who were similarly employed. Although such judgments were made, at least one woman was quick to suggest that her mother never made them outside of the family. This boundary was an important one to her. Despite the boundaries employed in some families, violations did form an important emotional part of the relationship between mothers, daughters, and sisters.

Supportive Mutuality

Mutuality within the triadic relationship also emerged in several themes. Mothers and sisters formed an emotional bond characterized by a sense of pleasant childhood memories and continuing emotional interdependence. Simply put, the women felt their sisters and mothers were always there for each other. This feeling of mutuality led the women to recognize the strength in difference. One part of the triad would contact another to encourage helpfulness between the other two. One woman's description of her mother's encouragement was based upon the difference in achievement. For example, creative sisters were called upon to help solve problems for more intellectual sisters. Pleasant memories from childhood included traveling together and playing games in the car, remembering similar outfits, and entertaining themselves with games prescribed by the mother while the parents were occupied with business matters. These pleasant memories were recalled between the first and second interviews, and the women reported reminiscing about their positive feelings toward the mother and their sister.

Complex Understandings of the Mother–Daughter–Sister Relationships

Understanding the connections between three or more women in a family was more difficult. Women seemed to spend considerable time trying to dissect the relationships. This understanding grew with age. The women also pondered how those relationships were affected by other external relationships. Most often these thoughts were related to men, as when brothers, fathers, and husbands influenced the relationship between the three women. Women described turning to their brothers when excluded by the mother–sister pair. They described defending their father's discipline to a sister and being encouraged to do so by their mothers. Mothers also admonished daughters to behave in the presence of their father. As one woman, raised in a traditional family, suggested:

> Looking back now everything was centered around Dad. [Mom would say,] "Now Dad's coming home, now don't fight [be]cause he's had a hard day" or "Dad's coming home; go wash and clean up because you want to be clean when Daddy comes home." (Lynetta-16)

One woman said that her husband functioned as the male presence in the family, doing handiwork for the two older sisters and their mother. Men were also excluded from the relationship between the three women. Insight from therapy led one woman to conclude that she and her mother had excluded her father from their family closeness.

Father–Daughter–Sister Interaction

Some of the main themes that typified the mother–daughter–sister relationship appeared in connection to the father–daughter–sister triad. The difference seemed to be in the details provided and the length of time spent discussing the relationship between the three of them as compared to the relationship with the mother. In regard to father–daughter–sister relationships, the notion of bonding as a threesome did not emerge, nor did a sense of mutuality. This triad was evaluated much more on the basis of favoritism by the father and alliance with a sister or father against the third. The father's favoritism was bestowed on the sister sometimes; at other times it was bestowed on the woman describing the relationship.

This favoritism seemed to affect and, to some extent, define the relationship between the girls. In some cases one daughter was favored due to her femininity, while a seemingly more masculine daughter was denigrated or ignored. This was especially poignant when the father was disappointed that the first-born child was not a boy. This disappointment interfered in the relationship between all three—father, sister, and daughter. The father expressed open affection for the younger daughter, but not the older one. Occasionally, one daughter intervened with her father on behalf of her sister. This example comes from a time of personal crisis for a much younger sister:

> Carol was sexually assaulted a couple of years ago and uh, that was a really, that was a big deal. She didn't want to tell my folks so she had me tell them. . . I'm kind of glad because my dad—I sort of had to chastise him into being understanding. . . She was all worried. . . that she was going to get in trouble or something. She was afraid that the police would call the house. . . to ask more questions and my folks would find out that way. (Jolene-52 and 53)

Sometimes the father or both parents unfairly compared one sister with the other. When this occurred it was likely to create low self-esteem in the sister who was disliked by the father.

Only one woman mentioned an alliance with the father. For her this included defending his parenting and disagreeing with her sister's perception of it. The mother sided with the other sister, so there was a division in the family between two unlikely pairs:

> We were little kids and my dad said, "It's time to eat dinner now." When my dad says, "It's time to eat dinner now," we marched our little bodies to the table. I mean, my mom had the dinner ready and we were to come to the table. My sister was playing the piano, and she kept playing. And Dad said, "It's time to come to dinner now, Sybil." And she didn't come. She kept playing the piano. And, you know, she went right direct against my father, and all of us knew, hey, you just don't do that. . . and he just lit into her and it was just, it was a bad scene. I mean he didn't physically abuse her or anything, but he was very, very, very angry and just lit into her, probably in a very vocal way. (Janice-49f)

At another time, this woman was allied with her sister and felt the sibling's overall influence was more important than that of her father. This suggests that her loyalties in the father–daughter and sister relationships shifted depending upon the circumstances and time.

Sisters were occasionally able to provide insight into the father–daughter relationship for each other. A poignant description emerges from the emotional struggle a father and his two daughters had in dealing with his wife's cancer:

My mom had cancer when I was 16 and Jane was away from the home, and she was living in another state. . . she was helping me figure out what was going on with [my father] [be]cause my father and I did not get along during that period at all. And she was just really helpful in gaining a perspective on why we weren't getting along, you know, and that my father was just totally freaking out. (Andrea-20)

As mentioned in the previous section, sometimes mothers and daughters bonded in a way that excluded fathers. However, sometimes they bonded in their attempts to make him feel welcome. This last was mentioned when a father came home to a traditional family environment at the end of his workday. Pleasant memories of this experience were reported. One woman described running with her sister to jump into her father's arms at the end of the day. Another described sweet treats that her father shared with them, and a swing he had obtained for them. Such interactions with father were brief but substantial to the women as they recollected their experiences of their sisters.

Family Interactions

As the focus of interaction widened to include other family members, major themes included family gatherings, perceptions, and structures. Family gatherings encompassed times of celebration. Holidays, travel, and reunions were mentioned. Memories of family gatherings sometimes created a sense of loss. Many differing perceptions were reported and the woman's own reconciliation of these differences was often included. Among the family perceptions mentioned by the women were the traumas of childhood and adult disclosure of previously secretive material. Family closeness was measured by the woman and compared to her sister's perceptions of that closeness. Difficulty connecting with family members was reported and evaluated by each sister in similar or different ways. The women were fairly detailed in their descriptions of family structure beyond the triads already considered. They weighed alliances with brothers, explored the brother–sister–parent connections, explained issues and conflicts related to families that share a business, and discussed inappropriate financial dependency. The family's pattern of achievement was considered, as was their adaptation to change. A specific adjustment warranted its own category: the separation of grown children from the family home. In addition, the women considered the multigenerational effect of their family's perceptions, structures, and allegiances. All of these themes emerged under the category describing the herstory of the immediate family relationships.

Family Gatherings

The women were careful to define what they meant by family gatherings. These included traveling, camping, holiday and birthday celebrations, and larger family gatherings such as reunions or simply having dinner together. At times previous get-togethers were recalled, or a family tradition was continued. Often these gatherings occurred because of similar interests. One woman described starting a new family tradition by taking her parents on a trip; she enjoyed watching their reaction to this new experience. Another mentioned traveling with her parents as an adult and felt it reflected her childhood experiences with them. Family gatherings also created an opportunity to feel sadness or loss. One woman felt just getting her family together would be difficult due to its size. Another said it would be hard to connect with her sister during large family gatherings, as they precluded intimate connection. For one woman, family gatherings caused her to remember earlier holidays and the role her sister played in them:

> I can remember Debbie as a teenager being really moody and often locked away in her room—going right to her room. . . to study or whatever. Or, at the holidays, you'll get family pictures—she was always sick—everybody [would] be dressed, and she'd be in her room and looking terrible. And when I think back on that, I wonder if that was another way of kind of removing herself. (Tracy-28)

On the other hand, one woman suggested that family gatherings provided an opportunity to look beyond her sister's difficult sensitivity and to just enjoy her time with her. These family gathering times seemed to raise a variety of emotional experiences for the women.

Family Perceptions

There were specific and general themes that emerged under the wide auspices of family perceptions.[1] The family often compared the sisters. These comparisons could be accompanied by judgments about the sisters. A sister was compared based upon school performance and found wanting; another sister was judged for her choice of husband:

> Michelle divorced the child's father, obviously. The child's six years old, and Michelle recently got remarried, and the marriage only lasted about a year. . . The whole family has had problems with the marriage. And the guy in particular is a jerk. . . Michelle was really just doing some really strange things. . . People in our family have a tendency to tell you they don't like what you're doing. They are very opinionated and not afraid to say how they feel about something. (Brooke -35f)

---

[1] Many of these themes are closely connected to other categories that evolved during the analysis, and repetition here will be kept to a minimum.

Comparisons took many forms. One woman's family expressed disdain about her sister's continuing relationship with the woman's ex-husband. When parents compared two teenagers based upon one's rebellious behavior and the other's obedience, the obedient sister covered for the rebellious one, trusting her in a way that her parents could not. Sisters were also compared based upon their similarity to the parents' extended families. For example, one sister would be evaluated as more like the Taylors; another was perceived as being like the Lecci's. Most often these attributes began because of physical similarity to one family or the other:

> Physically, we were quite different. I've always taken after my mother's side of the family. My mother was always rather slim and wiry and lots of energy, and my sister, Leslie, took after my father's side of the family.... And, she also took on that rather slow-paced, easygoing attitude, whereas I was always charging ahead and organizing everybody and planning every-thing. Not just for my sister, but for the whole family. (Janice-3 and 4)

Often the sisters saw things differently than the parents or other family members, bonding over shared perceptions. This was especially apparent as the sisters grew older. As they matured, each became more accepting. One said that she and her sister's perception of the meaning of family had altered. She said, "I think, as we get older, we tend to... appreciate family and... the meaning of family—especially being single [and] not having kids... of my own" (Tammy-6f). She also said that she felt this new perception of meaning was held by the rest of the family. A particular age might have marked this maturity: one woman sug-gested that it occurred at 40. Specific insights were an important part of this growth. For example, this woman described being able to take greater responsi-bility for her sense of alienation from the family:

> [N]ow I take some responsibility for that, but... on certain occasions, there wasn't tolerance for questioning. I mean, I was the one who was always questioning the way things were being done and always bringing up controversial issues and being critical... Anyway, that's the way I saw myself, and I felt like my mother was pushing me out. (Jean-32)

Differing perceptions between the sisters could be a source of conflict. This situation is an excellent example of how sisters might agree to disagree:

> Megan was really, really angry when... I said this to her.... I remember her saying, "How can you say that? How can you say that, that's not the way I... I saw it; that's not the way it was. All I wanted to do is be like you... I didn't believe Mom or Dad or anybody, you know, Mom in par-ticular was trying to push you out of the family." And what we finally came to is that I really pushed for her to see that I could have a different

perception than her, and that was okay. . . if we were going to be there together and talk about this, she needed to realize. . . that this was the way it was for me. (Jean-33)

Difference also emerged as a way of putting the family relationships of the two women into perspective. One woman described her new perception of her sister's strength. Another talked about the change that occurred when she recognized the jealousy between them and worked to understand her parents' perspective so she could let it go.

Such maturity was often accompanied by a sense that the older sister had paved the way for the younger. The parents' perceptions of acceptable behavior changed as a result of the older sister's actions.

But I lived with two guys in college. Well, Jane, my sister, lived with a guy when she was living apart from her husband for career reasons. . . So that kind of paved the way for me. But I lived platonically with two guys in college. My parents weren't real excited. (Andrea-11)

Just growing-up created changes. One woman said she and her sister could have a relationship only after the sister had left the family home.

Changing perceptions also occurred as the women considered their parents' favoritism toward one sister or the other. This favoritism was explained in terms of compatibility with the parents, rather than the superiority of one sister over another. The sisters discussed such insights and hoped to gain greater understanding of their parents. Sometimes this favoritism was attributed to a great degree of emotional separation from the parents. As one young woman reported, "I think at different points along the way,. . . we'll talk about our parents. . . or if something is coming up, like a decision to live with a guy or something like that, we'll talk about them and if they're being weird (Andrea-18). Sisters are often successful in this mutual attempt at altering family perceptions.

Childhood Pain and Adult Disclosure

Perceptions about sisters were also altered when a woman learned about her sister's previously undisclosed childhood traumas. One woman described learning about her sister's depression after she had suffered with it for nearly 9 years. Only a long road trip together provided them with the opportunity to share their emotionally difficult childhood experiences. She said:

And no one ever knew it. I mean, that was just really intense to find that out. I still remember, I was sad in the car and I'm driving. This was for 10 hours straight to Milwaukee and she just was crying and crying and crying, and on and off I was crying. It was like real intense. (Jean-35)

This experience created a new bond for the sisters and shifted their perceptions of each other. Likewise, she felt her sister knew her better when she expressed the reasons for her conflicts with her brothers. Their exclusion of her before the sister was born had created a sense of alienation her sister had not understood. Sharing some of their childhood pain and suffering transformed their relationship into a true friendship.

Sisters gained insight into each other's coping and personalities as a result of these adult shifts in perception. One woman became aware of her sister's attempt to be a perfect child and the internal turmoil that was hidden underneath. Another felt she needed to be candid and vocal in an attempt to unravel family secrets. For this she was ostracized, but until they talked in depth, her sister had only seen her as difficult. These expressions brought about a welcome deepening of the sister relationship. Such opportunities for deeper connection seemed to require some dedicated time and willingness on the part of both women. As these sisters unearthed their experiences together, they experienced the joy of discovery and the importance of shifting perceptions.

Changing Perceptions of Family Closeness

For the most part, family closeness improved with time and maturity—or at least it was thought to do so. One woman remembered her older sister's return from college and the importance of the gifts her sister brought as an expression of her closeness. Another described the developing friendships between all of her family members, including her parents and brothers. A third talked about the love between her family members and her husband. And a fourth mentioned the importance of being able to count on her sister's love during their mother's death. The importance of family closeness was considered by these women throughout their lives.

Difficulty in Connection with Family

While some women felt their parents were attentive to all the children, others talked at length about the difficulty connecting within their families. Families were sometimes described as less affectionate than families observed in friends' childhood homes. One woman talked about moving away to avoid her family's chaos. Another woman mentioned the outward appearance of a traditional family that lacked emotional depth and sustained interaction:

> My parents are both kind of standoffish—not really standoffish—they're not affectionate. They are pretty uptight. And I remember in comparing myself [and home] to. . .my friends' homes. They seemed a little more relaxed in their relationships and just a little less strained, a little more natural with their expressions of emotion than my family was. (Tracy-15f)

She did not feel she lacked this emotional closeness in childhood, but was able to see the missing elements of emotional family life in retrospect.

These difficult connections were attributed to some specific family members. The recognition of envy for her sister's relationship with her father and brother led one woman to conclude that she did not want a closer relationship with her family. One woman withdrew from her relationship with her parents during adolescence but was able to maintain closeness to her sister:

> I kind of withdrew during my high school years. I really wasn't around my parents. We had a TV upstairs so I would watch TV upstairs rather than be with my mom and dad watching TV or doing whatever, reading or whatever. So there were several years where I didn't really communicate with them. There weren't any problems. I just kind of withdrew into my own world and into my friends' world. Ingrid was always a part of that, [be]cause she was as much as friend as a sister to me. (Caroline-41)

Another woman described the intimacy two of her sisters shared with each other; this had the effect of keeping her at bay. When reflecting upon her current relationship with her sister, one woman mentioned that she was obligated to the relationship:

> If I met my sister at work and didn't know her, I probably wouldn't become friends with her because I feel like we are really different. She's very conservative. She's a real redneck. We grew up in Arkansas and [she] was never really interested in leaving that. (Tracy-16)

Connections between sisters could sometimes triumph despite family difficulties connecting; at other times the sister connection was not essential or important.

Sometimes the importance of the sister relationship was diminished by events that were hurtful. There was a sense that the sisters had to reconcile some difficulty in order to become emotionally solid again. These events included a specific wrong involving other family members. One woman remembers abandoning her sister to her parents during a difficult holiday gathering; the sister responded by giving her the silent treatment. Different coping strategies for dealing with thorny parents caused some sisters to misunderstand each other or argue for their own method of coping. One woman, tired of listening to her sister's attempts to get her parents to understand her, suggested that the sister just abandon hope as she had. Because the family members were never close, another woman felt she would have to initiate closeness with her sister:

> The family was never real close anyway in that kind of a relationship. . .
> So, I have a feeling that if we are ever close it will have to come from me, and that would be based on what I'm learning now. You know, from a psychological point of view how to deal better with her, [be]cause I think she's just not equipped to do that. It's not part of what she's able to accomplish. (Caroline-7)

Her need to work hard to make a substantial relationship with her sister seemed daunting, and she expected to have the primary responsibility for it. Such effort made a close sister relationship attainable for some women; it did not feel possible for others.

Family Structure

The family structure shared by sisters in childhood was a significant part of each woman's herstory. The threesomes formed with each parent were significant components of this structure, but there were also general structural elements, awareness of triads formed with brothers and an appreciation for parental involvement in those alliances. Gaps in the age of sibling groups also formed separate sets of children in a family. A much older or a much younger group of sisters were tightly bonded:

> We didn't have the same interests and things like that. The older kids got to do things that younger kids were too young to be able to do, so that kind of kept us from being very close. . . our interests and just the things that we like to do are a lot different, so we really didn't have that in common. The only thing we had in common is that we're in the same family so because of that we seemed to get along okay. (Brooke-10 to 13)

These sibling groups were sometimes difficult to bring together, and an intermediary was sometimes required. Intermediaries or moderators had specific roles within the family. The women mentioned the importance of moderating between family relationships. Moderators, in times of high conflict, were called peacemakers:

> She is the one that we all have described as the peacemaker, so to speak. Everybody in the family has contact with her. Although a lot of people in my family get sometimes angry, but we all keep in contact with Barb. (Chris-4)

Eldest siblings functioned as parents or were delegated that role by the mother. Roles might have shifted over time with antagonists becoming confidants, caregivers becoming dependent. Confidants, caregivers, mother substitutes—all were roles that were passed from one generation to the next, as nieces emulated the roles of their aunts and mothers.

Shared Work and Financial Dependency

Working together generated another family structure and sometimes brought financial dependency to the relationships. One woman described the important roles each sister had in managing a family farm, beginning as young as preschool. This job responsibility was related to the fact that older siblings had to attend school:

We had a lot of chores to do—kids back then, you know. Our folks milked cows for a living,. . . and we always had a lot of chores to do. . . and we'd have to go bring the cattle in. And this little girl when we were at school, Sadie, would. . . ride a horse, and our dad would put her on the horse, and she'd go bring the cows in when she was five or six. . . She came in when we got home from school. This was before she went to school, you know. So, we all worked, you know. We all did our chores and milked cows and fed the calves and the pigs—all that kind of stuff. (Thomasina-63)

Several women mentioned the financial dependency within the family. In one family all siblings were dependent upon the parents' business. In another, a sister and her husband were able to open their own business because of her father's insurance settlement. Two women mentioned brothers who were financially dependent upon their parents for support. One of those had supported her brother when he resided with her temporarily:

David, one of my brothers, also works with my parents. He has a vending business or something, I'm not really sure. . . He's tied to my parents with that—I think they own the truck or something. And. . . my younger brother is also working with them. He's living up there with them and works with them occasionally. He's still kind of a wanderer. He'll go and stay with them for a while and go work somewhere else for awhile. And he stayed with me for a few months, but now he's up there with them again and working with them. They're all so interdependent, and I wouldn't want to be that way. . . I don't want to be involved in their problems. There's always so much going on; it would make me crazy to be around there. (Tracy-16, 17, and 20f)

Importance of Brothers

Brothers were mentioned briefly in comparison to sisters. One woman felt there was a gender division between the children of the family. She described feeling that her brothers ostracized her in childhood. Some women bonded with their brothers against their sisters, particularly in relation to parental favoritism, similarity of interests, or age differences:

[My mom] and Sally both would be closer to the typical feminine-type things, and I would be more to the other side. . . There's just a difference. I was tomboyish, too. And I didn't really have that in common with them, but I had that in common with my brothers. So. . . we'd talk about basketball or we'd go to each other's games and talk about it, or I'd go out and shoot baskets with my brothers or play pick-up games with them, stuff like that. Well, my sisters weren't there. (Brooke-54 and 55)

Brothers who were closer in age were seen as allies against a younger sister who was a pest:

> Um, my relationship with Debbie, when I was living at home, was a care-taker relationship, because she's about 7 years younger than I am. So [when] she came to the family, my brothers and I were pretty close, and felt like we were kind of a unit. . . then we had this "trailer" who was kind of a surprise. Debbie was not planned and just didn't seem to really fit in with the rest of the family. (Tracy-2 and 3)

Another woman with a twin brother said she was closer to him than her sister, initially:

> [Todd], my twin brother, I'm a lot closer to him. He'd be the first person I'd turn to if there was a problem and I needed to share a problem with, or ask for advice, or help me work through something. (Tammy-9)

At follow-up, Tammy had reconsidered and suggested the relationships were different; the research had an effect on this awareness:

> I had more of a relationship with [Todd], my twin brother, than I had with Jamie in terms of sharing. . . I feel still more of a closeness with my twin brother than I do with her. . . [The research] did make me re-evaluate my relationship [to my sister] more. (Tammy-4f)

Sometimes, conflicts with brothers prevented the development of a strong sister relationship. The energy required to manage difficult brothers kept the sisters apart. At times, sisters bonded against brothers. These exclusionary bonds between the sisters were based upon similarity, familiarity, and jealousy of the brother. Molly (23) suggested, "I have two brothers and I think the bond is just completely different. There's a different bond that I feel with [Donna] than I feel with my brothers. Um, a tie—a closeness." Eve suggested that her brother's behavior was annoying:

> Josh always needed attention and he still does. He's always the one being stupid, and when someone comes to the house he overreacts to get attention. And when it got to the point where Ashley and I were bringing friends home, it. . . was annoying. He wouldn't go away. And so we both would get angry at him. (Eve-42)

Complex relationships continued into adulthood. Parental and extended family favoritism for a brother deepened the bond with a sister. Occasionally, the family favoritism toward boys enhanced the bond between sisters. Brothers and sisters also bonded to compensate for an ongoing favoritism toward one sister. When a parent continued to excuse the behavior of a favored child, the alliance between brother and sister sometimes targeted the other sister, and the two ill-favored siblings joined each other in anger against the parents. The origins of such alliances began in the differential closeness a sister might feel toward her brothers and sisters, which was often related to unfair parental treatment:

> So I didn't really feel like we were close like sisters, [not] like some people that I know—being close in age or feeling really close because they grew up in the same time, or when their parents were treating them the same way. She got totally different treatment than we did. (Tracy-4 and 5)

Anger, pain, jealousy, and humor all emerged in reaction to these complex dynamics between parents and children.

Another dimension of the sister–brother relationship was the notion that older siblings included or paved the way for younger ones. This mentoring occurred when a younger sibling considered school choices and experiences. One woman's sister and brother followed her into college. Another described the importance of including younger brothers and sisters in social activities. At the time, she felt her parents' expectations about this inclusion were unreasonable, but now she could understand why they insisted. As brothers were added to the discussion of the sister relationship, more intricate interactions became apparent; parental involvement in those interactions further complicated the picture, leading to a shifting structure that included roles that changed over time.

Family Achievement

Some of the women in the study commented upon their family's history of academic or occupational achievement and success. It is entirely possible that the context of being a research participant created some of this reflection. Nevertheless, they felt it was an important part of their story. Most insisted that the success of all siblings was celebrated regardless of ability:

> I was thinking about how Ashley's into her music. . . And I specifically remember when she was a senior, the full orchestra itself does a concerto competition where they have soloists who are backed by the orchestra. . . Her senior year she won, so she was going to play a violin solo with the orchestra, and they call it the Masterworks Concert. And I can remember sitting there and just being so nervous for her, you know. . . by then I'd had this all memorized, practiced it over, over, and over. I think my whole family could sing it still! But I think we were getting so nervous for her and then afterwards I got to bring flowers up on stage, you know, and give them to her, so that was really neat. And, uh, I thought about that. (Eve-38f)

There was often a family history of contributing to that kind of success by attending activities and providing practical support. When one sister was more successful than another, this troubled the women. The parents' method of handling that difference sometimes left one woman feeling entitled; sometimes she felt ignored:

> [B]ecause I don't think it's right to compare one child to another. It, it made me mad because I didn't want to be [compared], I knew that she would get angry and I didn't want it to be my fault because. . . I was smart. At certain times I felt like, you know, maybe I should get a B; you know, maybe it will make it easier for her. But she never really said anything to me. And usually when she got angry at me or something was wrong, I could feel the tension. (Eve-44f)

When Eve's sister began to change, it changed Eve's relationship with her parents; she no longer felt important to them:

> But Ashley changed; she totally changed groups of friends when she got into high school. So I think her grades went up, and I don't think it was ever really a problem again. . . After [that]. . . my parents weren't as interested in what I was doing, I think they dropped the grade issue. (Eve-48f)

Several of the women expressed being disturbed by parental comparisons based upon academic achievement. They were saddened by these comparisons.

Family Adaptations

A woman's family structure could adapt to difficult circumstances. This too was part of her story about her sister relationships. Adaptations occurred late in life in order to provide a home for ailing parents or partners:

> . . . until about seven years ago when we [all] started living together. We did that because [my sister Stacey] was getting ready to retire. . . we had our mother living, and her health was getting kind of bad. . . it was getting to [the point] that [my sister and mother] couldn't come to our home any more My husband was getting sick. At the time we thought he had Alzheimer's, but it wasn't. . . We decided that neither of us had a home large enough to accommodate all four of us, so I sold my home in the Duncan Ridge, and she sold her smaller home here in Colorado Springs and we. . . bought this home together. (Thelma-2 and 4)

Adaptations also occurred in midlife when one sister confronted the parents about their favoritism:

> I think after I complained to my parents. . . that I think you encourage Ashley more, I think they realized, and they kind of changed the way that they dealt with us. (Eve-31)

Adjustments occurred in young adulthood when one sister's pregnancy became the central focus of the entire sibling group. Adaptations also occurred in childhood when older siblings had to help with the day-to-day care for a much younger child:

> So Leslie and I. . . we did all the diaper changing. In fact to this day when. . . I have to hang towels out. . . I don't like to dry them in the dryer [be]cause it takes up so much energy, so I have a line in the garage, so every time I hang up towels in the garage I think about my baby sister Sybil, [be]cause when she was a baby, we used to have to hang up diapers. This was the days before paper diapers. And I remember. . . it was real hot. You know it could get a hundred degrees and we had a line out back. We did have a washer, which was the first time we'd ever had a washing machine, before that it was just a wringer and a tub. We had an automatic washing machine but we still had to hang these diapers up. And every time I think about all of those diapers. . . We would rock her to sleep, and we would help feed her and everything. . . In other words, we kind of participated in her upbringing in a sense. (Janice-19)

All of these adaptations were part of the family's day-to-day change and resilience, but some family changes were more difficult.

Permanent Departure of a Sister

The permanent separation of a family member across geographical distance led to resentment and pleas for a return. The return of an absent sister was treated like the return of the prodigal son, and celebrations of this return were often resented by the sister or siblings who had never left. A sister who had moved away was often left out of the family communication, as described in this story:

> Well, it felt kind of funny. I felt really left out when. . . both things happened this year. . . not knowing Susan was getting married until after everybody else, and then hearing that she had to have surgery. And that's another function of my being another step removed. Since I'm not in New England anymore, I haven't been in close contact with my parents or my other sister, so I'm not getting the news as fast as I used to. (Mindy-55)

In many instances, a sister had the ability to change the perceptions of and experiences with other family members. Her insight and understanding contributed to the overall awareness of those other family relationships. Sisters might direct their mutual insight toward their parents. Some helped to suggest methods of handling difficult conversations. They provided advice about how to manage a relationship with their mother. They provided reassurance at times of parental disapproval. Input was also given about life choices related to the family, such as returning to the parental home for a brief period after becoming an adult.

The family structures, roles, and relationship allegiances within the family boiled beneath the surface of the sister relationship—defining it, threatening it, shifting it—to create an ever-changing dynamic tension. Greater knowledge of the patterns and changes within the family helped to create a defining level of depth for the sister connection—an ability to see more clearly into the depths or a continuing focus on the surface tension. Parents, brothers, and other sisters added to the defining characteristics of the sisters' herstory with each other and the surface that stretched across their connection.

Family Substance Abuse

In some families alcohol or drug use affected the sister relationship. Women who described this problem always talked about it as their sister's problem, not their own. It is possible that the women failed to mention substance abuse or alcohol use of their own unless it had diminished or stopped. One woman said she expected her older sister to become a "bag lady" (Laurie-12) if her substance use continued. One narrator had stopped her own use, and this created a gulf between her and her drug-using sisters. Laurie also suggested, "My whole family has been drunk most of their lives, and I kind of see [my sister] Amy doing the same, and that really bothers me, and I feel powerless to do anything about it" (Laurie-13f).

Conclusion

The context of the family provided the women with primary evaluations of their sister relationships. Mothers, fathers, brothers, and the sisters themselves created an essential element of the story. This context held essential elements; it was also a context that allowed adaptation and change. It was a context that was predictable in its unpredictability. Against this backdrop sisters formed a lasting bond, complete with disconnection, maturity, and reconnection. Some women felt their sister was their primary confidant; others would not have chosen her as a friend. The rich variety of this experience found its depth in the story told by these 29 women narrators. That depth became a rich pool of partially dissolved understanding acting as a dark mirror, sometimes clear and sometimes opaque in its revelations.

5

Sister Extensions

"The days when the struggle was the hardest and the fight the
thickest; when the whole world was against us and we had to stand
the closer to each other; when I would go to her home and help
with the children and the housekeeping through the day and then
we would sit up far into the night . . . The years since the rewards
began to come have brought no enjoyment like that."

Susan B. Anthony (1902 as cited in Harper, 1908)

Extended family interactions were a significant component of the sister–sister understanding. The women mentioned grandparents, aunts, and cousins. They talked
about family members who lived close to one another and the importance of those
day-to-day connections. They also spoke a great deal about the relationship between
their own partners and children—the connection with their sisters' created families.
Specific relationships with the sister's partner, the couples' relationship with each
other, and the relationship to a sister's children were discussed at length. Nieces were
especially important in these discussions and formed the basis for a continuation of
the sister dynamic within the family. The complexity of these created family relationships was as rich as those within the family of origin. Specific events—divorce, death
of a spouse, birth of a child—formed anchors for the narrative. And there were always
the comparisons to the original family and the original sister relationship.

Extended Family Interactions

Grandparents were mentioned in passing. One woman said that her grandfather
was the only one to show her affection:

> I think I was angry, probably very angry, and took it out on her. I don't
> think I knew I was supposed to take it out just on Daddy, but I think I
> took it out on Opal because it made me mad that he liked her and loved
> her and showed her that he did. And, I didn't know that affection. I had
> to run across the alley to my Grandpa to get any kind of male affection
> when I was a little girl. (Martha-7)

Another recalled losing favor with her grandparents when an infant brother was born:

> [M]y father's parents, who lived in Arizona, they favored Josh and . . . they just loved Josh. And you know, Ashley and I, . . . we resented him because our grandparents, actually our grandmother really, liked Josh better . . . so I think we grew to resent them and him, because he was a favorite. And he was also named after my father, who was named after his father, and so they thought that was special that he was Joshua the III. (Eve-41f)

Aunts were described as the ancestors of the sister relationship. Their relationship with the woman's mother was a model to embrace or discard. A unique set of role models emerged when the mother had a twin sister. The connection between a parent and her twin created a different standard that was not well understood:

> I just see that my mother had her sisters and they were very close. Not because they've spent a lot of time with each other, but there was just, especially with the twin, there was such a kinship. You didn't have to say a lot of things. (Rebecca-62)

Aunts also played a role in the interactions between cousins. One woman described her aunt's displeasure with her behavior:

> I have been in fights to protect my sister. I can remember one . . . my great-aunt, Doris, was so angry at me; she would have shot me on sight. My cousin, Davey, slapped Opal for no reason that I knew of, but I saw him do it, and I being or trying to be a boy—I was a real tomboy—I fought with the best of them. I wrestled, I played football, I played baseball, anything a boy did, that's what I did. Dolls were out of the question. Anyhow, I fought Davey. I had him down and fought him, I mean fists, not slapping. Bloodied his nose, blacked his eye. (Martha-11 to13)

Cousins were sometimes favored over sisters. Guilt about leaving a sister out of playtime with cousins was described in this way: "I should have some real regrets about how we used to sneak away from her, but then she tells me, 'I don't remember'" (Rebecca-10). These extended family relationships provided a shadowy backdrop for the sister relationship—one that sometimes came into focus to provide guidance, chastisement, or support. The sister narrative was formed by these very significant others, who stood on the periphery.

Interactions between Sisters' Families

Relationships that were more central to the sisters' lives—those created by their partners and children—were also more central to defining the adult relationship between the women. Opportunities for greater contact with the sister were created by having adult families that lived near one another. This afforded the opportunity for traveling together or even residing together as adults:

> Sally is 5 years older, so in our family, especially the three older kids, her and my two brothers and then me and my younger sister were kinda grouped in a way . . . She has a child, a female, the first grandchild of the family. When she had the child after six months, she was divorced and she moved back into [my parents'] house. I was still in the house and she came back with the child for about six years and we kind of got a little bit closer as a result of that, because everyone . . . helped parenting the child and that caused us to get a little closer at that time. (Brooke-17 and 18)

Residing together as adults was often the result of an intentional decision. One woman moved across the country, following her sisters. Another woman explained the connection that occurred when sisters and brother-in-law lived together in adulthood:

> So I went back and stayed with my other [sister], Diana. She let me move in with her . . . My husband had to come back out to Wyoming then and herded cattle . . . for a living. So her husband and my husband came out, and we lived together in Laramie. I and her done real well. She had borne a girl and was expecting another, and then we got our own home, so worked out pretty good. (Thomasina-31)

Such day-to-day living brought with it an awareness of the family's daily struggles and triumphs. The emotional experience of any one family member was shared by all.

There were specific experiences creating the need for special contact between the sisters' families. These times together could be as simple as preparing food and having fun, or as serious as when a sister's professional husband performed medical procedures for her sibling. Special extended family celebrations were also noted. Graduations, Easter, Thanksgiving, and Christmas were all described as opportunities for interacting with the sister's family. One woman's youngest sister attended the high-school graduation for each of her six children. Thanksgiving was mentioned as a shared family holiday. However, most women with young children stayed in their own homes for Christmas. A cross-state visit occurred between some families at Easter.

These close interfamily connections resulted in a sense of support for the sister bond. The adult children of one pair of elder sisters were very grateful the two were residing together. One woman described her sons' attitude about her co-residence with her sister: "because they wouldn't like for me to live alone. They would worry... about Thelma if she were living alone" (Stacey-23). The same woman spoke at length about her husband's love for her family; he was like a brother to her sister and a son to her mother throughout 51 years of marriage. This type of support from others in the family seemed to recognize and sustain the sister connection.

Sisters and Partners

The connections between sisters and their husbands or partners were considerable and complicated. The detail given by the interviewees rivaled the detail they provided about mother–daughter–sister connections. Perhaps the male–female aspect of many of these relationships created a potential for great compatibility and great conflict. At any rate, the women talked about them at length. They mentioned the roles within the marriages, partnerships, and sister connection. There were confidences shared and broken. Sisters were betrayed and also allowed to develop or grow. Specific events in the marriage led to a series of differing responses.

When a sister lived with her sister's family, the roles that developed were both helpful and harmful. The reason for living with a sister and her family may or may not have been related to the parents' choices. Sometimes parental relocation created the need for the shared household. One woman provided childcare for her sister's children. The mother, father, and sister all functioned comfortably as co-parents for the daughter:

> Just in everyday living . . . the role Jackie plays . . . [she] can come in our house, and she can feed Angie, and she can give Angie a bath and that doesn't disrupt my life or disrupt Victor's life. It's like Angie has three parents. (Carla-52 and 53)

The narrator remarked that all three adults were non-authoritative with the little girl, using similar approaches to discipline. This allowed all three to function well as a team, without emotional distress. Their interactions with the child and with each other were characterized by non-interference. Carla did worry at times that Victor took advantage of this, and he was not aware of the extent of the requests he made of his sister-in-law. Carla also said, "It is almost like he's married to two women." This, too, created some interesting interactions.

Sisters who were close wanted their daughters to have sisters; husbands sometimes wanted a son. These gender preferences also affected the roles that each of the sisters and their partners played in the family. Sometimes one man provided assistance with household tasks and repairs to multiple female family members, including the sisters. Stacey perceived, "We had always spent a lot of time together.

My husband was sort of the man of the family. He took care of [my mother and sister] and us, too" (Thomasina-3).

Partner Compatibility

Partner compatibility was a strong factor in the ability to share life as adult women. One woman describes a lifelong connection between brothers-in-law. This connection included times of living together. Special occasions were shared. Sometimes husbands or partners participated in activities without their wives, freeing the women to spend time together, if they chose. This close relationship between significant others was compared to other extended families where the brothers-in-law did not like or appreciate each other:

> Well, our, you know, so many times when sis, . . . you know, you don't like the brother-in-law, so just being, being decent to them is all. But our boys loved one another. I mean they actually thought the world of each other. (Dorothy-57f)

In making this comparison, one woman spoke about the love and generosity between "brothers" who were present emotionally during the loss of the women's parents.

This level of compatibility was rare, appearing with only one woman during the interviews. Other participants spoke only about shared interests that made time together pleasant; some described a fear about brothers-in-law whose behavior placed their sisters in jeopardy:

> [I]t was almost like we had this family, and then my sister was just like no longer in the family for at least three years. The only time . . . that she really reemerged in the family was when he beat her up, and she was in trouble. When I think about it . . . Carol was back in the family again, but we had this big crisis to deal with. He'd always find a way to make her feel sorry for him, so she'd go back. When Carol left him, we went to the Bahamas together, and it was really kinda weird because I'd forgotten that she had a sense of humor. And we both like to read the same kind of books . . . I don't know, it just seemed like we were close there for a while and then I moved in with her. She bought a house, and I moved into the apartment next to the house. . . .we had a lot of fun. (Jolene-13 and 14)

Jolene and Carol's close sister relationship—one that included fun times of laughter—was dependent upon Carol's independence from a partner, since the partners she chose were frequently abusive.

Temporary Absence of a Partner

In one case, sisters lived together because of an absent or ill partner. During those experiences, the sister often needed practical and emotional support:

[M]y husband would go follow the harvest for, oh, maybe six weeks, a lot of times. He'd go on back into eastern Nebraska and then come west with the harvest. And this little sister of mine would come . . . we had cattle, of course, [on] the farm. And Sadie would come and stay with me while he was gone. And she was so little, but we had to drive the cattle to water. There wasn't a well by the pasture, so I'd have to go at noon and bring them into the water, you know, and this little girl would always go with me to bring those cows in. (Thomasina-64)

Some of the variation in the relationships with partners changed or altered the adult level of closeness felt in the sister relationship. If good, the relationships with partners brought adult sisters closer and created the possibility of time spent together; if poor, these same relationships could widen the expanse.

Crises Affecting both Families

Specific life crises diminished distance, as well. Death, illness, birth, and divorce all affected the women in this study and contributed to their feelings toward their sisters' partners. During the birth of a niece or nephew, the presence of the woman and her brother-in-law enhanced their connection. Death and illness affected their relationship in several ways. When a husband became ill, the sisters supported each other. When a partner died, the women became closer, sometimes living together:

[B]efore her husband died, Kathy had a heart attack, but she did live alone for a year or so . . . through the summertime . . . then she got real nervous, and she just couldn't stay alone anymore, so she'd come out and stay with me through the winter for the first maybe three years . . . [Kathy would] go home in the summer and come back out here in the wintertime. And then she got sick, and she just couldn't stay by herself anymore. (Thomasina-13 and 14)

The absence of a sister when a partner died made the burden of loss more difficult to bear, especially for young adult women. Often the sister was strongly affected by not being present:

When Anthony was killed, Donna had some problems with it. She was [undercover] at that point and so . . . we didn't contact her when that happened, although she was very close to him as well. And that was a loss for me not having her there to discuss . . . my feelings, the depth of my feelings—my loss . . . so that was one significant period in my life [in which] she was not involved. When she was told, she got upset because she hadn't been involved. And we hadn't contacted her . . . let her know. Um, but then, she also understood that we didn't want to do that for other reasons, as well. (Molly-14 to 16)

When a sister was ill, the partner and sister sometimes worked together to provide care. Sometimes the sister was able to do this more effectively than a male partner could. Pairs of sisters bonded to care for a dying sister in the ways that a husband could not, and he was grateful. In describing this, one woman said:

[T]o be together, to talk and to touch and just look at each other. We'll go over there and stay . . . and Ariel [dying sister] will lay there . . . half sleep. But she'll wake up and see [my sister] Liz . . . and she knows I'm there. And her husband is always [there] when Liz or I—either one—leave. Jeremy always pats us on the shoulder and says, "Thanks" . . . [be]cause . . . he is not a talker. (Lynetta-50 and 51)

Another type of crisis was experienced when a sister and her husband or partner separated or divorced. In some cases the loss was felt acutely by a sister who valued her relationship with the departed spouse. Women described difficulty and awkwardness surrounding the decision to have continuing contact with a sister's ex-husband. One woman described the temporary rift in her relationship with her sister when the sister entertained her former brother-in-law and his new girlfriend:

When we split, and he . . . brought around his current girlfriend and she was the cause [of the divorce]. He was seeing someone else . . . it was painful to see that Lila also invited him into her home. That [created] some really bad feelings, and I was terribly upset with her about it, because I felt betrayed. I felt she betrayed me. (Sheridan-21)

Other women welcomed the departure of a sister's difficult spouse. They expressed gratitude that their sisters had found a more suitable mate and were happy. Some commented on a cycle of abusive relationships:

[W]hen Carol divorced him [first husband], we got to be really good friends. In fact, we even lived together for a while, and she was really different. She had a sense of humor, and she was all free and easy and everything . . . When she married this other guy—her husband now—it's like she went back to being that sort of restricted . . . almost reclusive kind of person. (Jolene-8 to 11)

Relative Importance of the Partner or Sister

The women in the study wanted to provide comparisons between their sister relationship and their primary relationship. As with many of the other factors in this study, the women were diverse in their opinions. Some women felt their marriage was the most important relationship in their lives, and the sister relationship could not compare. One of them even described her marriage as "perfection," and said the close relationship with her sister could not approximate that. Other women suggested that their husbands knew better than to ever interfere in their relationships with their sisters. One suggested if she were forced to choose, her sister would come first:

> I don't think I would ever have to choose between the two, but if I did, I would probably . . . I've known my sister longer, I will always know my sister longer, so "blood is thicker than water" is really strong with me, and I don't know . . . how that's go[ing to] ever affect my marriage, but Jackie and I just have a unique relationship that I won't let anyone come between; nor will she let anyone come between our relationship. Maybe that's unhealthy, I don't know, but . . . Victor would never . . . ask me to choose between [him] and Jackie [be]cause I think he . . . would know the answer. I'd probably choose Jackie, [be]cause she's my blood. (Carla-60 to 63)

Seeing the sister relationship as primary may have contributed to the tendency to use a sister as a marital confidant. Sometimes the sister was the only one trusted enough to carry the secrets of the marital relationship. These confidences included transgressions by the husband or partner that caused pain for the sister. One woman described a series of financial problems that her sister, Bert, disclosed:

> [B]oth of them make good money, and [her husband] decided to [open] a travel business for awhile. And that was going all right, and then he decided to buy this outfitter store. Well, it was kinda throwing good money after bad . . . Things went from bad to worse, and they weren't getting any money, and they were spending all this money . . . They finally had to file bankruptcy, and she's trying to hang on to their house . . . This was after the IRS . . . I don't even understand it all, but the bank was taking them to court for some reason which seemed invalid, and Bert was going to be her own counsel. Now this is almost unheard of because you just can't win and she . . . told me later . . . "Nobody knows she's going through this" when she was going through it. (Rebecca-13)

Such discussions about partners were common, expressed sometimes with laughter; sometimes with tears.

There was also a direct relationship with the partner or husband of the sister. These relationships ebbed and flowed:

> And if it hadn't have been for our brothers-in-laws—the three boys . . . thinking so much of one another, we girls probably couldn't have been this close. Because, you know, if your husband doesn't like it, why then . . . you'd stay with your husband, but it wasn't like that. (Lynetta-30)

Limitations between the brother-in-law and the sister were created by context and life events. A relationship that started as a distant one became a caretaking relationship. A close relationship was lost due to divorce. A sister's loss during her sister's divorce was described this way:

> [B]ecause she was very close to my ex-husband. They were real[ly] good friends . . . She could call on him, and he would be there to help her through whatever . . . wire electrical, or mechanically, whatever. He was real handy in that respect. If she needed something done at the dress shop . . or something done on her car, around the house, she knew all she had to do was pick up the phone and call him . . . She didn't want to lose the friend-ship, and she sat and cried almost as hard as I did. (Sheridan-20)

The relationship between a sister and her husband was judged by the other sisters in a family. Sometimes this judgment was critical, as in the case of a woman whose sister disapproved of the husband's handling of the niece:

> I really disapprove of, not that she's doing it, but she's letting her new spouse do with the child . . . I want to say something, but I don't, you know, want to pick up the phone and say, "Hey, I heard that such and such" because I know she's hearing that from other people already. What is it going to do to help? (Brooke-36f and 37f)

Positive evaluation was also an important part of the narrative. Women judged their sisters' marital relationships as positive when they seemed support-ive and loving. The absence of critical judgment was also noted in the extended family. One mother's lack of criticism for her daughters' marital relationships was important. The daughter reported, "But, there again, Mom never talked about each of them, she never would talk negative about the girls to the other person" (Lynetta-42).

Betrayal and conflict emerged in the sister relationship as a result of the rela-tionship between a sister and brother-in-law. Sisters felt betrayed if their relation-ship with each other was secondary to a continuing relationship with a difficult or divorced spouse. The women also felt betrayed if their partner or husband were judged by the sister. This type of judgment was experienced as a betrayal, and the woman who said negative things about her brother-in-law was also quick to express remorse and re-focus on the positive aspects within the sister's marriage. Conflict between sisters and divorced partners was often solved by an ultimatum to the sister: "Choose between a relationship with my ex and one with me." Conflict between sisters and spouses was sometimes resolved through insight and awareness about how childhood roles had created the problems between them. One woman described her sister's optimism as a significant factor in resolving conflict between the sister and her husband:

> Finally, Kimberly said, "I just can't do this anymore!" . . . but the things that she has gone through and done . . . she's always pretty well done them on her own. But she told me one time—she was laughing when she was thinking about her marriage and the financial problems and stuff— she said, "You have to realize we're both babies in the family . . . We just think, well, it's gonna turn out alright. Somehow, it'll turn out alright, it always has; it always will. I know it's a dumb way of looking at it, but that's just their whole approach. (Lynetta-13)

The relationships between sisters and their spouses or partners had many dimensions. The variety of relationships was extensive. In general, the connections between sisters were influenced heavily by their marital or partner relationships, but sometimes the sister bond was described as rising above the fray—a constant in times of judgment, conflict, and betrayal.

Being an Aunt

Women talked spontaneously about their nieces more than nephews. This paralleled the focus on mothers rather than fathers in the family-of-origin relationship. While the male relationships were very important, perhaps the focus on sisters in the study created a greater awareness of the relationship between women and female children. Nieces were seen as part of a special bond and created a sense of continuity for sister relationships:

> I was at the birth of Jane's first daughter. I was one of her Lamaze coaches, and it was the most incredible experience I've ever had in my life. It truly was a miracle and I'm not a religious person, but it was cool. And so, I'm real tight with her, I really . . . I just love my niece. (Andrea-26)

This connection began at birth and was marked, often, by the presence of one sister at the birth of her sister's daughter:

> [I]t was pretty late at night and we were all pretty tired and after the baby was born and back in the nursery—several hours after the baby was born.

We were all sitting around in that hospital room. It was about 1:00 in the morning and we were talking about our feelings at the moment of the birth and it was so funny! . . . My sister basically said that she felt real strange. She felt like it was like a movie, [be]cause she was watching it and she couldn't feel it. But [what], I thought, . . . was so . . . ridiculous, was when the baby popped out, I thought, "Holy shit!" You know, there really was a baby in there! And it was such a funny thought because I was . . . taken aback and surprised. I had known for 9 months she was pregnant. I understand everything like that and I was like, "Wow! That is really amazing! It's a baby!" But just to watch, to watch that and see, you know, a live birth . . . it was like the most spiritual thing that's ever happened to me. It was like a miracle. And it was just truly—tears-to-your-eyes touching— moving to your heart. (Andrea-40)

The closeness of those connections was extended and included helping a sister manage her difficult child during adolescent years and judging the sister's parenting skills. Often the niece was a special ally within the family and this relationship was based upon the family's perception of strong similarity between the girl and her aunt.

Similarity to a niece was most often mentioned in terms of common interests. Several women talked about the love of the outdoors and athleticism as a common factor in the creation of their relationship. The relationship between aunt and niece was often based upon recognition of the similarity between the two—but also emphasized the difference between mother and daughter:

Anita saw things in me that [she did not in her mom] . . . Obviously she loves her mom. Anita is a real unique young lady. She may see me as being the single person going out . . . on three-week camping trips, taking off and doing this and that . . . the freedom, different lifestyle maybe than the typical family situation like she sees [with] her mom. Enjoying sports and being outdoors and nature and things like that . . . Anita and I have found a common bond. (Tammy-16f)

This similarity led some girls to confide in their aunts and ask that that confidence be kept from their own mother:

For instance, the same niece, Jo, got pregnant before she got married. She came to me and told me that she was pregnant. She said, "I'm not going to tell my mother because she'll make me get an abortion," and she said, "I want the baby." So, she said, "I'm going to go until past the time that they can give me an abortion before I tell mother." So she vowed me to secrecy, and I kept my mouth shut, and after the length of time went by where she could have an abortion, Jo told Opal, and Opal got on the phone and called me and she says, "You will never believe," and this is [a] quote, "what Jo has done to me." (Martha-24)

These connections were described as very important for the aunt. They were particularly poignant when a sister mistakenly called her daughter by the aunt's name, a tacit acknowledgment of their similarity and connection.

The relationship with the niece began at birth or even before. One participant described her dreams about the niece's birth defect, a premonition that came to pass. In that case, the management of the niece's physical rehabilitation bonded the aunt to her—and her to the aunt.

The same woman expressed concern that she might not be able to attend the birth of her sister's second child. She was afraid her absence would affect her lifelong relationship with the second girl. This awareness was causing her to rethink her choices about where to live. Both women were excited by the possibility of the girls sharing the same sister connection that they had enjoyed. Sometimes the decision to have a second child was fueled by the desire to recreate the sister relationship in the next generation:

> But the one thing that bothers me and is hard . . . I'm realizing, because the baby is supposed to be born in February. I think that's the first time I've really realized how far away I am, [be]cause I could conceivably not see this child for a year. And that's, that's hard. (Andrea-28)

The woman was also aware that her brother-in-law wanted a son. His feelings were contrasted with her own "secret" glee at the presence of another niece:

> But it's neat, . . . we've been talking about it, and I think it's neat that she's gonna have a sister. I caught a lot of shit [about] this from some of my friends . . . but I really hoped that she did have a girl, just so that relationship could repeat . . . There's not a lot of boys in my family, so I don't have a lot of experience with them. I don't really know. I guess little boys kind of make me nervous. I don't know what to really do with them. So, I kind of secretly thought it was cool that she would have a girl, and so did she. Her husband's not excited about it, though. Well, he's not, not excited about it, but he would have preferred a boy. (Andrea-29)

This continuity in the sister relationship from generation to generation was described as evoking a sense of posterity for the women in the project.

Several important dimensions of the relationship with the niece were described by the women. One was availability. The birth of the niece often led to more frequent contact with the sister's family or a desire for that contact when it was not possible. Several women mentioned the limited responsibilities of an aunt compared to a mother. "Sometimes just being an aunt is pretty fun too. You can play with them for a week or a weekend and give them back to Mom and Dad" (Tammy-26). This created a freedom between aunt and niece, but also limited the scope of their relationship. One aunt acknowledged relinquishing her own best ideas about interacting with a niece in order to comply with her sister's parental wishes.

Yet some aunts were able to fulfill maternal functions that did not suit their sister's personality or disposition. For example, one made clothing for her niece.

In addition to the special connections with the niece, there was also wistfulness about the missed opportunities to be present and an expressed effort at keeping in contact. One woman felt horrible missing her niece's eighth-grade graduation because of her own high-school graduation ceremony. When geographical distance kept the niece and the aunt apart, contact was maintained through holiday telephone calls. Assistance for this was required from the girl's mother. Other times, the aunt lived near the niece and participated regularly in the girl's activities. In one case, a young adult niece had moved to the town where her aunt lived in order to be closer to her. The limited and fun engagement with a niece was also recognized as being very different from the demands of parenting.

A variety of conflicts and difficulties with nieces were described. Family conflict erupted between sisters in the discussion of a child protective services report:

> [B]ut I just feel uncomfortable with the way she parents her daughter and the way she parents her son . . . (Jolene-11f)

Most often there was a sense of full family participation and support. In one case the brother-in-law's extended family was specifically mentioned:

> I had nothing to bring to the job market and I ended up on welfare, which is where my niece, Bertha, is at, and I worked through the Workfare program . . . You have to reach down and draw from within to find out what your strengths are, what your weaknesses are, and that is what I'm trying to share, what we're all trying to share, that she didn't need this dependence in her life. Bertha's a very smart young lady. We finally started to convince her. We're building her up, and giving her, like I said, whatever support we can, morally and financially. [Interviewer questions the use of "we."] My sisters and I. The rest of the family. Her dad's family. I know that her dad's family [has] been there for her to help her as well. I don't mean to sound like we're doing it all; we're not. They are doing their part as well. Everyone's just kinda banded together to do this, to make sure she doesn't fall back into the life that she was leading before. (Sheridan-31 and 32)

The aunt, the mother, the father, and extended family were engaged with the niece's growth. In this way, Bertha's needs, and the ways they were met, became paramount in the discussions between sisters.

Aunts were often involved in attempting to help a niece as she struggled with life choices and decisions.Extraordinary physical problems with a niece created an opportunity for the aunt to help. One woman said her relationship with her niece deepened due to her ability to give blood during a medical crisis. The need to help rebuild a niece's self-esteem sometimes became a family project. This was mentioned specifically in relation to Bertha's destructive relationships with men and the effect on the next generation of girls:

> Lila has an older daughter, Bertha, who has recently moved up here and she's pulling her life together—which has been a real mess for a long time . . . [T]hey're trying to help rally around her and help my sister give her all the support that we possibly can, in getting her daughter straightened out . . They have become estranged. [Lila] was doing the tough love bit in trying to teach her daughter that "You gotta stop what you're doing. Pull your life together! You've got two children, and you must think of somebody besides yourself." (Sheridan-28)

A similar theme emerged when a niece finally divorced an abusive husband. The family believed she was finally able to do so out of concern for her own children's lives. Throughout the description of difficult interactions, there was a sense of attempting to help without overstepping limitations placed on the aunt by the niece or by the sister.

Unlike their female siblings, nephews were mentioned rarely in the interviews. When they did appear in the dialogue, the nephews were mentioned explicitly in relation to medical or physical crises. One woman described her sister's impending death and her son's efforts to reach out to his aunt:

> Chase is very close to Ariel and . . . he'll call her instead of me, which I am glad because I find out how he is anyway, and he finds out how I am. It does Ariel a world of good to have him call her. (Lynetta-21)

Taking the Sister's Place as a Mother

Many women expressed a willingness to be a substitute mother for their nieces and nephews; some expressed concern about usurping the mother role. One woman described the love and discipline required to step into her sister's shoes as a mother. Facing her sister's death, another said she would be glad to step in permanently. Another said she would want her sister to take her place if she died early and left young children who needed her sister's care. "Like, if I were to die today, I know that Jackie would serve as a substitute mom for Angie, and it would be like I was still there. Does that make any sense?" (Carla-39f). Some women acknowledged this motherhood exchange as a mutual role, where each cared for the others' children. There was a desire to help but not to detract from the sister's primary importance as a mother. One woman clarified that she was not the mother in a public setting. Still, some women were judgmental about the requirement of taking over for a sister who was unable to maintain consistency in the mother role. One raised her nephew for 12 years while her sister tried to "find herself."

A few acknowledged that their sisters would be the first choice to replace them if they were prevented from continuing in their mothering role.

In one case, the sister also took over as substitute grandmother:

> [W]hen Chris, . . . Lorraine's grandson, was born, she had fell and broken her hip, or her leg, I guess it was . . . so I went over there and took care of the baby, [be]cause [her daughter] had a cesarean, so she . . . couldn't do much. I went over there and helped. And when Ariel son's second and third child were born, I went up there and took care of those kids. (Lynetta-33)

This exchange of maternal and grandmother responsibilities seemed to be valued by the women. Sometimes, it did require a delineation of the differences between mother and aunt.

Invariably, women evaluated their sisters' maternal performance. They judged sisters who failed to place their child's needs above their own vanity or selfish interests:

> No, I think that, I think it's too bad. [My sister's] missed a lot. She didn't really want either one of her children. Opal was very upset each time she got pregnant, and the kids have known this. I think that's hard for girls to grow up knowing that they really weren't wanted. (Martha-35)

In the research the women were not asked about their sisters' partners and children. However, they spent a great deal of time describing those relationships as a background for the sister connection. The relationships between partners, between sisters and husbands, and with the children of a sister were all very important to the women. Special relationships with their nieces were described; the way the nieces recreated the relationship of the sisters was important. There was also the need to compare the relationships between sisters and partners. Each relationship was evaluated as it related to the relationship between the sisters, whose relationship was being described for my research.

Sister's Relationship to Own Family

In the process of describing their relationships to their sisters and to their families, the women evaluated and commented upon the relationship their sisters shared with their partners and children. They described facts about the sisters' families. They explored dynamics between sisters and their husbands and sisters and their children. They determined whether children had the primary influence they felt necessary. They examined strategies used for resolution by the sister and by the sister's family of creation. Emotions were explored—the joy within the sister's family and the envy of it. Support between families was considered. Children of sisters were compared. All of these dimensions were an evaluation of the sister's family of creation and the manner in which that family lived.

Facts about Sisters' Families

Most of the facts about sister's families had to do with the number of children, grandchildren, and great-grandchildren. One woman's sister had six children but had lost a son. One woman had grandchildren, but none lived near her. Another woman's grandchildren had all married, save one. This recounting of the sister's progeny was a way of helping to define the family and its influence on the sister.

A sister's children sometimes affected her need for other emotional relationships, including female friendships. One woman tried to engage her sister in church activities but was unable to do so. She gave this rationale:

> Kimberly has her working relationships and she gets all of her social contacts at work. She has no need to go neighboring. She doesn't have close friends at church, particularly. Because when she comes home, she's totally honed in on her kids. (Rebecca-59)

The same woman suggested that her sister's family was "self-contained," with little need for other emotional investments.

The Sister's Family Conflicts

The women in the study looked inside those nuclear family relationships and attempted to understand the conflicts, losses, and methods of resolution that were employed by their sisters' families. Conflicts between a sister and her husband or partner were analyzed and attributed to lack of emotional or occupational support within the couple. In this case the conflict was left unresolved because of a sister's passivity:

> [O]ne of Kimberly's kids had to have tennis shoes. [His] dad wouldn't take [him] . . . She had only been home from the hospital about a day, and we had to go get this kid his tennis shoes; so there's where she's kind of weak . . . Is it because she works all the time? . . . Who can figure it out? But she just says, "It's just easier to give in." (Rebecca-30)

Concern about a sister's relationship with her family was most often centered on the relationship between adults, but difficulties between a sister and her children were also mentioned. These conflicts occurred with both sons and daughters.

One woman's sister was estranged from her daughter because the young woman refused her mother's advice:

> Lila has an older daughter, a daughter who has recently moved up here, and she's pulling her life together, which has been a real mess for a long time. [The family is] trying to help rally around her and help my sister give her all the support that we possibly can in getting her daughter straightened out . . . They have become estranged. [Lila] was doing the tough love bit in trying to teach her daughter that "You gotta stop what you're doing. Pull your life together! You've got two children, and you must think of somebody besides yourself." (Sheridan-28)

Another sister attempted to intervene to help her son, but he rejected his mother's offer of help. She remained supportive of him and a part of his life but was hurt by his rejection:

> Lila has offered Jonah everything she could to get him motivated. He won't take it. She just practically stood on her head for him, for which I feel that is something a mother would do anyway for a child . . . It hurts her. I mean [crying], he's changed a lot, for which she is really proud but . . . he's got a long way to grow up. (Sheridan-8 and 9)

The women in the study had sisters who had suffered great emotional losses through death or estrangement of their family members. Two described widowed sisters. One of them had remarried and was happy; the other was the recipient of her sister's empathy when she returned home alone after family functions. In the last case, the married sisters took it upon themselves to spend additional time with the widowed sister to minimize her sense of isolation and loneliness. Loss was also described in the case of children who had moved to a faraway city; their absence limited contact with grandchildren and great-grandchildren:

> Kathy has three great-grandchildren, three great-granddaughters, and they live in North Carolina. They had lived in North Carolina and then they moved to New Jersey. Now they've moved back to North Carolina, so she [doesn't] get to see them very much. (Thomasina-33)

Such losses seemed to be beyond resolution, but were managed—at least partly—through sisterly support.

Resolving Conflicts

When discussing internal conflicts in a sister's family, the sister's methods for resolving difficulties were described. Some women confronted their family problems boldly. One woman used a "scared straight" approach, taking her sons to their father's derelict habitats to demonstrate the likely outcome of their behavior:

Lila's had a lot of trouble with her sons, and to prevent them from becoming like their father, she has taken them to some of the places that they know that he has frequented, and those are not exactly places that you'd want your son to be, or even want to know that your father has been there, let alone your son. (Sheridan-8)

Another remained naïve and unrealistic in her approach toward problems:

Yeah. I think Bert has an attitude that just tickles us because . . . life is a surprise sometimes and that's part of her . . . just trusting everybody—trusting life in general. I mean when something funny happens, or something comes up in a near miss, it's like, "Oh!" I mean it's just like it's a big surprise. (Rebecca-43)

A third used her own behavior change in quitting smoking as an opportunity to assist her son with homework. The focus on his homework completion became her method for avoiding cigarettes. The woman reporting this was hopeful that her sister's coping was improving and believed the smoking cessation would have a positive effect on many other family problems:

Well, Bert smokes a lot and has since she was in college, so she's gone 9 weeks without smoking. Meanwhile she tried to plan that in with this 14-year-old son to get him to study. . . . They're kinda going through their suffering period together . . . I hope she's got him over the hump, and he's gonna start to bloom. (Rebecca-31)

Longer-term resolutions were also described. How did a sister come to terms with death, the decision to have children, and the effect children have on a marriage or partnership? Several women remarried after their husband's death. This was welcomed by the extended family but often came as a surprise or shock to them. This resolution by repartnering was an important step for the sister. Some women were childless while their sisters had children. This demanded another type of grieving and reconciliation. Childless women felt they had maintained some of their freedom and wondered if their sisters envied that:

Sometimes I think she . . . to a certain extent . . . envies . . . what I've done with my life in terms of still being single. Don't get me wrong, I think she doesn't regret having a family, but I think the freedom that being single—different options—that it can give you . . . different lifestyle, I think sometimes she envies that. (Tammy-14)

Tammy also reflected on her own sense of loss in being childless:

> But I think there are parts of her life that I envy too. Sometimes I miss not having children. Sometimes, I miss that closeness I think you can experience with kids. (Tammy-24 and 25)

Competing demands by a husband or partner and children were also described by one woman. Sometimes the sisters resolved those conflicts differently; this woman placed her husband first:

> [I]t never occurs to Kimberly to think, "Oh, gee, I'd like to go out tonight without the kids." She doesn't want to go anywhere without them . . . She has planned many more vacations with her kids, maybe day vacations or weekend or something like that, than we have . . . I'm the kind that if I've been home all the time, then I'd like to go out with my husband alone. They don't have that same kind of relationship of going out alone. In fact, he doesn't even remember her birthday, this last time. (Rebecca-22)

Emotional Reactions Within the Sister's Family

Grief and loss were not universal. Some women spent time describing the joy and celebrations in their sisters' families. Most often these celebrations involved the sister's children—a birthday celebration thrown by the children or a day-to-day enjoyment of couples and family who live nearby:

> Well, uh, we lived, then we lived in Juno and her and her husband would come for different holidays, for Thanksgiving, and I don't think they ever came for Christmas too much, because they always had their Christmas at home. But they'd come for when the kids would graduate. They always [came] for all the kids, I had six of them, and I think they came for every one of [their] graduations. (Thomasina-76 and 77)

These celebrations included the visits between sisters' families and the anticipation of upcoming family events:

> I've had a lot of communication with Sybil, too, because they're planning their summer vacation down here to visit with us. They have three small children, and they're really looking forward to their visit. We're looking forward to having them come because . . . they have such cute kids and we have a real good time with them. (Janice-41)

Relationships within the created nuclear family were examined by the women in this study. They expressed concern, joy, and bewilderment at the architecture of their sisters' families. These structures might be sound and emotionally stable or could seem ready to fall without much turbulence. In understanding these families, the woman describing them often went back to the blueprints—the collective experience of the family of origin for both women.

Effects of the Sister's Family on the Sister Reporting

The women described specific involvement with their sister's families. In a few cases one sister lived with another sister's family. Several women went to their sister's home to have a child. The result was a close relationship between the women and their sister's husband. In at least one case, the woman did not want to return to her own home, feeling her sister's family environment was a better place to care for her infant son:

> Well, I, in fact, I cried when I left there. I didn't want to even leave with my baby, you know. Course I was 20, but I still felt like I needed Jerilyn. You know, to be around her, I thought, "Land, I don't know how I would take care of a baby." I'd been around my brothers and sisters, but it was quite hard to leave. It wasn't that far, but then our cars [weren't] in very good shape, . . . so I didn't get to come very often up to see her. She came down a few times and saw me, when she could, but . . . they didn't get down to see me very often either. (Gretchen-32 & 33)

Rural women also made the choice to have their child at their sister's home in order to be closer to medical services during pregnancy. Sometimes, a married couple chose to live with a sister and brother-in-law for financial reasons. One woman mentioned this situation was preferable to living with the parents of either spouse. An arrangement like this was dependent upon the close relationship between the brothers-in-law. A unique reciprocal relationship between children and an aunt emerged when the living-together arrangement persisted. One nephew returned his aunt's care of him during childhood when she was coping with an illness later in life.

Sisters' families affected the relationship the women were able to maintain. The birth of a child to one created the possibility of a closer connection, shared emotions, and mutual learning. One woman felt she was influenced spiritually as well. She described the results of the shared experience and its impact on her, her sister, and her brother-in-law:

> [I]t was pretty late at night and we were all pretty tired and after the baby was born and back in the nursery—several hours after the baby was born. We were all sitting around in that hospital room. It was about 1:00 in the morning and we were talking about our feelings at the moment of the

birth and it was so funny! . . . My sister basically said that she felt real strange. She felt like it was like a movie, [be]cause she was watching it and she couldn't feel it. But [what], I thought, . . . was so . . . ridiculous, was when the baby popped out, I thought, "Holy shit!" You know, there really was a baby in there! And it was such a funny thought because I was . . . taken aback and surprised. I had known for 9 months she was pregnant. I understand everything like that and I was like, "Wow! That is really amazing! It's a baby!" But just to watch, to watch that and see, you know, a live birth . . . it was like the most spiritual thing that's ever happened to me. It was like a miracle. And it was just truly—tears-to-your-eyes touching—moving to your heart. (Andrea-40)

Sometimes sisters were able to maintain contact without their partners and children present, but most often the presence of a nuclear family resulted in visits with all members:

I like to do things socially with her. Not only because she's my sister; she's someone I enjoy spending time with. Most times, the things that we do are family-oriented kinds of things. It's not like we go out to the movies. Once in a while we'll go out to dinner or something, or we've gone on camping trips together. (Tammy-8 and 9f)

For one woman, new insight into the distress of her sister also influenced the attention she gave to her own children. She attempted to have unique and separate relationships with each of her daughters because her sister did not feel their parents had provided it. So the early childhood trauma of one sister may be brought forward in a productive way, influencing a positive connection between her sister and her sister's children.

In evaluating the importance of a sister's family and her own, a woman's emotions sometimes erupted. Some women expressed envy of a sister's relationship with her kids; others wished the sister had experiences more similar to her own. In this process, children were also compared across the families and to the original family:

I want to make sure that [my son] feels his place . . . feels comfortable about himself. So, I've always been . . . aware of that . . . because of my relationship to my sister and the things that I have found out since . . . I think that's important. You need to be aware, so that you can—in your dealings with your children—that you treat them each as individuals, as being very special people in what they're doing and not comparing them . . . [helping encourage] developing their gifts and their talents and their abilities. (Janice-43 and 47)

These comparisons, feelings, and insights were accompanied by a sense that the sister's family enjoyed support from the women being interviewed. Part of that support was the encouragement to take time away from the family for herself. Suggestions about family vacations or couples' getaways were seen as strengthening the family of the sister. Sometimes, the woman reported taking her sister's family on vacation. Support also occurred in times of need, like when a sister's family was strained by illness or by daily life. One sister who was dying gave gifts to each of her sisters and their children. All of them helped to care for her during the illness and death.

This support for the sister's family brought to fruition the importance of sister relationships in adult life and the influence of so many family relationships on the sister connection. The detailed interconnections between families in adulthood added the final texture to the photograph of the sister herstory. The nuance of the detail—caught in a frame of time and remembered exquisitely by the sister who was reporting—gave depth to the two-dimensional image. Layers underlying layers helped to create the meaning inherent in these women's words.

6

Time and Intensity

"We are caught in an inescapable network of mutuality, tied in a single garment of destiny. Whatever affects one directly, affects all indirectly."
Martin Luther King, Jr. (Commencement Speech, June 6, 1961[1])

The evaluation of closeness to a sister is inescapable, perhaps because of the interconnection that may be obtained or may prove elusive. Most women discussed their appreciation for the closeness of a sister or a nagging feeling of doubt about the distance from her. Were others closer? How should this be understood? Older participants described a dynamic unfolding of the relationship over time—sometimes emotionally very close and sometimes distant—constantly woven together across time and space. The women described elements of support, difficulty, healing, and loss. Embedded in their description were details about the pattern of communication required to enhance the tightness of the design, or to lead to its unraveling.

Measuring Closeness

It is not surprising that the attempt to understand the meaning of closeness was a dominant part of the sister's narrative. Emotional connection has always been measured using a continuum. How close is close enough? What is the importance of a connection that is close? Do you have to be physically present with each other to experience such a connection? How do connections survive across distance, and how are they made more important or deeper? If the herstory of a relationship emerges across a landscape, the closeness of a relationship emerges in its contours. It is the topographical map, one with all of the jagged relief and the exposed surfaces. It gives a sense of depth through color and communicates knowledge through dimension.

In attempting to verbalize their experience of close connection with their sisters, the women in the study talked about the notion of physical and emotional presence. They seemed to suggest that physical presence may enhance emotional closeness, but it was not required. When physically present, the sister became available for many of life's demands. There was a sense that the sister was emotionally and physically available when needed. This availability extended to the needs of others that might require the sisters to be present, like the illness of a mother. The availability of sisters changed over time. One woman recalled the importance of her childhood memories of being close to her sister. Another talked about the welcome presence of her sister during visits to their family home during their college years. Still others described the importance of being present as a witness for significant life events—the birth of a child and the initial weeks of caring for that newborn, or the loss of a partner and the attendance at his or her decline. Participation in the dying process of a sister was described in poignant detail. One woman even acknowledged that she and her sister had promised to return to reassure each other from beyond the grave. She said:

> If she would die . . . [be]cause we've talked about that before. If we would lose each other . . . through death . . . one time we'd promise each other that we would come back . . . in whatever form we would be in, to tell each other, "It's okay after you die," and that "I'm with you" and "I'm supporting you." (Vicki -51)

The presence of the sister was experienced with joy and anticipated with love. Many of the women talked about this anticipatory and welcome feeling—about being in the presence of their sisters. They acknowledged that the content of their conversation was different when face to face. Other family members could add excitement to that anticipation. Children, brothers-in-law, and brothers were mentioned as individuals whose physical presence with the sisters made the interactions light-hearted and joyful. Such interactions were so important that the absence of them was something the women felt they needed to defend.

When the sister was absent for extended periods, others were put in her place. Sometimes this gap was filled by a close friend or a sister-in-law. Similarity in experience often marked the choice of the "fill-in" sister, especially the presence of children of similar ages at home:

> I might be closer to my sister-in-law, Ricki, for some of these things, mainly because our kids are the same age. My sister's kids are younger than mine. And so [Ricki] and I are participating in church at the same level . . . Most of our activities are about the same. Our kids are in college the same time . . . That has . . . bound us together. Plus, Ricki lives next

door to my parents, so I . . . see more of her. My sister would only come down—like on a weekend . . . And so usually . . . it's hectic, and if there's a football game or baseball game then you don't talk. (Rebecca-20 and 21)

Although some of these descriptions clearly recalled the desire for an absent sister, the presence of some sisters was anticipated with dread. Some wished their sisters had not been part of their childhood experiences, while others described a closeness that was destroyed when they lived together as adults. Previous conflicts with the sister contributed to a sense of unwelcome contact. This woman avoided being alone with her sister by including other relatives in her visit:

[T]he last time I went, I went by myself. Because I'm a [businesswoman], I get all these free trips and everything. So I did go to visit by myself, but I said I would never go there alone to visit again. I'd either take my husband, or a child, or whatever . . . The last time I went, my mother-in-law and I were actually visiting my son in North Dakota, and then we went down and visited and stayed a few days and that was great. That was the last visit, and things went real well. (Janice-36)

A sister's physical presence could also lead to a sense of superficiality. The women were aware of this shallowness and felt cheated by it. The artificial contact was sometimes chosen by the women and sometimes imposed by circumstances or other people. The women most often compared the superficial tone of these encounters to other contacts that were more intimate or emotional. One woman felt closer to her brother; another described the important connection between her two sisters. Here is an example of a young woman's desire for a different level of intimacy with her sister:

I envy other . . . females that I have known and know in my life [who] have sisters [who] have real[ly] close relationships. I would like to have had that. So, maybe [laughter], maybe it will change; maybe it won't. (Caroline-20)

Large family gatherings almost always left women wanting a greater depth of connection, especially when they felt close to a sister. Family secrets that limited the conversation between sisters were reported. Third parties to the relationship sometimes asked one sister not to share with another. These circumstances and confidences most often occurred within the extended family context, as when a niece asked an aunt not to divulge significant information to her mother. All of these superficial or secretive experiences created a void and, in some cases, a sense of hope that someday, or in other circumstances, intimacy might emerge.

The depth of connection was enhanced by the relationship with a twin. Only one of the women in the study was a twin. Her experiences with her twin brother were described as unique and more important or closer than her connection to her sisters. Some women described their relationships as being "like twins" because their emotional understanding of each other was based upon shared experiences and deep intimacy:

> [I]n fact sometimes it's almost like a twin-type situation. Sometimes I'll want to call her, and I'll call her and she'll say, "Geez, Molly, I really need to talk to you. I have been wanting to call you" and the converse. (Molly-2)

Closeness, maintained by physical presence, defined by its qualities of depth and intimacy, is also enhanced by many kinds of communication between sisters.

Communication

Communication is anticipated or feared, instantaneous or delayed, secretive or direct. Whatever its methods and content, sisters are aware that their communication with each has an effect. Sometimes contact with the sister is anticipated with joy and is accompanied by visual memories. Sharing, talking, and laughing together were mentioned. One woman expressed a desire to share her research experience with her sister in hopes of enhancing their communication. Visual memories of communication with the sister were often accompanied by affection between them. Sometimes these were memories of actual contact; sometimes they were a condensation of shared time into one image:

> [It] is just the image of us . . . walking together in this field with our arms . . . around each others' shoulders and just talking and just being together, and just being really accepting of each other, wherever we were, in spite of the fact that we're real different people. (Jean-51)

Sisters are aware that their communication is affected by a number of issues. Honesty may be hampered by fear of the sister's response. The age difference between sisters provokes different attempts at communication. Giving direct feedback about a sister's behavior may be the hardest type of communication, and the women were aware of potential fallout from such confrontations. Sometimes sensitivity itself is the issue being confronted. One woman talked about a growing rigidity in her sister's sensitivity and its effect on her connections with others. In an attempt to help her sister, she confronted this sensitivity:

> I guess I want to give her good feedback about how sensitive she is, and how much it's hurting her and affecting her life. And so, I will just give her honest feedback and it upsets her a great deal. (Hillary-3)

The topics of communication between sisters vary widely. The women in the study mentioned issues related to gender, relationships with other people, and their shared experiences and memories. Gender issues included an understanding of workplace discrimination that some women had experienced and difficulties in communicating with men in their lives. Other relationships were often discussed in detail, particularly female friendships and issues with the women's parents. Children were important, as were shared events. Some women reported talking with their sisters about significant shared events such as the birth of a child or a family holiday celebration. Others spoke of the importance of discussing their memories with their sisters. Sometimes childhood understanding emerged and was resolved during this process:

> For years I felt guilty about [what I had done to her] until I finally . . . about two years ago, I just . . . talked to her about it and we worked through it . . . We laugh about it now. But, um, it was a horrible thing to do! (Jean-15)

Methods of communicating were also described by the women. Most acknowledged direct contact, or the lack of it. Cards and letters, messages, e-mail, and telephone calls were discussed specifically. They also mentioned nonverbal behavior, including watching each other's reactions to a third party or reading each others' eyes. Special ways of communicating included this description of a type of sister shorthand:

> Okay, for instance when I moved here, I got into some problems not being able to work immediately, and trying to get into my own house— then wheeling and dealing and doing all of these things to try and get money and try to find a place . . . I was just totally a basket case. Um, I needed somebody to tell me it was okay. I know that Barb's the one I usually come to. So, I called her and said, "I need my sissy." And she knew exactly what I meant . . . I need some comforting, or I need some someone to tell me I'm okay and it's going to work out. (Chris-29 and 30)

Many of the women talked about different forms of telepathic communication. Examples include the ability to answer an unasked question, a simultaneous sense of foreboding, a shared premonition, or an awareness that the sister was in distress. These experiences were not anticipated or planned—they just happened. The women learned to rely on these telepathic communications and felt they were legitimate yet out of their control. One woman wondered if the experiences were just based upon intimate knowledge of her sister, but most felt these instances were just another kind of communication that happened often between sisters who were closely connected.

The lack of communication between sisters was attributed to multiple factors, chief among them differences in temperament and a lack of mutuality in the relationship. One woman felt annoyed by the frequency of her sister's phone calls and found them difficult. Anger was mentioned as a barrier, especially when it shrouded the communication between the women. Sometimes these emotional reactions between sisters led to a total lack of communication. One woman's sister had not talked with her for years. She mentioned that she felt this was an immature response to a difficulty, but felt she would no longer sacrifice her own peaceful life by allowing the sister's anger to permeate it. Stalemates such as that one provided a direct contrast to the women's experience of growth-producing communications between them.

Growth in the sister relationship depended upon honesty and was marked by increasing insight and personal awareness. Late adolescence and beginning adulthood was a time of marked change in the communication between sisters. They began to emerge from conflicted interactions to a style of relating that reflected friendship. However, one young woman described the persistence of the little sister–big sister relationship:

> And there are still things that Ashley loves to bring up—things from when I was [this] really little kid—that I don't remember. [Something] I used to do that was really stupid . . . I don't even remember what it was. I remember them always talking about it, but . . . I think she likes to think of me as still being her little sister . . . she would call it my cat dance and I would walk around, trying to look like a dancing cat . . . and she still asks me to do [it] all the time . . . I guess we have two sides to our relationship. There's a side that is really serious, and we talk about our problems and things, but I think the majority of it is having fun and making me look like a fool. (Eve-24)

Most of the growth described by the women required honest interaction. The ability to be honest was dependent upon uninterrupted frequent contact between the sisters. Some women came to an increased understanding of each other and their respective relationships with their parents through insight informed by this honest communication.

Painful shared experiences were discussed between sisters, leading to a greater understanding of the different perspectives they had. These differing perspectives were enhanced by age differences within the family, when an older sister's insight allowed a younger sister to understand what she would face a decade later. Integration of this insight into the relationship deepened it and led to new respect among the women. Assumptions about how the other sister had understood the family issues were debunked by this honesty. Some women described the insight a sister shared about a parent, making it easier to interact with him or her.

> [M]y Mom had cancer when I was 16, and my sister was away from the home and she was living in another state . . . She was helping me figure

out what was going on with them [be]cause my father and I did not get along during that period at all. And she was just really helpful in gaining a perspective on why we weren't getting along, you know, and that my father was just totally freaking out. (Andrea-20)

Some women reported that their experiences were more similar to their sister's than they had imagined. For example, one woman seemed like the perfect child; her sister was the vocal, rebellious one. In actuality, both felt alienated. This was an insight they did not understand until adult communication replaced jealous rivalry. Insight, honesty, and growth were a hopeful and optimistic part of the communication for many of the women who described changes in their sister relationship over time.

More generalized family issues were discussed in the context of this honest interaction. The women who could talk honestly with their sisters compared their intimacy to other relationships where the same honesty did not exist:

My husband had two sisters and their husbands would not speak to one another. And the time of his mother's funeral . . . everybody eats [together at the wake]. [While] the one ate . . . the other one went someplace else. And they don't hardly remember what [the argument] was about. They really don't remember what it was about. But you see [his sisters] didn't talk it over. And we always talk everything over. (Lynetta-62)

Some of the women described a family communication pattern that relied on one sister who became the honest one for them all. She became the center of the family circle, managing the feelings of everyone else:

She has worked very diligently, and I have really accepted the work that she has done and tried to keep us all together. We have that continuity of a family that she and I both want. She, too, is a very loving, giving person. (Sheridan-5 and 6)

For one woman, honest communication with her sister was disrupted by another family pattern—an interfering mother. So honesty between sisters was described within the family context, its limitations apparent within the subtext.

One of the important elements of the communication between sisters was an underlying value placed upon the relationship itself. The time together was described as one characterized by happiness and a sense of comfort in each other's presence. In this context, the sister was appreciated as a person of value, someone the woman was glad to know:

I remember one time in particular: we were having lunch and somebody robbed a liquor store up the street. Barb's a paramedic, so she's used to being in crisis situations. The store robbers had a shootout in front of our house, and she administered first aid. The TV crews were there and she was calm and cool and even, never seemed to get flustered. And I was just, uh, you know, crazy. I didn't know what to do. I couldn't even talk to the newsmen. She was just there, and that's the way . . . she demonstrates herself in all situations. (Chris-22f)

In addition to individual value placed upon the sister, there was a sense of value within the relationship. The sense of support and the ease of being together were mentioned. The sister's ability to challenge and confront was a quality that some of the women enjoyed. The potential for happiness within a sister relationship was recommended for other families; when it was not realized, it was missed.

This value increased with time and maturity. Women at midlife and older mentioned the increasing appreciation for the value of the sister bond. It was strengthened by crisis and illness. The comfort in the relationship led sisters to want to reside together later in life. Even when living conditions might be more amenable somewhere else, the women lived near their sisters or with them in order to share time together toward the end of life. One woman did suggest that her own optimism might be coloring this view of her sister's value, but held it all the same.

Many different methods were used to communicate about multiple topics in these sister relationships. Some communications were clear, honest, and direct; others were indirect or even unspoken. The ability to communicate honestly and directly created a deeper and more valued relationship between the sisters as they matured. The loss of communication or lack of honesty was painful, especially because the relationship was valued so highly. Women mourned its absence or had chosen to be distant because the communication patterns were not positive. Communication, then, formed one of the critical components of the changing relationship over time.

Affirmative Understandings

Mutual understanding and reciprocity were expected from a sister. These attributes were based upon a sense of safety and trust, which made it possible for sisters to share emotionally laden experiences. A sister was also trusted to care for the other, if it became necessary. This close and mutual affirmation of the relationship arose from the emotional exchange between sisters. Often these exchanges were difficult but led to the deepening of the sister relationship. One woman was particularly eloquent about this mutuality. She described the nature of her relationship with her sister as reciprocal, based upon mutual trust and respect. Because her sister was not judgmental of her, she felt no need for secrets between them:

When one [of us] seems upset . . . it's kind of a mutual thing that we can contact each other and there is no judging. Barb knows everything about me. There is not anything that, I think . . . I've ever kept from her. She is the only person in the world that knows everything about me and is non-judgmental, and I try to be the same with her . . . when I've gone through periods between divorces—I've been divorced twice—where I have gone to a bar or something and have a one-night stand and told her about it, she didn't . . . get mad or have me look bad. That's just one thing that comes to mind . . . Or I've stayed in a relationship that she didn't approve of . . . we talked about it. She didn't tell me it was bad, or that she was mad at me or disappointed . . . She is not judgmental. (Chris-13 to 15)

For another woman, this mutual respect was shared among three sisters, with the outcome of mutual growth. Another woman, in her eighties, said that she and her sister had experienced reciprocal enjoyment throughout their long lives and now lived together. A visual image of this mutuality was made by her sister in the form of a plaque that hangs on the wall and is inscribed with the words "a sister is a forever friend" (Lynetta-61). The woman suggested that their candor was the basis for this friendship. One woman mentioned that adulthood had brought mutuality based upon similarity of interests and activities. All of these variations in experience suggested a degree of mutual sharing, trust, and support—an affirmative understanding between sisters.

Other elements of the mutual relationship emerged in specific circumstances. Mutual care was an important part of this reciprocal nature for several women. One mentioned that two sisters cared for each other until a third was born and shared this caring responsibility. Another young adult woman suggested that she and her sister even shared their envy of each other in a mutually respectful way:

Sometimes I think she . . . envies . . . what I've done with my life . . . Don't get me wrong, I think she doesn't regret having a family but I think the freedom that being single, different options that it can give you . . . just the different lifestyle—I think sometimes she envies that. But I think there are parts of her life that I envy too. Sometimes I miss not having children. (Tammy-15 and 25)

The mutuality of feelings was predominant in these themes. However, it did not emerge immediately in the relationship between sisters.

As sisters matured, their ability to be reciprocal improved. Mutuality grew over time. Three different women described an active intention to enhance it. One stated that she used to get defensive with her sister and had learned how to listen. She said:

[I]f she started making derogatory remarks about something I would turn it back on her and say, "Gee, I'm interested in how you feel about that. Can you talk about it more?" . . . that kind of thing. So that it now becomes . . . her place to explain, and I'm not the one on the defensive. (Caroline-18f)

As the younger sister, Caroline felt she enjoyed more equality with her older sister over time. She was able to give more feedback and experience more mutual growth. For her, the growth was anxiety-provoking but felt right. She described it this way:

> [S]o getting older, I feel like I can treat her more as an equal, as a friend, and not "Oh, my big sister. I need to . . . pay more respect," or something like that. And so I think that's part of the reason why we're having tension, because I'm not just nodding my head and letting things go by. (Caroline-25)

Another woman suggested that the mutual growth with her sister had emerged as a result of the important work she had done to resolve past conflicts with her family. Her conversation with her sister was described like this:

> [We] never really made it a point to spend time together, up until two years ago . . . I think it was two Christmases ago . . . I made a decision that I wanted to talk real openly with each of the members of my family and just talk about the things that happened in the past with each of them that I didn't feel comfortable about . . . that I didn't feel there were things resolved, so I did that with Megan. We went out for breakfast and I sat down and . . . we talked about the whole adoption scam and we talked about things that had happened in the past but that I still felt a little guilty about or I didn't feel right about [be]cause I wanted to get that all cleaned up. I wanted to make that right, and her response to me was very open. Megan said, "Jean, I really want to be, I want us to be friends. I don't want to just be your sister. I want to be friends." And, and I told her that that's what I wanted, too. (Jean-26 and 27)

Mutual growth was described differently at different stages of life. Another young woman described the conspiratorial nature of her mutuality with her sister, as they covered for each other with their parents in high school. Their relationship contact grew less frequent when one was in college and the other was still at home, marking a loss of daily mutuality. At the other end of the age spectrum, one woman described the mutual caring and caretaking that each did for each other. These live-in sisters were not financially dependent upon each other but lived together for the shared companionship and loving care they experienced. Caretaking was sometimes reversed as sisters aged. One woman had cared for her sister as an infant. Her sister took over caretaking for her as her health declined. She described the process in this way:

> Ariel and I have a different relationship than Elizabeth and I. Ariel says it's more like mother–daughter with Elizabeth and I, and it isn't really, but its big sister. And [Elizabeth] is the one that takes care of us [now] . . . I've had

three hip surgeries and I've been out at her house every time for six weeks. And she takes care of me. (Lynetta-27 and 28)

Such mutuality, when it exists, defines the sister relationship as exquisitely unique. One woman described the private language used only between her and her sister. Their special verbal cues indicated the need for support and care. Another woman's relationship with her sister was characterized by compatibility, open conversation, and similar opinions. She said:

> We just always seem to, to get along well . . . and talk about a lot of differ-ent things. . . We have so many similarities and our feelings about differ-ent life issues or . . . different opinions about whatever . . . and how special it was to always feel like I had . . . just an alliance—real strong bond—with someone, and that person would always be there for me no matter what . . . And I felt that way with my mother, too, but it was just a little bit different with sisters. (Vicki-21 and 22)

A third woman suggested that the sisters talk directly and honestly with each other, even when the information is difficult to hear:

> And she does the same with me. She'll call, she'll be depressed—she's been fighting depression, . . . she's on medication and sometimes it just doesn't quite grab ahold of her, and she'll . . . call me and I could tell she just needed someone to say, "Just hang on. It's going to be okay. You'll make it." . . . We don't do this with anybody else . . . whether brother or mother or anything. It's just between me and her, kind of our own per-sonal thing. (Chris-31f)

This special intimacy between sisters was important to the women. When it was not present with a particular sister, that was described as well.

The absence of reciprocal mutuality was experienced as painful. It was often based upon experiences of hurtfulness between the sisters. Some women felt there was little room for them in the relationship with their sister, whose own interests and ideas filled the room. Sometimes this was based upon jealousy of a younger sister's accomplishments, as described here:

> [S]he knows that I'm in graduate school to get a PhD, and she has never even asked me about it, never said one word about it. She will make a statement about something that she knows that I feel exactly the oppo-site about and wait to see what I will do with that. As I've gotten older, and especially now, I'm stronger in that situation and I don't fall for the bait. (Caroline-5)

Two of the women related the lack of mutuality to an age gap between sisters, with older sisters being less interested in younger ones:

> Marlene is 14 years older. There is a . . . kind of difference in our relation-
> ship. Perhaps I give her more respect, although she's always respectful to
> me. She doesn't ever [say], "Oh, you're a little girl, you wouldn't under-
> stand." Nothing like that, but there is a little difference because of the
> age. (Vicki-24f)

Mutual respect, growth, caring, and attentiveness were all a part of the special reciprocity between sisters. Most women commented upon its presence or painfully acknowledged its absence in the relationship. This reciprocity or its absence was inti- mately tied to mutuality in the relationship. The image these stories conjured was that of separated jigsaw pieces occasionally locking into place for a sense of shared history, closeness, and identity; each encounter bringing with it shared emotions.

Positive Feelings about the Sister

The predominant feelings about sisters included admiration and trust. Protec- tiveness was also a huge issue, and many women commented on it in various forms. Admiration of the sister was sometimes based upon age, sometimes upon talents, and, infrequently, a combination of these two. Younger sisters tended to admire older sisters from childhood. This childish desire to be like the sister gave way to a humorous understanding of older sisters, as this woman described:

> You know, she tells me now that she just was in awe of me that whole
> time—I mean, just looked up to me. And we laugh now about things that
> I used to do, and that were really adolescent, and she would want to do
> them too. You know, things I used to wear . . . or posters I hung up on
> my . . . wall. (Jean-18)

Admiration based upon talents was more enduring. One woman described her sister's excellent social skills and her artistic talent, wishing she had these traits:

> But I guess I always looked up to Karen because . . . I was always more
> successful in school, but she was more successful in friendships and . . .
> she has a lot of friends. And she was very artistically talented and still is.
> Um, and she had a lot of opportunities that I wish I had, had . . . For
> example . . . next semester in college, Karen was talking to a dean or actu-
> ally her watercolor teacher who said, "You know, if you can, you should
> study in England (because she wants to do visual arts for her major). And,
> you know, if you can, this is the time to do it." And so she went and

talked to all these people. Karen's very outgoing and I have trouble, you know, just going up to strangers and going, "Help me, I want to go to England, will you give me your money." . . . So she talked to all these people and wrote to . . . this world-famous watercolorist that she had exhibited with . . . He called her back, you know, and she was so excited! She called that night. And so it's probably going to end up that she'll go to England. (Eve-25)

Another woman suggested that her own experience and negotiating skills, admired by her sister, helped resolve a conflict when traveling. Intelligence and creativity were also admired by one group of siblings. One woman just said her sister, an RN, was likeable and skilled at her job. In this example of sisterly admiration, the reporter is careful to clarify that admiration goes both directions. She and her sister and brother respect their individual strengths:

I always knew Bert was a smart little kid, and I always think of myself as very average and I think of my brother as smart. Now, that doesn't mean I can't do the same things they do, but that's just kind of how you perceive it as you go through life. And scholastically both of them are better than I am scholastically, but they'll give me credit for being more creative. Bert was just out here last summer. She said, "Now let's see, last time I was here I went back and bought the kind of cheese you buy." . . . She had several things she liked that I did, so she said, "Let's see, what does it this time—rice vinegar?" She had been introduced to it . . . And there are several other things, so each time we gain something from each other. Or my brother, Larry, will call and say, "What kind of paint did you use for this or that?" So they credit me with being the creative side; however, they're both very creative themselves. (Rebecca-4)

The ambivalence about recognizing too much talent in one sister is clear from the quote above.

Sisters were also admired for their ability to endure a difficult period in life, caused by a partner or by an occupational stressor. One woman admired her sister for her strength in life trials related to her marriage, her children, and difficult business ventures:

I have to admire Kimberly . . . She has a good marriage, but it's different and she has three sons . . . [It is a] Catholic–Methodist marriage and my mother encouraged her, "Why don't you become a Catholic so you'll be unified? And his mother said, "Well, Tom, why don't you become a Methodist so you'll be unified?" He wouldn't, and she would've, but he doesn't go to church. So Kimberly said, "Why should I go to church there and be the one going, if he isn't going to go?" So she's always raised the kids Methodist, and he goes with her a good share of the time to a Methodist church, but every once in a while Tom will go over to the Catholic church. So Kimberly's primarily raised the kids in the church and . . . been responsible for that . . . They . . . make good money, and he decided to. . . he had a coffee business for a while, and that was going all right. Then he decided to buy this restaurant. Well, it was kind of throwing good money after bad, and things went from bad to worse. They weren't getting any money and they were spending all this money and . . . they finally had to file bankruptcy and she's trying to hang on to their house. I forget how many years, but then the bank somehow was trying to, this was after the IRS—I don't even understand it all, but the bank was taking them to court for some reason which seemed invalid. My sister was going to be her own counsel. Now this is almost unheard of because you just can't win, and she . . . told me later . . . nobody knows she's going through this, when she's going through it. Now she's working full time—she's got the kids, she got you know, and they go to court and her husband did go to one year of law school, but she said, "He did pull over a good one," and this was one time she was real pleased with him. But they went through, but she says, "I never knew ears could ring as badly as they did, and your heart can pound that bad," and she said, "If . . . I didn't have a heart attack then, I probably never will." [The judge] ruled against the bank, and then the bank wanted to sue them for court costs . . . and the judge says, "Okay, I'll tell them how much they have to pay for the court costs." So the lawyer takes it up there, and he put one big fat zero. So the bank indeed lost out, so I couldn't do anything like that. Now my sister made it through this. She has the smarts. (Rebecca-13)

While admiring her sister, the same woman describes concern for her, feeling that her husband does not participate as much as he should in the household responsibilities and work. Such admiration can distort perceptions or keep sisters from understanding one another. Some of the women recognized this and said so. Two sisters, who grew up separated by a large difference in age, experienced very different understandings of their family. As they matured, they were able to acknowledge this difference to each other, and the admiration the younger held for the older sister was no longer a barrier. Each was able to recognize the other's authentic experience. In another instance the jealousy accompanying the birth of a brother led to an increased admiration for and desire to emulate the sister:

But he was just an annoying person. Maybe it's his age. But Ashley and I would always . . . stick together and pick on him because that's what sisters have to do to younger brothers. But I think because I wasn't the youngest any more, I looked up to her—more because I couldn't be the baby and everyone didn't pay attention to me. So I wanted to be like her. (Eve-27)

These changing perceptions of the sister marked another element of the changing relationship over time: the ways in which the sister is admired and the feelings about that admiration.

Feelings about trust were not ambivalent. The strength of this trust was described as total and exclusive, with emphasis on sharing life's troubling circumstances. One woman talked extensively about the trust in the sister relationship and its uniqueness. She felt that her sister knew everything about her, and that she would confide details of her life to her sister that no one else knew. She contrasted this sense of trust to her distrust of other family members. She recognized that other sisters in the extended family did the same. Simply put:

> She knows everything about me, absolutely everything, and I feel like I know pretty much everything about her. I know a lot of things no one else knows. (Chris-20f)

Another woman made it clear that only her sister knew the intimate conflicts within her marriage:

> [A]nd I tell her things that are going on in my relation to Jerry that I don't tell anybody else in my family, when I need to talk to somebody, [be]cause I know that we have each other's confidence. (Jean-44)

Ironically, the same women who talked in detail about the trust in the relationship mentioned the limitations on that trust. One woman suggested that age differences kept her and her sister from confiding completely. She also suggested that their physical distance from each other might help them confide in each other and limit the time they had to share. Another woman said their trust depends upon complete honesty and would not exist without it. Here is an excerpt from her description:

> You know, I try to be honest and truthful in anything I do no matter what [the] consequences are. If she says, "Should I do this or do this?" and I see that the advice I'm going to give would be something she doesn't want to hear, she knows I would tell her the truth . . . I'd say what I really believed even if it's unpleasant. So she knows she can come to me for an honest answer, whereby I would never lie to her, and I wouldn't tell her anything she wanted to hear. I think it evens out. [Laughter] (Chris-28f)

Trust, confidence, and affection are apparent in the descriptions of these women's feelings about their sisters, but they spent many more minutes discussing their protective feelings toward their sisters.

Protectiveness

Sisters protected each other physically in childhood and emotionally as adults. For some women, their protectiveness of their sister came at a personal cost. Childhood altercations with neighborhood kids were often joined by the sister. Another woman told the story of "bigger boys" who took a swing at her when she was sick. Her sister stepped in to hit the boy and subsequently got into trouble. The sister, who was ill, felt terrible that her sister was disciplined for attempting to help. This scenario was repeated when another woman stepped in to defend her younger sister during an altercation with a female cousin. However scary it might have been, the threat of being hurt did not seem to be a factor in one sister's willingness to defend another.

Sometimes protectiveness was fairly benign. One woman recalled her experience protecting a younger sister; she would walk on the street side when they were on their way to school. Her younger sister came to rely on this defense and would manipulate others by antagonizing them and then saying her older sister would "get" them. The same woman also discussed the difference between a sister who was more her age and the protectiveness she felt toward the younger sister. Another woman felt a strong desire to defend her sister, since she towered over her.

Some sisters had a special need to be protected. Most often mentioned were the circumstances of acute or chronic childhood illness. Two different women talked about the need to care for a child sister after serious surgery. One much older sister moved her younger sister into her own home. A second described her sister's recovery from a dog bite, which required surgery:

> She was in the hospital for two weeks and when they brought her home my job was to make sure she didn't get in the corn crib with the dog, [be]cause she sat out in the hot sun talking to that poor dog because she felt so sorry for it. And she's never been afraid of dogs. (Rebecca-27)

This same woman cared for her sister during a major illness in adulthood:

> [A]bout five, four or five years ago, Kimberly went to the doctor and she was terribly sick . . . He took her in the hospital . . . she kept trying to suggest tests that they do because she works in the hospital field, and they didn't pay any attention to her. Now, she wasn't in the hospital that she works in; she was in one in her neighborhood, so that she thought her kids could come in and see her. Well, to make a long story short, it turns out she has a ruptured appendix by the time they got to it. Then after that was done, she said she laid awake one night, all night long, willing herself to stay awake because she couldn't get anybody's attention. She couldn't get any help and she was afraid she would die before

morning, she said, [laughs] because she was in such pain. She was bleeding internally but she had to call her doctor in Syracuse and say, "Would you check on this guy?" . . . I went back to Syracuse the day she was supposed to come home from the hospital and I went with her husband to go get her, and she looked like something out of a concentration camp. Kimberly's thin anyway; by this time she's nothing but skin and bones. (Rebecca-28)

Rebecca is a good example of a sister whose role as physical caretaker for an ill sister seemed to be consistent throughout life.

Accounts of physical protectiveness and risk to the defending sister persisted through junior high or middle school and into adulthood. In the adult stage, many of the women described a desire to absorb a sister's physical pain caused by disease or suffering. One of the women suggested that she would have gladly taken her sister's pain onto herself when she developed an aneurysm as an adult. Another woman described being willing to fight "to the death" for her sister, even though they were not close. Another kind of protectiveness emerged when a sister gave birth and was in great pain. As sisters grew older, younger sisters took the protective stance. This woman described her younger sister's growing connection with her and her protectiveness toward the older sister:

Now Lorraine is 14 years younger than I am, and we're friends, too. But she kind of looks out after me, and I look out after her. Not exactly a mother—I don't have a mother–daughter feeling with her—but I was so crazy about her when she was little, and she just has grown up to be real close . . . I mean, we'll go out there [to Lorraine's house] and she'll say, "Why don't you stay for supper?" Or . . . "Why don't you stay all night?" (Loretta-54)

This role reversal marked the sister relationship in several areas but was especially apparent in the desire of the younger sister to protect the older one.

Protectiveness took another form when an adolescent or adult sister "followed in her sister's footsteps." For one woman, her sister's entry into the same high school changed the nature of their relationship and made her feel protective of her younger sib. She stated:

I know high school is a hard time for her . . . It was a hard time for me, but having Sydney there made it a lot easier for me to, like, get through. You know, it's frightening, it's frightening your freshman year to go in there . . . I feel a responsibility to Victoria to make sure things are okay for her . . . and she feels comfortable . . . Now that I know some of her friends . . . I look at her as more of a person than, like, my little sister. (Diane-9 and 10)

The same young woman talked about the importance of helping her sister with course selection, school schedules, and the pragmatics of moving into the high school environment.

Sometimes sisters' internal reactions are checked in order to help a sister with difficult issues. One woman was shocked when her sister talked openly with her about sex. The younger sister wanted information about sexual experiences, so the older one recovered, giving her as much information as she could. She joked that she would probably still feel protective of her sister's sexuality even when the younger one is "40 and married." One sister talked frankly with her younger sister about the potential to be hurt by men. Subsequently, the younger one felt she may have been prejudiced against men by her older sister. On the other hand, she felt she had been forewarned and had passed that information to other women friends:

> [T]he issue of men [and] relationships: in a way it's helped me a great deal, . . . but in a way, it's almost made me put too much of a wall in front of myself in regard to relationships with men . . . dating intimate relationship with a man. I got the, a strong message that they often will use you. That sounds very negative. Whether it's for sex or for taking care of them—cooking their meals or being the mother figure . . . She just really tuned me into a lot of the negative things that can happen in a relationship. And it's helped me, it's helped me because . . . I'll notice it quicker than perhaps my friends of similar ages. You know, I'll say to Marlene, "Don't you understand that this is happening? He never pays attention to you unless he wants to have [an] intimate relationship." Or, "If he . . . feels needy, then he pays attention to you, but when he's feeling okay, he doesn't . . . . He's not verbal, he doesn't talk to you, doesn't share, he doesn't ask you how you're feeling." . . . I'll educate my friends on the information I got from my sister from a very young age. And it's made me more intolerant of just normal things. I always make sure that [men are] not going to get the best of me . . . I'm always going to be independent, never be dependent on a person in the relationship . . . It's always bad news . . . Being in a relationship means being dependent in certain ways, and so I've gone [to the] other extreme. So that's one thing that we would talk about. (Vicki-31)

Marlene's protection and advice in understanding relationships, men, and life is summarized like this: "[Marlene's perspective gave me] insight into a life that's a decade ahead of what my life is, and showing me the pitfalls and the good things" (Vicki-35).

When the sister was threatened by a combination of physical and emotional assaults, the older girl became her protector from threats within the family. Father–daughter incest triggered this protectionism for one girl. The mutual protection of the girls from their father is described, heartbreakingly, by one sister who described how she became a shield against her father's sexual abuse of the older girl and her sister remained vigilant to make sure the younger one was not harmed:

> Of course I don't remember this, but [Jackie] said that . . . times when my father was coming into our room. I think there was four instances when he came into our room, and we used to sleep in the same room. What we did is—we slept on cots. My sister and I would put our cots together and pushed them up against the wall, and she said when my father came in that night and molested her—fondled her, Jackie was sleeping on the cot closest. I guess outside . . . And she figured something out. [S]he knew that he wouldn't touch me, so Jackie put me on the outside cot, but when he came into the room, she was awake to make sure he wouldn't do anything to me. (Carla-50)

Potential physical abuse within the family was a reason for an older sister's defense of a younger one. One mother asked her older daughter to defend the younger one against an aggressive younger brother.

Protective roles were resilient. One woman had difficulty relinquishing the protective older sister stance and allowing a peer relationship to take its place. Protectiveness that persisted was described as "maternal." For most sisters the protectiveness gave way when both were mature enough to have a peer-like bond.

So sisters became each others' keepers in the need to protect each other from harm. This harm emerged from the greater community or the school, within the family, or from the women's own physical illnesses. The protectiveness persisted throughout life but on occasion shifted from an older sister to a younger as the aging process took its toll.

The feeling of protectiveness, the joy of mutual growth, and the shared emotions of admiration and trust were a part of the sister experience. These positive and affirming aspects of the relationship often led to a strong influence of one sister upon another.

Mutual Influence

The women talked at length about their ability to influence their sister and about her influence on them. Some times the influence was direct; sometimes it was indirect. This woman knew her sister depended upon her advice:

> When Barb has some problems . . . at work and there are things that happened to her, she will come to me for advice because I think she knows I can separate myself and see things real clear, or try to. And she respects me for that. (Chris-27f)

While the influence of one sister on another was often serious, sometimes it was funny. Another woman spoke about being a role model for her sister in adolescence and their shared humor at how ridiculous the modeling could become:

> You know, Megan tells me now that she just was just in awe of me that whole time—I mean, just looked up to me—and we laugh now about things that I used to do and that were really adolescent, and she would want to do them too. (Jean-18)

Another woman spoke about the influence her sister had upon her. She was aware of the importance of the sister's advice, even though their relationship could be problematic in other ways.

Some women reported their sister's positive influence in the development of skills; others suggested her advice and information may have biased them. A woman described her sister's influence on her own interest in music and the ways that influence spread to her own children. This sisterly influence was especially poignant since her father attempted to keep her from developing her musical interests. Another woman spoke about her ambivalence toward the sister's influence over her expectations and relationships with men. She felt the sister had both forewarned her about the potential abuse by men and had given her a set of generalized stereotypes about men. She expressed some ambivalence about this influence but concluded, " And it's helped me, it's helped me because. . . I'll notice it quicker than perhaps my friends of similar ages." (Vicki-31)

The woman felt the sister's feedback was helpful in some respects, but she was clearly biased to expect certain behaviors from all men because of her sister's influence.

A sister's behavior and the consequences of that behavior could create an indirect influence on a woman. Often the feelings attached to the outcomes created a desire to emulate or disassociate from the sister's experience. For two women, the decision to imitate their sister's behavior was rooted in the interactions between that sister and the parents of both girls. One woman described watching her sister suffer through unequal treatment at the hands of her parents and struggled to understand the different treatment. This created, for her, a desire to be a better mother and provide her own children with equal time:

> In looking at each [of my] kids, I'm trying to spend time with each of them . . . I'm sure my mom and dad never purposely [were unfair] . . . with Leslie, and Leslie brought a lot of . . . [mom's] reaction to us on herself . . . Maybe she did certain things because it was just her personality and temperament. (Janice-49)

Another woman learned from watching her sister's struggles and decided not to try to get help from her parents:

> So I have decided I'm not going to take that struggle. You know, if there's something about my life, or if I have a certain interest . . . with religion or with anything, political viewpoints—if I know it's going to clash, I just don't bring it up. Because why go through the . . . the heartache? They're the way they are; I'm the way I am. It doesn't mean that we still can't have a good mother–daughter, father–daughter relationship. (Vicki-37)

Different women described specific achievements and choices their sisters made, making it clear these choices caused them to want to move in similar directions. Two women mentioned that the decision to have children was partially influenced by their sister's role as a mother. One described her sister's ability to overcome the expression of anger and hoped she could manage her own in similar ways. She suggested:

> I have learned a lot from her, and she's been a real source of inspiration to me to keep my temper under control and to kind of let things not bother me so much in my family and outside. (Vicki-22f)

One sister wanted to copy her sister's social abilities and confidence when surrounded by others. She admired these skills and felt they came naturally to her sister. Another suggested that her sister influenced her fashion sense and hoped to repeat her sister's choice of style. She said:

> So I guess I've picked up a lot of the things from her, but I don't notice. But I know as she comes back from college she has some strange stylis-tics—fashion stuff—ideas that she really likes. And some of them, I look at them for a while, I guess. [I think to myself], "You know, that's really gross." And then I end up buying it a month later [be]cause I really like it! (Eve-28)

The influence of the sister ranges from the superficiality present in the imita-tion of fashion ideas to very important life decisions, such as the desire to bear a child. The influence was described sometimes as mutually beneficial and some-times harmful. Whether direct or indirect, the importance of modeling between sisters seems undeniable.

Difficult Understandings

The women in the study were very honest and often preoccupied with the conflicts in the relationship with their sisters. They described interactions

throughout life that created distance, hurt feelings, negative emotions, or difficult understandings. Many of them described sibling rivalry and its development across years of their lives. Some spent a great deal of their interview
discussing these difficulties and describing the attempted remediation within
the sister relationship. Many methods of reconciliation were required, and yet
some women did not achieve the desired harmony in the relationship. Guilt or
regret often accompanied the missed opportunities for emotional closeness. It
is difficult to capture the richness of the conflict and rivalry between sisters—
its maturation from physical fighting in childhood to adult resolution or
resignation.

Interactions between sisters often created a great deal of concern. Sisters had
clear memories of arguments and fights that occurred throughout life, becoming
less physically aggressive as they matured. Many women described actual physical
confrontation between themselves and their sisters in early childhood through
young adolescence. Some merely stated that physical fights occurred; others
described the detailed effects of those fights. In one scenario, the woman expressed
unfairness created by the size difference between her and her sister. She took
responsibility for this unfairness, stating:

> I obviously am two years older, so I'm bigger than Sally is, and she was
> kind of skinny then. I've always been kind of stocky and was just ten
> times stronger than she was, so when we'd get in a fight, I'd usually just
> kind of like hold her off, and she'd just be swinging away, you know, and
> I'd be holding her back and just laughing. That'd make her madder.
> (Brooke-71)

Childhood conflicts were often harmless clashes. Battling over childhood
games and goading a younger sister led to fights between them. Brooke suggested
that she merely held off her younger sister unless Sally resorted to scratching her.
In that case, the gloves came off:

> [B]etween the ages of eight and, like, thirteen or whatever, we were fight-
> ing all the time over those things. And I think it had a lot to do with, we
> were just in the proximity of each other all the time. We had to share a
> room. When we were growing up, we even had to take a bath together . . .
> When we were really little and really poor, we used to sleep in the same
> bed. It was like a little twin bed, and . . . you're obviously bound to [say],
> "Scoot over!" [and the other one responds] "No!" you know, and things
> like that. And you end up getting in a fight.

When giving details of these physical fights, one woman described the extension of rough conflict to the extended family. She described a time when she hit
her cousin and threw him into a ditch. Prevented from hitting a younger sibling,

one girl resorted to teasing and tickling her sister. She felt this was just as good, since the sister hated the tickling:

> She wasn't allowed to beat on me or anything, so the only thing she could do is tickle me. So she'd hold me down and tickle me really bad, and it was torture. I hated it. It was terrible. (Andrea-4)

Physical fights were not the only type of overt conflict that erupted between sisters. Several women said they hated their sisters when they were growing up; a few others merely said they were "mean." Conflict between the sisters was also reflected in uncertainty about how they were helping each other. In this description, one sister helped another cheat on her schoolwork:

> She would come home from school—I can still remember her with her calculus, throwing the books on the kitchen table, and saying, "Here, do my math for me." She'd get [an] A on her homework and D's on her tests, because I was doing her homework. And she was passing the tests by the skin of her teeth. Of course, now that I'm an adult, I realize I was just as much at fault for doing it. At the time it just seemed like the thing to do to keep Opal out of trouble. (Martha-32 and 33)

Another type of conflict described by one woman involved suffering in secrecy. For one sister the suffering meant hiding her depression; for the other it meant family status as an outcast:

> [O]f all the kids, I was the one that caused the most trouble and, and was trying to be pushed out of the family . . . What I found out from her is, as she talked about [her experience in the family], she began to realize that it was okay for us to have different perceptions and different opinions of that. (Jean-33)

The frequency of sisters' conflicts was not mentioned often during the interviews. One said "we fought constantly," but more commonly the frequency was not discussed. When it was, the women seemed to comment on the infrequent nature of the conflict they had described. One woman said they had only one fight, and it occurred on the day she left for college:

> I was ready to go away to college and I remember her pouting, because it was the very day that I was going, and I was packing my car . . . I was driving away in the late afternoon or maybe the next day, I don't really remember, and I don't remember a lot about it other than it was the first time she ever yelled at me. I don't remember what the fight was about . . . It was something silly. I mean, she was upset about me leaving, and she

wasn't coming, and she threw some pencils at me, and that is what I remember. (Tracy-47 and 48)

Many of the women questioned whether the fighting actually occurred or if it was just remembered and reported that way by others. One woman questioned her mother's report of their childhood physical fights. "Oh, the fighting? Something my mom always used to say... I don't know if this is her perception or this is what actually happened" (Brooke-39). Another discussed her tendency to hold onto an argument longer than her sister and to remember it in detail. A third suggested a similar process, admitting that her inability to let the fight go often led to additional conflicts.

The movement toward resolution of conflict could create a deeper connection between maturing sisters. If one sister attempted to understand the reasons for their fights, the sisters were likely to become more closely linked. One woman came to understand that her younger sister had picked a fight on the day the older departed for college because she did not want to be left alone. Two women suggested that their conflicts were, in large part, due to the need for sisters to live together in the same room. This lack of space was a common reason given for the eruption of conflict. Conflict also occurred when one sister felt betrayed by another. This could be as benign as defending a parent's right to express his or her feelings or as insidious as the allegiance with an ex-husband's new spouse.

With maturity, women felt their arguments became less intense and usually less physical. Some younger women felt they were less likely to "get away with" physical fighting. A teenager suggested that the presence of a mother or grandmother helped to stop the physical fights. An older woman described her experience of the diminishing conflict. It was both internal and interpersonal: "That doesn't mean that I see everything eye to eye with her, or she with [me]. We have little differences, but we don't let it become a big thing" (Stacey-12). She continued in this vein:

Well, if I don't think she's right, I'll probably tell her she's wrong, and vice versa. She probably tells me, and we'll probably... Well, it's just like little kids growing up. You know how you fight with a little brother or sister? Like that, but it's never... physical. (Stacey-14)

The fights that occurred between these sisters seemed to create disruption in other relationships.

Disruptions between sisters and families occurred and were described by the women in this research. One felt that her sister was not appreciated at work, but she knew that she must stay out of these decisions in her sister's life. She also suggested that it was important to respect the boundary surrounding the primary relationship in her sister's life. This boundary was set in response to the sister's sensitivity. The woman had learned how to avoid affecting other relationships in her sister's life and thereby maintain the peace between sisters.

Other women described the importance of threesomes. When a family had more than two girls, the situation was ripe for a conflicted triangle. Sometimes, one sister found herself in the center of a triangle between two argumentative or distant sisters and experienced pain at wanting to reconcile this difficulty. The women described feeling like they had to take sides in a conflict between their sisters. One woman said she expressed her position directly with the sisters and this helped to keep her out of the conflict. Another woman tried to stay neutral in the split between her sisters. Another tactic included developing separate and equal relationships with each of the sisters:

> It bothers me and hurts me to think that . . . I can't be with the two of them at the same time, rather than having to split my time into two different sections to be with one sister for a while and have to be with another for another; that really bothers me. That hurts. (Sheridan-2f)

For some women, the rift between sisters seemed hopeless. One woman admitted that her only avenue was to pray for a change. Sometimes, the rift between two sisters and a third created a permanent rift:

> Elise has always been a real high-energy person. So with this energy and all this motivation to better herself, she's always been just going at full speed—never slows down. And then when two or three things go real well for her . . . [and then] they don't . . . when those instances happen, she gets very, very angry. Typically, [she] takes it out on whoever's around. And she's very controlling, and she's been that way with her kids and her marriages . . . Everything has to be exactly the way she wants it, or she gets everything blown way out of proportion . . . I resist all attempts to be controlled, and I'll just back [away] whenever I feel that way . . . I think that's really angry. . . . I heard one time that she said she just "does and does and tries and tries," and she's just not going to do it anymore. [Barb and I] have no idea what that means, and when we try to talk to her, Elise gets angry and hangs up the phone or slams the door. And right now, I haven't spoken to her in over three years. I sent her Christmas cards or try to keep in touch with her kids, but she hasn't made any contacts to come back and talk to me, and it really hurts. It really makes me sad, because I have no idea what's wrong. (Chris-36f to 39f)

She was not the only woman who expressed dismay at a lack of resolution. When describing the relationship conflict between two of her sisters, Sheridan suggested the resolution would remain indefinitely, since neither sister could admit that she was wrong:

If it does, it's going to be a long time . . . Connie does not believe that she
was in the wrong. I don't agree with that, but, like I said, I'm not angry at
her. I'm trying to stay out of it as much as possible, listening to both sides
and trying to stay neutral, because I love them both very much and I hate . . .
to see that come about in their relationship. (Sheridan-10f and 11f)

Yet another woman described the triangulation occurring between two
sisters and a sister-in-law. The woman being interviewed was not involved in this
triangular conflict but did describe it as significant in the lives of all the women.
These disagreements became very complicated when extended family members
were involved. Arguments between sisters erupted at one family gathering when
one sister made a comment that was overheard by the other sister's sister-in-law.

Rifts in the relationship between three sisters can also occur because one shares
a meaningful life change with only one of the other two. This preference for one
sister as a confidant is described here:

When she was here to visit a couple weeks ago, she told me this major
thing that was going on in her life . . . It had been for three months and I
didn't know about it, and that was really upsetting to me, because I didn't
know about it . . . Then she didn't want to tell me on the phone . . . but
just the fact that this could have been happening for three months—it's
not a negative thing particularly, but a major life-changing thing—and I
didn't know about it for three months, was really kind of disturbing to
me. (Hillary-41 to 43)

These schisms occurred among sisters, or between sisters and others, at all
ages. Some felt hopeful about eventual resolution, but a few had just given up.
Some were able to step back and watch the progress of resolution between others;
some intervened. It was clear the separations from sisters were painful and the
lack of resolution left scars.

Process of Arguments/Fights

When the women described conflicts and disagreements, they seemed to tell them
in story form, each with a beginning, middle, and end. The initiation of the fight
or argument was described by several women. Often the argument began with a
verbal attack by one sister or the other. One woman described her sister's outrageous comments and the effect these had in starting a fight. Another woman took
responsibility, suggesting that she often started fights with her older sister by
saying something critical:

But sometimes when Sally just seems to say things that seem to be so
outrageous, and I just can't stand it . . . we end up fighting . . . or at least

snapping at each other, and it usually gets personal. So something personal is said and those types of things usually hurt the other person. It's
usually me saying something, you know, [like] "You didn't even do such
and such!" or something like that, and then she gets all upset. (Brooke-45
and 46)

Two women who lived together in adulthood began fighting when the older asked
the younger to perform a household task and she refused. Some sisters fought
because one was disappointed in the other's attention to their relationship. Critical
comments about this could lead to a fight or argument that lasted for some time.
Another woman described her feelings of remorse as she recognized that holding
back information to protect her sister led to a disagreement and hurt feelings. The
initiation of fights during childhood often caught the attention of the parents, who
intervened. Brooke, who acknowledged starting fights with her older sister, described
"getting into trouble" for those instigations. All of these methods of beginning an
argument with the sister recognized primary responsibility with one sibling or the
other; none of the women described mutual responsibility for this process.

After a fight had begun, the process of fighting differed considerably. The older
sister who wanted her younger sister to help with the housework took a parental
stance and was even abusive toward her sister to bring her into line. She felt
justified in using this approach to deal with the conflict. Parents actively solved
childhood conflicts. The woman who admitted starting fights with her older sister
described her mother's favoritism in solving the conflict:

Well . . . a lot of times, if one of my parents are in the room . . . they might
say something, especially my mom would really say something like,
"What'd you say that for? You shouldn't say that to your sister." . . . Then
Sally's crying, and it gets to be a big ol' thing, and we usually apologize,
and then it's done with. (Brooke-47 and 48)

Another woman just stated that she and her sister had learned to ignore their
conflicts until they went away. The active, aggressive, and passive methods of
moving through a conflict suggested that the women had a variety of methods for
coping with difficult interactions.

So how were fights and arguments ended? The conclusions or resolutions of
conflict were also varied. The woman who was abusive toward her sister described
the outcome as congenial. Her sister had learned to obey her and the two could,
therefore, live comfortably together. Brooke, who picked on her older sister,
recounted how Sally's tears brought the conflict to resolution and forced recognition that Brooke should apologize. A third woman mentioned her ability to talk
through minor scrapes with her sister, producing a clear resolution. Sometimes
arguments were not resolved. This woman suggests that her willingness to give in

to her sister had kept the peace in the past, but she was no longer willing to sacrifice her integrity for that peace, and the anger had persisted:

> We've had these problems, and especially in the last three years Elise hasn't even deigned to speak to me. I don't know how to get closer to her, but I can't get past her anger. And I feel like to get past it would be more than I would be willing to sacrifice—as far as my integrity or my conscience would allow. I feel like I'd have to go through a lot of abuse from her, verbal abuse. I'm not sure that I'm willing to sacrifice that right now. I'm not that forgiving. (Chris-45f)

These women understood that their arguments were not always transparent; sometimes the conflict was about something entirely different than the one that appeared on the surface. They demonstrated their insight into this process through stories and conjecture about the real reasons for their fights. These reasons sometimes dated from childhood; sometimes they were about recent encounters. One woman suggested their continued fighting was because of similarity of personality. Someone else was puzzled by her sister's personality—the underlying anger and its manifestations. She felt this style of relating had begun in childhood and created conflicts between the sisters, as well as between her sister and their parents:

> [S]omebody in church said that when they . . . sense that there's that need in a kid, they just really make an effort to pay special attention to that one child. [Be]cause they're really trying to tell [you] they need to be noticed, because they're acting out some odd behaviors . . . This was an interesting concept. (Janice-52)

Two sisters in one family were constantly in conflict. The woman who described this suggested they were just "not fond of each other." Insulting nicknames persisted (e.g., Miss Goody Two-Shoes), which made the conflict between the two fester. Chris also described her sister as controlling:

> I resist all attempts to be controlled. And I'll just back away whenever I feel that way. And I think that's really . . . [what]made Elise angry. (Chris-37f)

Several conflicts seemed to reflect underlying issues that were generated by present-day concerns in the relationship. One woman became very irritated with her sister's derogatory references to child protective services. She said:

> Myself, my mom, and Sally, we were upstairs just kind of watching TV and talking and just relaxing, and . . . for some reason we got talking

about CPS, Child Protective Services, and I just got really mad at my sister and just really yelled at her and lashed out at her and got really smart-mouth with her . . . I ended up leaving the room, and when I reflected on it later, it's like that anger was definitely displaced from something else, because it was too much for the situation. And when I thought about it a little bit further I realized, I'm really angry with the way she's handling the situation with my niece. (Brooke-39f)

That conflict presented the woman with cause for concern about her sister's daughter. Another woman felt her sister had displaced her anger about her disabling depression onto their relationship.

All of these insights demonstrated that the women in the study thought deeply about their conflicts with their sisters. Even when they were not sure of the source of the sister's anger or continuing conflict, they attempted to create a narrative for that anger that made sense to them. Their emotional connection with their sisters drove these attempts at insight and sometimes created a sense of resolution and acceptance.

When arguments and fights were not resolved, some women decided upon a strategy to minimize the likelihood or effects of their fights. One young woman had learned to be aware of her sister's unusual sensitivity:

We didn't really talk much the next couple of months, but then it started getting back to normal. But really we didn't discuss it much—just kind of like buried it—and didn't bring it out in the open. Because . . . it's hard to understand, but . . . that's kind of what I mean by feedback, just mainly her oversensitivity (Vicki -7)

A more mature woman had adopted a similar strategy, even though she was uncomfortable with it. She stated:

[W]ith my older sister, I have to tread a little bit lightly because I feel like . . . she probably had kind of a tough time growing up. And at the time I sure didn't know it, but Leslie was feeling so insecure about herself and . . . so I feel like I don't want to do anything to hurt her or anything. So I feel like I'm always treading a little bit lightly, like I don't want to offend her or say something that she might take in a negative way. (Janice-30)

Both of these women demonstrate a desire to avoid conflict in the relationship. They feel greater responsibility to maintain the peace with the sister. In these two circumstances, this need is created by an overly sensitive sister and an awareness of how she is affected by others.

These examples of fights and arguments provide only a beginning level of understanding about the difficulties in the sister–sister connection. The process of actual fighting—putting thoughts and feelings out into the open—is not the most common method for dealing with difficulty. Often conflict and rivalry create internal fissures in the sister–sister connection. The unsettled feelings smolder and stir beneath the surface, creating stress and an unexpected explosive eruption between the two girls or women. Sometimes others are devastated by the chaos; others are sent scurrying away. The aftermath can be ruinous across the landscape of the relationship or the entire family.

Conflict and Rivalry

Conflict and rivalry occurred on a continuum ranging from minor irritations to physical altercations. Here one young woman describes her sister's behavior during family gatherings. While anticipating having contact during the Thanksgiving holiday, she was fearful of her sister's unpredictability:

> Ninety-five percent of the time, there's always that expectation that everybody waits for the other shoe to fall, and I'm just as guilty of that as everybody else. She may start out being very pleasant and easy to be around and laughing and having a good time, and then all of the sudden— and who knows what that is . . . things will just completely deteriorate. And you don't want her to have to be around at all. (Caroline-14)

Most sister relationships do not span the entire continuum; their conflicts may hover at one extreme or the other.

Conflict in the sister–sister relationship had many causes, according to the women in this study. They speculated on the reasons for this in many ways. Starting in childhood, some felt their conflict could be traced to a parent or teacher who encouraged their competitiveness. One sister was usually seen as more competitive than another. One woman described this rivalry between sisters in much detail and had spent time in psychotherapy trying to understand the conflict:

> Well, it started back even when we were kids. You know, if I was sitting next to the car window on a family trip . . . If I did it once, then she wanted to be the next one. Whatever I did, Sybil wanted to follow . . . As far as our competitiveness, I'm not sure I even understand. In fact I've been going through therapy, and one of the focuses . . . is my relationship with her. (Chris-20 and 21)

She described this competitive narrative as the underlying reason for her sister's choice of careers, suggesting that the sister tried to best all of them by combining their career choices:

> If I did something or I accomplished something like I got my degree in women's studies, than she would make [women] her emphasis in

nursing . . . My other sister, Barb, became a paramedic, so Elise became a nurse. But just to better us both, Elise became an ob-gyn nurse. And one of my other sisters, Jonetta, said one time, well, she was going to plan on going on to law school, and Elise said, "Oh no, I don't want to do that." (Chris-27)

However, this description seemed to be extreme. Many women expressed awareness that conflict and rivalry between siblings was expected and normal. As a matter of fact, another woman suggested that her relationship with a much older sister was abnormal because fights were avoided. She attributes this to a huge gap in age:

[B]ecause when Marlene came home, she brought presents. She was the big sister, who was doing so much with her life, and she's so smart, and she knows so much about everything. You know, that's my image . . . And so, why would I want to fight with her—because she's like one of my best friends. She knows so much, she can tell me so much about things. (Vicki-45)

The inevitability of rivalry discussed by the women did not mean they experienced rivalry in the same ways. There were many different appearances for conflict beginning in childhood.

Yet in some families rivalry and conflict punctuated the childhood relationship with sisters, sometimes taking over as the dominant emotion between them. These childhood experiences of rivalry were couched in terms of relationships to others. Sibling dyads, relationships with other children, and the ever-present rivalry for parental attention were some of the dynamics these women described. In general, rivalry was described as unwanted and possibly unilateral. One woman described her hatred for her sister, but said her sister did not feel the same way toward her. When the rivalry and antagonism were present, they could overshadow any other kinds of contact between sisters. Sometimes it took many years after adolescence before women understood the jealous nature of this contention. These conflicts were sometime attributed to differences between the sisters, which were not reconcilable.

Rivalry for the attention or positive regard of parents was often mentioned by the women. One woman described this rivalry in great detail, adding that her sister was the perpetrator of it. In her words:

Ingrid always felt that I had—was born with—more good qualities and that I was the favorite child of our parents. She was the first-born and she felt she got all the ugly side of both parents, and that I got all of the good qualities, and she's always resented that. Ingrid always felt that I was favored in every way by our parents. I don't agree with that, but there's a lot of things she doesn't know that I didn't get, but [it] would have been nice if I had [gotten them]. (Caroline-2)

Caroline suggested that Ingrid sometimes set her up for parental disapproval:

> She would frequently do things like needle me, pick at me, until I would
> get angry or throw something at her—just continually picking—to get
> me angry. When I think back on that, I think it may have been so that I
> would look worse in our parent's eyes, which worked. (Caroline-4)

In this continuing description of rivalry, the favored sister described the
long-term consequences she paid for the conflict:

> I always felt that it was my responsibility—I frequently describe Ingrid
> as the squeaky wheel. She was always the one that caused trouble, usually
> at mealtime. And . . . I went way overboard the other direction to be the
> perfect child—hence, why she feels that my parents felt better about me
> than her. (Caroline-10)

Another woman talked about the effects of time and memory on the rivalry
between sisters. She suggested that the sisters fought constantly during childhood, but she cannot remember why anymore. Her thoughts about this interaction were expressed this way:

> We provoked each other. We did things we knew would make each other
> mad. I don't know if we consciously did it, but we . . . got to the point
> where we couldn't talk to each other at all without [arguing], [be]cause
> my mom told us we weren't allowed to talk to each other. We fought all
> the time. I can't remember about what, stupid things, but it seemed like
> a big deal at the time. (Diane-23)

In this situation the mother helped to reify the conflict by forbidding contact
and perhaps preventing a solution that could have been worked out between the
girls. Other women mentioned the same diminishment of conflict as an effect of
time and memory.

In retrospect, child and adolescent conflicts were often viewed as humorous or
unavoidable. This shaping of the experience by time and maturity were mentioned
by quite a few of the women. One described laughing with her sister when they
realized each thought the other had prevailed in their rivalry. Another described
the natural process of outgrowing a childhood conflict based, in part, on sharing a
bedroom. A third talked about the current amiable relationship between the two
women, but did mention that their childhood rivalry had sometimes escalated to
physical conflict.

Another theme related to rivalry was the manipulation of one sister by the
other. This was usually done as part of a competition for special resources or
sought-after positions. One woman talked about manipulating her younger sister

by giving attention when she wanted something that the girl could help facilitate. She said:

> We used to run away from her. She says, "I don't remember that." However, other times when we did little programs and circuses and stuff like that, we'd pull her in. She was always cute then, and the aunts and uncles and parents would think she was real cute. So she was our drawing card. (Rebecca-37)

Young sisters also manipulated each other to get more of the family dinner.

In adolescence, manipulation was characterized by playing tricks on the sister. One such episode was related to the sister's dating experience. The reporting woman remembered two incidents when her sister did this. Here is one:

> But I remember some of the ornery things she did to me. One time she had two girlfriends who were twin sisters . . . they were sisters of this guy I was dating and they were [in] junior high at the time, and I was [in] high school . . . Anyway, you had to go walk up the road to get the mail. Well, these three decided to walk up and get the mail, and when they came home they had opened a letter I got from a guy that I didn't like. He wrote silly stupid things in there . . . like, "I found one of your earrings in the car. I liked a chance to knock the other one off sometime." Well, you got these three girls reading this, and they're just dying laughing. (Rebecca-11)

In their adult years, the women reported less ongoing conflict and provided insights into their earlier childhood rivalries. Most women minimized their current conflicts:

> I think, on the whole, [I] kind of talked about the negative stuff. We do have just a wonderful relationship. We love each other very much, and we have a lot of things in common. We have so much fun. Every time we're together we just have just so much fun, [be]cause we're so close. (Vicki-13)

Some sisters have learned to handle conflict in a much more direct and mature way—eschewing the manipulative experiences of childhood:

> Now, it's more of a mind game. Ingrid will, for instance . . . make a statement about something that she knows that I feel exactly the opposite about and wait to see what I will do with that. As I've gotten older, and especially now, I'm stronger in that situation and I don't fall for the bait. (Caroline-5)

When women could not be honest as adults, they were regretful about that fact; some blamed the inability on their sisters.

Conflict and sister rivalry may be present throughout the lifespan, but they take on different forms in adult years, often accompanied by regret, loss, and awareness of difference. Sisters who were terribly conflicted as children were described as being close friends in adulthood. The late adolescent or college period was a time when this change was first apparent. :

> I remember going back and visiting her, and Megan skipping class to be with me! And that just blew me away. I mean, I could not imagine my sister doing that. She . . . just always did everything so perfectly, and she'd go out on a date in high school and come home and tell my mother everything that happened . . . Anyway, that was the first time that we really connected, I felt like. And that was really fun, to have a sister like that. And sometimes we'd talk on the phone, and she'd call me long distance and we'd talk. And she'd just go on and on about all this stuff that was happening. (Jean-24)

Another woman talked about an earlier transition in the relationship and the secrets that she kept for an older sister:

> [M]y sister got engaged to someone my parents disapproved of when she was 18, and she was really freaked out about it, and she told me. It was a racial difference—the guy was Asian and my parents were set on Mexican mates. And so she told me about it and asked me if I would stand by her. And I said, "Yeah." And I kept that secret for her and she was probably 17, and I was 11. And that was the time that our relationship changed . . . Ever since that time, we've just grown into being really [great] friends. (Andrea-5 and 6)

Irritation gave way to recognition when one woman and an older sister realized their conflict and avoidance was not necessary. Another woman talked with her sister, and everything worked out. A third discussed the childish competition between sisters, yet said they developed the maturity and skill that allowed them to resolve the issues in adulthood. Two other sisters transitioned from foes to closest friends almost overnight:

> [W]e can battle for years and years and years and hate each other . . . All of the sudden—one day it changes . . . [all] that fighting and that competition, and then one day, you just wake up and realize that that's over. [Your sister is] the best person in your life. (Andrea-53)

Perfectionism, childish antics, substance abuse, exploitation, differential achievement, and awareness of mortality were some of the factors creating conflict in childhood. The ability to understand these factors helped some women relate to their sisters differently as they matured and grew older. Interactions that followed such insights created the possibility of less defensive interactions, and some women expressed regret about those conflicts. As time passed it was as if these relationships developed elasticity, stretching to meet the challenges of the past and the present, and providing each of the sisters with opportunities for growth and the resolution of conflict.

Resolution of Rivalry

While some women developed conflict resolution skills, most often the parents had attempted reconciliation. Parents often tried to mediate jealousy and competition between their children by treating them equally. According to the women reporting, some parents were successful. Here is an interesting story about how far parents are willing to go to appear fair:

> Well, when Bert finally showed up, the folks looked at her . . . Of course, Larry and I are ready to really chew her out. They said, "Where have you been?" She said, "I told you. We were going out to get something to eat." [They said,] "Well, yeah, but we figured you were coming back." And she said, "You never said." And they said, "Well, we're giving this party for you." And she said, "You're giving this party for me? I didn't ask for this party." And they go, "Oh, I guess that's right." And often times parents do. They really think they're doing it for the child, but the child didn't ask for it . . . and I know that's a dumb way of looking at it, but this was her logic at 18 . . . This was her last chance to be with her friends. My brother and I . . . just had steam coming out of our ears that [my parents] were letting her off the hook on this. They said, "Well, we've got to agree with Bert." [laughter] (Rebecca-39)

Some parents were not at all successful at managing childhood rivalry. "Sydney's a little different, okay? Sydney and I never got along when we were younger. We constantly fought and constantly had to be kept away from each other, [be]cause we had a problem getting along" (Diane-7). During these rivalries, some women reported they had to remind their sisters about their parents' fairness. Thus, there were two mediators: the parents mediated between the siblings and one sibling mediated between the other sibling and the parent's sense of fairness. One woman even alerted her mother to the sister's hurt feelings so they could be soothed. The same woman admitted being surprised by her sister's fears that she was less favored. This is her experience:

> Jane's funny [be]cause she's so, she's so cool in so many ways and I just have a great relationship with her, and in a lot of ways I admire . . . her

relationship to my mom. Sometimes I think I'm a little too dependent on my parents . . . and I admire her independence . . . But there's that side to her that's very competitive, very sibling rivalry, very much. It's very funny. It's like this little kid. So I think that comes out more when I come home. (Andrea-36)

Jealousy and Rivalry

Jealousy was also a strong factor in the creation of rivalry between sisters. Some women just stated that they were jealous of their sisters—a fact of their relational lives. Other women suggested specific reasons for the development of jealousy. Different personalities or different talents and abilities led to different valuing by parents. Sometimes the differences between sisters created an alignment with a parent, as in this story of jealousy:

I mean, Megan was the youngest in the family. My Mom was the youngest. I felt like they really connected . . . Megan got a lot of attention that I didn't get . . . I remember before she was born, my mom doing things with me. I remember [Mom] . . . teaching me how to sew at a really, really young age. And then, once Megan came, that still happened, but there wasn't a connection. And I felt like that was because of her. That that was the way it was. (Jean-10)

Some women were jealous of their sisters' drive to achieve and determination rather than their actual achievements. Others felt their sisters were jealous of what they had managed to create in their lives. At times, the women seemed to be confusing jealousy with envy. This woman suggested she was jealous of her sister's personality—fun-loving and easygoing:

I always envied Lila because she was the one in our family that . . . didn't have to worry about weight. I guess she took after our dad. She was more outgoing. She was very popular in high school. Everybody seemed to like her. She never met a stranger. She could go everywhere she wanted to, and she was really popular with everybody. I always felt that was kind of neat, and I wished I could have been more like that. (Sheridan-24)

Rivalry also erupted between multiple siblings, including brothers. Sisters would align with brothers against another sister in an attempt to deal with their feelings about that sister's favored status with their parents. This sibling collusion created a difficult barrier for the sister connection. The closeness to the brothers was a defense and not one that was easily shattered. The favored sister was sometimes kept away from the older sibling group, and they considered her a pest. Jealousy leading to rivalry between sisters was sometimes heightened by the alignment with a brother and resulted in a sense of distance between female sibs.

Conflict Created by Family Changes

Conflict was more likely to emerge during stressful family events that strained a difficult sister relationship. The birth of a sister had the potential to create life-threatening aggression, as well as manageable rivalry. The older sisters who described these reactions justified them based upon loss of parental affection at the appearance of the younger sister. Even when parents attempted to anticipate this jealous rivalry before the arrival of the new sister, their efforts were not successful. Women in the study described hating their baby sisters at birth. Some expected the little sister to be a close playmate and friend but were disappointed at the reality of the infant's total dependence and lack of capacity for alliance. Anger erupted when one sister felt she lost her role as the "baby of the family." One woman expected her feelings to be different at the birth, but acknowledged the outcome that came with maturity. The jealousy upon the birth of a sibling most often subsided.

Childhood jealousy and envy did persist for some women as they and their sisters made different choices. The women were quick to add that envy in adult relationships was based upon personal choice. One woman suspected that her sister envied her childless lifestyle. Another admitted that she was jealous of her sister's motherhood. Many young women felt their sisters envied their freedom of choice. One woman felt that envy was normal in a sister relationship and nothing to worry about. The relationship roles of two sisters changed when the younger one became a caretaker for her older sister later in life. This role reversal was envied by the older woman. Other women envied their sisters' capacity for relationship with other members of the family. Specifically, this woman mentioned her envy of the sister's relationship with her father and brother:

> [O]verall I don't really want to be that involved; sometimes I feel envious . . . because I think there's a certain closeness that she has, especially with my father and my brother, that I don't have. (Hillary-12f)

These feelings of envy seemed to be based upon life circumstances, life choices, relationship significance, and loss associated with aging.

The balance of relationships within a family could lead to a specific type of rivalry and conflict when one sister lived far away from the family. One woman felt her sister and mother were fighting over time with her during vacations near her childhood home. She found herself in the position of mediating this conflict by trying to share time equally with each. Another woman said that stormy arguments emerged as a new force in a previously close relationship only after her sister moved far away. The experiences of these geographically separated sisters suggests that residing far apart may lead to greater difficulty in maintaining close relationships with all family members—especially sisters.

Death and the process of dying created the possibility of greater conflict and greater resolution. One woman was fighting with her sister when the sister died. She talked a lot about the conflict in her interview. She acknowledged trying to make the conflict unimportant so that it was bearable:

> I think . . . I may see things, may see the relationship as worse than it really was, because I'm so guilt-ridden over Kylie's death, because there was a big fight between the two of us before she left that day. (Laurie-15f)

At other times, she described punishing herself for not having a chance to make it right and recognizing, again, that the loss was permanent:

> [M]aybe just to [laughs] beat myself up for something . . . just try to justify what happened that day she left . . . saying that the relationship was bad, and the relationship was always bad . . . so that day really didn't, shouldn't be that significant . . . not being able to see her or having a decent conversation with her before she died. I'm so guilty that we had this fight before she left and that I'll never see her again. She's dead. (Laurie-17f)

Insight into these different ways of handling the emotional aftermath of the death was also present:

> So I never saw Kylie alive [again] except the time we had that fight, so it was almost like there was never an appropriate parting between us, and . . . that's what really bothers me . . . I think [I] would've been able to deal with her death a lot easier . . . had she left for the lake that day, had our last words together [been] pleasant ones, you know, but they weren't. (Laurie-22f)

There was regret about not having the ability to reconcile the loss before death came.

One woman described her inability to cope with the death of her sister due to lack of resolution of an argument before the sister died—but was also unable to see her sister in the casket. These two events left her feeling unresolved about the loss of her sister.

In contrast, the anticipated permanent loss of an older sister created a desire to understand the importance of sisterly presence during the loss:

> And . . . a lot of people aren't together as much as we are. You know sisters [like us] that are losing [one sister]. But Betty and I said we just have

to be there because we're available—and this way when we look back, we don't [ask ourselves], "Why didn't we do this?" or "Why didn't we do that?" So, she [dying sister] runs the show more or less. She's not a bit selfish, I don't mean that. But, I mean, whenever she feels like doing it, that's when we do things. And uh, we just need each other. (Dorothy-48 to 50)

Both anticipated death and unanticipated, traumatic death led to a desire for love and support, finalization of the connection, and a sense that the ending had been a good one. The denial of a final resolution created pain, rationalization, guilt, and self-blame, which never seemed to feel finished. Few women in the study had experienced the death of a sister, but many mentioned it and the fear of unresolved conflict.

Resolution of Conflict

Experiences handling conflict during childhood and adolescence prepared the way for a compatible relationship as adults. Nowhere was this clearer than when sisters shared a bedroom. The need to reconcile issues of privacy, sharing, and compatible use of limited resources helped the sisters to create a working relationship in adulthood. This woman describes the differences in her relationships with two sisters—one shared a room with her, the other did not:

I don't ever think Sydney and I had a fight where we weren't talking within five minutes. [We] . . . never . . . never had fights with each other. We basically got along really well [be]cause, when we were little, we shared a room together. Victoria was small. Sydney and I shared a room and learned to live and deal with each other. Then, I got to move upstairs. Victoria and I had a lot more respect for each other's privacy because we never really had anything together, but Becky and I basically come and go as we please between each other's rooms because we stayed in a room together. But it's not like we're invading each other's privacy or anything. (Diane-4 to 6)

Some women had to resolve conflicts alone. One woman described her experience of taking on the "good girl" role as a means of managing conflicts in the family. This role cost her some personal freedom and added stress to her life. In another case the loss of illusion with an idealized, older sister resulted in a more realistic view and closer connection between two sisters. Each had to learn to see the other's perspective. Resolution of conflict in the relationship was sometimes accomplished by allowing time to pass, confronting the problem directly, or ignoring the conflict. All of these childhood methods were transformed into fully formed adult coping skills.

When describing the details of how conflicts were resolved, additional methods became clear. Avoidance, dominance, direct confrontation, and the need to involve the input of others were all discussed. One woman simply stated that she and sisters avoided conflict by avoiding each other. She said, "They do their thing and I do my thing and that's basically it. We try not to cross wires too often" (Diane-15). Another woman said she would confront her sister about certain issues but was aware of her sister's sensitivity and tried not to go too far with her feedback. For a third woman, the avoidance was helpful, leading them to a point of recognition that the conflict was not necessary. One woman described the importance of minimizing future conflict by using physical force and dominance with a younger sister. The adage of *my house, my rules* seemed to apply to this circumstance, as the younger sibling had moved into the home of the older sister and her husband. Physical altercation put the sister in her place and left a clear hierarchy. However, such physical violence between sisters was rare when both were adults.

Many different women found a way to talk directly about their difficulties. For some the directness of conversation was simple and natural; for most, it was a skill that had been learned over the course of shared experiences and traumas. One woman considered giving up her moderator role and becoming more direct and honest:

> She's on a trip where she's needing my mom's approval, and I don't know why, and so I'm kind of caught up in that. But it's good, because I feel like things have changed a lot and I have been a lot more able to just not get in the middle of it and try to fix it, but kind of try to define my position in a thought-out way before it happens and, you know, clarify my position and not really solve it. (Andrea-36)

Another discussed her willingness to confront her sister when necessary. A third described becoming less defensive when she was criticized by her sister:

> Based on the way Ingrid treated me all of our lives . . . She would pick at me. Okay, I'm now more understanding of where that comes from. I always thought it was my fault, that there really was something wrong with me. And it's taken me a lot of years to get past that feeling. I now know it isn't my problem, and I think I could listen to her starting that same behavior with me again and not buy into it, and be able to turn it back onto her. (Caroline-17)

This strategy allowed her to respond directly to her sister. For some women, however, the ability to speak directly did not resolve the differences, but triggered hurt feelings in a sensitive sister. Learning to directly negotiate led this woman's sister to be impressed with her new skills:

> And we had conflict as well. And it was really interesting . . . because I'm older, but also because of what my studies have been in over the years, that I'd really worked on finding ways to work through conflict with people . . . I remember we had, probably, our biggest disagreement about what we were going to do when we got to Nashville and I wanted to stay with some friends of some friends and Megan was like, she was not going to stay with them. She wanted to stay at a youth hostel and just meet some other people and stuff. And, you know, she saw it real black and white and I was trying to negotiate this and say, "Let's look at what all our options are and see what the possibilities are being at one place and at another, or splitting up" . . . And it was interesting [be]cause what I remember is, we ended up staying with these people and she ended up being okay with that . . . Before that time came, I can't remember exactly how it happened, but I remember her just being in awe that we could actually work through this. And . . . it felt like a really major step to work through that together. For her to be able to do that, and for me to be able to facilitate that . . . By the time we left, both of us felt like we had gotten what we wanted, even though we weren't sure initially that we were going to get that. (Jean-30)

All of these methods of dealing directly with a sister were part of a growth process in the relationship between the women; they felt positive about the changes.

One woman described her inability to resolve conflicts without involving a third party. Her experiences with her sister were discussed in therapy, providing her with a new set of skills to use in the conflicts. However, having input from a third party like a therapist was rarely described during the interview process with the women. More commonly they talked about the importance of moderating conflict between others.

Sisters moderated conflicts between the sisters and their parents, exclusively. One woman described siding with her sister in a combined effort to understand difficult parents:

> [E]ver since that time, we've just grown into being . . . best friends. And it's real interesting to talk to my sister, because she's one of my best friends, but she's also the only person that shares my parents. So, through all this stuff, it's interesting to analyze our parents and figure out what's going on. (Andrea-6 and 7)

At another time, Andrea agreed with her parents and defended them to Jane. Andrea seemed to be suggesting that she could see both sides of the conflicted relationship and would respond according to the circumstances:

I mean, I've talked to my sister a lot. I've talked a lot to her on the phone . . . It's interesting that the holidays are coming up, and [I'm] talking to my mom and talking to my sister [be]cause they don't get along as well as I get with both of them. I guess in getting ready to go home myself, I guess I've been dealing with some of those issues with her. (Andrea-31)

This type of growth in the relationship was an important aspect of the ability to resolve conflicts.

Many of the women agreed that their adult methods were far superior to the way they had dealt with conflicts in their youth. In adult life the pranks and anger of youth had given way to a more congenial and direct method of dealing with conflict. Some women had to learn to compromise less in a conflict; others had to learn to be more giving with their sisters. Most felt they were generally closer than they had been. Physical attempts at solving problems had almost disappeared. For many, the competition for their parents' attention had been resolved. All of these efforts at conflict resolution were valued by the women in the study, but sometimes their best efforts did not pay off.

Other breaches in the relationship between sisters were perceived as irreconcilable due to triangulation within the family. One woman's experience of being with her sister was so caustic that she decided to avoid her. Jealousy, hurt feelings, and repeated poor interactions led others to abandon any attempt to mend their differences. This experience captures several of those emotions in a holiday vignette:

[W]ith the family, Marlene's oversensitive in every aspect of her life. I try to help her if Mom upsets her or Dad does or her brothers or something. I just try to help her not be so sensitive. [I say,] "Just go with it. That's life."

I think the biggest one . . . thing that happened [was] last Christmas. I left a day early because I was going to fly home on New Year's Day, and the person who was picking me up was having a party. And I flew into Santa Fe, but I live in Latham, which is two hours away. So I thought if I could change my ticket it would be good, because then that person who's having a party could pick me up a day early instead of the day that they're having the party. And, plus, I wanted to be there for the party and everything, so I left just a day early, and it hurt her feelings so badly that she won't even speak to me. So that's so immature I still can hardly believe it, but I guess it hurt her feelings so much that she couldn't even talk to me. She didn't even talk to Mom. She just pretty much sulked, and here she's 38 years old. But it was very serious to her and we had made plans when were going to go home, and when we're going to leave, and she only wanted to be home as long as I was home. We didn't talk much the next couple of months, but then it started getting back to normal . . . [We] really didn't discuss it much, just kind of buried it and didn't bring it out in the open, because . . . it's hard to understand. (Vicki-5 to 7)

This sensitivity was a major obstacle in resolving sister conflicts; it was mentioned by several women.

Resolution or lack of it was an important part of understanding the sister relationship. Smoldering fires, left over from childhood and youth, had the ability to create a backdraft when the wrong door was opened, inadvertently. Such explosiveness was rare, as most women found a way to decrease the flames or stop their spread in the adult relationship. Calmness seemed to prevail for most women dealing with the fires of a stormy adolescent or childhood relationships with their sisters. Yet some of these sparks remained to be rekindled as negative feelings toward the sister.

Negative Feelings

The relationships between sisters were punctuated by guilt and regret. Guilt was most often discussed in the context of childhood and adolescence; it was often related to the disconnection from the sister in favor of others. It could prevail in the persistence of a competitive attitude toward her. Two women described strong guilt in relation to their actions as children. One woman knew she had murderous impulses toward her infant sister. Her adult understanding of this urge and the actions that accompanied it, was described this way:

> [F]eeling terrible, terribly guilty . . . really being conflicted about, I don't know, I don't [know] whether I thought this then, or I've felt this since then, "I want to get rid of this girl, [be]cause she's like taking up space" . . . So, having a lot of really conflicting feelings about wanting her as a sister, but her not being the sister I wanted her to be. (Jean-9)

Another's guilt was partially assuaged by her sister's lack of concern about what she had done in abandoning her in order to play with others. The guilty sister suggested:

> I should have some real regrets about how we used to sneak away from her, but then she tells me, "I don't remember." Now mother remembers it, and I remember it, but Bert doesn't remember it. (Rebecca-10)

When guilt from childhood was discussed and understood with the sister, it often led to greater closeness and joy in the connection:

> And Sybil had . . . some real difficulties in her adult life, and she's kind of intimated to me that . . . some of her problems were because of me. And I guess sometimes I feel somewhat guilty about them. On the other hand I think, "Goll[y], I don't know if it's totally me." You know, she's been through some therapy and so forth . . . going through the divorce. (Janice-13)

Regret emerged in two contexts. Some women regretted not having a closer relationship with their sisters and wondered at the reasons for this, as in this synopsis:

> I would say it again. I would like for it to be different than it was, and I have some regrets that it was all the years behind. Can't do anything to change what happened before, but I would like to see it be different. I envy other females that I have known and know in my life that have sisters that have real close relationships. I would like to have had that. So [laughter] maybe it will change, maybe it won't. (Caroline-19 and 20)

Other women regretted their own erroneous beliefs about the relationship and wondered how those beliefs had created distance:

> [A]nd the same with one of my sisters, Jonetta. She had an emergency gallbladder operation that went awry, and we were all there for her. And even my sister was surprised at this, the amount of support she was getting from our family, [be]cause we all complain about what a dysfunctional family we have . . . It's just a real source of sadness that we can't be closer together. (Chris-12f)

In Chris' family, the four sisters had tacitly agreed that they would not be able to react in one's time of need, when in actuality they were able to do so. These feelings of regret and guilt were mentioned as part of exploring the resolution of conflict for women and as a way of understanding their closeness or lack of it.

Healing and Loss

The ability to resolve conflict, the reasons for it, the inability to deal with it—all of these themes form a prequel for the actual experience of loss and healing in the sister relationship. Many of these losses have been mentioned in other parts of this book, but here they are crystallized into experiences of losing something that was once held most dear. These losses are created by geographic distance, by illness, by mental illness, and by the death of the sister or others in the family. The attempts to heal such losses were successful for some, impossible for others. These are the stories told by the women about those ultimate losses and the effects of their healing efforts.

Geographic Distance

Geographic distance had an ambiguous effect on the quantity of contact between sisters. The ability to maintain connection across distance seemed more related to life circumstances and the motivation for moving than the amount of distance itself. In general, women felt emotionally closer to a sister who also lived closer physically. This geographic closeness allowed them to have frequent time together, shared experiences, and to participate in family celebrations and events. Sisters who did reside near one another became closer, while those who had been close and moved away became more emotionally distant. Yet some women who lived farther from their sisters felt the distance did not matter. They expressed understanding about the reasons for the physical distance. Family obligations, work, and career choices were all part of their explanation for living far away from each other. Most often this movement was charted at the end of adolescence and related to an opportunity or a partnership. Sometimes, a sister moved back to the area of the original family home, and this event was welcomed as a chance to be closer again. Still others moved to where their sisters had relocated when aging and retiring; the effects of separation from their previous home took a toll. In the consideration of physical distance, emotional closeness seemed to be defined and redefined by the women.

Some women felt their sisters were not close emotionally, even though they lived near one another. One complained that she and her mother heard from her sister only when she wanted something. Another woman said, regretfully, that she and her sister rarely saw one another, even though they lived within walking distance:

> In all honesty I don't think she has much crossed my mind. We just aren't that close, and we don't see each other that often. We live probably eight blocks apart. (Martha-4 and 5)

Often, a sister who moved away was noticeable in her absence at large family events and holidays. One woman talked about missing her brother's anniversary celebration as it was too far away. Another became more conscious of the physical distance after the birth of her sister's first child. One woman missed her sisters so much when they moved away that she moved across the country to join them. These experiences of sadness accompanying physical and emotional distance can be contrasted with the experiences of other women who felt the distance in the relationship was necessary. One woman enjoyed her sister's infrequent visits but found the constant phone calls from the sibling annoying:

> [Victoria] calls every day, and I could get a chance to talk to her every day probably if I wanted, but it's different when you actually see her and get a chance to talk to her than talking to her on the phone. Because she always seems to call when you're in the middle of something or doing something. (Diane-18)

Women who had moved away themselves felt they had an increased obligation to maintain the connection with their family members, including their sisters.

This description highlights the sense of homesickness felt by one young woman and her efforts to remain in connection with the rest of the family:

> I feel real discontent. One of my goals was to move out of Mississippi to get a better start, and now that I have I feel kind of like I'm lost out here without my family. Well, I do have a younger sister in Palo Alto, but she's my half-sister and even we don't get along, I think because I come across too much as a mother to her. But . . . the two sisters and brother that I have back in Mississippi I feel really homesick for. That's why I feel when I do make an attempt to go back it's going to have to be really a big attempt to get together with all of them. I don't see anybody else as an issue to me. (Chris-15f)

Women described ambivalent feelings when reflecting on the distance from their sisters. Sometimes they tried to replace their sisters with women friends. This woman created close confidants out of the women in her church:

> I'm isolated from family. Therefore, my friends at church are my family. So I try to tell my mother, I tell them these things because they're like my sisters. And she says, "Well, I certainly wouldn't air all my dirty laundry and say that my kid was gotten into trouble and did this and that." And I said, "Yeah, but these people support me. They understand." I under-stand when their kid gets drunk or something like that. And you figure [their kids] are not going to hell in a handbasket. [They made] a mistake, and you go on from there. (Rebecca-58)

Her efforts to explain the mutuality that existed with these women friends were not accepted by her mother, even though absence from her sisters made the need for female companionship evident.

Some women dealt with their geographic distance in late life by erasing the distance. The companionship of female family members was so important to them that some reported giving up their entire adult life and community to live with their sisters during advancing age.

Health and Mental Health of the Sister

The health and mental health of a sister were a part of the women's conversation about their relationships and loss. They seemed to appreciate alternative and holistic approaches, being aware of prevention and appropriate health practices by their sisters, as well as the effects of illness on the sister or her family members. The women reported concern about prevention, including an awareness of the need for regular medical care, healthy eating, exercise, and the importance of medication compliance. Their expressions included simple statements of health practices, such as daily walking. Sometimes, women shared the things they had learned from their own illnesses or physical discomfort. One woman described advising her sister on the appropriate diet for a particular health problem. Another described being subjugated to her sister's definition of health:

> Susan's also extremely thin. She's like the thinnest member of the family. Everybody in my family kind of has to struggle about not gaining weight except for Susan. And she was just real concerned about it. So when my year of school ended and I went to Italy to visit her, she paid for me to go spend like two weeks at a health farm, because she was so concerned about my having gained so much weight. To me, that seemed . . . like me taking care of Jane's business . . . She shouldn't be sending me off to some health farm and making me starve and do exercise and things. (Mindy-52)

Concern erupted when a sister's health was in jeopardy. One woman described her experience of sitting by a sister's bedside during treatment for an aneurysm. The women responded to the urgency of a sister's physical needs, but also the routine daily health care each maintained. Sisters were aware of each other's physical health and illness, which served as a catalyst for greater contact, or might have actually prevented it.

A partner's serious illness could have the same effects. The illness of one woman's husband kept her from attending a golden wedding anniversary of her sibling:

> It's been hard on everybody, a little bit, but nothing as compared to living alone and trying to cope, because I was close to my mother, too. I couldn't be down here [with my mom and my sister] when my husband got to where he couldn't travel. My mother got to where she wouldn't go up there, so it was just the feasible thing to do, and we did it! (Stacey-7)

Sisters also became each other's caretakers in times of devastating illness. A health crisis for one woman often mobilized her sister into a daily care role that she had not otherwise occupied. These caretaking roles seemed to span all time periods of life. Sometimes elderly sisters decided to live together for this reason. One sister cared for her young sister following surgery, feeling she would be more effective as a caretaker than their parents would be. She described the decision and her care for her sister:

> Lorraine had to have back surgery . . . She stayed with me . . . Somebody would go down almost every day to see her [at the hospital]. She was in a cast from here down [motions] and then after she got out of her cast she came to live with Paul and I. She could have stayed with the folks, but I talked her into coming to our house, because—uh, well, I don't know

why—just [be]cause I wanted her there, and we've always been so close. (Lynetta-26)

One woman described her childhood and adult interaction with a sister dealing with acute physical trauma. Her reactions included inspiration from her sister's stamina. She said:

This dog bite that Bert got when she was eight was a blessing. It was our family dog and they were coming up from the barn and she reached around and hugged this dog. It was a chow, and [she] must have stepped on his foot, and he turned on her and bit the whole cheek out. Bert rolled over, and it bit the top of her head, before my dad and my uncle could even turn around. So she had this huge scar all the time going through school . . . She was baton twirling all this time in these little towns in Missouri; they have these little homecoming deals and everything. So she was always in front of the public, even with this big scar. She had her picture in the paper countless times. She always liked when someone would come up to her [and] say, "What happened to you, little girl?" and then she would talk to them, so she kind of got out of her shell this way. Then, when she was in high school, she kept going to Chicago for plastic surgery, and that's kind of what led her into the work she does. She was in hospitals enough. So she says she really looks at this as a blessing, and she never blamed the dog. (Rebecca-26)

Bert's childhood experience of trauma was compared to her adult experience with emergency surgery, and Rebecca's response was the same:

[B]ut about five, four or five years ago, Bert went to the doctor and she was terribly sick and he thought it was female problems. He took her in the hospital, uh, she kept trying to suggest tests that they do, because she works in the hospital field, and they didn't pay any attention to her. Now she wasn't in the hospital that she works in, she was in one in her neighborhood so that she thought her kids could come in and see her. Well, to make a long story short, it turns out she has a ruptured appendix by the time they got to it. Then after that was done, she said she laid awake one night, all night long, willing herself to stay awake because she couldn't get anybody's attention. She couldn't get any help and she was afraid she would die before morning, she said, [laughs] because she was in such pain. She was bleeding internally, but she had to call her doctor in St. Louis and say, "Would you check on this guy?" By the time I got there . . . she was supposed to come home from the hospital, and I went with her husband to go get her. She looked like something out of a concentration camp. She's thin anyway; by this time she's nothing but skin and bones. (Rebecca-28)

Some women made choices to help their sisters in a way that changed the course of their own lives. This woman stayed with her sister even though she missed being near her own children as she grew older:

> I don't want to go back to San Diego and live in an apartment by myself. I would worry myself to death with Thelma here in Jackson. I wouldn't be happy at all with her down here. I don't think she would move up there. She's been in Jackson for too long—close to her doctors—and she does have a pretty serious health problem, which I don't have. (Stacey-46)

The acute need for care precipitated by emergency hospitalization was also described by another woman, who was called to intervene during her sister's heart attack.

In all of these cases, sisters at every age participated in the care required for a sister undergoing serious illness or trauma, but in some cases the partner of a sister or her husband became significant in the decisions surrounding care. One woman felt her brother-in-law welcomed her into their home and provided some of the care that she required. Another woman spoke negatively about her brother-in-law, who did not care properly for her sister. Still another mentioned that the health care choices made by her brother-in-law prevented the two sisters from being able to see each other regularly.

Like physical health, the mental health of a sister could influence the relationship and create a need for caregiving. Only one woman talked about discovering her sister's mental illness. Later in life, her sister shared the experience of severe depression she had experienced as a youth. The sister reporting this was shocked and had a great deal of difficulty accepting her own inability to discern the illness when it was occurring. "I think what chokes me up the most is that [the depression] went on for 9 years and it wasn't okay for Megan to talk about that" (Jean-39). Among these women, the awareness of mental illness in a sister was rare. Yet two young sisters had both experienced depression. Their method of caring for each other was to develop a suicide pact, with the implication that neither would act, or she might cause the death of the other:

> We have a suicide pact. I remember when we were both real depressed and both thinking of killing ourselves, we kind of convinced each other we wouldn't do it because we didn't want to leave the other one behind . . . I think we still honor it to this day, because I know there have been times where it's just kind of like . . . "Give up the show." And we talk to each other about it . . . before we'd do it . . . If we couldn't take it any more, we promised we would at least call the other first, and in a sense not do it because we know the other person would convince us not to. (Carla-54)

From these two examples, it is clear that mental illness and emotional pain can have profound effects on the sister connection.

Death and Trauma

In the life of these families, traumatic experiences and death represented additional losses from which the relationship was required to heal. Many women began talking about childhood traumas, such as the divorce of parents or the illness of a sibling. When those family disruptions occurred, sisters were called upon to help mend the breach in the family in various ways. Often, shared traumatic experience created greater understanding when the sisters remembered and felt similar about the experience. If perceptions differed or if these traumatic experiences were not shared, the girls or women became more distant from each other.

Shared trauma with similarity of experience was described in reaction to parental divorce and childhood illness:

> I think we need each other. We grew up together, we had very difficult childhoods, and we need that bonding to keep close together for some kind of grounding for all of us. We've all gone through our own personal trials and tribulations relating to our childhood, and I think it's important we keep together so we can comfort and talk to each other. (Chris-5f)

Difference in experience was created when the oldest sister had to take a parental role, thus creating a boundary between her and her siblings:

> And I think, in a way, Jonetta feels like I've been a real maternal figure . . . my mother was kind of a distant mother. She was bound up in her own problems, and she was a widow when I was 6 years old, and then Elise and my younger brother and sister were like my kids, my babies. So there might be a little bit of that, um, parent–child . . . resentment because I did have to tell her what to do a lot. I was left alone with the kids when I was little. I took care of them. That may be a source of it. (Chris-30)

Another woman described her young mother's widowhood as a trauma with which they all struggled:

> It made it bad on our mother. Well, you know, with the five children, and my mother had never had an education, so that really made it bad for her, and she just had a time getting by, you know. (Gretchen-30f)

Following the death or divorce of parents, the surviving parent often remarried. During those transitions, one sister sometimes became the stabilizing force in the new blended family. One woman dealing with the double trauma of her parents' divorce and her mother's early death became the central figure in the family headed by her stepfather. She describes struggling with him to gain control of the other children, especially her half-brother. She eventually threatened to leave the family over these conflicts and her stepfather relented, thereby re-establishing her "parental" authority in the family.

In a completely different solution, Gretchen left the family early, marrying young in order to reduce the burden her mother experienced as the widow of a large family:

> Then I got married real young. I decided, "Well, I'll get married. That'll make one less for Mama to have to, you know, support and worry about." So she, she kind of hated to see me get married, [of] course, so young, you know, but she said, "Yes, if you, if that's what you want." So, of course, I thought I did. (Gretchen-34f)

Her justification for this choice was based partially on her sister's absence. The older girl had gone to work to help pay for the family's needs at the age of 14, and the woman missed her sister so much that she decided to take a drastic step of her own.

Among the traumas experienced in the sister relationship, the premature death of a sister was the most difficult. In one family, two infant girls were lost before a surviving sister made it to childhood. The woman, describing the experience, said that she and her older sister were thrilled that they would be able to keep the next baby. The death of a sister in later life led two surviving sisters to attempt a closer connection. This did not work for all of the reasons that they had been distant before.

The loss or illness of a primary partner contributed to the connection or disconnection in the sister relationship. One woman's husband's illness prevented contact between the women. Another woman wanted to be close to her sister during her divorce but found it difficult:

> I guess [we] were as close at that period of time as any other time, but . . .
> I was sort of her rock at that time more than just a caring, loving person . . .
> I tried to be caring and loving but it was a difficult—a real difficult—time to see her go through what she went through. It was not a pleasant experience; it was the first divorce in our family, ever. (Janice-10)

Such traumas created the urge to mend an otherwise distant relationship between sisters, but in many cases the fabric was too torn to reweave or stitch together.

Healing also occurred when sisters bonded together to deal with traumatic experiences. One important aspect of this process included the use of second-hand information—a third party telling one sister, who reported to another. The reporter was usually a family member:

Like I say, [my son will] call her instead of me, which I am glad because I find out how he is anyway, and he finds out how I am, and it does Elizabeth a world of good to have him call her. (Lynetta-21)

Sometimes family members remained unaware of an emotional illness that had created separation, and healing could occur only when the information was discovered. This was true for several of the women.

Once aware of the crisis experienced by one sister, other sisters rallied to her to help her move through the difficult time. These efforts by one sister on behalf of the other could be as practical as financial support or relief from a caretaking role. Sometimes they were primarily emotional, but, on occasion, they were spiritual. When there were more than two sisters in the family, they usually joined forced to help the sister in need. These healing efforts sometimes were influential in the career choice of one woman; one woman became a nurse because her sister was in and out of hospitals as a child.

Financial support was provided to one woman by her sister:

Connie, too, spoiled me, [laughs] just like Lila did. She would buy little things for me and bring me gifts, and she, too, was very supportive when Andy and I split. Connie lives in San Diego and she made several calls to me, checking on me to see how I was and to see how my daughter Deidra was—offering financial support and moral support, uh, anything that she could offer to help us through it. (Sheridan-26)

Connie also gave Sheridan emotional support during the divorce. When a woman expressed emotional pain, her sister responded with emotional support, especially when those hurts were caused by life circumstances. Some sisters were available night and day during a divorce or significant loss. One woman recognized the emotional and physical toll being taken on her sister by her niece's protracted illness. She stepped into the mother role, giving the parents respite. Emotional support came in the form of listening; it could also mean stepping in with a certain degree of level-headedness when a sister was overwhelmed. Barb and Chris witnessed a bank robbery:

The TV crews were there, and she was calm and cool and even—never seemed to get flustered. And I was just, uh, you know, crazy. I didn't know what to do. I couldn't even talk to the newsmen. She was just there, and that's the way she just, uh, she demonstrates herself in all situations. She's even. I would say she's more even with me than everybody else. (Chris-25f)

Emotional support could be quite risky for the sister, going as far as a confrontation of an incestuous parent. Carla wanted to confront her father but was stopped by the sister he had victimized. Even when the trauma experienced by a sister was profound, some women had difficulty maintaining a caring attitude. After the initial intervention, the sisters' usual connection ensued, replete with bickering, irritability, and stubbornness:

> [Be]cause typically in the past if someone does have a crisis in our family—someone dies or something happens—we do pull together real well. Actually, I don't want it to be just in times of crisis or times of trouble. I want to feel we pull together [be]cause we care about each other, and I think deep down inside of all of us . . . just have a lot of stubborn streaks and tempers that we have to overcome. (Chris-9)

This long-term view of the healing in the relationship brought about by the response to crisis juxtaposed the quick response sisters had during other types of crises or trauma. Martha described her sister's struggle with an aneurysm and the misinterpretation of paramedics' arrival. At the request of her mother, she and her husband rushed to Opal's home to find her curled in a corner fearful of the paramedics, as if they were attempting to rape her. The sister's presence was enough to establish a reconnection with reality and allowed the paramedics to administer aid, transporting the sister to the hospital.

Spiritual answers to a crisis also occurred between the sisters. One woman hoped for a spiritual healing of her sister following their father's death, but she was disappointed, since the sister just attended church briefly. Other sisters joined forces to work together in assisting a fourth sister, who was dying. Their presence did not prevent the loss but did bond them in their connection to one another. "We just need each other. . . to be together, to talk and to touch and just look at each other" (Dorothy-50).

When the ability to help heal the sister was limited by knowledge or ability, sometimes a woman chose a career that would allow her to help others in a way she had not been able to help her sister. This was particularly apparent in young adult women who described childhood illnesses of their sister. One woman was attending graduate school in psychology at least in part due to her sister's bouts with depression in adolescence.

Sisters were not the only family members engaged in a crisis; they were often joined by mothers and extended family members. Families were particularly engaged in the developmental crises of their children. One niece had multiple birth defects. Another niece became involved with drugs during adolescence. A nephew lived with his aunt and uncle while his mother searched for her own life answers. These families provided a network of emotional and practical support to the children. All felt a responsibility to that next generation of children:

> Bertha's a very smart young lady. We finally started to convince her. We're building her up, and giving her . . . whatever support we can,

morally and financially . . . just being there, calling her long distance, letting her know that we care, providing . . . transportation if her car wasn't around for whatever reason. Just anything we could. (Sheridan-31)

Husbands and partners were an important part of this family safety net. They were present through illness and death and often mourned the loss as if they had been a lifelong part of the family. One woman described the close connection between her husband and brother-in-law and how his mourning for the loss of the brother-in-law was so profound that it would be second only to her own death. Another talked about the grief her husband experienced during the death of his mother-in-law:

[W]hen my husband passed away, why, Jeremy, my brother-in-law, he said, "Next to Lynetta, I think I missed Paul more than anybody else" because they had gotten to be close . . . The reason why we were close was because our husbands got along and loved one another too. (Lynetta-7)

Practical support was provided by these partners, who had become an important component of the family's ability to respond to crisis.

Family members also became easily frustrated with situations beyond their control. Others within the family could help by explaining the underlying causes of the expressed frustration rather than accepting the emotions superficially. This lesson was leaned early by one young woman, who described her experience of adolescence:

[M]y Mom had cancer when I was 16, and my sister was away from the home . . . in another state . . . She was helping me figure out what was going on with them [mother and father], [be]cause my father and I did not get along during that period, at all. And [my sister] was just really helpful in gaining a perspective on why we weren't getting along . . . and that my father was just totally freaking out. (Andrea-20)

The responses during a crisis, whether it affected the whole family or just one sister, created the opportunity for gathering the forces of love, support, and charity within the family. Some of these reactions were difficult to manage; others were temporary. However, the family's response to the finality of death seemed to produce some unique changes and the potential for integrated healing of the sister connection.

Death in the Family

Any death in the family ricocheted through the members, but the death of a mother was a time of great reckoning between sisters. They were given an opportunity to work together or understand one another in different terms. The dying process was often protracted and began with a long illness of the mother or the limitations of her aging. It sometimes began immediately following the mother's loss of her husband—when she was newly widowed, and the sisters worked together to try to fill the gaps left by that loss. Several women described physical conditions of aging that created a greater need for the sisters to provide practical and emotional support. One described her mother's failing eyesight. Another discussed her mother's loss of mobility. Still another suggested that her mother was able to do some things for herself, despite the imminent death:

> She was up and ate her own breakfast. I made her breakfast, and we were getting ready for a . . . Sunday party for her 95th birthday, because that was [the] only time all the kids could get here. And she had a[n] aneurysm and we knew that, but the doctor said she was too old to operate [on] . . . They said "Just let her [live] like that." . . . She started having that pain, and we gave her aspirin. It didn't help, so Paul took her to the hospital, and about 3 o'clock Thursday afternoon she died. (Lynetta-41)

A third woman explained her mother's decreasing will to live, which caused the sisters to have to perform simple tasks that the mother could still do.

In most cases, when their mother's decline required it, sisters cooperated with each other by sharing tasks and taking turns. One woman relieved her sister, who took primary responsibility for the mother's care. Another gave her sister respite by taking over on the weekends:

> And our mother lived a week short of being 95. She lived with me at that time. She had lived with Ariel . . . She took care of mother, as long as she was up and around and everything. Then we would go get her during the day, and she would come spend the day with me, and then Ariel would pick her up at night. Well, then she got so we didn't like to even leave her alone at all. And it was hard for her to get up and get in the car and go. And yet, she could get around much better than I can. She did use a cane at the last. (Lynetta-39)

Practical changes were often required when taking turns. One woman moved into her sister's and mother's home. Sometimes mothers would defer all of their financial and important life decisions to the daughters, who worked as a team to manage them. One woman described her sister as her best friends and found relief in knowing they shared the responsibility for both ailing parents.

Often sisters had to put aside their differences in order to care for their parents. This was true for one woman, even when her mother's personality was difficult for both of the sisters involved in her care:

> [F]or instance, my mother had an operation that was kind of an emergency where she had a stomach perforation. Where, even though we all

talk about our mother, and "She did this or that," we were all right there
on the scene, and we were all together, and we forgot all of our past problems with each other and just pulled together for our mom. (Chris-21)

However, critical judgment may become part of this process; some women
described the judgment levied against one sister for participating marginally in the
caretaking of the mother. One woman felt she did all of the caregiving while her sister
just "showed up at the hospital with flowers." Sometimes she wished their mother
would go to her sister's home for recovery, but this had not occurred. There were times
when the mother joined the sister in judging another sister. In this case, the mother
was hurt and would joke sarcastically about her other daughter's lack of attention:

I can remember Mother, who was quite the jokester, she'd say, "If I die,
you will send Opal a notice?" Or she'd say, "Send her a copy of the obit."
You'd have to know my mom, [be]cause she was hurt because Opal didn't
pay any attention. She'd go three or four weeks without ever calling
Mother. Here again, Mom was maybe two miles away from us. The only
time that she ever called either Mother or me on her own was when she
needed something. (Martha-28)

These judgments and disagreements seemed to erupt when one sister was close
enough to provide much of the practical support to their mother; the sister living
at a distance was not able to provide as much. Differential support included taking
the mother to doctor's appointments, getting her groceries, helping with house
cleaning, making arrangements for handiwork to be done, and providing daily
hygiene or nursing care. One woman said she had two households to maintain.

Sometimes the judgment was not there, though, if the sisters understood that
they were able to give different things to the mother. If one sister provided the
functional support, the mother might receive more emotional support from
connected sisters living at a distance.

These shared tasks and responsibilities could lead to a greater sense of connection and a differential understanding of the sister. Often, such understanding
enhanced the relationship.

The death of a parent during childhood resulted in a reconstitution of family
roles and relationships among the siblings. Often the oldest assumed responsibility for the younger children in the ways a parent would have, regardless of gender.
In one case, a young girl went to work to help provide income after her father's
death. Sometimes the dead parent's responsibilities were divided among several
children.

Any death in the family prompted a number of responses. The women described family rituals that had developed to help in the transition process. These
included attempts to be there with the dying person, gifts given to the family
members by the dying person, and a method for teaching younger generations by

the example of elders. This modeling created a set of expectations about behaviors surrounding death, and the ritual was followed in subsequent family death experiences.

Sister's Death

The women expressed strong desires to prevent the sister's death. Sometimes this prevention was very active, as when two sisters created a suicide contract—that one would not kill herself without the other. One young adult woman expressed her awareness that she had lived past 30, a time both sisters thought unimaginable in their youth. Their longevity surprised them and seemed to create the possibility of a much longer life.

Being present for a sister's death was a very painful and meaningful experience. One mature woman described how she and her two sisters were present for a fourth sister as she died. They provided mutual support and emotional connection for each other in their determination to be present during the loss. Their dying sister's needs and comfort determined their daily activities and schedules for a time, as all other responsibilities became secondary. Their emotional presence to the sister's experience was described as unique—one the husband could not provide and one for which he was grateful. The process of gift giving was embedded in this experience, as the dying woman gave gifts to her sisters and each of her sister's children. The surviving sisters expressed concern about the dying sister's children and wondered how the children would thrive or survive the experience of loss. During the interview, that woman's experience became so painful that she asked to switch the focus to her living sisters.

The healing involved in traumatic experiences, crises, painful losses, and death provided important opportunities for these women. They experienced a greater sense of presence and sometimes a greater sense of connection to a sister during and after these transitions. Sometimes they were able to resolve family difficulties or conflicts during these emotionally charged and demanding times; sometimes the women attempted directly to heal the breach in the sister relationship:

> I think mostly since Kylie's death. Amy and I . . . wanted so much to be very close to one another, and that's, to be really, really, really close together, and be . . . a confidant, and a friend, and everything else. It's just impossible. We are just so different, and that's the barrier. And there's a lot of jealousy between us. (Laurie-5f)

Attempts to Heal the Relationship and Self

The women in this study found conflict in the relationship with a sister difficult and wanted to repair it when they felt they could. Several different avenues were tried.

Being forthright often brought a more profound depth to the relationship. Many times direct discussions were focused on a history of competition and jealousy between the sisters. These discussions could lead to greater closeness or to continuing unresolved distance. Jealousy over friends was mentioned by one woman—competition for the attention of other girls in junior high or high school often led to estrangement that had to be worked through:

> [S]he . . . made me upset because they weren't just *her* friends. I felt like they're people—I can be friends with them, too . . . I think she had the attitude that, you know, "They were my friends first." And so . . . we might have sat down [and] talked about it. If I remember correctly, she told how she felt, and I said, "I understand, but they are allowed to be my friends, too. I understand that they're yours and I'm not going to get in the way or anything." I think after that we both got used to the idea, and it was okay. (Eve-15)

This became a long-term issue for the two women, as they continued to evaluate friendships based upon the connection a new friend had with the sister. In her next description the connection is related to boyfriends:

> I guess it was my freshman year, I started dating a guy, Danny, [who] was a junior, and his best friend, Jake, liked Ashley, and Danny liked me, and I didn't know that. So one night they called, after my father had taken my sister and I to the ballet. They said, "We're all going out." So we all went out and then we went somewhere to eat or something, and then we came back to our house to watch a movie. That was really weird, because I had never gone out on a date with my sister. We talked about it like a year ago, about how strange it was and that we had never done that, but it ended up I dated this guy for a while and Jake, he was this guy's best friend, ended up being my best friend and he just graduated last year . . . It's kind of nice . . . It bothered Ashley that I was friends with her friends, but Jake was really my friend first, but I really don't mind her being friends with him. We both share friendship, but he was my friend first. (Eve-21 and 22)

Other attempts to heal the relationship occurred when a woman gained personal insight that helped her to understand herself and her sister much better. This insight could include an ability to better understand their defensive reactions. One woman described becoming the good daughter; her awareness of this made her realize that each of the daughters had paid a price for this identity of hers. She also described the importance of recognizing her own quick antagonism and was able to replace it with an understanding and empathic question for her sister. Although some women describe this insightfulness as occurring privately, others required psychotherapy to understand and heal some aspects of the sister relationship. This often led to greater understanding and a sense of maturity in response to sister's emotional tugs.

Family limitations were a barrier to such healing insights. Sometimes distance in the relationship was due to the lack of emotional closeness in the family of origin. Healing the self might have helped heal the relationship, but such healing required the woman to reach out to her emotionally immature sister:

> [T]he family was never real close, anyway, in that kind of a relationship sort of thing. So I have a feeling that if we are ever close, it will have to come from me. That would be based on what I'm learning now . . . [be]cause I think she's just not equipped to do that. It's not part of what she's able to accomplish. (Caroline-7)

Another woman had given up, simply stating, "I don't know how to become closer to my sister".

Conclusions

The intensity of the sister connection drifted and dipped across the horizon, then rose again to a new height and a new understanding. It did this repeatedly over the years. Through the traverse, women learned to be better at many things. Navigating the conflicts in a family required skills that were developed over many years. Learning to accept a sister's distance and learning to respond to overwhelming requests took sisters to different extremes. Some had to learn when to let go and drift with the current constellation of things. Others fought to make the relationship closer and refused to give up, even during very emotional encounters. Change created by others blew the relationship here and there, providing little security. Yet most of the women remained focused on mending the supports, stitching the cloth and recreating the anchoring tail so that the relationship was capable of navigating the horizon again. A few just let it go with regret.

7

Time and Identity

"Narrative identity takes part in the story's movement, in its dialectic between order and disorder."

Paul Ricoeur (1995, p. 6)

The individual sense of self was partly defined by the sister's identity. Women wanted to know who they had become because of their sisters. They created these comparisons based partly upon facts of their existence, such as career choice, but also based upon physiology. Which sister was darker and which lighter in complexion and coloring? Which sister reflected her father's family identity and values, and who reflected her mother's? How did those identities lead to different valuation of the girls in comparison to each other? The answers to some of these questions created the basis for this chapter about identity.

Issues such as birth order and shared biology emerged as compelling factors. The women also gave great consideration to their age differences and the unique perceptions of family created by such changes. The characteristics of sisters were distinguished, including their talents, personalities, and moods. Sisters shared some aspects of identity, like those created by their common gender and their shared experiences. Roles developed within the original family became a part of identity and were often long-lasting. Women talked a great deal about the maternal role some sisters embodied for each other. Protectiveness was another common theme that shaped the sense of self.

Many facts were given. The women wanted me to have a clear description of the parameters surrounding their sisters' lives. These included statements about the number of marriages and children, years of education, types of careers, and organizations in which sisters were involved. Women also gave specific information about a sister's religious affiliations and her activity within the chosen spiritual practice. These facts were compared to facts about the woman's own life, forming the final cornerstone of identity.

Birth Order

Birth order was a constant factor in the women's descriptions. The place a woman's birth held in her family's biography created a lifelong role that seemed immutable.

The woman's position in her sibling hierarchy created a sense of leadership expectations for some sisters and the tendency to follow directions for others. These expectations were very difficult to change. Emotional closeness was often affected by these roles.

The oldest daughter was often viewed or viewed herself as domineering and organized, perhaps exploitive and having to take a leadership role. One woman described her role as the eldest and compared it to the role of her oldest child:

> I felt totally aware ... that ... first-born children sometimes are quite the leader type—can be very dominant, et cetera, et cetera. And I happened to turn out that way. I mean I am a first-born. And my first-born [child] ... is a very strong leader and ... should I say, not aggressive, but just gets things done and has no hesitation and moves ahead ... and just very self-confident, tons of self-esteem ... too much probably ... if that's possible, I don't know. (Janice-46)

Another woman talked about her suspicion that others might be jealous of her authority:

> Since Elise is [the] third kid, I've always hypothesized that she has always been mad at me for being born before her. She is the type of person that likes to take charge of everything and get family meeting[s] going, family reunions, get the family picture made at Christmas for my mother, or something ... She resents me being older than her. (Chris-18)

The role of leader might become stronger if one of the parents could not fulfill their roles, or might be created by the sheer number of younger siblings. The same woman discussed her feelings of resentment about being placed in the parental role by the ineffectual workings of her mother; that role carried with it expectations that continued into adulthood. She said:

> And I think ... she feels like I've been a real maternal figure ... My mother was kind of a distant mother. She was bound up in her own problems and she was a widow when I was 8 years old, and then Elise and my younger brother and sister were like my kids, my babies. So there might be a little bit of that, parent–child ... I'm not sure what the word is, sort of a resentment, because I did have to tell her what to do a lot. I was left alone with the kids when I was little. I took care of them. That may be a source of it. (Chris-30)

In adulthood, she is still expected to take the lead:

> Someone or somebody is going to have to take charge and start swallowing pride and I feel like—as the oldest—I might as well be the one to do it.

No one else is. And with my mother being the way she is, she's sort of a . . . she's kind of a . . . what you call . . . I hate to use the word *immature*, but kind of the innocent type that never really matured past a certain point. So it was like I had to be the mother when we were growing up. Alright, I think I'm going to have to take that role anyway. (Chris-13)

Often other siblings strove to be like this oldest sister, and she was the brunt of competitiveness. At times gender played a role, and the oldest girl would be discounted because she was "supposed to be a boy." Oldest sisters then faced a myriad of expectations and perhaps emotional reactions due to their position in the family.

Second-born or middle children were seen as somehow disadvantaged. Their competitiveness might stem from not knowing where they fit in the family. Chris joked about the middle-sister syndrome apparent in Elise. In this case the two older sisters were making fun of the youngest sister, who was also the middle child in the family:

She's been very competitive in that, uh, she wants to be the biggest and the best. And whatever Barb and I accomplish, Elise has to go way beyond that. It's just, we've always kind of chuckled about it. We thought it was kind of funny that she felt that she had to be so competitive. I don't know why. Maybe it's being the third child . . . middle kid or whatever. (Chris-35f)

Another woman discovered herself trying to move out of her mediator role. As the middle child, she had been the go-between for a sister and their mother. In this description, she talks about trying to change the middle-child role:

Jane's on a trip where she [needs] my mom's approval, and I don't know why, and so I'm kind of caught up in that. But it's good, because I feel like things have changed a lot, and I have been a lot more able to just not get in the middle of it and try to fix it, but kind of try to define my position in a thought-out way before it happens and, you know, clarify my position and not really solve it. (Andrea-36)

Youngest children have a special role in the family. According to the women in the study, they tend to be dependent and deeply loved. This woman described all of her siblings' roles, focusing on the youngest sister's dependency:

And Bert's still their baby. And with our lineup at home, I'm always the one who will cheer people up. My brother's kind of the steady one; he's the kind to say, "Mom, how are you?"—this kind of thing. I have a hard time emotionally with dealing with trying to find the right thing to say. Mine is to try and buoy up. And my brother can just sit there and pat

Mother's hand, and she just thinks that's just wonderful. And my sister's just been, kind of been dependent. (Rebecca-40)

Youngest children were often described as cute or diminutive. Being without a great deal of physical presence in the family, they sometimes learned to get their way by being manipulative of older siblings and parents. The special nature of the role made it difficult to give up, so the birth of a younger sibling was described as traumatic for the next younger one:

I think a lot of it had to do with my younger brother, whose name is Josh. He was born when I think I was like 6. He's 12. Maybe I was only 5. I'd always been the youngest, and so that kind of bothered me, and Ashley was kind of like . . . "I can take care of myself." But he's a very different person. He's—in some ways he's a lot like Ashley in that he's very creative, but he's an artist. But he was just an annoying person. Maybe it's his age. But Diana and I would always, you know, kind of stick together and pick on him because that's what sisters have to do to younger brothers. But I think because I wasn't the youngest any more, I looked up to Ashley more because I couldn't be the baby and everyone didn't pay attention to me. So I wanted to be like her. (Eve-27)

Changes in the birth order roles did occur, and this was often unexpected. This woman was surprised by the leadership ability of her younger sibling:

So Sybil's organizing a party for 350 people [for my parents' anniversary]. They're getting them a gift certificate for going on this trip, so she's going in with me on that. I would say . . . I think it's really neat what she's doing, because it's taken a lot of leadership on her part . . . [S]he came up with the idea and she's been planning it and carrying through on all the plans and doing all this. I guess I always think of her as my little sister, and I'm sort of proud that she's able to pull this thing off, especially with three small children and her busy schedule and everything. (Janice-42)

At other times the expectations of birth order went against type. In this example, one woman talked about unexpected role expectations created by being older than her sister: "When we were growing up, I always thought Kimberly thought I was pretty stupid, even though she's the younger one" (Rebecca-2).

Transgenerational similarities and differences in birth order were mentioned by a few women. Comparing her relationship to her younger sister, one woman commented on the roles created in her mother's relationship with her twin:

My mother and her twin seemed to understand each other—being kind of a counterpart. One was always dominant. Whereas with my sister, I suppose being six years older, you'd think [I would be] dominant. But, I have told you, I thought she was dominant. (Rebecca-63)

Another woman discussed the effect of her family's birth order on her approach to her children:

I was aware of [birth order], and I think that's important. You need to be aware so that you can, in your dealings with your children . . . treat them each as individuals, as being very special people in what they're doing and not comparing them to the other. [It's important to develop] their gifts and their talents and their abilities. (Janice-47)

Birth order was a contributing factor for a woman's identity in relationship to her sisters, but it certainly did not tell the whole story of the underlying identity. With time and new shared experiences, the sisters' birth order could become less significant in defining their relationship to each other.

Effects of Age Spacing and Age Difference

The amount of time between sisters' births created a disparity in their experiences in the family and helped to form the foundation for differences in individual identity. There seemed to be a developmental window for these effects. Spacing had a prominent impact upon early childhood and adolescent relationships, due in part to different interests and activities at these developmental levels. This woman put it simply: "I think [be]cause of the age difference—Jamie will be five years older than I—our interests are different. She was basically a teenager and I was a little kid" (Tammy-3f). However, this impact diminished with time until it became less significant in adulthood. At follow-up the same participant said:

I think as we get older we tend to, at least I have, appreciate family and the meaning of family especially, being single, not having kids . . . of my own. And I think family is real important and [have started] appreciating her as a human being and not just as a sister. (Tammy-5 and 6f)

Yet most of the women reflected in detail on how these age differences created difference in activities, friends, and goals. This woman described the ambivalent feelings she had about having to take her much younger sister along for teenage outings:

One thing that was real tough, I think . . . when she was a little older and say, I was about 15 or 16, a lot of times my mom and dad wanted us to take her with us when we were going somewhere. And . . . the three of us were going to go to the lake because my brother and sister and I had a lot of the same friends. And we'd want to go to the lake. And, "Well, why don't you take Sybil with you?" And we didn't want Sybil with us because we were all a bunch of teenagers, and we didn't want our baby sister with us. The thing was, Sybil was such a cute little kid, and all of our friends really liked her, and they sort of wanted her to come. But we were like, "Ahhhh!" (Janice-20)

Having a much older sister could create a kind of heroine worship—a desire to emulate the sister:

But I guess Ashley's influenced me in a lot of ways like that. I think her music [did], because my father's very musical, but he didn't do it while I was old enough to remember. He used to be in plays all the time, and he used to sing. And . . . he still does it . . . for fun, but he doesn't do it as seriously as he used to. He'll sing around the house. He'll play classical music until it comes out his ears. But I don't . . . think that influenced me as much my sister being very successful. I mean, she was playing solos . . . during band concerts when she was in sixth grade, which is very unheard of, and that really impressed me. So I decided that I wanted to play something. (Eve-29)

These experiences could be reversed, as when a much younger sister was talented in a unique way and the parents encouraged her older sister to be more like the younger girl. Such comparisons often included academic or athletic performance.

Large age gaps between sisters could create a sense of sibling groups. Sisters in the older group experienced their parents quite differently and had more difficulty forming bonds with those in the younger group. These large age differences often led to closer bonds with sisters in the same group, who shared bedrooms. At the extreme, one sister may have left home before the other was capable of having much of a relationship with her. Memory was affected. Shared fun and play occurred primarily with the sibling group closest in age. This woman's recollection of the experience was particularly descriptive:

I don't have any memories, really, of positive connections with Megan. It was like . . . maybe we were sisters; we weren't friends, and that was appropriate, I think, for the age difference at that point. So I kind of feel like . . . she was my sister, and she showed up as a part of the family for different kinds of events and stuff like that. It probably wasn't until . . . in between my second and third year of college—I was living in Australia for a year and a half and working there—and she came over with my family to visit me. I don't remember anything significant happening. She was just my sister. (Jean-20)

For some sisters, their older siblings had already established a set of relationships that did not allow much room for them. Yet some sisters bridged this gap for specific activities and events. Rebecca and Kimberly included Bert in their childhood plays because adults were drawn in by the "cute" factor (37).

Closeness was sometimes more possible with much younger or older sisters. The absence of daily conflict and lack of competition for the same parental resources could create a much more affectionate bond:

> [M]y images come from my friends and their relationship with their sisters. And if there's a couple of years difference, they'll maybe steal their sister's sweater and not tell her. Those type of interactions . . . Or they may think the same boy is cute and . . . both may like him, and then they get mad at each other. The jealousies, um, around boys, clothes, attention from their parents . . .
>
> Since there is a 14-year age difference, we were getting different amount[s] of attention. As a grade-school girl, I would get different attention as opposed to a college-aged girl who's away from home. I've never felt like I'm competing with her for my parents' attention. The fighting that is normal among siblings that have similar ages, like my brother, who's 3 years older than me—we fought all the time, and we had a really rough relationship for quite a long time— . . . A healthy amount of fighting, I suppose, is fine. I never had that with my sister. (Vicki-43 and 44)

Much older sisters were often revered, and this reverence took many forms. Being a role model or a maternal figure for the younger sister provided ways to bridge the age gap. One narrative described a younger sister missing her older sisters when they departed for grade school and waiting anxiously for their return. There was a sense of longing in one description of a small girl climbing to a high tree so she could watch for her sisters' return. In another narrative, a young girl was carried in the heat by her much older sister. A third woman described her ability to confide in her much older sister in a way that seemed impossible with her mother:

> Also, my mother had me when she was 39, and so there is this 40-year difference in our age. It made a difference, and I was the youngest. So I think that Mom was a different parent than she was to . . . Jill, who is the oldest. Mom wasn't, I don't think, as available as my sister was. So I think I felt more comfortable discussing things with Jill, because I thought she would understand; and somehow I didn't feel that way with Mom. (Vicki-40)

In addition to affecting the relationships during childhood and adolescent development, large age gaps also seemed to naturally create different family perceptions for sisters. The older girls' view of their parents was markedly different from the younger girls':

> Kathy's 4 years older, and we've never gotten along very well, from the time I was very young until [now] . . . She always felt that I was born with more good qualities, and that I was the favorite child of our parents. She was the first-born, and she felt she got all the ugly side of both parents

and that I got all of the good qualities . . . She's always resented that. She always felt that I was favored in every way by our parents. I don't agree with that. (Thomasina-1 and 2)

In another case, one sister was abused by her parents while the other one was not. These differences in perception seemed to persist during childhood and adolescence, but for some women the differences seemed to shift following the departure of the older sister from the family home:

I think Jane broke away from my parents a lot more, and [she's] a lot more . . . pragmatic, and she's a lot more comfortable . . . We both overachieve, I think for self-esteem reasons. She just seems different about it. She seems a lot more comfortable. She just turned 35, and I think it's been in the last year or so she's started to really question values and question what she's doing . . . For so long she's been really set and felt like she was really successful . . . She knew exactly what she was doing. And I think I've always questioned, and never felt comfortable, [with] what I am doing. That's the basic difference between us. (Andrea-16 and 17)

Next Andrea described the importance of their relationship and how it has deepened since the shift in Jane's identity:

[T]he best thing about her is, like I said, we're best friends, but we also have the same ties. So . . . approaching my parents' aging and things like that, I'm really glad that I have her, because she's a lot of support, and . . . we can go through a lot of that stuff that's going to be hard together. (Andrea-24)

The importance of age spacing and its detrimental effects on closeness seemed to diminish with time. This woman began her interview talking about the closeness across age:

I don't know how to describe it. It's close, but yet we keep in close contact with each other, but we don't get to see that much of each other. I don't talk to her [regularly] . . . maybe once every 3 months, something like that. But when we do, we pick up exactly where we left off. And since she's six years younger than I am . . . you'd think we'd have nothing in common. (Rebecca-1)

Age spacing seemed to have a variety of effects on the relationship. For some women the lens of the older sister's life allowed them to see more clearly into their own futures. For others, it clouded their vision, creating a blurred image against which they wished to stand in contrast. Older sisters were able to re-vision their own direction by observing their younger sisters' thoughts and feelings. The vision of the sister changed with time; sometimes closer affection and shared experiences were more likely as the image cleared.

Characteristics of the Sister

The women described their sisters as representing the diversity of human nature. Valued qualities, negative traits, differences in personality, and even pathological habits were described. All of these formed part of the sister's identity and seemed to help establish the identity of the woman describing the characteristics.

Sisters were valued for so many traits. One was a sense of humor:

> So she's, um, she's funny. She's got one of the funniest sense[s] of humor . . . my daughter, Kimberly, who I named after her, has much the same kind of sense of humor. It's really funny, I think. (Rebecca-8 and 9)

Sisters were described as caring and interested. One woman merely said her sister was popular. Another, while valuing her sister for her talent and gaiety, said she valued her sister's overall goodness. She credited the interview with bringing those qualities into focus for her:

> The feelings that I left with at the end of the session last time were that I felt really fortunate that I had her as a sister. I think she's really a good person and a good person to know . . . That was confirmed . . . when I spent time with Leslie over the holidays and shared some things with her, and talked with her and laughed with her. (Jean-49 and 50)

Another woman described her sister as strong, intelligent, and family-oriented—all traits she admired. These uncommon sisters were seen as important contributors to the family and their world.

They were also valued for the ways they moved through life. One woman said she valued her sister's coping in the face of difficult experiences. Another sister approached the world with innocence and curiosity toward life. A third was energetic and aggressive in her approach to the world and her career. Others were carefree or shy. Embedded in these descriptions was a sense of how the woman herself might be different and, thus, have a separate identity from her sister. Here is an example:

> If we're feeding the ducks, I'm out there with my arm out there feeding the ducks, and Leslie's standing back in the back, kind of holding onto her bread . . . to kind of look at the whole situation, cautiously thinking, "I'd like to do it, but I don't think I really have the nerve to stick my arm out there." We have a lot of [home] movies . . . There were some movies of us kids when we were little and I was always just out there, you know [saying], "This is great!" and Leslie's just kind of standing back a little shy. You know, those kinds of things manifest themselves later in life. How you grow up and how you respond to new environments and new experiences a little differently affects you as you grow older. (Janice-55 and 56)

Some characteristics were disagreeable. One sister's aggressive, competitive nature was described as follows:

> I felt like she's always been in competition with me, and we have always had a lot of problems. She is very angry. And a lot of her anger hasn't anything to do with me, per se. She is very competitive, and I have been a big focus of that. (Chris-20)

Other differences between sisters created concern. The narratives contained several references to sisters' reactions to drug use, eating disorders, smoking, and other habits that the sisters, presumably, do not share:

> [My bingeing on chocolate when we traveled] really bothered Cindy because [the] people that I went with didn't drink too much, and I liked to drink, and it really bothered them. So instead of drinking I started eating a lot of chocolate . . . So I'd eat, like, one or two of those [large chocolate bars] a day, and it was weird because I had never done that. I mean, I never went to the store and bought a candy bar. I mean, that was so unlike me that I just really got into eating a lot of sugar, especially the chocolate. I think that was sort of upsetting to her because it was . . . unusual for me to do. (Morgan-14 and 15f)

Family members sometimes share traits. When an assumed family trait was not present in the sister's character, the woman judged her sister as lacking a family connection. This could be positive or negative. This woman said her sister lacked her family's temper:

> She never showed, outwardly, any signs of being upset or angry at all of us. She said she would just not let it bother her like we do. We all, typically, have bad tempers. So Barb was always the one that would never get upset or angry. She was the one we could always go to if I wanted to talk to another family member without talking to them directly. I could tell her, and she would initiate something for me. (Chris-17)

A sense of humor, the motivation to excel, and the desire to help others were found lacking in some sisters and commented upon by the women. Sometimes resentment developed when the differences were not recognized by others:

> We have a lot of differences. Like . . . when I go back to Mother's, I feel like I should be in the kitchen all the time, especially when you've taken six kids with you through the years. Even now that I don't have the six kids that travel with me, then I figure I should be the one to be helping Mother. My sister can sit in and watch a basketball game or football game and it doesn't bother her one whip, but my mother will always say, "Let her go. She's tired." (Rebecca-6)

Another sister was seen as responsible for creating competition in an otherwise harmonious family:

> My sister's funny because she's so . . . cool in so many ways, and I just have a great relationship with her, and in a lot of ways I admire . . . her relationship to my mom. Sometimes I think I'm a little too dependent on my parents . . . and I admire her independence and things like that. But there's that side to her that [is] very competitive, very sibling rivalry, very much—it's very funny, it's like this little kid. So I think that comes out more when I come home on the holidays. (Andrea-34)

Sometimes, the woman describing the relationship was the one who felt she missed out on a family trait:

> So growing up, I always knew she was a smart little kid, and . . . I always think of myself as very average, and I think of my brother as smart. Now, that doesn't mean I can't do the same things they do, but that's just kind of how you perceive it as you go through life, and scholastically both of them are better than I am scholastically, but they'll give me credit for being more creative. (Rebecca-4)

For some of the women in the study, their sisters represented a personality type created by a unique set of traits. These traits were assumed to be readily identifiable to others. One woman called her sister a "cheerleader type," describing her as driven to be popular and wanting to be the "center of attention" (Chris-26). Another woman described her sister as the perfect "minister's wife"— constricted by role expectations. Certain traits led to a personality type within the family as well. One woman felt her sister's drive and energy created a family leadership role for her. Not surprisingly, the role of family rebel was used to describe an independent-minded sister. This woman made it clear that her sister's naïveté had led her to take adventurous risks and to have more global values:

> [S]he's been in some really, really strange situations because she is extremely trusting of all people. And I don't know if that comes from growing up in the rural area, and my parents have worried about her going through the Black areas of Cleveland. And she says, "Hey, those are the same people who shoveled me out of the snow, the same people that have . . ." . . . I can honestly say color makes no difference to my sister. She was going to go sing at a Black church about the time [of] the race riots, and they finally said, "No, Kim, you can't come." She says, "Why not? I don't care." They said, "You may not care, but they'll take it out on us." So she couldn't do that. . . As I say, she's seen more of a cosmopolitan world than I have. (Rebecca-42)

These social roles and identities seemed to form a detailed character description for some of the sisters portrayed in the study. Other women merely described an individual trait, not connecting it to a larger image of the sister.

Jealousy sometimes erupted between sisters with different character traits and abilities. Often these traits were related to the way parents valued one sister's gifts or identity over another. Academic success was contrasted with athletic performance; musical talent was compared to gymnastic ability. Many women discussed the parental attention given to one sister over another, like in this example:

And at one point in time her success on that really bothered me . . . I guess it was my eighth- and ninth-grade year, she started studying with [this professional musician]. He's the first chair in the State Symphony. And she started working with him and she'd win all kinds of contests. She'd do well in district and state band. And my dad would drive her 30 minutes every Saturday to . . . study with him, who'd spend all his time there with her. [My dad would] spend all this money. I was still doing gymnastics and I was doing well enough, but my parents [said], "I don't want to stay at a gymnastics meet because we get bleacher butt," as they called it . . . And it was at the point when I was still doing compulsory gymnastics, which is every single competitor is doing the same routine on everything . . . [My parents would say] something like, "I don't want to sit there for 4 hours watching the same routine and listening to the same music." And they'd do it, but I could tell they were doing it because I was doing it—to make me happy. And so I got really jealous, you know, and I'd yell at my mom . . . "You just don't care what I'm doing" because they'd go for 2 hours to listen to Karen play for some competition . . . So that'd, that made me angry, but then I'd started going to gymnastic meets watching friends of mine, going, "You know, this really *is* boring." I realized that they were going because they knew I wanted them to. I knew that I was successful, but in different ways. And so, I think, that didn't last very long, but it made me angry for a while that she was so successful. And now when she calls me saying [some professional musician] called me, you know, I get really excited for her. Because I know that's exactly what she wants to do. And I know it's not what I want to do. (Eve-30)

As can be seen from the picture painted by this participant, the handling of jealousy by the parents many help to manage the potential estrangement of sisters. In the follow-up interview Eve was careful to clarify the mature attitude she and her sister have toward their differences now:

It's not really an issue anymore because Karen is doing what she likes. She's doing very well at it . . . Basically what she's taking in college [are] music courses . . . and she's doing really well so . . . it's not really an issue anymore. It's just me worried about passing this year. (Eve-49)

One sister's character traits may have led the other to approach her in a certain manner; they may have written the recipe for one sister's attitude toward the other. All of the women who discussed the effect of their sister's traits on their approach to her described their sister as sensitive or insecure. For most of their lives, this led them to approach the sister gingerly. Conflict was avoided and she was not given clear feedback. For some women, this changed with time: they became tired of walking on eggshells with the sister and became more confrontational. Here is one woman's description of an earlier approach and her subsequent confrontation with her sister:

> Ingrid would pick at me. Okay, I'm now more understanding of where that comes from. I always thought it was my fault, that there really was something wrong with me. And it's taken me a lot of years to get past that feeling. I now know it isn't my problem and I . . . think I could listen to her starting that same behavior with me again—which she still does, even today—and not buy into it and be able to turn it back onto her. (Caroline-17)

Attitudes credited to the sister's traits were described. One woman, again, mentioned jealousy; another discussed a lack of empathy. "I had a hard time understanding her before, because things she did . . . I felt like everything she did was to bug me and . . . I don't think she intended it really, but everything she did was to make my life miserable" (Diane-12). A third woman said it was hard to watch her sister's negative character traits becoming more rigid with time.

Still, some women remained hopeful—describing changes in the sister's personality characteristics or their own. Such changes often helped to re-image the identity of one or both of the sisters. One woman physician said her career choice was related to a sister who had been ill as a child. The frequent hospitalizations put her in the role of communicator and helped her to overcome shyness while fostering her interest in medicine. In another instance, one woman became aware of her sister's developing insight. As Andrea became aware that her sister was developing higher self-scrutiny, she felt that was a positive development for Jane. Andrea anticipated that Jane's questioning might led to closer identification between the two. Some women felt their sisters had developed greater control over their tempers or become more independent with time. These and similar changes established a different identity for the sister, which created a potential difference in the sisters' way of relating to one another. When the identity of one changed, that change created the potential for growth in the identity of the other.

Gender Issues

The importance of gender in the lives and identities of women took several forms for the women in this study. There was a concern that gender-identified traits and interests made it difficult for a tomboy to relate to a more feminine girl. Childhood identities such as those created a rift that could be hard to breach. There was also a sense that sisters were closer to each other than they were to brothers by virtue of sharing their gender identity. Some women talked about gender-related topics that they discussed—a shared viewpoint that meant they were close. There were also women who were stigmatized in the family by virtue of biological sex—often the first-born who was "supposed to be a boy." Other women discussed their preference for male attention and friendship. This male identification created a distance in their relationships with their sisters. Thus, gender and gender identification could either enhance the connection to the sister or diminish it.

Women who were "tomboys" most often discussed gender differences with their sisters. One woman described her differences from her more feminine sisters in stereotypical terms—her interest in sports and their interest in playing with dolls. Another woman mentioned being closer to her brothers, with whom she shared childhood activities. These alliances, created by gender identity, shaped a sense of place in the family. The fact that nontraditional women seemed to comment upon these differences suggested a sense of being excluded or perhaps misunderstood.

Problematic family interactions could also arise when a first child was a girl. One woman talked about her father's mistreatment of and lack of interest in his first-born daughter. Another suggested that she and her sister received male attention and affection only from their grandfather, being ignored by their father because of his preference for male children.

A bond of feminist sisterhood was created by some women who experienced such rejection. They also became bound by other mistreatment based upon their sex. One sister's negative experiences with men could influence the other. A woman discussed her increasing awareness of sexual harassment in the workplace following her sister's experiences with that kind of discrimination. She said:

> She has gotten her PhD, and she's a professor, and the different problems in being a female versus a male in the same profession, like being a teacher and her co-workers being male, [they] would get keys to their own class-room, and she wouldn't get keys to her classroom. There's just so many different things that's an eye-opener that things still really continue. And, it's just, it's amazing. So that gives me sensitivity to that and the struggles that she has gone through—different sexual harassment things. (Vicki-32)

Such bonds could also create prejudice against men. The same woman talked about her feelings regarding her own developing bias:

> In a way it's helped me a great deal. For sure it's helping a great deal, but in a way it's almost made me put too much of a wall in front of myself in regard to relationships with men . . . That sounds very negative, but whether it's

for sex or for taking care of them, you know, cooking their meals or being the mother figure . . . Marlene just really tuned me into a lot of the negative things that can happen in a relationship. And it's helped me. It's helped me because . . . I'll notice it . . . for my friends of similar ages. (Vicki-31)

She was ambivalent about how her sister's negative experiences with men might affect her but appreciated the education.

The opposite gender bias seemed to be formed for women who preferred the company of men. One woman admitted this preference and tied it to her early childhood connection with her brother. Here is her description of the inherent comfort she feels in the company of men:

[T]o be very honest . . . I honestly am more comfortable with men than women . . . Even in social settings and just friends, I've always enjoyed being around men. And it's one of the reasons I'm not real fond of women's groups and so forth. I find them, for myself, just a little boring. I like to be with either mixed company or preferably with men. I just really enjoy their company . . . I don't really have . . . many really close girlfriends. I really don't. In fact, a lot of the guys that I used to date or go with, we were such good friends . . . really close friends that now, when I want to see one of my old friends, it's like seeing one of my old boyfriends. (Janice-26)

The same woman felt strongly that her husband was her best friend, suggesting she would always confide first in him, even about having an affair. At least some of this preference was related to being "left out" of the connection between her sisters:

I think that I've always been that way. I gravitate more towards the male than the female and consequently, too, that plays down into the siblings with the sisters. I think that because Leslie and Sybil were such close good friends, I mean I was almost like a third party in there . . . as adults anyway. (Janice-28 and 29)

Gender issues contributed to the sense of a woman's identity. Gender identity and gender preferences could create a close relationship with the sister or they could provide a push toward the preference for male companionship and activities, just as gender discrimination could create a closer bond.

Development of Separate Abilities

Related to the topic of gender and also of personal characteristics was the notion of separate abilities. Families supported the women in the development of individual identities. Childhood identities could be supported or denigrated by parents, but provided a chance for each girl to come to know herself as different from her sister. Some developed their creative talents when they felt overshadowed by their siblings' intelligence. Their families often used them as creative resources for problem solving or interior design. In this case it was to create a float for a college parade:

> [W]hen Kimberly was in college, she called Mother one time and she said, "We have to find something for a sorority float." She couldn't come up with any ideas, so my mother said, "Well, call your sister." So after Kim got done with me, she called mother. Kim said, "Rebecca gave me five ideas right off the top of her head." (Rebecca-16)

Sometimes creativity was contrasted not with intelligence, but with practicality:

> Bert's also creative, only she's the kind that will get into doing crafts. Now I do my own wallpapering. She does her own wallpapering. She refinished a whole stairway—all the spindles on the stairway—I wouldn't want to tackle that for love or money. She has bricked a wall. She fixes her own washing machine . . . She's working on her gas grill. She could do almost anything. I mean she's put in tile, and I would never approach anything like that . . . She's had to do it because she can't get her husband to move. He won't do some of these things, and she can't really afford to go out and hire somebody. (Rebecca-18)

These differences between sisters could minimize conflict that might have been created by competitive similarity. Rebecca also summarized the effect of separate abilities and identities on her sisters, herself, her brother, and their children:

> [W]hen I think of my sister, my brother, and me, and most kids—you each find your own little niche, and . . . I can honestly say . . . for my brother, my sister, and myself, there is no jealousy. I mean, uh, my brother has children that are extremely bright—two National Merit scholars— whereas my sister is sitting there with this kid that she doesn't know if she's going to get him through high school. But we all suffer with each other for various things. Maybe the one that's really smart isn't real social, and the one's that social . . . I think it's [important] to find the good points in each person and let them enjoy that. I think that's basi- cally the way my parents have raised us. I just don't see . . . I have a lot of cousins that are that way, too. Everybody just enjoys who they are and where we are. I don't see anybody clamoring to get to the top and trying to beat somebody else out or thinking that you have to have this or you're not as good. (Rebecca-33)

Similarity of Experience

The identities of women within their families are informed by similar experiences. While families often seem different from the perspectives of individual members, the women in this study described how similarity was a part of their development and identity. Sisters participated together in family events across time. They shared an interest in understanding, even analyzing their parents. High school years represented a pivotal time for the participation in this shared experience. In adult life, sisters gave each other advice based upon having parallel incidents or experiences.

Sister relationships were distinguished from most friendships because the women shared this common past and parentage. The commonality led one woman to say that her sister was the most important person in her life; another suggested she and the sister had fun together, perhaps too much: "Barb is a lot of fun. When we are getting along, we have a blast together and that's why I've always thought maybe we were too much alike" (Chris-23). Identities were founded upon that commonality. Growth came from understanding a mother's cancer, a father's reaction to his wife's death, and the growing importance of the blood connection over time. A sense of family dysfunction gave way in the face of newly shared experiences that only a family member could understand. This woman described that process:

> I think we need each other. We grew up together. We had very difficult childhoods, and we need that bonding to keep close together for some kind of a grounding for all of us. We've all gone through our own personal trials and tribulations relating to our childhood, and I think it's important we keep together so we can comfort and talk to each other. (Chris-5f)

For at least one woman, her sister's move into high school was central to their sense of shared identity. This transition increased her empathy for her sister. She became more helpful, providing her sister with rides to and from school and advice about class selection and coursework. Old arguments were forgotten as childish skirmishes gave way to shared experiences of adolescence:

> Now that Victoria's older and I'm older . . . it wasn't until just recently we started getting along a lot better. I think it's because she's in high school . . . or is going to be in high school. Now I feel a little more responsible for her. But before, I can't even remember what we used to fight about, but it was constant. (Diane-8)

Helping her sister ease through the entry to high school was significant. That time period when girls are susceptible to ostracizing by other girls or being disappointed in first love was important for these sisters as well. A woman got to know her sisters' friends and developed a greater sense of responsibility for her sister's adjustment. Another woman described comparable inroads during the early college years. Similar school transitions were heralded by the advice of the older sister to the younger. Common activities and interests generated a greater sense of shared identity for the young women as they grew into adulthood.

In adulthood, similar experiences converged, creating even more elements of shared identity. Greater connection between the women occurred and was reinforced by advice from one sister to another. This advice could be mundane or profound. Some women advised their sisters about diets; others talked about childrearing and marriage. Being married and having children was often a part of that similar experience:

> They're [sister and family] coming down now for a couple of weeks this summer, and they'll stay here with their three kids. They have three kids. And her husband is a teacher, and my husband is a teacher. And she's . . . graduated from college in counseling, and we have a real nice time together. We really do . . . She's a good mother, and she's a very domestic person. She stays home with the kids and does a wonderful job with raising her children, so . . . we have a lot of things in common. (Janice-24)

Shared trauma could be a part of that identity as well. One woman understood her sister's newfound widowhood all too well; another revealed a shared history of divorce for three of the four sisters. "She lost her husband . . . all three of the girls—no, our one sister, Virgie, her husband is still living—but Kathy and myself and Diana have all lost our husbands" (Thomasina-80). One woman was shocked when her younger sister revealed a long history of depression, leading to a greater understanding of the family's role in creating it. One woman hoped for resolution, imagining that shared older age and maturity might cause bygones to be bygones. These shared experiences created the context for similar components of identity among the sisters in a family.

Family Roles and Contexts

One sister understood another, in part, by placing her identity in a present and herstorical context. Among other things, the context included portrayal of family roles, residences, occupations, health issues, aging issues, and losses. All of these factors contributed to a sense of the sister as a unique individual. According to one of the women interviewed, one of her sisters struggled with alcoholism, and the family's history of chemical dependency defined her identity. The interviewee said that she feared her sister would become a bag lady and spend all of her time in bars. Such family roles were considered immutable. The roles were created through consistent family labeling and interactions. Some sisters were leaders; others were playmates. Caretakers and natural mothers were described; the absence of these traits was also noted. Moderators emerged from conflicted mother–daughter relationships. "Good children" were identified, but these were not always the parents' favorite child. Sisters were also portrayed as airheads, aunts, travel guides, trophies (fought over by family members), perfectionists, peacemakers, artists, rebels and intellectuals. Some were the hubs of family communication. These roles were created based upon the expectations of the family, but also the expectations of other people important to the family. Here is a sample of these roles and their perceived paths to fruition. One woman described being the carefree sister, while her sister was the responsible mother:

> [T]o a certain extent she envies . . . what I've done with my life in terms of still being single. [I think she sees] different options that it can give you, just the different lifestyle. I think, sometimes, she envies that. (Tammy-15)

Another woman suggested that her role as the family favorite was ironic:

> So there's a really interesting push–pull in our family because Jane's the model child in a sense, but I'm the favorite and get along a lot better [with the rest]. So I don't know; it's just real[ly] interesting. (Andrea-15)

Here is a sister who liked to pretend she was stupid:

> Michelle kind of plays the dumb role to her advantage, I think. I remember one time she's like, "Well, how do I get a smog check?" I'm like, "Look in the phone book? [My sister said,]What do you mean, how do you do it?[I said] Okay, forget it. I'll just do it for you." She's used to doing that, and after a while I kind of caught on to that and went, "You're just doing this because you want something done." And she's like, "Yeah, well, it's worked for twenty-some years. [I] might as well keep it up!" (Brooke-86f)

Peacemaker roles were mentioned in several families:

> She is the one that we all have described as the peacemaker . . . Everybody in the family has contact with her. Although a lot of people in my family get . . . angry, but we all keep in contact with Barb. (Chris-14)

In many cases family roles are mutable with life experience. Some women were able to forsake their family's expectations from childhood and create identities that did not include those expectations. For example, one woman said her sisters were always driving her to achieve and perform academically. In this story, she grows weary of their demands that she continue the role of excellent student:

> [I]f the three of us are together—say, like, if Marilyn is visiting and Susan is there and I am there—those two are fairly competitive with each other. They live similar sorts of lifestyles: Marilyn is a real estate broker and

Susan is a controller. Marilyn recently got married, but prior to that they were both single. They just had . . . a lot more drive to competitive instincts that comes out with each other. Lately I watch them, and it's like I can't even deal with it anymore. It's too much.

I can't keep up. Sometimes when the entire family is together, I feel like I start to disappear. It's just too much effort to try to get heard, because they never stop talking and there is all this competitive energy going on. (Mindy-45 to 47).

For some women, their roles in the family were too tempting to resist. Thus, one woman described her sister's desire to hold onto the airhead role around the family, even though it was no longer part of her personal identity.

One family role has been discussed in a previous chapter but is a significant part of some women's identity. That is the role of caretaker, particularly caretaker for the aging or ill mother. There seemed to be ambivalence about a sister who filled this role. It was appreciated by the other sisters, but sometimes it was envied. Sometimes, the caregiver became controlling of others in the family:

Sometimes Carol becomes "Carolish." She has been the one that has been . . . the caretaker of the family . . . makes sure . . . that people wouldn't fight between each other and so forth. And sometimes, around that, she would become real testy . . . vitriolic, very inflexible in her thought processes, and all the rest the family members—we joked about that with her. And [we] call her on it, and not necessarily just joke, but we'll call her on it: "Carol is being Carolish again." (Jolene-17 and 18)

The recognition of family roles and responsibilities may have been extended to the ways in which one sister acted like the parent of the other. These roles sometimes included a protective stance toward a sister who was deemed more vulnerable than the others. Later in life, those roles could switch, with the younger becoming the protector of the older.

Parenting Between Sisters

Physical protectiveness between sisters was often a part of the role of older sister, yet emotional protectiveness had no such designation. The role of parent substitute could include providing basic assistance, such as food or transportation, for a much younger sister. The role was often assumed at the behest of parents who left one sister in charge. It was also a role that assumed far more significant responsibilities in some cases. One woman discussed her role helping to raise her younger sister:

I remember taking care of Debbie as a youngster, when she wasn't old enough to take care of herself, but I don't remember ever playing with her like I played with my brothers, or doing things even with the family

unit—my sister being part of that . . . Most of the memories I have of her
are being [too much] younger. [We would be] playing football or baseball,
and I don't remember her being part of that. (Tracy-37)

This role of parental assistant or parent in situ was often established in infancy
or childhood, yet it persisted into the adult years. One woman described that
watching her sister struggle was much like watching her child struggle: "With
Brooke I feel almost more like a close friend—upset for her or with her. With
Gina, I feel . . . a lot, in some ways, like a parent feels watching their child going
through difficulty" (Hillary-55 & 56).

The role of substitute parent was also created by family dissolution. When
a father left the home, the mother was sometimes a single parent with few
resources. Older sisters stepped into the role of parent to help the mother in her
attempts to manage the family, particularly if there were many children. One
older sister went to work to help earn money to buy food. These pragmatic needs
were one factor in moving the older sister into a parental role. But the mother's
emotional reaction to an absent father could also make an older sister into a
parent.

Likewise, age differences in the sisters could contribute to the assumption of a
parental role. In this case, the age of the mother, combined with the age of the
older sisters, created such a relationship:

> [Mother] was 42, and so any thought of ever having sisters or brothers
> was kind of out of the question. So . . . we, being 10, could . . . really have
> a comprehension and understood a little more of what was happening.
> So we were really thrilled. We were so excited and went through this
> whole pregnancy with my mother and preparation, etc. for this impend-
> ing birth, and it was a big deal . . . We all helped out with Sybil a lot
> because my mother was older. (Janice-17)

Age was not always the defining criterion for a substitute parent. When the
sister's primary needs were emotional, sometimes younger sisters filled a parental
role. Some younger sisters cared for older sisters who suffered from mental illness
or severe emotional distress. One sister took care of an older sister who had
suffered from depression and an eating disorder in her teenage years. In most
cases these sister–parent roles finally ended.

Women also assumed the role of parent to their sisters when parents were
unavailable because of work-related issues. One woman's parents worked on a
farm in another community and both were gone all day, leaving one sister to care
for the other in their absence. Such instances were rare among the women and,
when mentioned, did seem to relate to a rural agrarian life.

Many women described the sister–parent role as diminishing with time. This
was a welcome change in the relationship, a relief. Sisters became more capable
of relating to each other in a mutually satisfying way. They became peers. They

sometimes functioned as role models for each other but no longer felt the neces sity to be their sister's keeper. One woman said merely, "This is the way it always should have been."

Self–Sister Comparisons

Identity was partly created by comparing the sister and the self. Such comparisons were founded upon many things: characteristics, interests, values, lifestyle, the importance of relationship, the evaluation of others. Sometimes similarity created a sense of shared identity; sometimes difference allowed for a greater sense of connection. These evaluations were based partly upon who excelled and who did not, but generally they were merely a statement of the reasons for the connection's strength or lack of it.

Sisters were compared by others as well as themselves, particularly their parents.

At times the comparison was based upon traits that were passed down from one side of the family or the other.

Some comparisons were based upon academic achievement. Those comparisons might lead to a feeling of being less important to her parents or lower self-esteem; other comparisons had an even more sinister outcome. One woman described her sister as her father's favorite because the younger girl was quieter and less boisterous than she was. She also postulated that this was the reason her sister was molested by him and she was not. The assumed parental comparison was important to her for understanding her own guilt and sadness about her sister's molestation. While women assumed that parents made these comparisons, they were not the only ones. One woman described the recognition of her sister's attractiveness and superior fashion sense, adding that they shared similar mannerisms. Because of this comparison, she admitted trying to emulate her sister's behavior.

As the women compared themselves to their sisters, they also sought to uncover similarities. Similarities in interests, values, perspectives, attributes, tastes, energy level, adventurousness, and activities created depth of connection between sisters. The women talked about the importance of sharing the same perspective about life with their sister. Feeling optimistic and lacking complaint or criticism was a very important bond between sisters with similar attitudes:

> [T]here are also a lot of things that we're similar about . . . The reason for doing what we're doing is to make an investment in ourselves, as well as make an investment in other people . . . Megan teaches, she is a T.A. at Michigan State, and she's always having her professors tell her that she's spending too much time helping her students, but she loves doing it. I can identify with that. She gets real turned on by that, and I can identify with that, so I know what she's talking about. (Jean-53)

Having a nonjudgmental attitude toward others was also significant in the shared optimism between women and their sisters. In this description the woman expounded on her shared outlook with her sister, but part of the comparison was still focused on the difference between them: "Kimberly is not a critical person. I don't think I am either, particularly. Not that I won't talk about somebody, but I will give them the benefit of the doubt . . . I think all of us in our family are that way, but there might be extenuating circumstances for everybody" (Rebecca-14).

Shared values were also important. Women experienced a strong sense of values and often tied that to their shared religious beliefs. This sometimes included going to religious services together, participating in activities provided by the religious institution, or just being aware of each others' faith: "But we all have similar interests and I'd say our similar interests. . . are house, our homes that we make, and we all get into the French motif. We all like that, and family's a primary thing; church is a primary thing. So we have those similarities" (Rebecca-5). Shared values could also be related to the importance of education or the characteristics of a suitable mate. Those values were one reason that a sister relationship was compared to other sibling relationships and found to be stronger. The similarity with a younger sister's personality and temperament were contrasted with the distance one woman felt from her other sister and brother. She also felt more similar to the younger sister than she did to her mother.

One woman suggested that she and her sister were like "one and the same person" (Carla-41f). Another said that she and her sister were friends as well as sisters because of their shared temperament. One closely bonded sister had trouble leaving her adult sister who was suffering; she felt she would not be so conflicted if it were her other sister. Some women felt closer to their sisters throughout life's stages. They identified with each new transition that their sisters faced. For example, they enjoyed similar games, gave similar importance to academic pursuits, examined college experiences, discussed boyfriends, and worried about children. These comparisons all created a greater sense of connection in the sister relationship when evaluated against other relationships.

Differences were also explored and sometimes led to distancing from a sister. The women recognized that some difference was necessary to define separate sister identities, yet they feared their effect on the relationship. Major differences were hard to reconcile. Several women described the distance created by a drug or alcohol addiction. One of them discussed the importance of the substance abuse shared by her and her sister when they were teens. As she grew older she stopped using, and this created a gap in the relationship that could not be spanned.

Many women examined these differences with sisters and found they precluded the kind of relationship they wanted with their sisters. One said that although she would defend her sister "to the death," they had nothing in common (Martha-5). Admitting the same lack of commonality, Martha regretted that they "had no joy together." Anticipating contact with a sister, a third woman described her disappointment as their differences quickly emerged.

Sometimes the differences between sisters were created by their choices or fundamental differences in their lives. Here, the secrecy around a lesbian sister's first relationship was described as creating a temporary separation:

> I don't really feel that the fact of her involvement with that woman affected our relationship. I feel like the fact of her not having told me for so long is what affected our relationship, [be]cause it had been a pretty significant thing in Gina's life for, you know, three to four months before she told me. We've talked about it a lot, and kind of worked it out. (Hillary-29 to 31)

Other issues related to partner transitions were also seen as a difference between sisters. One woman had remarried after a divorce, but her sister was widowed and "too old to remarry," so they no longer shared the common bond of being partnered. Such life transitions created distance, different values, and a different focus in life. This did not always have to create a sense of separation for the sisters, but frequently it did. The differences between sisters consumed a great deal of their narrative about the relationship. Perhaps differences were troubling to them, or they had worked hard to reconcile them. Whatever the reason, the women gave a great deal of detail about the sense of difference and how it created separate identities.

Some felt envious of a sister's gifts; others felt sorry that they had superior talent that cast the sister in an unfavorable light. One woman justified cheating by doing her sister's homework on the basis that she loved school so much and her sister hated it. Sisters were acknowledged as calmer or quicker to anger when compared to one another. Stubbornness was decried; intensity was evaluated. Creativity was examined alongside pragmatism. Some women felt their sisters were more social, while they remained shy. Others remarked that they were less independent. There was also fluidity when understanding these comparisons: the trait or talent may have become less of a differentiating factor over time. Some women described how differences in their youth had made them stronger allies as adults. All acknowledged a developmental path for the comparison itself, with it becoming less important or more rigid over time.

Attempts to understand the differences in how their parents raised them often led sisters to a different perception of their shared herstory. Their perceptions of these shared events shaped their world and their sense of the relationship. At times, a woman reconciled the differences in perception by acknowledging they would not change. Two of the dimensions used to examine the differences in traits between sisters were the dimensions of traditional masculinity and femininity and the dimension of political/religious conservatism versus more of a free-spirit adventurer. One woman called her sister a bigot. Several talked about one of them being a tomboy and having little in common with the feminine interests of the other:

Brooke was athletic. She ran track. That was really all that she was really good in . . . The other sports . . . she really wasn't that good in, but track she was really good in . . . Gina tried but just didn't quite have it, whereas I was always doing something athletic. I was always at a softball game, or a basketball game, or volleyball, or whatever else . . . I was tomboyish, too. And I didn't really have that in common with them. (Hillary-53 and 54)

Another frequently mentioned dimension was related to being driven by ambition versus being carefree. These differences were often recognized by others who compared the sisters, especially teachers.

Sometimes sisters were aligned with characteristics of one branch of the family, while their sisters were aligned with the other. In this case, the woman drew the distinction based upon physical traits with each side of the family:

Physically, we were quite different. I've always taken after my mother's side of the family. My mother was always rather slim and wiry and lots of energy, and my sister Leslie took after my father's side of the family. My father's side of the family always sort of had a little bit of a weight prob-lem, and she was always kind of the plump side. So physically we were quite extreme. (Janice-3)

These family characteristics formed the basis of a comparison that made the sisters different physically, but also seemed to predict their nature, behavior, and compatibility:

Now my sister Leslie and my sister Sybil are like peas in a pod. They are out of the same mold. They both have always had this little weight thing. I mean, they're not obese or anything like that, but just always . . . put on the weight, love the sweets and all the rolls and all the [fattening] stuff . . . They both get real tired, very easily . . . My mother and I have always had a bundle of energy: go, go, and go! So our temperament[s], I guess you would say, are very different. (Janice-22)

In addition, there was an apparent continuum regarding each sister's level of commitment to career, primary relationship, and parenting during her middle years. Greater distance on the continuum seemed to create a greater separation of interests and, potentially, closeness. One woman suggested that her sister was more traditional, with a husband and children, while she was footloose. Differences in career choice also shifted this continuum toward one end or the other:

Actually, we're real different people. I guess that means that the direc-tions in our lives are going [differently] . . . She was trained to be a writer, and that's not what I'm trained to be. Then I'm in a primary relationship with somebody right now, you know, I'm married to somebody, and she's not, so that's what I mean when I say that we're different. (Jean-52)

Having a different relationship status was only one part of this picture. Commonality was also based upon how much each sister valued her primary partner. The significance of that connection could bond the sisters more closely or drive them apart as each identified differently with the role of partner/spouse.

The relative importance of the relationship to significant others could be very different for two sisters. Parents, children, partners, and friends were all mentioned as evidence of the importance placed upon relationships. The relative importance of children, partners, or parents could have been grounds for similarity between the adult sisters. They might have shared similar values about the importance of being a mother. One woman clearly missed being a parent and felt the difference from her sister, who had recently become one. She said, "But I think there are parts of her life that I envy, too. Sometimes I miss not having children. Sometimes I miss that closeness I think you can experience with kids" (Tammy-24 and 25). When a sister was favored by parents, this could create a barrier between the sisters. It could also make the favored sister want to distance herself from her parents for fear of being overwhelmed by them. One woman said her relationship to her parents was better than her sister's because she valued it more. Even when both sisters valued their family relationships, one might emphasize the connection to her primary partner and the other might value the connection to her children more:

[I]f I've been home all the time, then I'd like to go out with my husband alone, but [Kimberly and Tom] don't have that same kind of relationship of going out alone. In fact, he didn't even remember her birthday this last time. So she has a son who has moved back home with them now. He graduated from Whipple College and he has a job now with an auto shop, and so he's living at home. So he took his mother out. Well, I admire her for accepting . . . the way her [life] is, and the way she enjoys it is great. I mean, there's where I see the only differences in the two of us. We both enjoy our kids absolutely. I mean, I hurt for her when Tom doesn't remember or when he doesn't do anything. I mean, it was her 50th birthday! [Laughs] You would have thought . . . She kind of kidded him, saying, "Oh, going to have a party tonight?" He said. "Well, I'm going to work," which he does. He works at night, so there was not a whole lot he could have done, but he could have taken her, sometime. (Rebecca-22 and 23)

The women also differed from their sisters on the importance of friends. For some these friendships were essential, while their sisters did not seem to need them:

But [my mom and Kim] are also living in a different situation, in the Southeast, where everybody knows everybody. Not my sister, Bert. She's in

Minneapolis, but she has her working relationships, and she gets all of her social contacts at work. She has no need to go neighboring. She doesn't have close friends at church, particularly. Because when she comes home, she's totally honed in on her kids. (Rebecca-59)

The continuum formed by the importance of other relationships and roles was another kind of comparison between sisters—one that created a specific identity for each woman.

Other comparisons focused more on individual traits, including intelligence, creativity, and humor. These comparisons seemed to provide documentation of family characteristics that continued in the sisters. The traits may have defined the identity of one sister more clearly than the others. Some sisters wrote, and some liked to read. Some intellectual sisters like to read more; some connective sisters wrote more letters and e-mails to each other. Comparisons were also formed on the basis of the development of relationships at certain times in the women's lives. The sisters evaluated each other regarding the advent of dating relationships. Some began young and were more popular and social; others started later in life. When interviewed, some women listed a whole string of traits and experiences that differentiated themselves from their sisters:

[Jane] was very shy. She had great grades. She was real thin. She ... didn't have many friends growing up. She was Gamma Delta. She met her husband when she was 17 or 18 and married him when she was 20. She and my Mom just had a horrible time when she was an adolescent. (Andrea-9)

When a woman compared herself to her sister and felt she had fewer gifts or talents, she reacted with initial envy or distrust. Sisters may have envied each others' accomplishments based partly upon how their parents felt about those accomplishments in childhood. However, this envy did occasionally give way to appreciation of the difference:

I knew that I was successful, but in different ways. And so, I think, that didn't last very long, but it made me angry for a while that she was so successful . . . I didn't think that I was, but I just was in a different way. And now when she calls me saying, "Michael X [famous musician] called me," I get really excited for her, because I know that's exactly what she wants to do. And I know it's not what I want to do." (Eve-30)

All of these criteria for comparing the self and the sister provided women with a unique sense of identity. Those identities balanced similarity and difference across experiences, traits and life decisions.

Physiology

Sisters share biology and they share "blood." The women commented upon the shared biology of gender, but also of family genetics. They also made it clear that a relationship with a sister was a blood relationship, which took precedence over other relationships, even if the emotional closeness between them was found wanting. One woman noted monthly hormone fluctuations and said she and her sister were similar in mood during those times. "Jackie and I are on the same menstrual cycle, too, so, we're bitchy together. We're both . . . in a bad mood together." (Carla-43)

Blood relationships were compared to non-blood relationships. Interestingly, this was done twice by the women, both times in relation to a primary attachment with a man. One woman said that her husband knew better than to interfere with her sister relationship. Another one shamed her sister for continuing a friendship with an ex-husband of hers:

> But at the time I couldn't handle it, so it [was] like, "Either [him] or [me]" [laughs]. "You chose him or you chose me; after all, I'm blood." I guess I probably gave her an ultimatum. (Sheridan-26f)

Blood was also mentioned in relationship to half-siblings. As Chris stated, "I do have a younger sister in Los Angeles, but she's my half-sister, and even we don't get along" (15f).

(The study did not evaluate sisters who were not full-blooded, so comments about the nature of these half-sisters may have been a product of the research itself.)

Sometimes the blood relationship was the entire reason for the connection, but not always. One woman suggested that she would not be friends with her sister otherwise. Another said her emotional connection to her sister was so strong it would not matter if they were sisters or not—they would still be close. In other cases, the women mentioned the blood relationship to establish mutual responsibility. In this example, it was the basis for coming together to support ailing parents. Brothers and sisters were also defined by their blood connection. A woman described their mutuality with the phrase "all for one, one for all" (Stacey-27).

Sister identity emerged from these comparisons. The abilities of one versus the abilities of another, the roles each held and their importance to them, the perceptions of shared herstory and how they differed, and the characteristics that were unique to each sister defined them. Some were contrasted with their sisters; some were similar. The image that emerges is one of an identity coming into focus slowly, with many complexities, a fair degree of shadow, and some blurred lines all informed by the connection between the sisters.

Factual Information

The final category in this chapter is related to the facts women told to describe their sisters' lives. These facts were both general and specific. The facts were used at different points in the interview to give me a sense of the sister as a person. Therefore, they are included here as a dimension of the sister's identity. Facts about the sister's level of activity, her qualities, marriage, birth of her children, her occupation, health, herstory, geographic location in relation to the sister, birth of grandchildren, and other major life transitions were given as background for the description of events, feelings, and connections with the sister.

The level of sisters' activities varied a great deal. Some described sisters who ran their own businesses. They were involved, sometimes with their husbands or partners, in community and church activities. Occasionally, women worked with their husbands on a family farm. Some were homemakers, primarily focused upon their children. Women held down the home front while husbands were gone for business reasons. Changes across generations became clear as women described the introduction of new technologies that changed their lives and those of their sisters. One of the older women talked about the arrival of their combines and how it affected her sister's family life: her younger sister spent much time with her when her husband was gone harvesting, until the combines arrived: "But I think it was only a year or two 'til they got the combines, and then [of] course he'd just go with the combine, and the harvest didn't last near so long as it did in the earlier days" (Thomasina-57).

Family life was also described with many facts. The number of sisters a woman had, each sister's successive partners, and the number of their children and grandchildren were all covered during the interview. Suggestions of difficulties were presented as facts. One woman's sister had an ill daughter; another had lost a child. Confusing relationships were created by one sister when she married her daughter's father-in-law, making her the young woman's mother and mother-in-law. The women in the study felt a need to explain such anomalies to make their sisters more fully seen during the interview.

A chronology of the sister's moves was sometimes given, often described in relation to the geographic location of the woman describing it. The nature of the sister's life transitions in those locations was described. A child might have been born in this town; a marriage might have lasted for 50 years in that one. Sisters moved because of their partners or husbands, their work or careers. Some left the family home and returned; others moved away and never came back. Such transitions were also important in defining the sister connection and the opportunity for contact.

In addition to other facts, many women mentioned religious affiliation as a part of their sister's identity. For two women in the study the religious beliefs shared with a sister were a source of strength and comfort, on a daily basis and in times of crisis. These two women discussed the importance of shared beliefs, shared activities, and shared values. One said she did not understand how anyone could survive without a religious identification:

> We're Christian people . . . and we marched to a different drummer. I mean, they just do . . . We have resources that the average person who is not a Christian, they don't know about, and they miss out [on] so much. When you're a Christian you can make things work, with the Lord's help. (Stacey-42)

Struggling with the loss of her husband and their mother, these sisters found comfort in their shared faith—another important part of their identity.

Conclusion

Identity flows from intimacy within the sister connection. The sense of self is defined in relation to the sister's presence or absence. It is as if the journey toward identity begins in lofty ideals and flows down the mountain, negotiating a unique path by circumventing the obstacles around which it must flow. Some obstacles, like boulders, are hardened and immoveable, altering the direction that must be taken. Other obstacles give way and can merely be towed downstream along a newly defined course. Obstacles may be created by the sister connection or sometimes are a natural diversion, providing a new tributary defined by the self. Trauma runs rapidly and dangerously, threatening the safety and security of the self. The rapid pace is managed initially through quickly learned strokes, often without reflection; but trauma, shared with the sister, may pool into dark depths and offer the chance for recovery and respite. Shared joy and celebration provide brief eddies, a way to move out of life's course and find a different aspect of the self— more playful and relaxed—before merging again with the continuous journey downstream to a greater understanding of the self and of the sister.

PART TWO

EXPANSION OF OUR UNDERSTANDING

8

Sisters of Difference

"They resemble us just enough to make all their differences confusing, and no matter what we choose to make of this, we are cast
in relation to them our whole lives long.
                                                        Susan Scarf Merrell (1997, p. 8)

While phenomenology has provided a clear understanding of the essence of sisters
as portrayed by the women in my research, it seemed important to acknowledge
the context of some sisters' lives not represented. At first, this seemed contradictory, as phenomenology purported to engage in the uncovering of universal
essences. However, hermeneutic analysis has been used to provide an integration
of the findings of phenomenological research with the greater literature. In my
research, a hermeneutic interpretation had the potential to add a greater texture
by exploring identities that may have created great disparity between the experiences of sisters in any particular family. Here, that texture was added by including ways that sisters differ from one another within the same family based upon
identifying dimensions that challenge the similarity between sisters in specific
ways. The research literature suggested that disabled and able-bodied sisters
might have these differences, as might lesbian and heterosexual sisters. Such
strong identifiers were not fully represented among my participants and have
been analyzed here by comparing my research themes systematically to those
gleaned from the research literature.

There are always differences between sisters, yet some are more clearly defined
by cultural demands and traditions than others. Such differences in sexual orientation or disability have had the potential to create strong disparities between
sisters. They have also separated women from their families and often made
women seek artificially created substitute families. These separations have been
merely pragmatic (as when a woman needs accommodations in her living environment) or have been purely emotional (as when one sister's religious beliefs have
not allowed her to recognize her sister's partner as a member of the family). The
differences have sometimes created an opportunity for enhanced intimacy and
closeness when sisters have talked honestly about the differences. Some women
manage to maintain close connections across these identity differences despite
cultural reactions that may have caused one to experience more discrimination

211

and prejudice than the other. Strong differences in identity and community have sometimes enhanced the sister connection. Such variations in adaptation to profound differences have formed a backdrop for the ever-changing narrative of sisters' lives.

Differently Abled Sisters

The relationship between disabled and non-disabled siblings has been explored more than any other sibling difference. The importance of being raised with a sister who has special needs creates unique family dynamics and sister demands that have caught the attention of theorists and researchers in psychology for over six decades. The first articles and book chapters appeared in the early 1950s. Senapati and Hayes (1988) documented this history and the methodological problems they found. According to those authors, most research examined only the effects of the disabled sibling on the non-disabled sibling but did not evaluate the effects of the able-bodied sibling on her brother or sister. The focus of most articles has been upon the negative effects of the relationship; the positive outcomes of having disabled children in a family have not usually been considered. Many research articles have failed to integrate their findings into existing conceptual or theoretical models. These problems were consistent through 1988, but many have been addressed since the Senapati and Hayes article was published. It is clear from examining the literature that many authors have failed to address the effects and perceptions of having a disabled sibling throughout the lifespan. Still fewer have examined gender differences and the specific effects of disability between sisters.

How have children understood the abilities and disabilities that exist in a family? It has been documented that this understanding changes over time. The perceptions of children who have a sibling with a disability have altered as they have grown up. Very young children have given explanations for impairment that were not factual; for example, they may have thought their sibling was disabled because he or she was bad or naughty (Stalker & Connors, 2003). Some siblings described their disabled sister or brother as different, but they did not feel the difference was negative. Most, however, were concerned that their disabled sister experienced prejudice and worried about how that prejudice would affect her (Stalker & Connors, 2003). Many children feared they, too, would develop the disability, even if there was no basis in fact for this worry (Bank & Kahn, 1982b). As children grew older the facts started to emerge for them and siblings developed a more accurate representation of disability and the sources of such differences.

The reactions of people in the environment helped to shape these feelings and perceptions toward a disabled sibling. In an evaluation of disability between sisters, one article suggested that older siblings—looking back on childhood—were aware of stigma toward their disabled sister (McGraw & Walker, 2007). Sometimes this stigma resulted in sisters being seen as exceptional, which had negative connotations for some women. Stalker and Connors (2003) found that children's perceptions of their disabled siblings were shaped by the way that others perceived those siblings. Children attempted to normalize what others saw as abnormal. Some sisters have found that activism against cultural bias helped to reconcile conflicting emotions about disability. However, the type of disability made a difference in this reconciliation.

Factors related to specific disabilities have made them easier or more difficult for sisters to handle. The age of onset made a difference. When a young sister had a disability early in childhood or from birth, the other sisters adjusted to this fact as a part of the family history. When an older sibling became disabled, family structure and roles had to be realigned, creating a disruption that was more difficult to manage. The chronicity and degree of difficulty in managing the disability created ripples in the adaptation to living with a disabled sibling (Bank & Kahn, 1982b). The "degree of embarrassment" (Bank & Kahn, 1982, p. 235) associated with a specific disorder also affected the ability to handle the emotional and practical consequences of sibling disability. Several types of disabilities have been evaluated by researchers, and their work has given a clearer picture of specific differences based on specific abilities.

These specific studies have usually included developmental disabilities or mental retardation in siblings as a comparison group for non-disabled sibling adjustment. One study compared the relationships between three groups of sibling pairs: siblings when one had autism, one was intellectually disabled, or none had disabilities. There was a lot of variation within groups, but the between-groups differences were not significant. This suggests, but does not prove, that the type of disability does not determine the effects on the sister relationship. In the study, the relationships between siblings were highly positive overall (McHale, Sloan, & Simeonsson, 1986).

More recent research developments have suggested a major difference between developmental disabilities and mental illness in a sibling, especially for sisters. Siblings with developmental disability were more likely to have strong emotional connections with non-disabled siblings than siblings with schizophrenia (Pruchno, Patrick, & Burant, 1996). A comparison of siblings with mental illness and siblings with intellectual deficits found different caregiving expectations (Greenberg et al., 1999). The age of onset for such disorders created differing opportunities for adjustment. Adult siblings who cared for siblings with mental retardation were socialized to do this during childhood; those with mentally ill sisters were not socialized to care for them as adults. When compared to earlier research, there was a major difference in Greenberg's study. The majority of the research participants were women, so this study suggested some gender significance. When only sisters were considered, there was an expectation of caregiving to intellectually impaired sisters, but not to mentally ill ones.

What other roles have been expected of sisters? How have their lives changed when a sibling was disabled? These questions have been the focus of some research interest. In contrast with researchers' biases noted by Senapati and Hayes (1988), most brothers and sisters seemed to focus on the positive effects of the disability. The participants in several studies have described developing compassion from a young age (Bank & Kahn, 1982b, chapter 9; McGraw & Walker, 2007). The researchers found that sisters and brothers had more responsibilities, but only after their mothers assessed that an older sibling was capable of empathy and "negotiation skills" (Senapati & Hayes, 1988, p. 108). Likewise, the participants suggested that closer relationships within the family were generated because of caring for a disabled sister or brother (McGraw & Walker, 2007). They reported that the existing family closeness provided a template for their involvement in the care of a disabled sib (Greenberg et al., 1999).

Another research theme described how sisters seemed to "minimize the personal consequences" of having a sibling with a disability (McGraw & Walker, 2007, p. 491). This consensus was supported by McHale and Pawletko (1992) who compared siblings who had a disabled brother or sister to those who did not have any disabled siblings. Their findings described the ability of non-disabled siblings to overlook the favored status of a disabled child. In families without disabilities, there was little acceptance of a child who was favored by the parents. Older children expressed the idea that "fairness does not always mean being treated the same" (McHale & Pawletko, p. 80). These comparative studies have created a more detailed view of the way that sisters deal with the abilities and disabilities of their siblings.

Sisters without disabilities have not been naïve about the effects on their lives. According to McGraw and Walker (2007), women described "personal hardships against a backdrop of benefits, highlighting the complex nature of these connections" (p. 491). Some children and women were more troubled by the nature of the sibling relationship when it occurred against a background of disability. They complained about limits, losses, and frustrations created in their own lives (McGraw & Walker, 2007; Stalker & Connors, 2003). In numerous studies, the identity of the non-disabled sibling was influenced. For example, just the label of "non-disabled sibling" created a specific set of identity characteristics that would not otherwise have been present. The identity of the disabled sister is also affected by having a sibling without disabilities (Bank & Kahn, 1982b; McGraw & Walker, 2007; Stalker & Connors, 2003). Thus, the identity of one sister may have created a unique identity for the others.

Likewise, the family relationships may have developed in multiple ways, creating some unique and not-so-unique roles and interactions. Most researchers have subscribed to the theory that parents assign family roles to specific children early in life. In families with disabled children, the roles assigned by parents have been created with a consideration of the differential abilities of the children. Non-disabled children have often been placed in dichotomous roles—compassionate helper to or isolated from the disabled child (Bank & Kahn, 1982b). The siblings with impairments have been described as favored or treated as scapegoats (Stalker & Connors, 2003). When a disabled sibling had difficulties with her parents, sometimes a sister or brother mediated between the parents and that child. Likewise, the "well" child might have striven to be perfect in order to limit the stress on parents created by the disability of a sister or brother (Bank & Kahn, 1982b).

Enmeshment—a family's potential for suffocating closeness—has developed between sisters with and without developmental disability (Bank & Kahn, 1982a). Although not confirmed by research, many authors have expressed a concern that such enmeshment might keep all sisters from developing their unique identities. This concern has been rooted in a worry that one daughter's emotional reserves will be used to benefit the disabled sister rather than herself. Thus, the complicated expectations of a sister who is also a caregiver have been difficult to untangle.

Even though many disabled sisters have become independent, the literature has focused primarily on caregiving issues. Aging mothers have often relinquished primary caregiving for a sibling with disability to a sister (McGraw & Walker, 2007; Orsmond & Seltzer, 2000). Bias against disabilities within the larger cultural context has not always been supportive of the caregiver role. A nonsupportive culture may turn a sister into an activist against discrimination related to disability. Yet most of the research is presented in a non-gender-specific way, as if brothers were just as likely to fill the caregiving and the activist roles. A few studies have examined the specific roles expected for sisters. McHale and Pawletko (1992) documented no main or significant gender effects when evaluating older and younger siblings in households with versus without disabled children. The only finding was a tendency for older girls to be "more involved in chores and conversations" with their mothers than younger children or male children were (p. 72). This study did not focus specifically on disability, but this finding emerged as part of a larger study on the evaluation of favored children in a family. A contrast emerged from a review article by Eriksen and Gerstel (2002). They tracked the gender-specific nature of caregiving expectations, documenting a 48-year history of expectations that, for sisters, are quite different than those for their brothers. Three aspects of caregiving differentiated the sisters from the brothers: they gave more care overall, they gave different kinds of care, and they were more likely to give practical support (childcare, grocery shopping, etc.) than brothers. The significance of gender was empirically supported by other researchers (Greenberg et al., 1999) who demonstrated that sisters were expected to care for a disabled sister more often than a brother was. Perhaps the family expectations for this caregiving have actually resulted in more caregiving between sisters because there has been a stronger emotional connection between sisters than to a developmentally disabled brother (Pruchno, Patrick, & Burant, 1996). Emotional connection may form the foundation for the provision of practical support from one sister to another (Eriksen & Gerstel, 2002). Certainly, the gender-specific family expectations have played a role as well.

Some other things seem to influence the caregiving role between sisters. Age, race, and social class have all been evaluated (Eriksen & Gerstel, 2002). Race has not seemed to differentiate the willingness to give. Women of higher means have been more likely to give support, perhaps because they have had the financial ability to give practical support or the leisure time to be present. Women at midlife have been more likely to provide support if they do not have children at home. Other caregiving responsibilities have been likely to push or pull a midlife woman toward providing instrumental support for her sister (Greenberg et al., 1999). Aging mothers who cared for disabled adults have said that their non-disabled children did not provide functional support. The mothers acknowledged that sisters did supplement the mother's caregiving by providing emotional support to their sister or brother (Pruchno, Patrick, & Burant, 1996). This finding was contradicted, however, by Eriksen and Gerstel (2002), whose review suggested that adult siblings gave some kind of care to all siblings, disabled or not. The vast majority of siblings gave support within the past year; others gave as often as once a month. What's more, the care was perceived as reciprocal regardless of ability. In an attempt to reconcile the contradictions, it is worth noting that other authors found older women have been less likely to give support to their sisters, perhaps because of physical limitations on their ability to do so or because of their geographic distance from the sister (Pruchno, Patrick, & Burant, 1996). Clearly sisters have provided care to their disabled siblings. This provision of emotional and practical support is often reciprocal but not universal.

Disabled and able-bodied sisters have helped to construct each other's lives and identities. In early life those influences have seemed to be magically understood. As an able-bodied child grew, she came to a more factual basis for her understanding and may have had many demands from the family. In addition, she may have developed an enhanced compassion for others. Maturity has found sisters attempting to reconcile caregiving roles within the family—for children of her own, her disabled sister, and aging parents. Many of these roles have been conflicted, and the stresses on a woman's identity and life have become numerous. Yet there has been little discovered about the sister who removes herself from such responsibilities, and even less about how the disabled sister is affected by these roles. In older life, sisters have been less able to provide care. Different life stages provide life course choices in relation to the disabled sister and the able bodied one. Some women are likely to have moved away from the family to avoid the responsibility of caring for a disabled child; others may stay close to the parental home just to take on that responsibility. Maturity may lead some to regret the decision they have made in relation to their connection to a disabled sister in later years. Others are likely to feel good about the decision to be available to take a role of support to the disabled sister. In the process they are likely to reap a different kind of sister connection that is mutually beneficial.

Lesbian and Heterosexual Sisters

Sexual orientation adds another variable to the sister relationship. The existing literature has provided several themes about this difference. Differences in sexual orientation have affected the sister relationship, the mother–daughter–sister relationship, and many relationships within the extended family. Most families have expected their children to be heterosexual (Mize, Turell, & Meier, 2004), so research has centered on the disillusion of that expectation. The process of coming out or disclosing sexual orientation within the family has been the subject of such research (see Green, 2000, for a review). Disclosure of lesbian orientation by one daughter has had multiple effects in the family. According to Mize et al. (2004), negative parental responses that varied "from disapproval to profound distress" could result in a sister relationship that was stronger and more emotionally supportive. Some lesbian women have expressed gratitude for the support of a sister in the face of parental rejection. When a disclosure was made, the family system has sometimes become divided into two groups: those who knew and those who do not know (Crosbie-Burnett et al., 1996). Occasionally, a sister has been placed in the position of keeping secrets from others in the family out of respect for her lesbian sister's wishes or to protect her from family rejection. These secrets have created in-group and out-group divisions, which have caused discomfort when the groups are mixed at family functions and events. Heterosexual sisters have also been mediators, giving advice to their lesbian sisters about how to disclose and to the parents about how handle the disclosure. For some women, the process of adjusting to "finding out" (Beeler & DiProva, 1999) required additional time because of their parents' negativity. A sister's ability to stay connected to an "out" lesbian sister has been hampered by those changing dynamics in the family and by the reactions of others.

The decision to disclose her sexual orientation to family has most often begun with the selection of one trusted family member. Mize et al. (2004) concluded that most research has focused on parental reactions, and siblings have seldom been mentioned. They discovered that when the sister was told first, this initial disclosure and the communication about it usually led to greater emotional closeness between the women. In telling any family member, a lesbian woman may have been afraid of disappointing her family by being different (Mize & Pinjala, 2002; Oswald, 2000). Some have expressed stronger feelings: one of Mize's participants suggested she experienced the "pain of feeling isolated, crazy and very different" (Mize et al., 2004, p. 3). Most often mothers and sisters have been told before fathers and brothers, since there has been a general assumption that heterosexual women are more supportive of sexual minorities than heterosexual men (Oswald, 2002). Green (2000) summarized the previous literature about disclosure and concluded that 62% to 72% of lesbians have come out to their siblings, roughly equal to those who are out to their mothers (62% to 69%) but much higher than those who are out to their fathers (39% to 55%). This percentage has been quite different based upon specific ethnic roles and expectations.

Among some Asian Americans, siblings were much more likely to be told than either parent. The majority of gays and lesbians who said they were Asian American were out to at least one of their siblings; only 27% were out to a parent (Green, 2000, p. 261). Green concluded that social support from other sources may be more important or necessary, especially when family and siblings responses had been very homophobic or detrimental. This awareness was also reflected in Hancock's (1995) advice to her therapy clients. She suggested selective disclosure for managing potential negative reactions by some family members; she has encouraged lesbians who have "difficult" families to tell only one person and ask him or her to keep the secret. Hancock mentions siblings as potential trusted confidants within the family.

Once told, heterosexual sisters have experienced a process of adjustment and identity change. A family once viewed as typical may have been redefined (Crosbie-Burnett et al., 1996). This redefinition may have created a loss of status for the family, and the sister may have developed strong feelings about that loss. In an interesting extension of the coming-out process, the heterosexual sister had to decide whom she would tell. In considering this, she may have wondered whom her sister would want to tell. In some small research studies, sisters have given details about their own adjustment to a lesbian sister's disclosure (Oswald, 2002). Some of their reactions are unique to this minority culture. Usually sisters share a minority culture, but when a sister has devoted much time and attention to the lesbian, gay, bi-sexual and transgendered (LGBT) community, the other sister may have felt left out or ostracized, creating a sense of distance between them (Crosbie-Burnett et al., 1996). Some sisters have admitted questioning their own sexual orientation based upon the lesbian sister's disclosure. This has been especially true if the disclosure was about bisexual identity (Oswald, 2000). Some unique aspects of sisters' relationships and closeness have been created when one sister comes out to another.

The age of disclosure has also made a difference in the sister relationship. The effects of disclosure have been handled differently based upon the developmental level of the heterosexual sister. "Adolescent siblings are likely to struggle with identity and intimacy issues" (Crosbie-Burnett et al., 1996, p. 401). Younger children may not understand the significance of the information and may not be told, thus making them an unintentional part of the out-group within a family. Secrets kept from younger sisters have often created dishonesty and suspicion. Some family therapists have suggested that clinical work with children and families should provide support to the heterosexual family members, including sisters who have lesbian siblings.

Sisters, whether heterosexual or lesbian, have relied upon each other. In the narrative studies completed by Mize and colleagues, heterosexual sisters were often an important component of the social support for lesbian women (Mize & Pinjala, 2002; Mize et al., 2004). In focusing on the process of disclosure and adjustment, the literature has been short-sighted. Laird recognized this as early as 1996, when she suggested that psychotherapists needed to understand the complexity of relationships between lesbians and their families of origin. In some ways, the designers of research and the writers of theory have missed the point. According to Laird, lesbian and heterosexual sisters are role models for each other. They keep some secrets and share others. They participate together in family rituals and are evaluated for that participation. Their kinship ties are not well understood or ethnographically explored. National survey results from Bryant and Demian (1994) suggested that siblings rank after LGBT friends, LGBT organizations, heterosexual friends, and co-workers as sources of support. Which siblings? Were brothers and sisters the same? Generally surveys have not differentiated between parents and siblings either, lumping parents and sisters together in the description of family support (e.g., Rostosky et al., 2004).

The complexity of the relationship between lesbian and heterosexual sisters has been partly illuminated by the way sisters include each other in their lives and rituals. Oswald (2002) evaluated inclusion of partners in family celebration rituals. The survey suggested that gay and lesbian persons with partners were more likely to have their partner included if they were "more visible" and parents and siblings were "more supportive" (p. 432). Inclusion was not affected by the visibility to extended family members. Thus the gatekeeper status of siblings has been acknowledged, and in this study the difference between sisters and brothers was not clear. Beeler and DiProva (1999) examined that gatekeeper role for the sisters' own families. They suggested that some sisters work with their husbands to gain specific support for a lesbian sister, including the introduction of a lesbian sister and her partner to others; disclosure to their children is also discussed by the couple. Many lesbian women have heard the phrase, "Do you want me to tell _____?" Sisters have asked such a question so they may follow their sisters' wishes; sometimes they engage in "stigma management" for the sister (Beeler & DiProva, 1999, p. 452). This process of dealing with others' bias about the lesbian community is a significant and specific type of support. Also related to disclosure, stigma management recognizes the complex and ongoing awareness of prejudice in the lesbian sister's life. In these ways, the inclusion of sisters runs in both directions—disclosure by the lesbian sister and stigma management by the heterosexual sister.

Like many other issues in the sister relationship, the relationship between a mother and her daughters has been affected by the sexual orientation of all. Similarities and differences with mothers have been evaluated in relation to sister relationships. Some of these have been the result of orientation; others have just been about generational differences that create closeness between the sisters. The relationship with the mother and her reactions have often defined the relationship between the sisters (Mize et al., 2004). When the mother has been accepting, a reluctant sister may be able to move through her own ambivalence. When a mother has not been accepting or integrative of the lesbian couple, however, the sister may compensate for the mother's reaction. In a third possible reaction, a mother who is rejecting may have required a similar response from her hetero-sexual daughter in order to continue their close connection. In some cases, a lesbian sister was helped to set generational boundaries by her heterosexual sister. She and the sister bonded as age peers as well as sisters. Keeping the parents in their own generational space helped to solidify and create respect for the lesbian partner relationship (Mize et al., 2004). Mothers and daughters struggled to find the unique method for having the three-way relationship. Sometimes a pair has formed, excluding the other. This exclusion has occasionally followed generational lines, or it may have developed based upon similarity in sexual orientation. A third possibility is that it has followed compassionate acceptance—one person was left out because the other two have bonded to create a compassionate and accepting relationship regardless of similarity or difference.

In some families sisters with different sexual orientation face bias and pre-judice of another nature—one based upon gender. The stories of lesbians and their sisters have been negotiated in a family context with its own potential for oppression on the basis of gender and sexual orientation. This potential affects the telling of family history from the point of view of two women, raised in the same family with different sexual orientations (Mize et al., 2004).

English (1996) described her personal story, replete with gender differen-ces across several generations of homophobia. She documented the difference between her heterosexual sister and herself and tied those differences to early childhood. They first appeared as opposing interests in dress and activities. The author wanted to be like her father and would give her sister any gifts she received that were connected to femininity. Her first sexual experiences were with her sister's best friend. The two hid from her sister, slept together during sleepovers, and lied about time they spent together. The relationship was not disclosed until years later. In this family the father's own gay identity emerged when he devel-oped AIDS. Thereafter, the heterosexual daughter avoided her father. That daugh-ter and her mother denied the gay identity of the father even when it was revealed to them. English became the focus of her sister and mother's rage when they could not direct it toward the ill gay father. She described her sister's unwillingness to let her son visit or travel to spend vacations with the sister and her partner. All of these family reactions were tied to gender and sexual orientation. In this case the prejudice was more easily vented at the lesbian daughter (who had become very open about her life) rather than the gay father (who remained secretive despite his revelations).

Mize et al. (2004) documented another aspect of gender discrimination within the family. Their participants suggested that differences in gender expecta-tions were experienced by both heterosexual and lesbian sisters. A generational influence played a part: women born after 1970 felt they had fewer gender-biased expectations. The majority of all participants, however, expressed awareness of limitations due to engendered roles and attitudes in the family. This narrative research reflected the complexity of the relationships between lesbian and hetero-sexual sisters differentiating their shared and conflicting values. In completing this narrative research, Mize, et al. accomplished some of the objectives set forth in Laird (1996) when she suggested a thorough ethnographic study was necessary to fully understand the relationships between lesbian women and their sisters.

Similarity of values between sisters seemed as significant as their differences in sexual orientation. Beeler and DiProva described one sister relationship where both the heterosexual and lesbian sister shared the need for privacy—a value that made the adjustment to sexual orientation easier. The authors' narrative study included only one sister among all family members who were adjusting to lesbian disclosure. Similarity of values also emerged when dealing with cultural bias. One woman decided to terminate her affiliations with businesses that had a history of lesbian or gay discrimination. This decision was based upon a social outing with her lesbian sister and consideration of her comfort (Mize & Pinjala, 2002). Another values issue affected the frequency of contact between sisters. Women found their own unique balance between the families from which they came and the families they had created. Sometimes this balance created struggles between sisters when they found a different way to balance the two (Mize et al., 2004). Sister relationships seemed to continue despite these struggles, and several authors commented upon the strength and resilience of the connection.

Resilience was also strengthened by the challenges of difference in sexual orientation (Mize et al., 2004). In a testament to this resilience, Laird (1996) described an interaction between a heterosexual mother and daughter. During the interaction, the mother was judging the lesbian sister's sexual orientation. Rather than joining her mother, the heterosexual sister used this opportunity to confront her mother's tendency to be judgmental with both daughters. Such resilience has also been present in the need to understand the sister. Beeler and DiProva described the heterosexual sisters' need to place their memories in context. Many have attempted to create a "coherent narrative" (p. 452) of the past, describing and rewriting the presumption of heterosexuality in the original sister narrative.

A similar rewriting takes place when the competitive strivings among young sisters were abandoned in favor of greater emotional closeness. This seemed to exist across geographic distance (Mize et al., 2004). Laird also suggested a type of resilence when she described families with lesbian sisters as bi-cultural. Those families had to negotiate the difference between living in heterosexual culture and living in lesbian culture. For example, a sister with close friendship networks might have to decide whether to spend the high holidays with her Jewish family or with a chosen family close to her. Such choices reflect the cultural tension similar to those occurring in cross-racial or bi-ethic families with differing traditions for hoiday celebrations. The navigation of this must occur for the lesbian woman but may also be negotiated by the supportive heterosexual sister Families who are capable of negotiating bi-culturalism are often capable of superseding sexual orientation politics (Laird, 1996).

Lesbian life courses often include a conscious decision about whether to have children. When a lesbian woman made a conscious choice to have a child, her sister's role in the child's life became important. Even though sisters' acceptance was not considered separately, Gartrell et al. (1996) traced the important role that families of lesbian women have played in the adjustment and acceptance of children within the lesbian family. During Gartrell, et al.'s research, some lesbian women expressed fear that no one in their extended families would accept their children. Exploration of relationships between children in lesbian families and their adult female relatives were explored in another study (Patterson, Hart, & Mason, 1998). Thirty-two percent of children in the study had at least annual contact with female relatives who were not their grandparents. When family members had more frequent contact, children had fewer behavioral problems. Patterson, Hart and Mason's research concludes that the connection of blood relationships seems important in the amount of time siblings participated in their niece's or nephew's life. The authors found a significant difference in the integration of siblings and parents of the biological mother versus those of the co-parenting lesbian partner. Since the research was correlational rather than causative, it is impossible to be certain how the factors were inter-connected. It is possible that a woman was more likely to have a child if she felt assured that the sister and family would support her decision.

The complexity of the connection between lesbian women and their sisters seemed to have an effect on other relationships, within and outside the family. Developmentally, the sister relationship may help to create an imprint for adult intimacy whether that intimacy is with a male partner or a female one. For example, a sister's compassion may have been an important quality desired in a lesbian partner, or a sister's emotional presence may have been an important quality desired in a male partner. In addition, the connection to sisters may have created a desire for close female friendships; a herstory with sisters has sometimes enhanced those friendships. Sometimes sisters, especially twins, have felt an emotional competition with a sister's partner or husband (Mize et al., 2004).

In other ways, the sister relationship may have generally enhanced the contribution each sister has made in the larger world. Berzon (2004) discussed the role her own lesbianism played in the support her sister, a psychologist, gave to students on a university campus. Other authors have acknowledged the important role played by a sister-in-law as either accepting or rejecting of their lives (Raphael & Meyer, 2000). In this case example, the lesbian woman remained close to a niece, even though her brother and sister-in-law had not integrated her and her lifelong partner into their lives. The sister-in-law mimicked the reaction of her in-laws and husband—rejecting her sister-in-law's relationship. The knowledge of such effects has been limited by the lack of more comprehensive studies with many women. Yet these narrative approaches do give a window into the possibilities of the strength and complexity of the sister connection across the sexual orientation difference.

Conclusions

To some, the pairing of sexual orientation and disability in one chapter may seem odd. Yet the relationships between heterosexual and lesbian sisters have mirrored the differences between disabled and able-bodied sisters. Both relationships have reflected a difference that emerged for women and had to be integrated differently—differences that could occur at different life stages. Often disability was present from birth, while the awareness of lesbian sexuality did not fully emerge until at least adolescence. Yet there have been times when a disability occurred much later in life and affected the relationship then. Likewise, sometimes a young girl's sexual orientation becomes clear from a very young age and the sister has experienced the difference between them without a clear name for what it was. The disabled and non-disabled sisters may have found their lives and identities defined by being one or the other; similarly, the lesbian and heterosexual sisters may have been defined by their difference. Yet each set of sisters has shared far more similarity than difference based upon their family connection, genetic material, and primary ethnic or cultural context. Developmental stages have affected the relationship and seen it change. The role of caregiving seemed to emerge for sisters whether one was disabled or not. And the role of confidant was often required by sisters, whether the issue was coming out or something else. Sisters have often been called upon as confidants and helpers. These differences seem essential to the nature of the sister connection. Do they really define the relationship more than other differences? To truly understand the importance of these identities, it seemed important to compare them to the findings of my original research and to ascertain the significance that might be unique to ability/disability and sexual orientation. These comparisons have been drawn through a hermeneutic process in Chapter 10.

9

Cross Cultural, Racial, and Ethnic Perspectives on Sisters

The most authentic thing about us is our capacity to create, to overcome, to endure, to transform, to love and to be greater than our suffering.

Ben Okri (1999[1])

There is always a danger of stereotyping ethnic or racial families. The diversity that graces the United States and the perspectives of immigrant sisters vary in astoundingly different ways. With that variation come some general truths about sisters within ethnic groups and from the same nation. Like the sisters in my research, the stories of these sisters represent all potential combinations of closeness, distance, love, absence, and estrangement.

Sisters of African Ancestry

Much of what I know or have learned about sisters in the Black communities of the United States has not been apparent in the theoretical or research literature of psychology. Like many other kinds of sister relationships, those between Black sisters have been diminished, ignored, or combined with the relationship between brothers and sisters. In distilling the information for this chapter, I found it most helpful to expand upon what has been written and question what might be true for sisters of African ancestry living in the United States.

Black sisterhood has been described as powerful. The interconnected women in a Black family have created a model for the development of connection and community. Their efforts have helped to shield children from prejudice and discrimination. Aunts and cousins have become part of a network that is dependable and extended across time and distance, providing child care, social support, shared financial resources, and sometimes shared living arrangements (Ugarriza, 2006). Many have fictive relationships in which every closely held woman is a sister,

[1] from Mental Fight by Ben Okri used by permission of The Marsh Agency Ltd.

an aunt, or a grandmother to those in her kinship circle (Boyd-Franklin, 2006). This community or urban village has helped to raise Black girls and has provided a strong model for the development of interwoven lives and stories. Young girls have learned to count upon many mothers and sisters to hold them, groom them, and help them achieve and to provide examples for how they might live. In many ways a Black woman's strength has been fostered by an interdependent and complex web of female relationships, of which the sister relationship, blood or fictive, has been a strong part.

Family Structure and Sisters' Roles

The family structure and values associated with recent U.S. immigrants of African ancestry have been quite different from those whose families have lived in the United States for generations and have survived slavery. The importance of slavery, the relationship of White and Black persons, a culture of hatred toward Black women and men, and the development of strong ethnic identity have shaped the experiences of families and sisters who have been in the United States for many years. Language, translocation, loss of national identity, late experiences with prejudice, and the specific national religious and cultural values are predominant for recent immigrants. Thus Black American women are made up of many subcultures, and the relationships of sisters within those subcultures have developed in significantly different ways.

Family structure and living arrangements have changed for Black women throughout their developmental history (Boyd-Franklin, 2006). As young girls, Black sisters may have been raised in families that encouraged them to provide for each other, care for each other, and groom each other. The older sister has often been encouraged to supervise the younger sister, functioning as a second mother at one moment and a playmate in the next. Such responsibility has often been referenced with language that diminishes its importance and pathologizes the role. The *parentified child* has been a concern to family therapists. As part of an extended family kinship network, these roles have often had a positive effect, giving an older sister the opportunity to develop "responsibility, competence and autonomy" (Hines & Boyd-Franklin, 2003, p. 91). Parentified children have developed partly because of single-parent families. These roles have developed intentionally or because the parent was not responsible enough, and the older girl has taken the initiative to fill in for her mother. Older girls in such a family have become overburdened in parenting their parents (Boyd-Franklin, 2006; Hines & Boyd-Franklin, 2003). The opportunity to be a mother to a sister has not been unique to the Black single-parent family. With it have come unique opportunities and some potential burdens.

In adolescence, older sisters have often been encouraged to set an example for their younger sisters; sometimes this example is positive and sometimes it is negative. High-achieving and socially active sisters may have led the way for younger sisters to follow in their footsteps. This role may have been very important if their mother did not have the opportunity to succeed and could not be such a model for academic achievement herself. Drugs and promiscuity or straying from tightly held spiritual beliefs may have created an unintended role model for younger sisters who follow older ones into those arenas. One author suggests that high school dropouts who used drugs and hung out in the neighborhood were much more visible than those who left the neighborhood to work and would return at the end of the day. These models may have been counteracted by a sister who was more present, attended school, and paid attention to her homework and grades. Adolescence has sometimes presented a difficult transition in this older sister/younger sister relationship. Identity and intimacy issues may have taken a sister away from her younger sibling, and the younger one may have felt abandoned. Likewise, the need to understand and develop her own ethnic identity may have led the older sister to pull away from the family in recognition of her differences from them.

Ethnic Identity Development in Black Sisters

The development of ethnic identity in American Blacks has been explored by many authors (Cross, 1971; Helms, 1995). Ethnic identity for women, especially young women, may be different from that of Black men, yet gender differences are not often mentioned. The stages of nigrescence have been described as pre-encounter, encounter, immersion/emersion, integration, and integration/commitment. Pre-encounter includes a time of innocence, when a child does not experience herself as racially different from other children or denies that difference and has had no direct experiences of discrimination (although it is hard to imagine a U.S. Black child who has lived for very long without encountering prejudice). When it occurs it ushers in the next stage—the encounter. The encounter awakens a sense of difference and vulnerability. Reactions to that encounter may help a Black girl remain in denial of discrimination or she may face it and move to the next stage— immersion in the Black community and, in some cases, isolation from any other racial groups. This involvement may give the young woman the opportunity to form a new sense of herself, and this sense, it seems, has always created a unique connection with community—a community that may have defended her from the anger and hatred of others and allowed the expression of her own joy and rage.

What might happen as an older sister enters this stage while a younger sister remains in the pre-encounter stage of ethnic identity? Their relationship may become more distant, with each trying to get the other to understand her perspective. Or the encounter with hate by a younger sister may create the first encounter for an older sister who had not experienced prejudice as directly. For example, Shantelle, who was an excellent math and science student with a desire to become a pilot for the U.S. Air Force, has a teacher who says to her, "No Black girl has ever been a pilot in the Air Force; very few Black men have" (actually neither statement has been true, but prejudice has rarely cared about truth). This discouragement and the double blow of racist and sexist attitudes may crush the girl's dreams and cause her to question her abilities, even affecting her grades. What happens when Shantelle tells her sister Desiree about this? The older sister may react in anger and with some shame for her younger sister. Her own encouragement of Shantelle may be overridden by the sister's experience with her teacher. The interruption of her influence may directly affect the sense of self-worth held by Desiree. Thus, both sisters may have their pre-encounter illusion broken when one of them encounters prejudice or hatred.

Immersion/emersion may occur or recur at any stage of development, but it is often associated with Black adolescence. The desire to immerse herself with other youths who have experienced the hurt and distrust created by discrimination is a natural one. The young Black girl who seeks this immersion may find it in the neighborhood, the church youth group, or the self-defeating drug culture. She may also subjugate herself to the misogyny inherent in much of rap music or demean her gender in order to be accepted by her racial peers. For her, immersion may mean the loss of individual strength and identity. Conversely, the encounter with prejudice may provide an outlet for that strength within her and the association with a positive sisterhood of peers. Her attitudes toward those options and her feelings about the other ethnic communities that surround her may have been partly determined by her sister's navigation of immersion before her. Likewise, she may have set the example that her younger sister chose to follow, or not. In many ways, her mother's, aunts', and fictive elders' ways of navigating prejudice will have been strong factors. Their own struggles to be honest about those experiences of racism will have played a part. Many elders have had to manage the conflicts created between wanting to honestly prepare younger women for their own encounters with racism, yet wanting to shelter them from it (Boyd-Franklin, 2006; Mize, Turell, & Meier, 2004). All of these factors may have culminated in the young woman's choices about how she navigates immersion/emersion.

Another possible outcome of Black female adolescence has been early pregnancy (Boyd-Franklin, 2006). A young girl who has given birth may be raised next to her own daughter by her parents, so she is both mother and sister to the infant. This relationship may have been openly acknowledged or hidden from the younger sister/ daughter. As the young mother reaches adulthood, she may have wanted to shift her role and relationship with her sister/daughter. In doing this she may have caused problems between her mother and her daughter, whose grandmother was functioning as a mother. Such relationships may have been fluid and such transitions managed easily, or, if the grandmother did not relinquish her primary role as parent to the younger child, the conflicts may have been difficult to manage. Usually these relationships were not formalized. The young girl could have felt betrayed by a secret that was held by her acting mother and her actual mother/sister. Boyd-Franklin suggested this can be especially problematic when the mother was not able to mother her older daughter early in life because of similar circumstances. The relationships and understanding of mother, daughter, grandmother, and sister have sometimes become difficult to rearrange, and a permanent rending of the kinship community may have been the result. Thus family roles and relationships have played a role in the navigation of adolescence and may hinder or assist the movement from racial immersion/emersion to that of integration.

For Black girls and young women the movement from immersion/emersion toward integration has been changing. Many new opportunities have been signaled by the election of the first U.S. President of African ancestry, Barack Obama. Michelle Obama and their two daughters, Malia and Sasha, have created strong, determined, and loving role models for girls and young women. Their integration into the U.S. and the world culture has added a new dimension for the development of an integrated identity and for the inclusion of relationships with others outside of one's own race and nationality. The First Family has provided a model for a loving and committed long-term marriage and the possibility of giving back to the communities of the neighborhood, the country, and the world. The "first sisters" may well be center stage in much of this exploration and may be the archetype of a new generation of Black sisters. Their examples come beside examples of powerful local women who—acting as sisters—penetrated the veil of racism to find meaning and purpose in a multicultural world.

Black Sisters and Gender Expectations

What have Black female kinship networks taught their children about gender? According to Kamya (2003) the answer has varied greatly for immigrant Blacks and American-born Blacks. For those who are born in the United States, so many people, including older siblings, have helped to raise Black girls. The influence of so many has created fluidity about the roles and responsibilities associated with gender. Older brothers or older sisters have been equally likely to change diapers, find schoolbooks, cook a quick meal, or transport them to school. Yet there have been differences born of American racism, and the differential impact of that racism and hatred on Black males and females may have affected the sister role.

Because of the number of young Black men who have been shot, imprisoned, or lost to drugs, a gender ratio inequity has developed, with many more young Black women surviving to adulthood than young Black men. In these circumstances Black sons have been treasured in a different way and may have been raised with different expectations. Girls have often been raised with the expectation that they need to achieve independence from male support and with an eye toward self-sufficiency. Early studies (Hare, 1985) suggested that the self-esteem of boys and girls were attributed to different things: girls were more likely to feel good about their achievement but to have some anxiety about it; boys were more socially skilled and had more social self-esteem. These gender variations may make it likely that young Black girls have more female role models of success and greater pressure to prove themselves.

Unique Pressures Among Black Sisters

The pressure to succeed, coupled with the demand for caregiving and shared responsibilities within the female network, has sometimes created an overload for Black women. Generally, mutuality and reciprocity have been expected in female relationships, but sometimes one person has become the central conduit of communication. This has been especially likely when sisters and community were spread across the country. In those cases, one woman may have experienced an overload in her responsibilities for the rest of the extended family.

One aspect of Black culture has created disharmony and difficulty between sisters of African ancestry. The internalization of negative attitudes about skin color and hair texture has led to favoritism and privilege for one sister over another. Despite strong feelings of pride and community within the Black sisterhood, lighter-skinned women and girls have often been favored within the Black community as much as outside of it. Within families, one girl may have been more highly regarded by parents or grandparents who have internalized this prejudice from the White culture. As Boyd-Franklin wrote, "The lightest or darkest child in a family may be seen as `different,' and therefore targeted as the family scapegoat at an early age" (2006, p. 42). Girls may have been valued more or considered more intelligent than their sisters who have darker skin or eyes, with more traditional African hair or facial features. Likewise, some young women may have been considered "not Black enough" by peer groups because of their Caucasian-like features and coloring. These differences between sisters may have been difficult to navigate and could have created lifelong feelings of inferiority or superiority for a sister who looked different. Sometimes paternity was challenged on the basis of these differences. This, too, has its roots in the misuse of slave women by plantation owners and family members. Thus, racism and internalized racism created difficult understandings between sisters who do not resemble each other. These prejudices have arisen from nearly two centuries of degradation of the African image in White America.

Social class has also been a barrier for many women and girls of African ancestry. Racist policies and unstated doctrines that keep African American women from earning to their potential have arisen as a direct psychological outgrowth of slavery. Boyd-Franklin (2006) discussed some of these outcomes. The history of selling parents like chattel shrouded the background of families and created estrangement from sisters. Sometimes sisters were separated from each other when parents were sold to different masters. This was a standard practice used to discourage families from developing an identity and strength together.

In more recent decades, extended family structures have been created by informal adoption of children within the Black community. This has continued to occur because of more subtle undermining by the dominant culture. More recently, the source of estrangement has been the problem of early Black male mortality. Many single or young mothers have been unable to live and raise their children alone.

Sometimes informal adoption occurred because an older relative wanted to have a child, or may have simply wanted another child to raise. Problems might have arisen when sisters were informally adopted to different relatives (although no examples were given of this). More commonly, older adult sisters lived together and were helping to raise each other's children, sometimes in their parents' home. So, extended family structures created the possibility of many role models for a sister relationship born of the relationship between many sisters and cousins as well as their mothers and aunts, who may have all lived under one roof.

Jones and Shorter-Gooden (2003) have described another pressure that can occur for Black women. "Sisterella" has been defined as a complex created when social status and the stress and pressure of high achievement create a special family role for a Black woman. In their exploration of Black women's identities, they discovered the complexity of the roles that Black women attempt to fill—one of them being sister, not just to the immediate family but to an extensive kinship network. The authors suggested that these ingredients create a specific kind of superwoman complex for the woman of African ancestry. She has been required to keep up appearances for the sake of the community, often camouflaging depression and anxiety. In describing this, the authors mentioned a woman in medical school whose depression was partly caused by accidentally receiving an e-mail sent from her sister to her cousins suggesting that she considered her career too important to be bothered with family obligations. This left the high-achieving sister feeling hurt and outcast from her kinship network and the community that could have supported her, and depression ensued. This potential for too many roles and relationships contributed to this young doctor's stress. She was a clear case of the phenomenon described as "Sisterella" by the authors who provide another unique role created for sisters within the Black American community.

Sisters of African ancestry have created their relationships amidst a palette of choices. Surrounded at times by the foreboding nature of a racist culture, they managed to create a vivid terrain for relationship, built upon the strength and resilience of many sisters. These sisters are considered no less significant if they were created in friendship or by blood. Close connections have been necessitated by extended family living arrangements, often born of the continuing subtle prejudice of racism in the culture. They may have been reinforced or denigrated by the misogyny in much of rap music. All of these influences may have served to strengthen a sister bond unique in its resilience and so strongly desired that many "sister" relationships have been formed in addition to those created by natural circumstances.

Latinas

Within the United States the majority of Latinas have come from three different cultural and national traditions: Puerto Rico, Cuba, and Mexico. These nationalities share some values and cultural roots, but often their many differences have been overlooked. Each of these nationalities has different immigration patterns, achievement orientations, family structures, and religious variations that have made them unique cultures with individual expectations for family structures, male–female roles, the development of girls, and therefore the relationships between sisters. Most of the literature has not provided detailed information about these sister relationships, and it had to be extracted again from personal stories, clinical vignettes, and what might be assumed based upon knowledge of the relationship between male and female siblings.

Garcia-Preto (2003) discussed the overarching and shared values and experiences of immigrants to the United States from Latin American countries. Many resented the failure to honor and appreciate their unique cultural origins. They have shared a degree of social oppression and discrimination that has, for the most part, marginalized them in the United States. Many women have come from histories of constant migration across national boundaries that produced a different sense of biculturalism—one that was transnational, with identities in both countries and ties to both sets of values. In addition, the United States has persisted in referring to this group as Hispanic, a term associated with the oppressors who murdered them and raped their women and children, whose blood flowed in their veins and has, at times, poisoned the indigenous and African parts of themselves and their cultural worlds.

Mexican Americans

Mexican Americans have been the largest group of immigrants and transnationals from Latin America. The fluid boundary between the United States and Mexico, historically through the present, has been a possible reason for the high number of immigrants. Becerra (1998) suggested that Mexican American immigration has always been the result of the demand for cheap labor during westward expansion and for use in the fields of the southwest, but this pattern has reversed during times of high U.S. unemployment, resulting in forced migration back to Mexico during the 1930s. Proximity to the United States along with the migration back and forth has reinforced prejudice against Mexican Americans. Continuous contact with Mexico also maintains strong connection to their cultural values. Their unique migration history has created a continuous bias against and a dependence upon Mexican American men and women.

Mexican American Family Structure and Roles

Likewise, family structure and assimilation were different for different waves of immigrants and have been related to the ease of immigration. Three primary principles of Mexican family relationships were outlined by Becerra (1998): (1) male dominance; (2) rigid sex and age grading so that "the older order the younger and the men the women"; and (3) strong family orientation (p. 159).

The family orientation includes living near kin and receiving practical support for everyday life from each other. For example, Angelica and her sister, Theresa, have lived within 1 mile of each other and their two brothers. Their mother and stepfather live about 10 miles away. The sisters have been close in age and were close emotionally as they grew up, although they went through some tumultuous experiences. Each took over portions of the parental role. Theresa took over some of the mother's responsibilities for cooking, cleaning, and minding the younger children, while Angie filled in the vacant stepfather and absent father role by being the protector of her brothers.

Throughout life the sisters have depended upon each other for counsel, feedback, and practical support. Each helped the other with child care and financial needs in an emergency, and both provided their homes as havens for the other's children and grandchildren. In addition, they have had sister getaways once a year when they go to a nearby town for relaxation and shared activities like theater performances. The entire extended sibling group has gathered for birthday celebrations, holiday meals, and other activities. Sometimes, they have discussed their religious and spiritual beliefs, although neither attends the Catholic church, in which they were raised. The sisters seem to have split some of their pragmatic functions along gender role lines, but the emotional support and practical support have been common among sisters whose families have emigrated from Mexico.

The family of Angie and Theresa represents the Mexican American immigrant family in several ways. Their mother and stepfather have a long marriage; this cultural group has lowest divorce rate of any in the United States. Likewise, for a portion of their youth, the girls filled in for a mother who had to work because of an absent father. Many Mexican American women find themselves single for some period of their life due to immigration patterns that disrupt the male role as head of household and force women into the labor force, before or after immigration to the United States. Even though divorce rates have been low, the functional single parent has existed in many Mexican American immigrant families.

Gender Roles and Mexican American Sisters

Gender roles have been misunderstood in Mexican culture. The term *machismo* is overused and misunderstood. It has stood for the strength of the man and his role as the father in a family; however, it has been primarily defined by the expectations he shoulders to provide for his own children, as well as his parents, his in-laws, the children of relatives, and sometimes his siblings. He has been expected to set an example of achievement for his children and be a provider for his wife. The role of women has not been so controlled by machismo; rather, the concept of *marianismo* has been the complementary strength for women. It has stood for her female strength and authority, as well as her caregiving and child care roles. She may have been stereotyped by this cultural role. The first definitions of this role occurred in a 1973 article in which Evelyn P. Stevens defined the cult of marianismo as it related to the Mexican woman, and traced historical roots in both Europe and Middle America:

> It is the cult of feminine spiritual superiority, which teaches that women are semi-divine, morally superior to and spiritually stronger than men. (p. 4)
>
> The roots of marianismo are both deep and widespread, springing apparently from primitive awe at woman's ability to produce a live human creature from inside her own body. (p. 5)
>
> Beneath the submissiveness, however, lies the strength of her conviction—shared by the entire society—that men must be humored, for, after all, everyone knows that they are *como niños* (like little boys) whose intemperance, foolishness, and obstinacy must be forgiven because "they can't help the way they are." (p. 9)

Oldest daughters are expected to be trained in these values and roles by their mothers, often taking some responsibilities for younger siblings. So an older sister might well have functioned as her younger sisters' second mother. Her authority may or may not have been challenged by them. Certainly, the culture, as well as her mother, would have supported her in the role. Or a set of older sisters might divide parental roles, as in the example of Angie and Theresa.

Cuban-American Sisters

As I was writing about the relationships that might exist between Latina sisters, the political and cultural map was changing for Cuban American sisters. Long denied the right to visit their homeland, the barriers have just begun to lift. Against this backdrop of political strife and advancement, women with Cuban ancestry have experienced family separation. Even U.S.-born Cuban American women have not been allowed to visit their home country. Sometimes sisters have been on opposite sides of this political and geographic divide with no ability to have physical contact in over five decades. It is hard to imagine the type of longing this might have engendered for women here or in Cuba. However, the relationship between Cubans, Cuban Americans, and recent Cuban immigrants has been a tumultuous one that may have left sisters estranged on the opposite sides of an internal cultural war.

Cubans who arrived in the United States during the first wave of immigration have been supported and have been financially successful in the United States. However, Cubans who arrived in later waves, especially those who came as "boat people," have been devalued by the Cubans already here (Bernal & Shapiro, 2005). This distinction has occurred between siblings if they immigrated as adults, or one child was left in Cuba while another was allowed to immigrate with parents, uncles, or cousins. Generally, those who came in the first wave had more financial ability to leave Cuba and did so to escape the seizing of their goods and money by the new communist government. Suárez (1998) suggested that each wave of immigrants was lower on the socioeconomic scale, creating a class divide, at least partially created by communism. Despite these differences within the culture, an extreme cultural pride dominates across classes. That pride has developed against a landscape of discrimination etched across the horizon by the larger U.S. culture.

Cuban Family Structure and Sisters' Roles

The primacy of an extended family structure has been common for Cuban Americans. *Compadre* and *comadre* roles have been very important in this structure. Cuban godparents have functioned as second parents, not just as spiritual ones. They may have taken over parenting if required by family separation, divorce, or parental absence. The extended family structure has begun to fall apart in successive generations, related to the migration north along the Eastern Seaboard of the United States. Even in Northern cities, however, older and unmarried women have continued to live with their parents rather than move into their own apartments or homes (Suárez, 1998). These older sisters have also played a role in the development of the family and its structure.

Gender Roles and Cuban American Sisters

Gender roles have been somewhat resistant to change among Cuban Americans for several reasons. Gender equality was a part of the communist agenda under Castro and continued to be associated with all that went wrong with that political approach for those who fled. First generations to immigrate have remained less flexible than later generations in this regard. Girls in later generations have been supported in academic and business achievement, which is highly valued among Cubans. However, when it comes to dating and sexuality, the strong double standard has not changed. Initially, this cultural tradition led to chaperoned dating, but it has more recently been defined as restrictions on sexual freedom that are different for women than men. Only girls have a *quinceanera* (a formal dance with 15 couples on her 15th birthday). This tradition is a celebration of her eligibility for marriage and her virginity. These restrictions have continued at other life stages as well (Suárez, 1998).

A Cuban American pregnant teen has been expected to keep her child, but unlike in many other Latina cultures, she has not been discouraged from choosing abortion. This has most likely emerged from the combination of Spiritism and Catholicism within the Cuban culture. However, it has also been attributed to the focus on individual achievement and success. Despite this individualistic nature, girls have been more likely to continue to live with their parents and have been likely to move back home after a divorce. This coming and going of sisters within the family may have created unique and specific expectations for the relationship.

Imagine this set of Cuban American sisters. Cheena and Estelle are sisters in their mid-fifties. Cheena is the oldest by 4 years. She remembers her family's piecemeal immigration to the United States, but Estelle was born shortly after the immigration. The family suffered from poverty and discrimination within and outside of their own cultural groups. These factors led to Cheena's decision to quit school at 17 to help provide for her family by working in a local restaurant during the week and a hotel on the weekends. Partly due to this sacrifice, the family's socioeconomic standing was raised and Estelle was able to continue her schooling in a junior college, earning a degree as a nursing assistant. The sisters' relationship has always been close, but resentment festered within Cheena for the sacrifices she made to help her sister succeed. Likewise, Estelle felt guilt at the opportunities her nursing degree has offered her and the continued difference in social class that has been generated by the simple matter of birth order and expectations of the oldest daughter. Both maintained pride in the achievements of their own daughters, but in some ways Estelle's were less inclined to attend college than Cheena's. The sisters' feelings of resentment and guilt may have been continued in the self-defeating or achievement-driven behaviors of the next generation of sisters.

Puerto Rican Sisters

Puerto Rican sisters have been unique in their citizenship status and the ability to travel easily back and forth between Puerto Rico and the mainland United States. This may have contributed to their higher level of education when compared to Mexican Americans. The immigration from Puerto Rico occurred in waves that were socioeconomically reversed from those of Cuban Americans. The poorest Puerto Ricans immigrated when the coffee and sugar plantations that formed the base of their economy fell apart due to the Great Depression. Those who worked in the fields moved to the mainland looking for work. Later immigrants have been professionals trained in Puerto Rico looking for a higher standard of living in the United States. About 95% of those in the latter waves of immigrants live in the greater New York City area (Sánchez-Ayéndez, 1998).

Puerto Rican Family Structures and Sisters' Roles

As in Cuban American families, the Puerto Rican family structure has been defined by extended kinship circles and gender roles. However, the Puerto Rican family has been more likely to stay in a neighborhood community that provided its members with a sense of shared values and common history. Extended families were likely to contain godparents and fictive siblings. Sometimes these siblings have arrived by virtue of informal adoptions. Sisters and fictive sisters may not have been treated differently by parents in this structure, but neither was their birthright confused. At least one author suggested that more may be demanded of naturally born sisters than of fictive kin. Women may be quite aware of how their herstory is shared by their blood sister. Interactions with the extended family may have been frequent. Many trips have occurred to maintain connections between the island and the mainland. It has not been unusual for a Puerto Rican family living in New York to travel to Puerto Rico for a family funeral or wedding. The role of women in these events has been described in this way:

> Women, as part of their female role and interrelated with the domestic domain, are seen as responsible for establishing the bases for good relationships among family members. (Sánchez-Ayéndez, 1998, p. 212)

Gender Roles and Puerto Rican Sisters

Sister roles in Puerto Rican families have been partially determined by the gender expectations of the culture and neighborhood. Again, *marianismo* has provided a stereotype for these gender-based roles. There has also been a double standard related to sexual behavior and family authority, with men having more freedom and control. As the time since immigration lengthens, the assimilation into U.S. mainland culture has led to greater freedom and equality. Often these changes were forced, caused by the necessity for a second family income and the role of Puerto Rican women in the workforce.

In the Puerto Rican family, daughters have generally received more affection than sons, particularly from their mothers. This preference may be translated to sisters as well, where affection may be more freely shared among the female members of the family. In many Puerto Rican families both emotional support and practical support have come from the women, creating a female unit bound by affection, emotional sharing, and practical assistance. The Spanish equivalent of superwoman is *hembrismo*. The Puerto Rican woman, more readily integrated into mainland culture than the Puerto Rican man, has maintained the role of caregiver while becoming the primary breadwinner. Precious little time may remain for the fostering of a sister connection amid these superhuman demands on the Puerto Rican American woman.

Unique Pressures for Puerto Rican Sisters

Another potential stress on the Puerto Rican sister relationship is related to U.S. mainland racism. This racism has differentiated Puerto Rican women and sisters on the basis of skin color. Lighter-skinned sisters may have been favored in their families, jobs, and schools. Sisters with fairer skins may have been more valuable as heterosexual mates to men in the culture, thus favoring one sister over another. How sisters have managed these issues, and whether these stresses affect the sense of intimacy in their relationship, has not yet become clear. Some experiences of cultural favoritism have definitely created difficult communication, a sense of unfair advantage, and guilt about being the one favored.

Relationships with family members, including sisters, have been compared to friendships with the common use of the phrase *como de la familia* ("my friend who is like family"). It has often been individualized for a specific relationship and accompanying qualitative judgments about the closeness of the friendship. Therefore, *my friend who is like a sister* connotes more intimacy and expectations than *the friend who is like a cousin*. These distinctions have been an important way of making it clear that the sister relationship has greater emotional valence for Puerto Rican women than the relationships of other relatives.

Dominican and Haitian Sisters

Dominicans have been traditionally associated more with Latina groups, while Haitians, occupying the other half of their shared island, have a history and skin color more closely associated with individuals of African ancestry. Because of these identifications and the proximity to Puerto Rico, Dominicans have often attempt to enter the United States through their Puerto Rican neighbor. The family structure of Dominicans has also often been extended, with clear half-siblings, godparents, fictive kin, and actual aunts, uncles, and cousins living together under one roof. This structure has created the possibility for partial immigration of the family with some, but not all, of their children to the United States. The intent has been to bring the others later, but this may not actually occur. As a result, sisters may have been separated at a young age and not reunited for many years, if ever.

Because the island was the center of a colonialist struggle between France, Spain, and Great Britain, those of fairer skin have often been valued more highly, again setting up potential jealousy and guilt among sisters. Other values within the family have affected the relationships of sisters. These include *familialism*, *marianismo*, and *machismo*. As for many Latina immigrants to the United States, Dominican women have been expected to be primarily mothers and caregivers, but the U.S. prejudice against men of color has led to dual roles and responsibilities for Dominican women. This created a need for sisters to be even more present—to provide practical support—while having less time in which to assist.

The Dominican population in the United States has been considered transnational—they have frequently journeyed back to the Dominican Republic. This frequent contact has helped separated siblings stay in touch. Indeed, it has been important for those working in the United States to send money back to relatives who have assisted them in their immigration. In this way, a sister who helped to finance her sister's move may then be supported partially by the money her U.S. sister sends back. Such international interdependence has become very common, but how frequently it occurs among sisters remains unclear.

Immigrant Sisters from Central America

Many women from Central America have migrated to the United States under terrible circumstances, and many have suffered torture and rape at the hands of those who had promised to help them immigrate. Kusnir (2005) described the experiences of Maria, an isolated immigrant who saw her sister killed in front of her as she hid under a bed. She was forced to hide for 5 years until she could immigrate to the United States safely. Such stories are not uncommon. Women immigrating alone from other Central American countries, first through Mexico and then into the United States, have required the assistance of a *coyote*, a man who knows how to help them manage the illegal routes to safety. These women have often been victimized and sometimes robbed by these coyote guides. They have to make two border crossings, and often they cannot afford the second one. Many women have remained in Mexico for long periods of time before they could complete their migration.

The reason so many women have attempted solitary migration has its roots in the history of civil war and the huge ensuing cost in terms of human life. Salvadorian women were not recognized as war refugees in the United States due to our political leanings at the time. They were forced to become undocumented workers, leading to further vulnerability.

The relationship and connection of sisters in these women's narratives are likely to be filled with pain and sadness—loss and survivor guilt. Many could not maintain contact with their sisters during immigration. The next generation of sisters in the United States has created a very different relationship experience. The relationship of sisters who experienced horrific trauma as they immigrated together has been constructed as a close, indeed indivisible, bond, but one in which the women remain silent about its roots and its strengths.

Women of Asian Ancestry

Women of Asian ancestry in the United States have generally been discussed as geographic clusters, based partially on location and partially on the time of their primary immigration. These divisions have grouped Chinese, Japanese, and Korean women into one group (West Asian); Cambodian, Vietnamese, and Laotians in another group (Southeast Asians); and women from Hawaii, the Philippines, and Malaysia (Pacific Islanders). Indian and Pakistani women are a fourth group that is sometimes included with Asians and sometimes considered separately. Those groupings will be used here, but with a clear understanding that each of these countries has its own unique history, spiritual beliefs, and gender-related practices—all of which may affect the sister relationship.

Sisters from China

Lee and Mock (2005) documented five separate waves of Chinese immigration to the United States. Some of these waves had specific gender implications that affected sister relationships and the relationships between husbands and wives.

During the California Gold Rush and the building of the transcontinental railroad in the United States, there was a need for cheap labor. Chinese men were brought or recruited to work in the gold mines and on the railways. When the Gold Rush ended and the railway was completed, many men wished to bring Chinese wives or future brides to this country to continue their lives here. In fear of a mass immigration of more Chinese, whose cheap labor was no longer needed in the United States, the U.S. Congress passed laws limiting the immigration of Chinese families. This had several effects on the women in China and eventually became a part of the Chinese American experience.

Women bonded more closely to their children. Traditionally, Chinese women have been subjugated to male authority, including that of their father-in-laws and sons. The forced estrangement between men and women in the Chinese American history may have created stronger ties between women, whose support and friendship would have sustained them through the absence of a son or husband. Perhaps this historical chapter provided a wedge that has allowed the eventual influence of Western culture in China itself.

Modern Chinese American women have evolved into very diverse communities. Some have become feminists, and some have emerged as lesbians. Many young Chinese American women have remained single for much longer and do not take a traditional role in the lives of in-laws. Transitional generations have suffered with the pressure of the old, traditional expectations on women and the newer immigrant demands on women in the United States. The support and encouragement of a same-sex sibling may have made this transition easier or more difficult. If the sister supported the traditional role of women in Chinese culture, she may have judged her sister and may have remained estranged from a self-directed sister. Older sisters traditionally have a responsibility to care for all younger siblings. They become second parents to them, providing nurturance, support, and direction. The birth order of sisters may have been very significant in this dynamic of traditional versus acculturated Chinese American sisters. Older sisters who are traditional may not be able to accept the differences so easily, influenced by being the socializing force for younger siblings in the family. On the other hand, an older sister who became more acculturated may have provided a model for the younger sister's own ventures into a different life.

The traditional Chinese value of high achievement has transferred to Chinese women in the United States. They have often been encouraged to excel in their education and rewarded for doing so. This educational experience may have altered the understanding of their place in the world and in their culture, paradoxically putting them at odds with other traditional values like subjugation and community centeredness. Sisters who achieve at different levels in the United States have experienced a sense of shame related to failed competition. In some cases, they may also experience differential treatment by their parents based upon that achievement. The effects of these differences on Chinese American sisters have not been well documented in the research or theoretical literature. Yet the presence of tensions from immigration and Western influence suggest that sisters have become estranged from one another and in some cases remain out of connection with each other.

Another factor that has affected recent generations of Chinese American sisters is the adoption of Chinese female children in the United States. In 1970, the Chinese government, concerned with overpopulation, began to limit the births of children to one child per family. The higher value placed on boys in the Chinese culture, especially in rural areas, led to the wholesale abandonment of many female children or abortion of female fetuses. Parents hoped to have a son instead (Wei Xing Zhu & Hesketh, 2009). Orphanages filled with these Chinese newborns forced the Chinese government to allow out-of-country adoption for these female babies and toddlers. Many Chinese female babies were brought to the United States to be raised by both heterosexual couples and single parents (often lesbians, until recent changes in the guidelines allowed adoptions by married couples only). Since 2002, an average of 5,000 to 8,000 Chinese infants and children were adopted into the United States per year, 91% of them girls (Department of Homeland Security, 2008). Frequently families adopted more than one girl, creating Chinese American sisters raised together from infancy who usually had no blood relationship.

These girls have been growing up in the United States with the awareness that they were abandoned by their birth parents in favor of a male child. Many have realized they were brought away from the country where they were born because of gender discrimination. How has this affected their sense of self, their shared ethnic identity, and the closeness of their bond to one another? These facts of their life and birth will differentiate them from most of their classmates in school, from their peers on the softball field or in youth groups, and most importantly from their parents. These differences seem likely to create a very close sister bond that is a primary source of identity in their development—bonds created in the loss of their country and in the adoption of a new culture. It is not clear how the older sister's role might have been present in these newly constituted Chinese and American families. That has depended upon the socialization of the parents who are raising them in the United States. Many factors, then, affect the adjustment and shared relationship of Chinese sisters whose relationship was created and continues to be created by adoption into U.S. families.

Chinese American sisters have relationships developed by great variation across situations that have led to a potential for extremely close or very distant relationships. Traditional values may have created a strong bond for older sisters, but those same values have limited sisters' relationships across large age differences. Infants who became sisters because of U.S. adoption may be the closest siblings of all.

Japanese American Sisters

In this century, most Japanese Americans have been born in the United States. Their history of immigration to the United States, like that of the Chinese, was strictly and prejudicially restricted by U.S. law for many years. Like the Chinese, they were ostracized from citizenship and immigration, with resultant effects on family relationships. Among Japanese Americans, the immigrant generations had different names by which they were recognized within the Japanese community. Shibusawa (2005) traced this historical naming and related it to a unique chapter in U.S. history—the internment of the American Japanese during World War II. Out of the camps came a generation of American heroes who were allowed to leave their confinement only if they joined the U.S. military. They were restricted to fighting in the European theater during that war. This generation is referred to as the Nissei generation. Their parents (too elderly to fight or prevented from doing so), who remained and often died in the camps, were known as the Issei generation. However, the tracing of these generations is focused primarily upon male Japanese Americans. Less known are the experiences of the Japanese American female Nissei, who were allowed to leave the camps to become educated in service to the United States or to join the military as translators or clerks (Moore, 2003). Many became nurses (Matsumoto, 1984) to assist in the war effort, yet unlike the Fighting 442nd Division, they were not later acknowledged as heroes or honored for their contributions to the war.

Japanese sisters of the World War II generation were also greatly affected by the nuclear bombs that were dropped by the United States onto Nagasaki and Hiroshima. Sisters were no doubt annihilated during that attack. Many others were left burned by radiation or horribly maimed. How did sisters—some in the United States—begin to fathom the loss for their Japanese sisters and kin? There was no permission for open mourning of those losses in the United States. During recent commemorative events, a Japanese woman named Hirata described her experience in this way:

> There were dying citizens outside the doors, begging for water. I had difficulty believing that their voices were coming from fellow human beings. One of my sisters did not return home that night . . . Four days later, my sister thanked everyone and died. She was 19 years of age. (Ricci, 2005)

How does such grief become absorbed in the collective memory of Japanese American surviving sisters? How does a country overcome such losses and move on?

Another part of Japanese American history that affected sister relationships was the use of "picture brides"—women whose pictures enticed Japanese American men to bring them to the United States as wives. It was traditional in Japanese culture for marriages to be arranged. These women were bought for the betterment of their families in Japan and for the perceived betterment of their own lives. In the process, women gave up their own needs and desires for the betterment of the family and the two families that would be joined. Such sacrifices were not new to the culture, but the move across an ocean into a different cultural world required a new level of self-sacrifice and separation from sisters. This process came to an end due to immigration reform in the United States. In the 1950s, the immigration ban on Asian families was lifted and Japanese families were able to immigrate together, thus relieving the need for picture brides.

The theme extracted from this history has been one of separation of the Japanese American woman from her own family of origin and thus from the comfort and support of her sisters. My own mother had a Japanese Nissei classmate in nurses' training. Beth was moved from the camps to a city 2,000 miles from her family in her late teens. She lived in a nursing dormitory and then worked at the local hospital. Eventually she relocated back to California, but she maintained ties with some of those nursing school "sisters" throughout her life. How many Japanese Americans of that generation were similarly separated from their families and from their lives? In the book *All Good Women* (Miner, 1988), the author traces a group of women living in San Francisco during the 1940s, their struggle to survive during the later years of the Great Depression, and their shared sisterhood. One of these women was a Japanese American who was removed and placed in a camp, disrupting the sisterhood of the good women who fought to try to prevent her internment. These anecdotes bring to light the need that Japanese American women feel for a sister or sister-like connection and the cultural disruption of those relationships.

This history suggests that Japanese American women may have a deeply engrained distrust of stability within the sister connection and a constant fear of loss or removal from those they love. Certainly the Japanese American women of today lead lives that provide for a greater connection between them and their sisters, yet many Japanese Americans experienced cultural post-traumatic stress disorder during the internment of Arab American citizens following the events of September 11, 2001 (Kim, 2006). In the shared cultural experience, women became aware of the ways in which ethnic discrimination and distrust may exact specific losses between sisters. Japanese American women have developed this awareness and the knowledge that they may be forced to leave sisters behind or may be forced apart from them by tradition or by trauma and war.

Another factor affecting the lives of Japanese American sisters has been the cultural drive for achievement and success. Not all families have experienced extreme sibling rivalry, but it has happened often enough to be documented as a cultural trend (Pilisuk & Hillier Parks, 1986). Some authors suggest this rivalry was not experienced personally in Japan, since one child's achievement there was recognized as an achievement by the entire family because of the communal principles of Japanese culture. Thus, a sister would have benefited and shared in her sister's recognition. However, acculturation in the United States provided some loss of this shared recognition, while the fierce sibling rivalry may have remained. Sisters may have developed strong negative feelings about the academic or occupational success of another sister, especially when it eclipsed their own. Many forces have driven sisters of Japanese ancestry apart and created the potential for a distant relationship between them.

Sisters from Korea

The issue of division and loss has permeated the relationships of sisters from western Asian nations. Certainly, the division of Korea into two separate and opposed countries split not only the country but many of its families. The same war that created that division also created many bicultural Korean American families: those whose parents came from other cultures within the United States of 1950 and those who came from Korea itself. Many service members came home from the Korean War with Korean wives or husbands. Once again, these members of an Asian country—usually the women—left their homeland and family to travel to a distant land. Few U.S. citizens remained in Korea to continue their marriage or romantic relationship there. Another outgrowth of this war was the adoption of Korean orphans into U.S. families. Nearly 157,000 Korean children were adopted overseas between 1954 and 2007. Fifty-five percent were girls (Overseas Adopted Koreans, 2010). A meeting with adoptees in the year 2000 reported that "slightly more than half of the respondents (52%) had at least one sibling who was also adopted from South Korea" (Freundlich & Lieberthal, 2000, p. 6). Twenty-six percent had siblings who were the natural children of their adoptive parents.

A unique factor in Korean American acculturation that affected such changes was the use of the Korean language. Many Korean American immigrants have struggled to learn English due to the extreme differences in the articulation and writing of the two languages. This has often resulted in a loss of self-esteem during immigration and a tendency to be isolated from the larger U.S. culture. Freundlich and Lieberthal reported that 47 percent of the adopted Korean Americans had never been married, and 70 percent had no children, despite an average age of 31. Korean American immigrants who have not learned to speak fluent English have often been the victims of occupational and peer discrimination.

These opposing factors—the loss of country and culture in Korea and the isolation of Korean American culture within the United States—has created opposing forces for closeness in the sister connection. Women who have immigrated without a good command of English may have found shelter and support in relationships with female peers, including sisters within the United States. However, sisters may have been separated during immigration, particularly sisters of the Korean War generation. Likewise, children adopted out of Korea may find solace in a sister adopted with them, or they may feel estranged from their Korean roots by the forced removal from their own culture and country. How have these Korean adoptees viewed sisters who were born into their American families? Some have been in bitter conflict about their own identity and their sisters. They may have experienced feelings similar to those of any adopted child when comparing themselves to biological children in the same family. Depending upon birth order and age differences, the sisters may have felt closely connected or very distant. The notion of feeling like an outsider permeates the self for Korean American women and may, indeed, create a sense of joined isolation and community with a sister or "sisters" of similar origins.

Gender issues within the Korean culture are also significant in terms of their effects on the relationship between sisters. The role of women in Korea has traditionally been symbolized by the concept of *jeong*. When practicing *jeong*, a woman:

> [E]nriches and humanizes social relationships and makes life meaningful. [*Jeong*] is expressed by attention to the small but important details that show concern for another person's comfort and well-being . . . a combination of empathy, sympathy, compassion, emotional attachment and tenderness, in varying degrees according to the social context. (Kim & Ryu, 2005, p. 355)

Such an approach to relationships may provide a rich and fertile land for the growth of the sister connection among Korean American women.

Freedom has changed for Korean immigrant women. In the United States, women have been encouraged to become educated. Gender role tensions were created by the continued expectation of caregiver roles within the family. Korean American women, like many other immigrant women in the United States, had to face the struggle to be a breadwinner and caregiver. Add to this the expectation that the Korean daughter-in-law has been required to be the primary caregiver for her husband's parents, and the tension became multigenerational. Korean American sisters may be able to commiserate about these demands and the negativity they feel within a tight cultural group. Alternately, one sister who has more traditional Korean values may have judged the other sister and caused her more angst. Therefore, the freedom felt by Korean American women has led to either closer or more distant sister relationships.

Korean Americans have continued to value males more highly than females. While both genders have high expectations for educational achievement, a son's achievement has been valued more highly. In some families, the son and father have joined to become the primary partnership in the family, replacing that of husband and wife. The submission demanded by these values has been strained by the woman's acculturation to the dominant culture in the United States. Those have included a presumed equity for women and acceptance as an equal partner in relationships. Sisters may have filled the gap when support and understanding have not been forthcoming within a given peer group. Like many of the sisters in my study, those Korean American sisters may provide a model for the next generation of Korean American girls. These girls, born in the United States, are fluent in English and can support each other in violation of the culturally defined limitations on women.

Spiritual beliefs have also played a strong part in determining gender and peer relationships for Korean American women, and thus they affect the sister relationship as well. Many Korean Americans have become Christians, yet all are influenced by the underlying values of Confucianism; both of these spiritual belief systems have relied on a strong patriarchal influence (Moon, 1998). Korean American Christian churches have maintained a more traditional and conservative view of gender roles. Women have remained subjugated to their husbands in this belief system. Likewise, this patriarchal structure permeates Confucianism. That belief system has defined the importance of attitudes toward five key relationships that deserve respect. Within the prescription for appropriate family relationships, the younger brother has been expected to hold specific respect for the older brother; this has been called the fourth relationship. It has been elevated over other peer relationships, while the sister relationship remains unspecified or is just another version of peer connection. In Korean American culture the Korean tradition of referring to all women as "sister" has persisted, but the same has not been true of men. To lead a valuable and balanced life, these relationships must be honored. Thus, the strongly held communal values that assist in the maintenance of relationships within the Korean American heritage may have extended to sisters, but this has not been specifically articulated as the one between brothers was.

Sisters who have lived in the United States, but whose ancestry originates in western Asia, come from a history of division and loss. These divisions were often the result of aggression or intervention on the part of the United States and other countries (e.g., Japan's colonial history with Korea). For native Korean Americans or those who have immigrated to the United States, their country has torn their families and their lives asunder. At the same time, the United States may have provided a haven from war and an opportunity for the achievement of dreams. This schizophrenic heritage has affected the west Asian woman's sense of herself, her role in her culture, and her family relationships. Sometimes, the resilience she has demonstrated in the face of such loss has come from the sister who suffered similar disconnection from her culture and family. Sometimes, the sister became a source of judgment and criticism related to right choices within the bicultural context. In many instances, a sister provided a refuge or an opportunity to see the world reflected in another's eyes, but always there has been the feared loss—the sense that others may take her away permanently.

Sisters from Southeast Asia

The variety and diversity of Southeast Asian family structure is not well understood in the United States. Each country—Cambodia, Laos, and Vietnam—has had very distinct cultures and traditions, and within those countries there have existed unique peoples. Most immigrants from Southeast Asia came to the United States as refugees following the wars in Vietnam and Cambodia (which were at least partly a result of U.S. colonialist policies and the aggression of China). Until those wars began, the Vietnamese had enjoyed both a rich shared heritage from China and a tumultuous relationship with her. The many sources of stress following the division of a country, the polarization of its neighbors, and the wars to settle the dispute among giants have left their scars on the family structures of immigrants from Southeast Asia.

Vietnamese American Sisters

The Vietnamese arrived in the United States in two waves. The first wave, as is often the case, represented the higher socioeconomic classes who fled in advance of the war and communism. The second wave was composed of war refugees who survived countless assaults on themselves and their families. Their homes, fields, and businesses were the location of the war, and their children were conscripted into service. There was no battlefront in this war, which raged among their houses and tore apart the bodies of those who resisted or assisted on either side of the conflict.

The Vietnamese American family has been founded on the principles of Confucianism. Respect for others, placing community ahead of the individual, honoring one's ancestors, knowing one's place, and serving others have been valued by the culture. That culture has determined the relationship between Vietnamese American sisters. Vietnam had a history of legal polygamy (for men only) prior to the war. These values were carried into the United States. For Vietnamese American men, having a mistress is acceptable if they cared well enough for all of the children and women dependent upon them. Divorce has been fairly uncommon in Vietnamese American families. Yet women have had some independence and self-direction by owning and running their own businesses.

Among siblings, the oldest has the most authority, and that authority was much higher if the child was a boy. Oldest sisters were to be respected and served as models for younger sisters. The oldest also had the responsibility to care for elderly parents. This structure created a unique set of stresses on the sister relationship. An eldest sister has unquestioned authority over her younger sisters, yet younger brothers may have been allowed to treat that elder sister with less respect.

Many Vietnamese families in the United States have immigrated together, either before or after the war, but the battles have left many marks for the generation who immigrated and those who are their children. Vietnamese Americans who migrated here as refugees left a war-torn country (Leung & Boehnlein, 2005). Sisters may have left other sisters behind. They may have been raped or seen a sister, a mother, or an aunt raped as they journeyed from Vietnam to the Cambodian refugee camps and then finally to the United States. Many used boats to escape in the final days of the war. When intercepted, the women were often killed or raped and placed in camps. Such vicious aggression is all too common in war—but that does not tell the whole story. Sisters experiencing that kind of assault watched each other either experience it or escape it. When one was victimized, the other sisters have a shattered sense of self and an uncertain identity within the culture.

The failure to talk about such emotional difficulties may have prohibited sisters from experiencing connection through the trauma. Each was likely to suffer such insults alone. If sisters of those older generations survived together, they may have been separated upon arrival in the United States. This final traumatic loss in the sister connection has to be understood by the next generation. The women who experienced these tragedies have reached middle age and have become mothers to the next generation of Vietnamese American daughters and sisters. How have they passed down the horror of war to sisters in the next generation?

It is very likely that older generations of sisters try to shield younger generations from their own experiences of being refugees. Living closely together in confined spaces, perhaps working at shared businesses, the Vietnamese American sisters have remembered the traumas in their bones, even if their voices have been silent. The shared experience and the resilience of survival have been interwoven in the connection, but they have not been acknowledged. Have the younger sisters in a family experienced this bond and wondered about its unspoken depths? Did they develop greater awareness of the conflict-born rivalries of other American families? How have they assessed the importance of the sister connection?

Large families have sometimes made Vietnamese American sister relationships very complex. Eldest sisters have still been placed in a position of authority, but that authority may not have remained absolute as it was challenged within the context of the U.S. culture. Most Vietnamese girls have had more than one sister from whom to select a confidant, playmate, or business partner. Still, it is likely that the gender disparities in the culture persist in the United States and that the modern Vietnamese American woman is more likely to cast her lot with her husband and their own children rather than depending upon her sister.

Cambodian American Sisters

Cambodians, like the Vietnamese, migrated primarily following the Southeast Asian wars. These refugees experienced many of the same traumas, yet there was a very significant difference: many of them suffered family losses because of their own governments' use of murder and torture against them. Pol Pot's Khmer Rouge regime ruled Cambodia following the Vietnamese war. Its campaign to destroy family relationships and punish successful achievers was an outgrowth of distorted socialism. To achieve this end they executed millions of their own citizens. Those who were the most highly educated were targeted in order to drive all citizens to a similar level of work and productivity for the Khmer Rouge government. Women were forced to spy on their husbands and children on their parents, with secrecy, betrayal, and distrust permeating families.

While family structure had been a significant strength of the Cambodian people and a stabilizing force for their country, the Khmer Rouge dismantled it. They forced children into labor camps, separating them from their parents and each other. They killed and raped family members in front of each other.

Most Cambodians who survived this onslaught and were able to immigrate came as a part of a female-headed household. A book by Loung Ung (2005), based on her own experiences and those of her sister, tells the story of two sisters, one who stayed in Cambodia and the other who immigrated with her brother and sister-in-law to Vermont. They reunited 15 years later. Both sisters suffered post-traumatic stress and flashbacks as they relived the nightmares of that time and their separation—yet their experiences were markedly different, as Loung Ung attended college and became a successful author. Chou, her sister, almost starved to death many times and was denied an education or adequate medical care. Their story is told by Loung in her book (2005); the narrative provides a clear view of the contrasting life course for these two sisters.

The Cambodian American family of today is often headed by an immigrant grandmother and her eldest son and eldest daughter. He became responsible for his siblings upon the death of his father, most likely during the war or the Khmer Rouge campaign (McKenzie-Pollock 2005). He may have been born in this country or survived as a young child. The eldest daughter also had a unique and honorific role in the family, providing a model to her younger sisters. The Cambodian Americans have a special set of terms reserved for these two eldest siblings. Other specific terms have remained in use for their younger siblings. Each term retained a unique designation for the place in the family. Cambodian American families also include fictive siblings—"sisters" and "brothers" who are not a part of the family line but who serve in similar roles and are geographically part of the Cambodian American community.

Against this backdrop, older and younger sisters shared in silence the devastating memories and emotions associated with the torture and loss they experienced prior to their immigration. They would rarely have spoken about it to each other. The book by Ung has provided rare understanding. Yet like the Vietnamese immigrant sisters of the same generation, there has been a shared sense of deep understanding and grief. A sense of wonder has been created for the life they have now and the sacrifice that made it possible. Guilt and shame have become everyday companions, but not ones that are shared openly. And these women quietly keep these secret torments from the children who have become the next generation of Cambodian-American sisters.

Sisters who were born in this country have grown up with all of the benefits of education and opportunity. Pride about those accomplishments may have been diminished by a family that remembers how such accomplishments led to death and torture in the Cambodian countryside. Has this fear been transmitted between sisters of that next generation, or was a safety net created against such trauma and subjugation? The strength of the women who survived must have been transmitted down to them. The abilities of their surviving grandmothers have remained in their blood. The unexpected effects of the Khmer Rouge might have been an increased confidence in the next generation of Cambodian women.

Hmong American Sisters

The Hmong are an immigrant group who served the United States from the hills of Laos during the Vietnam war. When the war ended and the United States had lost, the Hmong were left homeless. They were at the beginning of the war a peaceful agrarian society without a written language. Thousands of Hmong were brought to the United States at the close of the war, but thousands more suffered in Thai camps until they could be processed out (Faderman, 1999). The Hmong family has always been multigenerational, with several generations living in very close spaces. In the United States, Hmong Americans maintained their clan structure and celebrated holidays and rituals related to arranged marriages between men and women. Girls have traditionally been married at very young ages, as soon as they are capable of bearing children. The average Hmong family has 10 children; Hmong Americans have 4 (Vang, 2004). Perhaps the difference between the traditional culture of the immigrants and the next generation has led to a larger gap in values than in any other Asian American culture.

Sisters of the next generation of Hmong immigrants have found themselves in the position of translating for their parents and grandparents. They developed an unusual role and cultural sophistication at an early age. Valuing education, their parents, who primarily farmed or ran small businesses, pushed both girls and boys to achieve, but the girls have been expected to stop their education when they get married. Elaborate presentation rituals occur each year during the Hmong New Year, but many young women have begun to opt out of the cultural demands for early marriage and children, pursing master's and doctoral degrees for the first time in the history of their culture. This change, having occurred in only one generation, has made it difficult for families to adapt.

Sometimes, sisters have been in concert about their adoption of Western ideas and sometimes they have not. Recently five Hmong sisters completed their degrees in the same year (Tharp, 2009). Ranging from an M.D. at Georgetown to a special education high school diploma from the local district, the sisters fulfilled a family dream of education and change—goals and achievements that they shared, encouraged by the tales of their parents' flight from Laos into Thailand and finally to the rural community of Merced, California. Each recounted the loneliness of education far from sisters, family, and clan and the intent to return to the family. Using modern technology, the sisters were able to encourage each other daily via cell phone. These sister separations occurred in ways that have not been typical for the Hmong people, and their inventive ways of continuing their connection has sustained them.

Unlike these sisters, many girls have experienced cultural shame and humiliation. On some occasions Hmong girls find their way into Southeast Asian gangs as a way of recreating a family structure more consistent with the younger women's new-found values. Yet this has become another avenue of victimization, where young Hmong women may be gang-raped or forced into prostitution; they are often led into that life by other Hmong girls (Straka, 2003). Such trauma has occurred when first-generation women attempt to find a place in the culture of the United States while still retaining ties to a values system that is broken by war and is based on gender.

Sisters who have been taught to suppress their emotions by their families may have desired contact with families who are more emotional. This need has sometimes placed them in a different cultural context and isolated them even more from those they love. Trust has been inhibited by all of these factors, yet a young woman who has sisters or a sister-like friend has found support. That support has extended to her desires and goals and provided a new avenue toward the belief in trust between women. The cost of her dreams and desires has sometimes been the loss of her family, community, and clan in which she is embedded. Yet the sister connection has often remained strong.

For all Southeast Asian women in the United States, their heritage has been darkly colored by the palette of war, trauma, rape, conflict, deceit, and guilt. For those who have found their place, the role of the sister relationship has been elusive. Tempering the colors of these emotional traumas has been difficult. True and honest sisterhood may have to wait for future generations who are further removed from the horror, where the palette may again be brightly colored by shared joy, hope, and fulfillment.

Pacific Islander Sisters

Pacific Islander sisters originate from wide-ranging groups of islands like Indonesia, which is the fourth-largest nation on earth (Piercy, Soekandar, Limansubroto, & Davis, 2005). Those considered here also come from the islands of Hawaii, Malaysia, and the Philippines. These three countries and one state have some common and many diverse features. The most significant link has been the role they have played as a crossroads between many countries—each of which has left its ethnic mark on the islands. Pacific traders included travelers from Europe in search of the New World, conquering East Asian nations, and Middle Eastern merchants. The islands also suffered from infighting within their groups, with constant conflict between warring tribes or individually defined nations. Yet each group of islands also has a unique history and set of family relationships contributing to the role that sisters play in each others' lives.

Hawaiian Sisters

Kanuha (2005) described the core values of the Hawaiian family:

> The foundation of *nā 'ohana* is its children and their relationship to elders (*kapūna*), their ancestors, and their physical, spiritual, and material surroundings. Core values that maintain the necessary balance between

family members and their natural environment include *aloha* (love and affinity), *mālama* (care), *kokua* (help, aid), *lōkahi* (unity, connection), *loko-maika'i* (generosity), *ha'aha'a* (humility), *ho'omana* (spirituality), and *pono* (righteousness or "right"). (p. 66)

These values were not traditional in the typical sense of U.S. roles. They were not defined in terms of specific couples. Hawaiian tradition permitted more than one lover. Marrying relatives was permitted within the Hawaiian royal family. Family members have been expected to care for each other in times of illness or death. Conflicts emerged when the traditional Hawaiian family values and specific gender roles were not fulfilled by individuals. Gender variations were made acceptable in order to maintain the consistency of the family's importance and centrality to the individual. The conflicts may also have been partially created by the lack of self-acceptance for one's indigenous roots.

Two sibling traditions that are prominent in the Hawaiian family have made their way into the relationship between sisters. One of these cultural traditions was the imperative for forgiveness within the family. This process has been ritualized in the ceremony of *ho'oponopono*. To teach this process to their young children, parents have often used it to resolve sibling conflict. The need to forgive a sister in a ritualized way may have contributed to the strength of Hawaiian sister relationships. The need to value ancestors was another ancient Hawaiian tradition. In some cases, this respect led to the delivery of one child to the grandparents, who then raised it. This practice is likely to separate sisters from one another.

Historically gender has not been a deterrent to real power in the Hawaiian world, as some of the strongest cultural beliefs were embedded in the goddess Pele, the maker of volcanoes. Hawaii has been viewed as a peaceful paradise, but it has welcomed outsiders only reluctantly. Travelers from other lands, including representatives from the country in which Hawaii now resides, have brought hardship, war, and leprosy to its shores.

Hawaiian sisters have shared the family respect and love of the islands that is natural to many, but they may long for a greater view of the world and more opportunity than the small chain of islands affords. These Hawaiian sisters have been very much the same as other American sisters in their beliefs, values, and drive. They may have had more distrust of outsiders, creating a stronger bond with the siblings and sisters within the islands.

Filipino American Sisters

Filipino American sisters tend to be very Westernized due to the occupation of the island by U.S. troops during World War II and the continued strong military presence of the United States in the Philippine Islands. Colonization has had some benefits but clearly has stripped the Filipino culture of many of its ethnic roots. It has indoctrinated the Philippines with U.S. educational values. Travel between the United States and the Philippines has been nearly as easy as it was between the United States and Puerto Rico. Family members in the United States are considered transnational and often send support back to family members in the islands. Yet there are ethnic values related to the family that have remained a strong part of Filipino culture in the United States.

Divorce is not legal in the Philippines, making marriage a stronger bond for Filipino American or bi-ethnic families in the United States. Families have often been multigenerational and extended, with large households. Women have held traditional roles as leaders in the Philippines and were by and large responsible for their family's financial management. The tribal traditions held women as chieftains and religious leaders. Some authors have suggested that the Filipina loses freedom during U.S. immigration compared to the freedom she had in the Philippines (Root, 2005). Sibling relationships have been specifically defined among Filipinos. The terms *sister* and *brother* have been used broadly to refer to anyone who was a part of the tribe or cultural group. Boys' education has been considered more important than that of their sisters, and sisters may be called upon to sacrifice their own opportunities for the good of the family. Sisters were traditionally valued for being beautiful, but also revered for their intelligence. As teens girls have been expected to take on adult responsibilities in caregiving but are not allowed sexual expression. Thus their roles have been established with a mixture of traditional and modern expectations.

Filipino American sisters have found some joy in shared strengths and intellectual curiosity. In a sister pair, both were expected to succeed, but the drive for competition did not seem to be present as it has been in some cultural traditions. The fondness for the term *sister*, reflected in the use of it for even elders in the tribe, suggested an ongoing appreciation for the blood sister bond. For Filipino American sisters, the history of colonialism may have created an internal dichotomy that each has solved in her own way. Too much identification with the colonialist values in the United States may have brought one sister into conflict with another, especially in the realm of sexual activity. Likewise, lesbian sexuality has not been accepted in the Philippines. The sexual orientation of one Filipina may bring her into conflict with her sister's religious and cultural beliefs. A middle-aged sister who has divorced her husband will have contradicted Filipino traditions. If she is a first-generation immigrant, she has also broken the laws of her homeland. Most other Pacific Island cultures have not forbidden divorce, making this a unique aspect of the relationship between Filipino American sisters.

Indonesian Sisters

It is hard to capture any of these traditions in a few pages or paragraphs, but the diversity of Indonesian sisters makes it especially difficult. Thousands of islands make up Indonesia, and only about one third of them are occupied. The religious beliefs of Indonesian people have varied widely; there are Hindus, Muslims, and

Spiritualists. *Malu*, meaning shame, has been a strong controlling function. Indonesian women were taught not to bring *malu* on their husbands or their families. Women were expected to defer to their husbands and lesbians had to remain closeted, often marrying in order to avoid detection.

In a world where women were controlled in this way, the potential for trust between sisters may have been damaged. This real anecdote represents the intricacies of life for a few women from Malaysia, a neighbor of Indonesia. Three college women came to the United States to complete their education. When I met them, three things seemed remarkable for me. One, they were all wonderful cooks (okay, not relevant). Second, two of them were sisters and all three did everything together. Third, their mother came and lived with them for 6 months of the year. At the time I was fairly naïve about the cultural traditions that might have created this situation, but as I got to know them, I began to understand more about the reasons for their behavior. Of course they were attempting to survive in a culture that was not always hospitable, and there was safety in numbers. More importantly, they were responsible for each others' behavior. Having their sister and cousin present meant that they were not likely to bring shame upon their families. The mother came for 6 months of the year to make sure they were continuing to fulfill their cultural traditions.

The three had a number of secrets that emerged as they began to trust me. One sister and the cousin had become aware that they were attracted to other women, and they were, of course, fearful of revealing this to anyone in their country. The sister who identified as lesbian was beautiful. She explained that a marriage had been arranged for her in Malaysia that would bring great honor to her family. She desperately wanted to defy tradition and stay in the United States. Both sisters explained that their brother was a celebrity in their country. Not only that, but he was transgendered; that was accepted because he was male and very successful. For two years the sisters struggled with their decision about returning to Malaysia. Finally, they went back, and the one woman married her predestined husband. I never heard from them again. Their love and support for each other was as natural as their mother's decision to cook for them 6 months out of the year. I wonder if their shared secrets survived the trans-Pacific crossing.

U.S. Sisters from the Indian Subcontinent

Asian Indian Sisters in the United States

In the subcontinent of India, religious preference has interacted with nationality to produce specific gender variations for women. Most Asian Indians have been Hindu, but there has also been a large Muslim minority. Hinduism has required that families practice their religious beliefs in the home, and the lack of socialization to a larger religious community has sometimes created very rigid family rules

(Almeida, 2005). For Muslims, the laws of the Indian democracy have not supported their faith through a theocracy, but they also have not impinged upon the practice of it. Religious law has been given precedence in religious matters. One of the significant issues for women in India has been the use of the veil within Muslim traditions. Some women who have worn the veil have felt it is protective. The Muslim tradition has defined the use of the veil as an attempt to suppress individuality, not to suppress women. Segregated women have suggested that their segregation provided them with a sense of protection against male aggression or rape, freedom to be educated without interference, and protection from being sexually controlled by men. Indian women have had have equal rights in India, but that equality varies by region, social class, and religious tradition, as it has, to some extent, in the United States.

The roles of Asian Indian women who immigrate to the United States are full of contradictions. In Asian Indian tradition, marriages have sometimes been arranged, and the choice of a wife was based partially upon the lightness of her skin. This tradition has been less related to internalized oppression in the Asian Indian culture and more related to religious and spiritual beliefs about the darkness and the light. In the United States, immigrant women have remained highly valued for their ability to provide sons. However, most have been free to marry whom they choose, to obtain higher education, and to earn a very good living as professionals or business owners. Asian Indian immigrant women have been the wealthiest immigrants in the United States (Almeida, 2005). Of course, these opportunities have been strictly limited by social class structure in India. Immigration to the United States has been a luxury only for the rich or those capable of paying for higher education in America.

Family roles and relationships have been deeply affected by immigration to the United States. Sisters coming from this diverse country to the United States may have immigrated with their families or alone. They may have come for higher education and remained afterward. Many were capable of living alone and providing for their own and their children's welfare. Often, they have provided for the welfare of their parents who remained in India. This role reversal has sometimes been difficult to manage. The degree of acculturation to U.S. gender roles has been unclear. Sibling relationships within Indian American families have traditionally been clearly defined. A woman had to remain under the control of her eldest brother, especially if she had a large dowry. That dowry was technically part of his inheritance, and he had a vested interest in its security. Within Indian tradition, this brother–sister relationship has been ritualized through the process of *Rakhi*. The brother and sister pair celebrate their relationship through the preparation of food by the sister and the giving of money by the brother. The cross-gendered relationship between siblings has been held in very high esteem and may have diminished the importance of sisters for U.S. immigrant women.

Traditionally, unmarried sisters have been supported by their brothers and have resided with him, his wife, his in-laws, and the extended family. This practice has continued for many Asian Indian women in the United States. The brother's extended family continued to provide support to other brothers and sisters in India, thus creating an international link between siblings that has not been easily broken. Sisters have usually left their family or their brother's family when they marry, although sometimes they stayed with the family of origin until their own children were born.

These traditions have created a time extension of the original family, with brothers and sisters living together into middle or young adulthood. Traditionally, the close ties of the Indian sibling group actually began at the age of 10, which is when older Asian Indian sisters began to take over care of their younger siblings. Recent research by Ramu (2006) suggested that this practice of living with extended family may be changing rapidly, both inside and outside of India, due to Western influence.

Pakistani Sisters

Unlike Asian Indian women, Pakistani women have been severely controlled by their culture and religious tradition. The country of Pakistan split from India to form a Muslim state in a bloody and violent civil war. For women, that war meant the loss of family members to one side of the border or the other. Women were also raped and forced into marriages. Women in Pakistan have become dominated by the Muslim tradition, which provided separate and unequal spaces and opportunities based on gender.

The Muslim tradition that is most predominant in Pakistan is the Sunni tradition. In 2005, only 22% of women in Pakistan were educated, compared to 49% of men (Nath, 2005). Polygamy has remained common, with men having up to four wives. All marriages were arranged and were not considered valid until a contract was signed and the marriage was consummated. Women remained virgins until their wedding day. There was little escape from this determined life for women, as they have generally not been allowed to hold jobs or support themselves. All have been subject to violence within the home and within the culture, with as many as 80% reporting domestic violence of some kind (Noor, 2004). As a result, depression and suicide plague women in Pakistan, sometimes related to the inability to marry the person of their choosing. On average, Pakistani women have seven children. All of these factors make it very unlikely that Pakistani women will migrate independently to the United States. The effects of such patriarchal dominance have had a deep effect on sisters and sister-like relationships of co-wives. The sister relationships that develop between wives of one husband may replace the lost sister relationships in the family, but this is not an easy transition. Relationships between wives have been complicated by jealousy, envy, and alliances among the wives.

In direct contrast to the brother and sister relationships of Hindu Asian Indians, Pakistani siblings have been separated by gender. They have not been allowed to eat or worship together. Sons often continued to live with their parents throughout adulthood, while daughters had to leave for their husband's households. Women who did not marry often lived with older relatives and became caregivers. How can sisters in such a culture survive in each others' lives? One woman quoted in the *New York Times* (2008) during the decline of Musharraf's popularity in Pakistan described the abduction of her brother on his wedding day, the despondency of her parents, and the plea that someone had to recognize the helplessness of her and her four sisters. Even the close connection between them may have threatened this patriarchal culture; most likely, it was severed in the service of marriage. Continued contact with a sister remained doubtful, especially with geographic separation.

Since the Pakistani family has been large, a woman may have many sisters, and it is likely there was a close bond with one or two of those sisters. Two or three sisters might have formed personal pockets of resistance, silenced by the domination of a patriarchal regime that intensified with the recent resurgence of the Taliban. These bonds may have helped provide the emotional strength needed for survival when women felt a complete lack of control over their lives. The knowledge that men (fathers, husbands, brothers, religious leaders) may terminate the contact with the sister at any moment has not always damaged the emotional strength of the connection, and that emotional lifeline has continued in the face of great loss and potential abuses. There have been no connections quite as strong as those forged by the heat of shared threat. Nath (2005) gave an example of an immigrant Pakistani woman in the United States who helped her sister, still in Pakistan, to escape from an abusive husband. The bond in that story stretched across time and distance to provide the lifeline one sister needed from another.

Some Pakistani women have remained single and been assigned as caregivers in the homes of other family members. Unmarried sisters, daughters-in-law, and extended female family members have helped to care for the elderly at home. Pakistanis have avoided nursing homes or assisted living facilities as much as possible. These caregiving roles may have kept sisters in physical contact with one another, even after marriage. One sister could have lived with another and cared for an elderly aunt or grandmother, although it is more likely that this would have occurred in her brother's home. It would have been a break in tradition for a Pakistani woman to care for a relative in her sister's home, since women follow the family of their husbands rather than their own kin. Sisters-in-law may come to play a much more important role in the lives of married Pakistani women. Co-wives may also form a sister-like bond, but this would require an unimaginably difficult transition. Sisters have been much less likely to take on parental roles with each other, since a man often had more than one wife or was very likely to remarry if he has lost a wife; an older wife might have been like a parent to a younger one. The presence of half-sisters has been greatly expanded in the polygamous families of some Pakistanis. Relationships between sisters and half-sisters may not have been differentiated in a culture where only paternity matters.

Sisters of the Middle East

Conflicts surround the nations of the Middle East as they have done for centuries—in fact for most of recorded history. How might such conflicts provide a context for a close family bond? The countries that have remained predominantly Muslim have been patriarchal and hierarchical in structure, but some have offered much greater freedom for women than others. This variability may have created stronger bonds between women and between sisters. Some women who have experienced the tightest of controls may have bonded in much the same way as sisters in Pakistan; others who experienced much greater freedom may compete and be more distant or may bond out of shared dreams and ideas.

Arab American Sisters

While most Arab women have been Muslim, those who immigrate to the United States have been predominantly Christian. Both faiths have been practiced within the context of Arab culture with stern parental control, very clear hierarchies making for clear generational boundaries, and a definitive role for women (Abudabbeh, 2005a). Families may have been shamed by one of their children, and the punishment for doing so may be severe. Arab women generally have been assigned to arranged marriages, although they have the right of refusal. Even though polygamy is practiced, women may insist that their marriage contract has a termination clause if the husband takes a second wife. Divorce has generally been prohibited by Christian Arabian sects and has been rare among Muslim couples. Fathers have generally taken custody of all children after a divorce.

The labels *brother* and *sister* have been used for all members of an Arab's *umma* or nation. Yet siblings of one family have often been kept together following a family dissolution. This manufactured very strong female bonding between sisters, without fear of disruption due to male or religious interference. The increased control that has been experienced by Arab women suggested they may maintain contact over some distance. The threatened loss of the mother following a divorce may make the sister tie even stronger. In such situations, an older sister actually assumes a maternal role. In a clinical case described by Abudabbeh (2005a), a father was encouraged to strengthen the bond between sisters who had experienced a difficult adjustment to the loss of their mother and their country following a divorce.

Armenian Sisters

Like many women from the Middle East, the relationship of Armenian sisters was formed against a backdrop of war and conflict. Their bond has been further distorted and perhaps strengthened by the presence of a contested genocide in 1915. Many older Armenians were the only survivors of their families and may have witnessed the murder and rape of many female family members, including mothers, grandmothers, aunts, cousins, and sisters. Survivors were quiet about their experiences; retelling was believed to create a continuous reliving of the trauma, as if it were still occurring. Most were the only surviving sibling and therefore, the only surviving sister.

An exception is the story of Vehanoush "Rose" Torosian and her sister Seranouch "Sarah" Panosian (Graybill, 1985). These two young sisters, along with many surviving members of their families, were forced out of their homes and completed a 6-month death march to Syria. Along the way, a 5-year-old sister was given to a Turkish soldier because the survivors were too weak to carry her. The two sisters did not know of her ultimate fate. They also described the abandonment of a boy in a river because no one could carry him any longer. One sister witnessed Turkish soldiers taunting children with promises of bread and then dousing them with gasoline and setting them on fire. When they were forcibly separated, the girls each survived as domestics in Turkish homes for the next 4 years, until one found her way to the United States. She worked very strenuously to help her sister get married in Cuba and then immigrate to the United States. The two lived in Midwestern cities about 3 hours apart until both were widowed. Then they moved in together, continuing their connection to their Armenian heritage by preparing traditional dishes and being active in the Armenian Orthodox church. Living through such trauma left them with many scars. Their survival created the same sense of guilt and ambivalence that has characterized most holocaust survivors. Independence and self-sustaining hard work became hallmark values of such an experience.

Multigenerational households were common before the genocide and continued with the immigration of widowed grandmothers and single parents into the United States. Family, therefore, was more important than individual experience. The gender gap among Armenians and Armenian Americans has followed traditional lines, with men being recognized as the head of the family but women being the head of the household. Siblings were very important and shared many gender-specific tasks. They also provided a strong sense of connection to the family's survival. Armenian sisters were likely to live near one another even after marriage and to participate frequently in each others' lives. The need for self-sufficiency drove extended families to share business responsibilities and create financial stability for one another. Thus sisters might have continued to work together in a family-run operation. One of the outcomes of the genocide was a strong emotionality that flavored Armenian interchanges. This emotionality may have resulted in high levels of conflict, followed by a gracious outflow of emotional generosity between sisters. Such dynamics may create heated and colorful relationships bound by the strength of emotional connection. The loss of generations of sister relationships may have left Armenian women without adequate role models for the relationship. The mandate for valuing the connection may have been both internal and external. In these ways the genocide raises the stakes of the sister connection, adding a specific dimension that enlarged the bond.

Iranian Sisters

As I write this, the women of Iran are being murdered in the streets for protesting the democratic election of 2009 that has reasserted a government that supports strict controls on women's lives. This new violence against women (and all of the protestors in Iran) has added a new chapter to the misogyny that many sisters will encounter in their lives. Traditionally, Iranian families were structured by the philosophy of Sufism. Enjoyment of life in the present, forsaking material things, and the diminishment of the self have all been hallmarks of this tradition. Classes were distinguished and kept separate from one another. Add to this the patriarchal nature of the Shiite Muslim tradition, and most women have been expected to subjugate their lives to the betterment of the family and of Iran.

Iran itself has remained very self-sufficient and independent. Authoritarian, often religious, leaders have inspired self-control in service of the country. Mediators were often used to deal with family and community conflicts that sometimes resulted in required silence over a period of years. Iranians who have immigrated to the United States are the most prosperous of all immigrant groups. They often live close to extended family members and maintain close contacts.

Iranian American women have the experience of both control by others and limited self-determination. Some of their experiences parallel those of Arab American women. Marriages have been arranged in Iran, and this practice may continue in the United States. Such arrangements were done to benefit both families. Polygamy was practiced in Iran, but is unlikely to persist for most Iranian Americans. In their tradition, the first wife has always remained more important. In the case of divorce, the children have gone with the father in Iran, but U.S. courts do not support this approach and have granted joint custody to both parents. At times the practice of paying the ex-wife and keeping the children may persist; this payment is referred to as a *mehr*.

Paternal custody was challenged in the case of two girls, Sarah, age 6, and Yasmine, age 15, whose mother was Belgian and whose father was Iranian. After the divorce, the girls were taken from Belgium to Tehran by their father (British Broadcasting Company, 2003, Dec. 3). Both parents claimed custody under the traditions of their nations. One day the girls left the father's house, hailed a cab, and were taken to the Belgian embassy. The wily sisters escaped their father's control but were held in Tehran at the embassy for 5 months while their release was debated on the international stage. Their cross-national heritage created an international war and a separate peace for them, joined only by their relationship with each other. They were surrounded by strangers while the world waited for their final disposition (BBC, 2004, May 6). While they had two staff members attending to their needs, their emotional connection would have been with each other—older and younger sister surviving and determining their own fate in a country that did not recognize their ability to do so.

Women who remain in Iran find other ways to exercise control within the family. They may ask other female family members to exert their influence on their behalf. Wives do this on behalf of their children. This tradition bonds women and girls in an extended family and creates the potential for a negotiated connection that benefits all of the women. Close and intimate bonds exist between friends and age-peers that follow gender lines. Women are connected to women and men to men by this intimacy, but gender valuation clearly favors males. They inherit twice as much as their sisters. Brothers become the keeper of their siblings at the death of a parent or at the death of a sister's husband. This relationship may not be close emotionally but is required financially and politically by the culture.

In the United States the relationships with other women and with men have been altered by a woman's potential to earn her own income, and many Iranian women who have migrated to the West have received professional educations. The close female–female bonding that was traditional back home may have remained unchanged by such opportunities, and the environment has been rich for the strong connection between Iranian sisters. Bonded by the tradition of close intimacy between same-gender peers, Iranian sisters may become inseparable. Sisters and lifelong female friends have provided an opportunity to challenge and intervene with hierarchically valued husbands, brothers, and fathers. The relationship has served both a practical and an emotional function. This may even extend to the professional development of sisters and women, offering continuing support in the face of potential abuse. Some authors have suggested that this abuse is more likely in immigrant families where the women have become more successful and adaptive than the men (Jalali, 2005).

Lebanese and Syrian Sisters

Lebanon and Syria were formed in modern times when the French colonialists were forced out during World War II. Prior to the French occupation, these countries were part of the Ottoman Empire. However, Syria—specifically Damascus—has an extensive presence in history and has existed since 2500 B.C. This recent independence has created a backdrop for the development of the cultures of Lebanon and Syria. The infusion of different traditions and faiths has resulted in democratic countries with a predominance of Christians but a sizeable minority of both Sunni and Shiite Muslims, all of whom hold power within the government. This structure has given refuge to immigrants escaping religious persecution in the region. Lebanese and Syrian tradition has become localized in the structure of family rather than in the traditions of any particular faith. It is the family that has formed the primary basis of individual identification.

The gender issues in these two countries have contained much that is modern and progressive and much that is regressive and controlling. Women or men who have affairs can still be stoned to death, but usually this punishment is meted out only to women (Minces & Pallis, 1982). Women are expected to be virgins on her wedding day, and some of the wealthiest women undergo hymen reconstruction. Yet women's work has been valued as another source of monetary income, and they have been encouraged to receive higher education as well as to complete professional training. These educational practices provide greater strength for the extended family, a family that has stayed connected and has provided financial support to all its members. The family has also provided child care, emotional support, medical support, and socialization to any given nuclear family. Brothers have still maintained control over sisters and inherit twice as much from a family estate. The relationship between brothers and sisters in Lebanon was developed as a replication of the masculine hierarchy in the Muslim tradition. Brothers have developed close emotional ties to their sisters but also control them with violence (Joseph, 1994).

Within the context of such divergent views of women and with the close ties of the extended family, sister relationships are likely to flourish. These values may persist in Iranian immigrant women. Sisters might have provided role models for educational endeavors, assistance with child care, emotional support for loss of safety in a violent family, and practical support during a health crisis. How might an Iranian American woman react to the stoning of a woman back home? What if her sister had been the victim of an "honor killing"? Some sisters might support the patriarchal intent of such a stoning; others would be appalled at the punishment. Both are likely to be devastated at the loss. Many experience tremendous grief and ambivalence. Some women may blame a sister for putting herself in harm's way. Little has been written of such experiences by sisters. The typical Syrian American or Lebanese American sister has known little of this type of intervention. Those who have migrated to the West have been likely to view such practices as a part of a horrific past where women were controlled more by such extreme punishment.

Sisters from Palestine

How can a woman come to understand a homeland that has a dubious existence? How was it defined, and what must be done to secure it? Such uncertainty has created a people who are determined and adaptive. The values they have endorsed vary based upon the countries to which they have adapted. If they resided originally in Saudi Arabia, they tended to be more conservative. If they resided in Lebanon or Syria, they tended toward more democratic and progressive ideals. Uncertainty permeated their lives and their consciousness. Families from Palestine have been defined by a continuous threat to the lives of their children, who have been targets in conflict after conflict. Losing their country has become a part of their consciousness and makes all things unpredictable (Abudabbeh, 2005b).

With this as the backdrop, the Palestinian family has been besieged. That sense of constant threat has been at least partly translated into the control of Palestinian women. They are expected to repopulate the country as it continues to lose its children. More children mean more likelihood of eventual success as a people—a re-establishment of their homeland and success as a nation. All of this pressure has created a demand for childbearing within Palestinian families, but it varies a great deal by region: urban women tend to enjoy more freedom than their rural sisters. This sets the stage for sister relationships that may be formed on the basis of shared household responsibilities. One such story is recounted in a review of two books on Palestine by Nancy Murray (2008). She tells the story of six sisters living in Palestine who are controlled by the patriarchal values of their father. One sister is forced into a marriage that becomes violent, but a younger sister rebels. After she proved her virginity, she was allowed to remain single and retain some control over her own life. When the father died, the sisters had to fend for themselves, with the entire group being more able to help the first sister out of the domestic violence.

In another page from Palestinian life, imagine two sisters living in the rural countryside of a Palestinian settlement. They have had many children and live side by side, hypervigilant yet terrified of forces they cannot control in their children's lives. Bombs and rockets arrive without warning, killing the child next door or two young sisters walking in the street. These threats have formed a shared trauma and potentially a traumatic bonding between women who see each others' children as their own and who attempt to protect them together. Even this bonding may not be enough to replenish what has been lost—a child, opportunities for education, or the freedom to stop bearing children who may die young. The loss of such a sister would be devastating, the experience of grief overwhelming. Yet such losses are common among Palestinians. Those who migrate to the United States arrive with such sadness. They have come to a country that does not fully understand and has not been able to fully embrace their sense of loss and isolation—of country, children, family, and sisters.

The sister connections for women who emigrate from the Middle East have been defined and controlled by many forces. These include wars and conflict, centuries of patriarchy, multiple losses, and diminished opportunities. Yet they have been strengthened by the need for each other. They have epitomized the survival of sisters who have lost so many significant others. They have been replenished by limitations, replaced by some opportunities for education and career, and always by the importance of keeping family close.

European American Sisters

Early in life I learned the importance of variations in the ways that White Americans live. This variation had created religious and family turmoil on both sides of my father's family: the English-Welsh integration with Polish-Czech did not come naturally or easily. It cost my paternal grandfather his 12-member immediate family and my father his grandparents. It also cost my grandfather his Catholicism. As for my grandmother, she was an outcast for marrying outside of her "race" in the early 1900s. Her mother lived with the young couple all of their married lives but never forgave them. This conflict is not unusual in recent history. The integration of various ethnic groups across Europe and in the United States has a long and dismal history. Many U.S. citizens who come from European stock do not even know their heritage, but all Europeans do. In the United States, as of 1990, 50% of European Americans were integrated by marriage; it seems amazing that the remaining 50% are not. The relationships of Europeans and European sisters have as much variety as those from any other continent, based upon history, religious preference, and the conflicts surrounding their ancestral countries.

Sisters from England

It is perhaps the English who most dominate the cultural scene in the United States. They have also for centuries attempted to dominate or colonize the world. This reputation is built upon certain British characteristics and has created a negative attitude against all that is "Anglo" in the far reaches of the old British Empire. Modern British and British Americans bear the guilt of those transgressions. In many cases they have moved from the role of conqueror to that of humanitarian, their ethnocentrism giving way to egalitarianism in the 20th and early 21st centuries (McGill & Pearce, 2005).

The dark side of this egalitarianism is the belief that those who suffer have brought it upon themselves. To understand this view, it is important to appreciate the fierce independence of the British. Accompanied by emotional stoicism, principled self-reliance, and the core value of hard work, the British and British Americans were able to leave family and home for decades. They colonized other countries and conquered their peoples. Because of this strong tradition of leaving home for new lands and warring with other peoples and nations, the connection with family is more easily severed by the British.

Initially dependent, British American women had to become much more independent. Those who remained in England were divided by class, with upper-class women being much more tightly controlled through Victorian times. Changes in British and American feminism in the mid-1800s and the again in the early 1920s forged the potential for independence. In addition, women were expected to contribute to the household and the farm on the frontiers of America. They held jobs to help pay the rent in the lower-class neighborhoods of London. Their role outside of the home became as important as their role inside of it. Independence and stoicism combined to minimize the likelihood of emotional closeness and connection. For Americans of British ancestry, the sister relationship may be appreciated without words or emotional expression. Conflict is often avoided or dealt with through silence and distance. Inadequacy and perfectionism may accompany sibling competition. Sisters may be more comfortable being in competition with each other than they are in connection with each other.

The translocation of British women throughout the former British Empire and the American colonies may make them less connected to their families of origin and more connected to their families of creation. Such an attitude would be consistent with the ever-expanding landscape that women of British descent have populated. Those who immigrated early to the United States, of course, came for religious freedom and the right to practice their self-determined faith. All of these faiths were presumed to be varieties of Christianity, although some may have been Wiccan. The modern British American, then, inherits a commitment to freedom of expression, especially in religious terms. This issue may be very complex for sisters who attempt to navigate different versions of Christian religious practice, let alone a combination of other faiths that have become common in America (e.g., Mormonism, agnosticism, or atheism).

How have British American sisters maintained relationships? Much of their connection may have been about the correct form—keeping contact at holidays and birthdays, sending thank-you notes promptly, providing invitations to major family gatherings. Some British American sisters have lived near each other and were able to converse regularly or spend time together, but little in modern America supports staying near one's home and family. The British interior has seemed to call for adventure and movement away and out, rather than in and toward.

Irish American Sisters

The Irish, while they remain next-door neighbors of the British, have a personality shaped by British policies about Ireland and enforced by British rule. Irish Catholics have experienced the brunt of this discrimination and prejudice. Two factors have formed a basis for the identity of Irish Americans. One was the seizure of Irish Catholic land in Ireland and the accompanying punishment of Irish Protestants who supported or were married to them. The second was the removal of Irish wheat, which could have fed the population during the Irish potato famine in the 1840s. Many Irish Catholics immigrated to the United States during that famine. The Catholicism traditionally practiced in Ireland had some unique features that influenced individual identity and family life. Jansenism, an Irish Catholic derivation, suggested that people are evil and deserve to be punished. This approach seemed to be interpreted in different ways for Irish men and Irish women.

Irish women have been perceived as strong and Irish men have been perceived as weak. Perhaps these are remnants of the matriarchal religious culture that once inhabited Ireland. Men's weaknesses have been related to laziness and drinking.

They were treated and discussed as if they were overgrown boys, without mature capabilities. Irish women were expected to overcompensate for them by being saintly and sane, as well as sober. The Irish have in some ways internalized the British oppression, believing they are inferior and need to compensate for that failure. They have done this very creatively through poetry and a tradition of oral history (Delaney, 2008).

McGoldrick (2005) has suggested that Irish men were socialized in pubs and Irish women were socialized in church. This guidance for individual development and the resultant division of labor seemed very one-sided, but it has left Irish women with much freedom and power. Many Irish women did not marry and were not expected to do so. Some assumed caretaking roles in the extended family but may have resented doing so. More single Irish women have immigrated to the United States than any other Irish group. Sons and daughters have been treated differently. Sons were overindulged and closest to their mothers. In Delaney's fictional account of Irish oral history traditions, a confused young man does not understand his mother's distance from him throughout his childhood. His father does what he can to provide nurturance, and he receives some from his mother's younger sister, Kate, but the feeling of being unwanted drove him to follow a storyteller and to attempt to learn that craft. Only years later does he discover that the triad of parents in his home were misunderstood—his aunt was his real mother. The complicated relationship between the two sisters, one married to the boy's father and the other living with them as the boy's aunt, unfolds and forms a backdrop for the entire historical novel.

Despite the usual closeness of a son to his mother in the Irish American family, the daughter has been the one likely to be her mother's caretaker in older age. Daughters were expected to achieve, were not required to marry or have children, and were likely to be educated. Other than the mother and son relationships, children have been closest to their same-gender relatives. This means that aunts, sisters, and female cousins evolve into the young girl's social group and may remain so throughout her life.

Irish American sisters have been fiercely independent but are likely to stay emotionally connected to each other. They have depended upon each other, but probably not too much. The eruption of Irish anger and venting of frustration may have been barriers to the relationship between sisters or may have no consequence—an understood part of the Irish personality. Many Irish women have learned to suppress their emotions but may hold them tightly in order to keep them under control. If they feel inadequate, they may express those feelings to a same-sex peer or sibling, as the gender divide has remained so strong in Irish American families. Irish American parents have often divided children into good and bad, labels that stick throughout life. Such dynamics may have created distance between sisters. Some sisters have come together primarily out of family obligation; negative feelings tied to previous parental favoritism may continue. Internal conflict, parental favoritism, a culturally induced sense of inadequacy, and a mandate to carry the moral fiber of the family have combined to create a heavy load for Irish American women. Even the high value placed on the friend-ship of a sister may not be able to overcome such odds.

Sisters from the Netherlands

Dutch women have enjoyed a degree of independence but are likely to value mutual respect as much as equal opportunity. As a people, the Dutch come from a small country that has been overrun many times by numerous invaders. This has created a nation of tolerance and adaptability. The primary faith has been Calvinism, which provides core values of tolerance, family, community, and conservative per-missiveness (De Master & Giordano, 2005). The strength of their beliefs has led Dutch people to rely on their own conscience rather than a set of religious rules. When the conscience has been unclear, the individual has suffered. Faith rested on the notion that others should be left alone to believe as they see fit.

Roles for men and women have been clearly defined among Dutch American immigrants. Each has enjoyed mutual respect for those roles. Men were not likely to make major decisions against the desires of their wives. This tolerance of gender expression has extended to sexual orientation, as Amsterdam became an early supportive urban center for the gay and lesbian population in Europe and the world. There has also been a great deal of support for leaving home and returning to the fold. With this as a backdrop, sisters of Dutch ancestry who live near one another have provided a great deal of mutual emotional support and acceptance. Judgment among sisters has been replaced by tolerance for difference and change. Mutual respect within lesbian and heterosexual marriage may have resulted in lower divorce rates, but the decision to divorce would most likely have been sup-ported by the sister. In short, Dutch American sisters seem likely to have a strong emotional and practical bond that adjusts well to changing life circumstances. These bonds have not been greatly influenced by age differences, education, or similarity but do reflect differences in childlessness and partner status (Voorpostel, van der Lippe, Dykstra, & Flap, 2007).

Sisters of German Descent

Germany will forever be associated with its role in modern history as an axis of evil. The aggression of Germany against the rest of Europe in the conflicts that became World War I and World War II have created an enduring image in America of treach-ery and assault. The result was a divided Germany that was not allowed to mourn its losses or its tragic division. Of course, this reputation, while temporarily deserved, has not been the sum total of the German contribution to humankind. German contributions, including symphonies, plays, philosophy, psychoanalysis, and art, have been downplayed as a result of the transgressions perpetrated against others, especially their own Jewish citizens (Winawer & Wetzel, 2005). Those of German descent in the United States and throughout Europe have desired nothing more than to blend into the background and to minimize the heritage they share. If they are Jewish, they may have wanted to minimize the suffering of their grandparents and great-grandparents, preferring to focus on present opportunities more than historical atrocities.

Emotionally, this burden is similar to the one European Americans have felt for the history of slavery. It has brought guilt, disconnection, sadness, depression, and an inability to embrace the gifts of life. The struggles inherent in this process have left German American sisters with a self-critical attitude that may become pervasive and accompanied by severe guilt and shame.

Family closeness and connection have remained a strongly held value for Germans. Nuclear and extended families were important, and each has been maintained by clear boundaries with the external world. Individuals have had their own clear boundaries within German tradition and have held closely a desire to create a home space for the individual or family. German American women have been encouraged to seek an education, and that education has been highly valued by their peers. Gender roles have required that women keep a clean and orderly home containing well-behaved and high-achieving children. German American fathers have tended to be severe and have used firm discipline. Children in the typical German family learn have learned to suppress emotion and avoid conflict. Friendships have been considered a unique form of intimate relationships and have been clearly distinguished from relationships with acquaintances. Sisters, within such a context, have become close but emotionally removed from each other. They have been likely to defend each other to the outside world but may have remained curiously unaffected by each other in the home. The desire to avoid conflict and to achieve high honors could have led one sister to be competitive and conflicted with her same-gender siblings. Forging a close emotional connection within these cultural and familial boundaries would have been difficult and may not have been desired. The intact nature of family relationships and spending time together were far more important than the sharing of emotional closeness.

In a rare analysis of the development of sister relationships, Braunbeck (1993) detailed the communication of two central themes related to sisters in German films created by Margarethe von Trotta, a female director. The first theme was the theme of differentiation—the need to create a polarity from the sister to define the self. The other theme was the threat of symbiosis—the merging of the sister with the self. Both of these themes have been important in the context of Germany's geographic division and the effects of that division on the psyche of German American sisters.

Greek American Sisters

The importance of Greek extended family is forever embedded in the consciousness of Greek Americans by the film *My Big Fat Greek Wedding*. In that film, a non-Greek man who married a Greek woman came to an understanding of how differently tradition and family may be defined across Europe. There have been many divisions of Europe through the centuries—northern and southern in the Renaissance, for example. After World War II, Europe was divided literally into east and west. The eastern part of Europe became associated with communism and socialism, the western with democracy and independence. This division persists in the minds of many American immigrants from Eastern and Western Europe. It has led to a feeling of great pride and concurrent inadequacy on the part of Greek Americans. Greeks were the founders of democracy, but this role has often been forgotten by others in the subtle prejudices that persist about east and west (Killian & Agathangelou, 2005).

Greek Americans have often maintained a closely connected community in the United States. This has been evident in the persistence of the Greek tradition of naming children for grandparents. The first boy is often named for his paternal grandfather; the first girl is named for her paternal grandmother. The process is repeated for the maternal grandparents. This has created, for sisters, an automatic identification with their father's or mother's side of the family and a favored relationship with their grandparent of the same name. Greek American men were given more sexual freedom, both within and outside of marriage. This was attributed to the widely held belief that Greek men were incapable of resisting their sexual needs. Greek women were expected to maintain the family household and give children their spiritual and moral education. Because children have been highly valued in the Greek American world, this role of the primary parent was also highly valued and powerful. Greek sisters often raised their children together and lived together in older age. Due to the tight closeness of the Greek extended family, many of the elders have lived nearby and assisted with the care of children, especially those named after them.

Even the sister role has had some ritualized functions. If a sister was the matron of honor at her sister's wedding (and it is expected she would be), she was also the godmother to the first child. Thus, a girl in a Greek American family has been likely to grow up with a defined and specific connection to a community of women—a grandmother for whom she was named, an aunt who functions as her godmother, her own sister who has shared these same supports, and a mother who was the axis around which all of these relationships pivoted. Sisters may have shared the role of preparing traditional Greek foods and helping to provide service at Greek festivals, most often connected to the Greek Orthodox Church.

The history of democracy and independence may have also informed young Greek American sisters' lives, promoting individual academic achievement and shared business achievement. Their mother's and father's side may have claimed greater accomplishments for the female children identified with their side of the equation, and this may have promoted competitive feelings between the sisters.

Sisters from Hungary

Hungary has had a mixed personality as a country (Laszloffy, 2005). It has been associated with both eastern and western divides in Europe. It has been both pagan and Catholic in its primary religious faiths. It has trusted outsiders and been suspicious of them. Many have felt that this mix creates a unique tension for the individual Hungarian, who may have suffered from internal conflicts leading to depression and suicidal ideation. Some have even suggested there might be a cultural link to bipolar disorder. On the positive side, Hungarians have a unique language that is dramatic and tends toward the highly enthusiastic. There have been two different waves of immigrants from Hungary to the United States. The first were economic refugees fleeing during World War I. The second group included wealthy business and professional people who fled during the failed attempt for Hungarian independence following World War II. Both groups have assimilated into the European American culture of the United States, but with very different results.

Laszloffy (2005) described two sisters who personified this emotionally defined aspect of Hungarian sisters. Both were dramatic and artistic performers. Each excelled in a different aspect of drama, and their competition was minimized by the elevation of both sets of skills within the family. Hungarian American sisters with internal conflicts that find emotional expression through dramatic activities, storytelling, or myth making have engaged in the cultural traditions of Hungary. The potential for over-dramatization may make it difficult to maintain connection or may make these connections volatile. Hungarian American sisters, then, have inherited a cultural tradition that endorses dramatic re-enactment of the sister connection, with much emotional upheaval likely to occur.

Italian American Sisters

Like Hungarian sisters, Italian sisters inherit a divided sense of self from a divided country. Italy has long been separated into northern and southern, separated by beliefs, values, and nature. Northern Italy has been the home for the prosperous, the artistic, and the successful; southern Italy has been the home for the poorest of its citizens. They were the ones repeatedly driven from their homes by earthquakes and volcanoes. They were also the ones invaded repeatedly by those from across the sea and those next door (Giordano, McGoldrick, & Klages, 2005). In the face of such turmoil has stood the Italian family—always constant, never changing. It provided the foundation for the individual woman and drew her back to the clan. This has been just as likely to be true for Italian families in California as it is in Italy. Italian American families in the eastern portion of the United States have tended to live in neighborhoods where generations have grown up with the same families for neighbors and friends. Italian Catholics have worshiped a very different God than the one worshipped by Irish Catholics. This God was benevolent and forgiving. The Italian Catholic church was more ecumenical in the inclusion of pagan traditions, mysticism, and even some Muslim beliefs. However, this flexibility did not always extend to gender roles in the Italian or Italian American family.

Gender roles in Italian American families have remained traditional, with men maintaining the power in the family and women minding the home. Education was provided for boys, and girls were allowed to attend college only if the funds were available after educating the boys. This has been changing rapidly, but the change has created great discomfort among traditional Italian Catholics. Extended families have provided a great deal of support for sisters within the Italian culture but may have limited their freedom to choose the life they wish to lead. Girls have been raised to stay close to the neighborhood, leaving for education or marriage temporarily but then returning to live in the close connection of the family and community. Failure to do so may be seen as a betrayal and has sometimes created great strife. Sisters living through such a family quarrel may have periods of protracted, emotionally charged silence between them. Since a girl's most trusted advisors have been her family members of the same gender, the loss of a sister may have meant the loss of a friend, confidant, and ally within the tight family circle. On the other hand, sisters who have not experienced this separation may remain close to each other, both emotionally and geographically, throughout their lives.

Conclusions

Cultures have envisioned different roles for women and for sisters as well. It has been difficult to embrace and understand the commonalities across cultures, let alone the potential differences. Of course, women have defined themselves and their relationships apart from the influence of culture or ethnicity. Those are merely boundaries, established to be respected or to be broken down. As women's roles have begun to change around the world, the ways that sisters continue to hold each other close, to fight, to forgive, or to separate have continued to evolve, each variation conducted by the woman who was called sister.

10

First-Stage Integration

"What difference is there between us, save a restless dream that
follows my soul, but fears to come near you?"
Kahlil Gibran (1961/1994, p. 11[1])

It was important to me that the words of the women not remain stagnant in a
world that is changing too fast for words. On the one hand, it seemed that the
women's words and feelings were universal and timeless, involving issues like
sibling rivalry and the importance of lifelong connection. Yet the stories were
primarily those of White women in America. What might be gained by completing
a hermeneutic analysis that included some material from the previous chapters
and expanded the scope of this work to include considerations of diversity among
and between sisters? To accomplish this hermeneutic analysis, I collated themes
from the previous two chapters and integrated them with the primary themes
from my research, using specific examples from the women in my research project
to provide illustration.

The structure of this chapter emerged from both sources as I extracted the
themes of different cultures, discovering the points of similarity and difference
with my project's findings. This integration eventually emerged as an understanding of difference between sisters, similarity across differences, and differences
within similarity. I hope these themes have come to represent some of the possible understandings that a more diverse perspective on sisters has to offer. I was
aware as I worked on this chapter that the task of explicating all themes from all
cultures would be the subject of another entire book. This, then, is the beginning of
integration—pointing the way forward for a more cross-cultural understanding
of sisters.

[1] Reprinted by permission of Penguin Books Ltd. from The Vision: Reflections on the Way of the
Soul by Kahlil Gibran, translated by Juan R. I. Cole (Arkana, 1997). Translation copyright © Juan R.I.
Cole, 1997.

Identity and Facts About Diverse Sisters' Lives

The complexity of the sister experience has not always been fully understood or evaluated by researchers and scholars. This theme was present for much of the cross-cultural writing, and it was also present in the issues surrounding lesbian and bisexual sisters. The presence of a bicultural or tricultural identity for women creates different shades of similarity and difference, adding new components to the diverse personalities and interests that sisters possess.

Biculturalism calls for the ability to blend more than one world and worldview into identity, and sisters have reconciled this in many different ways. In the process they may have become quite divergent in their values, as one remains more traditional or ethnically specific in her approach to life and the other grabs hold of Western influence and adopts it wholesale, rejecting much of her cultural tradition. This biculturalism or triculturalism may also involve a cultural community that is not defined by national boundaries but by life condition, as one sister embraces a deaf culture or another immerses herself in lesbian life. Some of these communities may exclude the sister or include her as an honorary member, but she will not be fully integrated into a culture to which she cannot belong. Yet each sister may share similar identities that are governed by ethnicity, race, and nation. These similarities may help to sustain the connection between two sisters, alike in some of their cultural affiliations and different in others.

There is another part of life in which sisters share an identity. Their lives are often interwoven with bias, discrimination, and gender-specific trauma. They may have a shared history of discrimination based upon gender, class, ethnicity within country, race, marital status, language use, immigration status, or religious preference. Many sisters share these traits and have experienced bias and even hatred directed at them because of substantial difference from the country or culture where they reside. Korean American women face bias because of their language use. Many are fluent in English, but those who are not may remain isolated in a community that does not embrace their native tongue. This isolation may actually increase the close relationship of immigrant sisters who remain close geographically and closely connected to a larger community of Korean women and men.

Specific examples of gender inequity emerged from the literature and from my research. For some women gender equity was symbolic of the negative experiences they shared in Cuba. It was associated with socialism and the reign of Castro—a negative affiliation for many Cuban Americans. In the research project, some sisters acknowledged support for gender-based roles in their families and in their religious practices.

These fears of gender equity stand in contrast to global issues, where women and girls are demeaned or diminished. Gender inequity has been ritualized in many cultures, including Pakistan, where separate and unequal practices exist for women and men. The experience of Cambodian women, whose own government turned against them, was similar to that of Pakistani women, whose freedoms have been limited by the Taliban. Gender inequity was present for the women in my research, although not usually as dramatic or sweeping in its effects. Their experiences of inequity were not so ritualized or nationalized as those experienced by some immigrant women from more gender-polarized countries of the world.

The underground nature of gender discrimination in world democracies may mean that covert bias has not been easily uncovered or understood. Individual women may not have considered the discriminating aspects of gender at all, but those biases have still been present in some subtle ways. Many of the women in the research project mentioned health care issues and financial concerns related to older sisters. These challenges may have been rooted in the combination of gender and age discrimination for women. Benefits may have been withheld from the elderly in the United States. Since women live longer, they are differentially affected by these losses. Similarly, lesbian women in the United States have experienced nationalized discrimination by their own country. Without the freedom to marry and receive full financial and social benefits, they have been marginalized within their own democracy. Unlike the national discrimination experienced by women in Pakistan or the older women in the United States, this discrimination is not something that has usually been shared by sisters.

There have been other types of hatred and violence against women that not all sisters share. Different herstories of domestic violence, rape, sexual assault and molestation, scarring, and shaming have occurred throughout the world. Many examples of culturally supported rape and violence were described in the literature. Most often these were related to war, refugee translocation, and toppled governments. Nicaraguan women witnessed violence against their sisters at the hands of *coyotes*—the men who were supposed to help them cross multiple borders to immigrate into the United States. Cambodian women experienced the state-sanctioned rape and murder of successful and intelligent individuals under the Pol Pot regime. The women interviewed in my research also mentioned the awareness of these differences when one sister had been sexually assaulted or raped, and another had not.

In some instances, sisters have been placed in the position of supporting or abetting violence against their sister. This has occurred among the second generation of Hmong immigrants to the United States. In an attempt to adapt to the U.S. culture where they were forced to immigrate after the Vietnam war, Hmong adolescents have formed gangs, and this gang subculture has supported the rape of many young Hmong girls as part of an initiation process. Girls who have endured this process have been used to find other girls for the gang to rape, and in some cases sisters have identified sisters as victims for the gang. They have done this for fear of their lives and out of their own resignation. Sisters have also been placed in the position of supporting culturally sanctioned deaths of their sibling in some countries. For example, sisters may still witness their sister's stoning in Syria and Lebanon—punishment for an extramarital affair. In the film *The Stoning of Soraya M.* (Burns et al., 2009), which has just been released in theaters, an aunt pleads unsuccessfully for the life of her niece, who has been sentenced to such a death. Such examples may be rare but do occur.

Most often, sisters have played a supportive role in helping each other to overcome culturally sanctioned abuse or violence. Polygamous families in Pakistan or Iran may have permitted abuse of wives, and this practice may have bonded sisters together if they were allowed to maintain contact with one another. Fear that her sister might be abused in such contexts has persisted for immigrant women who left these countries to go to countries where domestic violence is punished by law. One woman described her attempts to help her sister from afar. Like women in the study who attempted to intervene in cases of domestic violence, these attempts were not always successful. Sisters from many nations have shared the frustration and grief of being unable to make a difference in protecting a woman from abuse by a violent brother-in-law or partner.

Guilt and grief have also permeated the lives of women who have witnessed the atrocities of war and violence against their sisters. Palestinian and Israeli women suffer continued threats to sisters, children, and nieces from the violence between their peoples in a fight for a homeland each believes belongs to them. The women of Israel and Palestine have shared overwhelming grief at the loss of life and have often called for peace in the Middle East to stop this violence. Similarly, a woman who lost a sister in war may feel survivor guilt. Surviving Armenian sisters who witnessed the holocaust of their people may feel guilty about their own survival. Women who survived the wholesale rape of Armenian women have persistent memories of trauma. The younger women in the Armenian American culture have lost a generation of role models for the sister relationship, as generally their great-aunts and grandmothers did not survive together.

While most of the women in the study were not subjected to the violence of war in their own land, similarity to the ravages of war can be found in other experiences. Those interviewed mentioned domestic violence, sexual crimes against sisters, and molestation during childhood. Women whose sisters were molested during childhood felt survivor guilt if they escaped the abuse. Violence within the home was the primary source of this type of hatred against women. Rape of one sister also triggered guilt in her sibling, who became aware of her sister's rape only much later. The sadness that became a part of the sister relationship was profound. There was no pervasive threat to all women, like those reported for sisters in nations under assault or war, but traumatic survival seemed to bring about the same feelings of loss, sadness, guilt, and shame.

Against the bloody pages of these shared herstories, the shared strength of the sister relationship emerged. Resilience was present in the surviving Southeast Asian mothers and grandmothers who immigrated to the United States and France. That resilience has been passed down to sisters in the next generation. The buoyancy of surviving Armenian sisters bonded them to each other as they tried to stay geographically close and often shared a business in the United States. Over centuries of being conquered and re-conquered, the potency of support, acceptance, and tolerance infused the relationships of Dutch sisters. In my research, the women reflected a similar resilience in many ways, as they discussed the lifelong relationship between sisters and the forming of female subgroups within the family, which provided emotional support and strength.

Subtle forms of violence have led to an increased reliance upon family and community relationships with other women. The longstanding division between northern and southern Italy may have created closeness with extended family members and a desire to keep the sister close. A similar dynamic was apparent in the participants of my study who described farm families. Their survival depended upon having many hands to complete the labor-intensive work. Such bonding may have created greater emotional closeness. However, it might have limited opportunities for girls, who were supposed to stay near the neighborhood in urban settings or close to the farm in rural ones.

Sometimes sisters helped each other to overcome engendered cultural mandates. This has been demonstrated by women from Hmong families who helped a sister achieve high goals in the face of family and cultural bias against those goals. Likewise, the community of women provided a backdrop for daily life in Pakistan, whether of half-sisters in the original family, the sister-in-law (wife of the eldest brother) and her female children, or co-wives to one husband. Although there were no women in my research who came from polygamous cultures, one woman had established such a strong link between her sister and her husband that she felt like he had two wives. Among study participants, the unique ability of a group of women to bond in the face of cultural discrimination arose in the tight female bonds between mother, daughter, and sister or sisters and nieces. The power of these female connections provided the opposing force and the emotional depth required to fight prejudice, hatred, and the aftermath of violence against women.

Sisters of Difference

Identity and facts about sisters' lives have been affected by the differences that define them. Chapter 8 reviewed these differences in relation to disability and lesbian or bisexual identity. In the midst of such life-defining identities, there were similarities that united sisters and produced a desire to understand how the differences could be managed within the sister bond. Some of these similarities appeared in my interviews. The evaluation of those similarities in identity across profound differences in identity provides a deeper understanding. Sisters found a way to transcend difference. Secrets were shared with the sister first. A lesbian may be most likely to disclose her identity to her sister, especially if she expects critical reactions from parents. While acknowledging the difference, family rituals were still shared.

Similarly, women in the research project described secrets that were shared. Sometimes this occurred due to difference between a young daughter and her mother. The women in the study also had shared secrets with sisters and asked them not to divulge them to a third party, sometimes the mother. The disappointment they experienced when this confidence was violated was very similar to the experience of being "outed" to other members of the family. Family beliefs and mores were often shared despite differences. Among the women in the study, some values were shared, but often very different values had evolved. For example, one sister called another a bigot, indicating that shared early beliefs might be altered as life unfolded.

Parallel responses to prejudice may also harden the sister connection. External prejudice against a sister can heighten family cohesion, while family prejudice against a lesbian sister may heighten sister support and emotional connection. Likewise, the women in the sister project reported sticking together through difficult family issues like parental divorce during childhood.

When those differences that so profoundly affect identity have not been shared, understanding takes more effort and wears on the sister connection. This was somewhat true of disabled and non-disabled sisters. Perceptions of disabled sisters changed over the lifespan, as did perceptions of sisters in general for women in the study. One factor affecting this was the age of the sister when she became disabled. If a sister was disabled from birth, the family adjusted to her because she had the experience of disability all of her life. Those with later onset of disabilities required the family to mourn and adapt to the changing identity of the sister. These emotional changes were harder to manage than the gradual development of identity in a sister who was disabled from birth.

Related changes caused by unforeseen difficulties that were encountered in any sister's life affected the sisters in the study. For example, a young adult sister with mental health or chronic health issues that emerged may not have been understood until much later. Some non-disabled sisters or heterosexual sisters had resentment or anger at being defined by their sister's identity. They may have experienced uniqueness in their own identity that was entirely constructed by the sister's disability or lesbianism. They may have had thoughts like, "I am the able-bodied sister" or "the intellectually normal sister" or "the emotionally normal sister" or "the heterosexual sister" only because the sister is "other." A straight sister was required to deal with her own coming out related to her sister's experience as a lesbian. For some sisters, a lesbian sister's coming out caused them to question their own sexual orientation. In somewhat similar terms, an immigrant woman from west Asian might have found that her sister's balance between traditional and assimilated values also generated a need to adjust or question her own identity. These experiences could create a unique identity for some—one that was not about their own development but about the life circumstances, proclivities, and choices of the sister.

Sometimes differences between sisters required caregiving. Most of the litera-ture has suggested that sisters feel good about the benefits of the caregiving role. Older sisters in single-parent African American families have provided care to younger sisters and valued the increased sense of responsibility they learned. They have also described feeling more mature because of the responsibilities they shouldered. Caregiving may have been required if a sister had a disability. The non-disabled sisters who provided such care have reported developing greater compassion. Beyond caregiving itself, the sister may have developed a sense of protectiveness around issues of prejudice and discrimination. The women in the sisters' project demonstrated similar protectiveness when defending sisters who were smaller, younger, or more naïve.

Women with profound differences were also likely to find a platform where they could rally against seemingly universal prejudice for a sister. She may have joined her disabled or lesbian sister in the fight for equal access or equal rights. The degree to which each of the sisters participated in such activism and how each was present for caregiving may be judged as sufficient or not, just as similar activ-ities were judged by women in my research. Extreme differences in the identity issues of sisters may have called for different levels of response and adaptation than have usually been required, because of differences in choice or life circum-stances individually affecting sisters.

Caregiving

Caregiving emerged as such a large theme in the literature on difference that it is important to discuss it in some depth. The kinds of care varied from physical to practical to emotional. Much of the time the description was rooted in the mother–daughter–sister triad and described the changing interactions involving caregiving over the lifespan. Women in my research also described these dimen-sions in relation to caregiving and had many of the same things to say. Some of these were about the judgments rendered toward the adequacy of the sister's caregiving role. Nowhere was this more apparent than the description of depen-dent disabled sisters in the literature and mothers or sisters who were becoming increasingly disabled by aging in the research project.

There were gender differences in these roles. As the mother of a disabled sister aged, the sister took over responsibility much more than the brother. A similar dynamic was reported by the women in the sister project as it related to the care of aging mother—daughters provided more care than sons. Most of the time women began to feel this increased responsibility at midlife. As they themselves aged, they were less able, or perhaps willing, to take on caregiving roles for the mother or sister. One woman I interviewed discussed her sister's absence from her mother's care—she was there in the hospital but not for the long haul. Interestingly, the research has suggested that mothers have this same perception of a sister's care for her disabled sibling. It was reported that sisters think they are doing far more than their mothers think they have done. So the demands for care-giving and the comparison of willingness to be a caregiver provided similar themes in the literature and in my research.

Some specific caregiving roles were present in the ethnic literature. It has been very common for older African American sisters to provide care and grooming for younger sisters. This became ritualized as a part of sharing a specific cultural similarity. A similar cultural demand required older Filipino sisters to provide pragmatic care for their younger sisters. In the research project, women reported providing practical care for their sisters by feeding them and bathing them, but the ritualized nature of that caregiving was not described. Practical care was also given to sisters who had to manage prejudice and bias within the culture and were not fully self-sustaining because of it. This was clear from information related to immigrant Dominican Latina women. Dutch sisters also typically provided practical care to each other. The Dutch, among others, have tended to have very strong emotional bonds with their sisters. This experience was similar to experiences mentioned by women in the study who said things like, "I would do anything for her" or "I would give up my life for my sister."

In evaluating the literature about sisters of difference, it was possible to unearth ways in which sisters stayed the same and continued to share important moments and experiences. Sisters whose lives were not parallel sometimes found profound strength in being understood by someone close. Most of the time those sisters did not share a defining life characteristic like sexual orientation, degree of assim-ilation, or disability, but they were still able to find deep connections and corre-sponding experiences that tied them together across difference.

Differences Within Similarity

Defined primarily by a shared ethnic, national, or racial identity, sisters may have had differences that defined the essence of who they were. Sisters within a family may have been differentially affected because of their age. Their sense of self may have been altered by the way they each experienced an alcoholic mother who became sober or a father who molested a daughter and then left the family to avoid prosecution. If one sister was young when the mother was an alcoholic and the other wasn't born until after she became sober, the differences in their psy-chological identities may have been immense—even if both were Irish. If an older sister was molested yet managed to keep her father from her younger sister by telling and being heard, the younger sister may have grown up without the shame and secrecy that often accompany such abuse—even if both were Cuban.

Ethnic identity has been understood as the cumulative effect of a set of experi-ences and the integration of them into the sense of self. This development has not always followed neatly defined stages, but if major events occurred that affected that identity, the adaptations may have created strain for the sister relationship.

African American sisters' first encounters with prejudice may have occurred years apart. Such an event was expected to awaken ethnic identity and may have created a rift in the sister relationship if those encounters and the emotional reactions to them were not well understood by the sister. In my research, sisters reflected upon specific profound events that formed them that the sister did not understand fully, like the experience of giving birth and being a parent. In Cuban families, older and unmarried sisters may have continued to reside with parents or extended family. Divorcing sisters may have moved back into the parents' home in Latina families. These experiences of migrating home were mentioned in the study related to financial needs or need for additional help, like on a family farm. Economic necessity could certainly be the reason why some women from other nations live with their parents for extended periods, but the move has more often represented the implementation of a culturally specific gender belief.

Sisters who share a common ethnic or cultural heritage can also differ in terms of appearance, experience of prejudice, and discrimination. Racial features that are traditional for African American women (darker skin, highly textured hair, darker eyes) may have created less favored status within the family or larger community. If sisters were substantially different in these physical characteristics, these differences may have defined a significant part of their identity. Historically, the lightness of skin, hair, and eyes has created wide differences in opportunity for African American women who could "pass" as White. Similarly, my research participants described differential treatment by parents for girls whose features or personality characteristics aligned them with their father's or mother's family. Such alignment, depending upon the values of the family and community, may have created greater rewards or isolation. Immigrant sisters may have differed from one another based upon religious preferences, and the sister whose preferences were aligned with those of the family may be favored. For example, an immigrant Latina woman who moves away from her Catholic family history to embrace an evangelical tradition or to become an agnostic may have experienced isolation and distance from her family. Differences in religious identity may have meant that some sisters shared holidays with their parents and extended families, while others have not. Women in the research study identified similar potential for isolation when one left the family's tradition. One suggested that similar strengths and experiences were created by shared religious beliefs. The women also mentioned rifts created by religious differences with their sisters.

Family History and Difference

The ways that families have managed diversity among sisters may be similar to the ways they have managed bigotry and hatred in the larger community. If parents have provided a strong model for maintaining self-respect while confronting prejudice, family cohesion may have grown. Parents able to do this may have been able to mange prejudice within the family in a similar way. Such abilities have usually required a continuing attunement to the ways that discrimination can permeate the culture. Recent difficulty understanding that bias against gays and lesbians has been wrought of the same cloth as racial hatred challenges parents to manage both with equanimity. Parental favoritism related to cultural bias may create rivalry or conflict between sisters who differ because of skin color or sexual orientation. Yet this has not often been the case: parents who have managed one prejudice external to the family have not always done so within it.

On the other hand, the disability of a sister may have called forth family cohesion. Occasionally, parents favored the disabled sister to compensate for the prejudice of the larger culture. The disabled sister's reaction to this bias may have helped to bridge the gap created between sisters of differing abilities. Cultural values that were held in high esteem may have, paradoxically, created the same effect. The desire for academic and occupational achievement among some Western Asian families may have created a bias in favor of the more intelligent or highly achieving sister. Such favored status has also been created within a family, as was seen in the differential value given to musical, intellectual, athletic, and artistic gifts among sisters in my research. A similar dynamic may occur in Hungarian American families, whose tradition may highly value a dramatic approach to life. This could create a competitive reaction among sisters with the demand for such thespian expressiveness.

Again, mother–daughter–sister triads have formed in the management of this kind of difference. The literature reported this in relation to lesbian and heterosexual mothers and daughters. Triads of all kinds formed, including the alignment of similar mothers and daughters or dissimilar ones (e.g., lesbian mother and daughter, heterosexual mother and daughter). Of course, personality characteristics may have been more important than identity after families have adjusted beyond the coming-out period. It is also possible that the cross-identity barriers have remained.

The parental role in managing difference takes several forms. Parents who share an ethnic and cultural heritage with their children may actively manage the prejudice experienced by a child within the larger cultural context. This is frequently true of African American parents. In the research project women described similar management on the basis of being global nomads if they were "military brats" or if they moved frequently within the United States. This management may have been required when children experienced prejudice because of poverty and exclusion based upon religion. On occasion, parents have also made matters worse. Parental favoritism has been something most parents try to avoid, but sometimes identity differences have reinforced parental bias for one daughter over another.

Parental favoritism has been ritualized among some Greek Americans due to naming practices. The eldest daughter was traditionally named after the paternal grandmother and the second daughter was named after her maternal grandmother, creating an automatic identification with one parent. This may have created a divide between sisters, as each was expected to defend different sides of the family in internecine disputes. This type of dispute has not been limited to the Greeks, of course: it has also been present when one daughter was closer to the father and one was closer to the mother for other reasons, as the women in the project described. Some Irish American parents label their children as good or bad; either label might have been the preferred one, depending upon the family's rebellious or conformist leanings. Such favoritism was expressed in my study by several women, particularly the woman who said her sister labeled her "goody two shoes," reflecting the sense that she behaved as expected in order to receive favors from her parents.

All of these differences between sisters and the ways that parents have managed them have created an enhanced or diminished sense of closeness between sisters. Some cultural biases and familial prejudices may have made equal treatment unlikely. In those cases, parents have had to work hard to try to compensate for the biases they felt. If they could not do so, it may have been up to the sisters themselves. Some of my participants described just such a process as the sisters learned to manage their differences over time.

In-groups and Out-groups in the Family

Several types of in-groups that are related to diversity were created. Often the division in the family was unintentional, but sometimes it was carefully considered and implemented based upon one member's specific characteristics. An in-group could have been created when a lesbian woman came out to only certain members of her family and asked them to keep the secret. Younger sisters or children may have been left out because family members suggested they may not have understood the issues related to gay or lesbian identity. Similarly, a teen pregnancy that is terminated or ends in adoption may not have been shared. One sister's history of being raped or experiencing other sexual violence may not have been shared with a younger sister. Such secrets and the resulting in-groups may have been created because of concern about how children would understand and integrate the information, but they also might have left a younger sister with the sense that secrets were being kept from her for an unknown reason. This division may be created by the relating of trauma and rape during refugee experiences of Southeast Asian women. Has the next generation been told about the horrors of their experience? Was the gang rape of young Hmong women in part the re-creation of unconscious knowledge about the horrors of women in war? Within the research project, in-groups were also reported. This creation of an out-group was reported by my interviewees. One witnessed incest but was forbidden from confronting the father. Another was aware of her sister's rape but was asked to keep the secret from their father. In all of these local and migratory instances, the secrecy, not the original issue, was what created distance and a sense of disconnection among sisters when some were not told.

There are also several situations in which out-groups were created by gender. Lesbian women have been much more likely to come out to their mothers and sisters than their fathers and brothers. If they have told the men in their family, it was usually after the women were told. This dynamic was similar to a major theme in the study, when women felt closer to their mothers and sisters than their brothers and fathers, forming a gender-based bond that may have excluded men. In a different twist on that exclusion, sometimes girls were excluded from a favored group created by their mothers, fathers, and brothers. Such division has occurred in African American families. If so, these out-groups may have represented the parents' attempt to compensate for differential racism against young Black males. This may have inadvertently created an out-group in the family where the sisters reside.

Likewise, young women in several Latina cultures have been restricted from dating and sexual relationships, leaving them out of the frank discussions of sexual experience that have occurred between brothers. These divisions have varied between and within families; some Latinas have more freedom. In my research, some women felt an older sister provided a bridge to family secrets by charting new territory. Once she was allowed some freedom related to her sexual experience, the younger sister might have had more opportunity to date or to discuss frankly sexual material. In these ways, gender and sexuality may have formed the basis for a family in-group and out-group. In some families, either the brothers or sisters were excluded from secrets, experiences, or conversations.

In-groups have also been formed by siblings who left out their parents. This was fairly typical, but when the basis was a diversity issue, it may have presented a unique set of challenges. Chinese American or Korean American sisters adopted into White families or lesbian families may form an in-group from which their parents were excluded, based upon ethnicity and national heritage. This bonding of children who are different from their parents may have felt more like an out-group if other siblings were present who shared ethnicity and national origin with their parents. Such bonding occurred for women in the study during periods of parental abuse of children. One sister helped to protect another from sexual abuse. Another felt she was part of an out-group because she was abused by her mother and her sister was not. The sister needed to deny that the abuse existed and sided with her mother, who also denied it. The abused sister became a family outsider who had been the target of the violence.

There were times when a family's national history created a strong desire to keep others out. This type of division has made the family the in-group and shoved others to the outside. Or the family may have created an impermeable barrier that others could not breach. Such a division seemed to be common among German American families, whose history of being denigrated for starting the world wars in Europe created a sense of distrust. The division of the country into East and West Germany for many decades did not help matters. Likewise, the divisions of Korea and of Vietnam may have created similar desires to maintain strong family boundaries. In each of these cases, some of this mistrust was also rooted in guilt about the impact of their nation's aggression on the rest of the world.

In a parallel process, the sisters in the research described themselves as united and bonded by shared guilt for their aggression against a sister or a cousin. All of these family divisions have created phenomena in which sisters may have found themselves bonded more tightly within an in-group. They also may have been separated because one was "in" and the other was "out" of the favored group within the family. Secrecy, exclusion, and loneliness may have been the hallmarks of this experience for sisters who found themselves outside, while sisters who shared the secrets and membership of the in-group enjoyed a sense of camaraderie, collusion, and excitement.

Family Roles Changed by Differences and Culture

In the literature as well as my research, new family roles may have been created by bias and discrimination. Existing roles may have changed because of difference and advocacy. In general, the effect on roles included the arrival of a mediator, the diffusion of the parental role, new opportunities to serve as a role model for a sister, and the development of many alternatives to gender-based roles. Most of these role variations were mentioned in some fashion by women in the study. They talked about sisters who were peacemakers in the family, as well as occasions when they had been mediators between a sister and parents. Often parental roles were fulfilled in order for a sister to have a more comfortable pregnancy, learn to adapt to school, figure out how to choose a career, etc. Sisters were certainly role models for everything from dating to career choice. How has diversity changed these roles for women?

According to the literature, a sister may have become a mediator between family members who accepted a lesbian's coming-out process and those who did not. Often this was not a typical role for this sister but one she adopted out of love and understanding for her lesbian sister. In my own experience the depth of that role emerged for my twin sister, who best understood the bias and discrimination with which I have lived. In the research study, sisters became mediators in reaction to their sisters' life experiences—divorce, custody, or domestic violence served as a motivator for decision making.

Parental role diffusion was common and seemed to provide strength in African American single-parent families. An older sister was both a playmate and substitute mother. This effect also occurred due to translocation history and refugee status for Latina and Cambodian American women; the immigration of women from these and other cultures resulted in many single-parent families headed by mothers who work. This role diffusion created responsibility, maturity, and patience in older sisters, traits that serve them well throughout life. Such a process seemed to occur for the women I interviewed as well. If a parent was not fully present because of work, divorce, or single status or was just not very interested in being a good parent, the older sister often stepped into the breach. Although the family therapy literature has frequently suggested that such roles are not healthy because they violate generational boundaries, in reality much strength and support, as well as enhancing of personality traits, may emerge from these responsibilities.

Sisters have served as role models in so many respects. Older sisters were emulated and sometimes used as an example of how *not* to grow up. These role model relationships seemed to emerge regardless of culture, heritage, or diversity issues, both in the literature and in my study. The older African American sister provided a role model for her younger sibling, for better or for worse, leading her to a life of achievement or one of drugs and gangs, or something in between. Indonesian women have been given specific responsibility for their younger sister's behavior that is proscribed within cultural mandates. In a similar vein, the women in the study talked about the effects of difference on the ability of a sister to be a role model. If a sister had a special skill or admirable trait that could not be easily imitated, the younger sister wanted to grow in a different direction. Sisters became compensatory role models, providing an incentive to follow a different path.

One of the most specifically mentioned roles related to sisters were those defined by their gender. In many nationalities and cultures sisters were expected to follow specific gendered paths. For Latinas across the spectrum, gender-based roles may have been split between two sisters in order to provide constancy and support in a tumultuous family. Some Asian sisters may have exhibited confused roles because they were expected to be submissive and traditionally feminine in most family circumstances, but maintained a high drives for achievement. A similar gender-based conflict occurred for sisters from Syria and Lebanon, where women were given educational opportunities that conflicted with demands to be submissive at home.

This confusion caused by culturally prescribed gender roles was also present in my research. Some women felt their assigned gender role in the family was related to the absence of male children. In an attempt to manage conflicting gender roles, some unique solutions emerged. Hmong women have been known to dichotomize such conflicts by choosing either extreme of the gender continuum. Some have become highly instrumental, seeking doctoral degrees, whereas a sister may marry at age 14 and have many children. This disparity related to gender roles was also seen among my study's participants; they mentioned many times this primary division of caregiver and career-focused roles.

The role of superwoman emerged in many traditions but has been specifically mentioned in relation to Latina and Black cultures. The term "Sisterella" has been used to define a set of interlocking demands for women in the Black community (Jones & Shorter-Gooden, 2003). A Sisterella has the task of maintaining kinship ties to a remarkably large group of kin, both biological and fictive ones. The management of this family structure may become overwhelming.

Likewise, some Latina immigrants were able to find work when their male partners could not. They served as both primary breadwinners and primary caregivers to a large extended family. Sister relationships in each of these scenarios may have been negatively affected by the role demands and emotional drain. Or sisters may have shared these roles, helping each other cope with the overwhelming responsibilities for emotional connection with so many people. These dynamics and the response of the sister relationship to them were expressed by women in the study who led very complicated or stress-filled lives.

Gender-based roles that seem to provide strength for instrumentality come from Greek and Irish cultural prescriptions. Greek daughters have been encouraged to reflect the pride of democracy, which originated in Greece, and to be high achievers. This may create competition and distance among sisters. The presumed maturity and responsibility of Irish women in relation to men suggested emotional resilience, practicality, and compensation for boyish men. Irish sisters may have become closer to each other and female relatives, who were seen as part of the responsible, dependable, and mature family group. Women in the research project described a similar group of responsible sisters when others failed to fill the role, or when a large family had essentially two cohorts and the older took on the more responsible roles.

Family roles may have been changed by immigration or legal differences between nations. For example, the eldest sister often had a specifically defined role within the Southeast Asian cultures in Vietnamese and Cambodian families. Special words were used to define this role of the eldest sister in the family. Her authority was unchallenged. This may not have been sustained during immigration or after a family began to adapt to a new country. Legal differences may have affected sister roles. In the Philippines there was no divorce, yet those who immigrated to another country could divorce their husbands. This created a challenge to the role of wife, and it is not clear what effects this might have on the relationship between married and divorced sisters.

Role changes, especially when related to gender, have required family resilience. Sisters seem to have managed those changes as long as deeply held values or beliefs were not too strongly threatened. Many of the women in the study and much of the international literature have explored the conundrum of gender-defined roles, which change rapidly when cultures collide or sisters differ.

Bias Affecting Closeness and Distance

Often women have become closer to their sisters if they were able to negotiate differences and understand bias and discrimination. Research by other authors suggested that the strength and resilience of the relationship persisted despite differences in sexual orientation or disability. Similarly, women who developed identities that were specific to certain regions of the United States learned to communicate across the geographic abyss. One woman in the study discussed the time when her sister was negotiating her sexual orientation; together they arrived at a closer understanding and connection. Some sisters felt distant from a lesbian sister during her immersion in gay culture. The identification with different communities of peers created a sense of separation and loss. The corollary occurred when a woman watched her older sister move into a different life stage; one younger sister described her older sister's departure for college and the sense of abandonment she felt. An African American sister may have been emotionally removed from her younger sister during a similar period of ethnic immersion that created a new and exciting part of her identity. All of these experiences of difference have required a resilience and flexibility in the sister connection.

Throughout history and across geographic divides, women have been separated from their sisters with cultural approval. Many instances of this loss occur all over the world. In the United States, Black sisters were frequently separated during slavery—a direct attempt to undermine Black families. Another instance occurred due to the discrimination against Japanese Americans during World War II. Sisters were sometimes adopted out of the camps by a sponsoring White family who educated them. Frequently they moved to the Eastern or Midwestern portions of the country, far from the conflict in the Pacific and from the western coast of California, where most women's sisters would have been interred. Adoption of orphaned children has also been a factor for some Romanian, Korean, and Chinese American girls, who may have sisters they have never met.

Immigration and class have combined to separate sisters of Cuban, Puerto Rican, Nicaraguan, and Southeast Asian extraction. An early part of U.S. history resulted in the separation of British and Spanish sisters as they immigrated to avoid religious persecution, sometimes leaving other sisters behind. Indigenous peoples were removed to reservations and schools. Some never saw their family members again, although siblings were sometimes kept together. In many of these cases, economic or political circumstances kept sisters apart for decades and may have formed the basis for stoic acceptance toward the loss of a sister's presence. One specific variation on sister separation occurred in Hawaii. Traditional Hawaiian families sometimes gave an eldest child to the grandparents out of respect. Girls were separated from their sisters, although each remained with part of the extended family. In my research, older sisters sometimes raised sisters apart from each other, or aunts did—again because of economic circumstances or specific family dynamics.

Separations from a sister have also occurred when the relationship between them was less valued by the larger culture than other relationships. Pakistani and Indian sisters may have been separated during the formation of Pakistan, based upon the particular religious tradition of their husbands. Likewise, the Taliban control in parts of Pakistan may place one sister within their scope of gender discrimination and another outside of it. Similar separations occurred for African female slaves who were housed with families in the North versus those in the South during the U.S. Civil War. The continuation of arranged marriages may separate sisters in parts of the Indian subcontinent and Middle East. Across the globe, many influences have conspired to remove sisters from each other for much of their lives.

Sometimes cultural traditions have helped keep sisters together. In some Arab-speaking countries, the father has automatic custody during divorce, bonding the sisters who have not been separated from each other, even though they have lost their mother. In America, most states have instituted joint custody, requiring that siblings be kept together, with equal access by both parents. One woman in my research reported that her sister bond was strengthened when both girls were forced by joint custody to go for an unwanted visit to their father's home.

These traditions of keeping sisters together during family disruption have not been globally adopted, however; separation of sisters during family discord has been much more common. The tradition of migration to the family of the husband separates sisters. In Pakistan, the eldest brother has had control over his sister until she marries. This dynamic has created a closer relationship with the brother and his wife than between sisters. For the most part, the women who were a part of my study felt forced away from their sisters only because of their own choices or those of their husbands and partners. Separation forced by parents or partners often led sisters to bond in a strong and rebellious fashion—holding tightly to the connection. At times this type of close attachment was due to gender-based favoritism in the family.

Cultural expectations have played a large role in how sisters express their feelings of closeness. In some Latina cultures women show a great deal of affection to each other. Korean women and their sisters are expected to show emotional tenderness and empathy, as they do with all relatives. Confucianism has provided five major pillars for adult conduct in relationships; sisters are not mentioned specifically, but peers are. For cultures influenced by Confucianism, the relationship with one's peers must be maintained, and this fundamental principle has strengthened the sister connection in a unique way. In another unique mandate for relationship health, the Hawaiian family has developed a cultural imperative to forgive. This imperative has become ritualized in a ceremony that may strengthen sister bonds. A Hawaiian cultural mandate forbids walking away from the sister connection. Such mandates were not mentioned in the research project, although some women mentioned the need to stay connected because of the blood relationship alone, and others suggested that religious values required them to forgive. Some of them never healed the breaches between them and their sisters.

The emotional intensity or personality of some cultures can dictate the closeness or distance between women. British women have generally been more comfortable with competition than connection with their sisters and more connected to the families they create than the ones from which they originate. Some women in this study mentioned how British ancestry affected their lives. They also felt that their husbands were more important than their sisters. German women have often become very critical of their sisters while at the same time avoiding conflict with them; some authors have suggested this is a projection of cultural guilt related to Germany's aggression in Europe. This critical stance between German sisters may help to minimize pain and manage distance. One woman I interviewed was very apologetic that she was so critical of her sister, so such tendencies are clearly not limited to sisters of German heritage. Irish and Italian sisters may express much more emotionality toward each other. These expressions vary widely, from dramatic outbursts of rage or charged silences. Some of the women in the study reported losing their tempers with sisters and feeling badly about it, often making excuses for the anger and subsequent guilt. Emotionally laden methods of communicating in all of these cultures may have determined or given voice to the type of affection, arguments, and love that were expressed between women.

Cultural and Family Extensions of the Sister

The importance of extended family members could have been suggested or dictated by cultural mandates. For example, different cultural expectations may have suggested the importance of a sister's children and husband. In the cross-cultural literature, the children of a sister were considered most often. Childless sisters have often been included with those who have children as second mothers or fill-in care providers. This issue used to arise among lesbian and heterosexual sisters before the widespread use of in vitro fertilization. Differences in identity have often been substantial when one sister is a mother and the other is not.

Many lesbians today have their own children or have adopted children. Sometimes, families have not accepted lesbian couples who are parents. In some research studies, the variation in acceptance among family members has been related to having a blood relationship with the child. A woman would be closer to her biological niece and more likely to accept the lesbian parents if the child was her sister's biological daughter. Conversely, she might not have accepted the biological child of her sister's lesbian partner in the absence of a blood-related niece or nephew. In my research, the women were biologically related to all of their nieces but found a closer connection when they could identify with her.

That transgenerational identification was affected by cultural mandates as well. In Greek tradition a woman is automatically the godmother for her sister's first child if she is the maid or matron of honor at her wedding. This has created an automatic link to the niece or nephew. Much was said about nieces in my research; the closeness to them seemed to vary with a whole host of factors, such as presence at the niece's birth, having a niece named after the aunt, similarity of interests, gender identity, etc. Sometimes the aunt and niece shared more values and personality characteristics than the mother and daughter did.

Sisters-in-law and fictive sisters have also extended the sister relationship in various cultures. Some researchers have suggested that a lesbian couple will be more integrated into the family when a sister-in-law has been accepting of them. Sisters-in-law have been openly accepting, willing to integrate the couple into the extended family, or they may reject the couple, the partner, or both. A similar diversity was found in my study, where some women felt very close to a sister-in-law and others avoided family gatherings because of a sister-in-law's presence.

Fictive sisters have played an extensive role in sister relationships. They sometimes take the place of a blood relative but most often just increase the network of connected women. Latina and African American women have had many fictive kin. Among Filipino women, all female tribal members have been called "sister." No similar terms were used in the sister project, but friends and co-workers were sometimes described as being "like a sister."

Extended family members have often gathered for social and recreational experiences. In many cultures specific rules prescribe the activities, events, foods, and interactions that take place at these holidays, picnics, roasts, Shabbats, barbecues, Sunday dinners, or other events. Some events have been formalized with specific cultural traditions. Almost all cultures have such traditions for weddings, religious holidays, fasting periods, reunions, or deaths. For some women, these rituals and activities have generated an extended family interaction, providing an opportunity for sisters and fictive kin to gather. In some cultures, however, such rituals protect against emotional expression and affection. This superficiality and formality was specifically mentioned in relation to British families. The women in my research mentioned large family gatherings as times when they would see their sisters but often lamented the lack of connection when the extended family was present. Some felt these large gatherings were superficial and did not allow for the intimacy that was usually present in the sister connection.

Conclusions

The integration of my research findings with the information about diversity in the literature provided many similar themes. Women immigrating from around the world and those living in the United States carefully consider the level of intimacy in the sister relationship. Emotional expressions, affection, manner of relating, and special use of language have all been part of this analysis, whether in Singapore or Tehran, Dayton or Amsterdam, Beijing or Manila. The intensity of the sister attachment is a way of measuring its importance and the extent to which it fulfills the desire for a sense of sisterhood. Many cultural variations, as well as the dynamics of disabled and non-disabled sisters, have provided an analysis of the mother–daughter–sister triad. There were also many other family dynamics present in the literature. The role of the father or eldest brother played a part in helping to define the importance of same-gender closeness between the women in families. Rituals and gatherings enhanced these relationships and may have been very meaningful, as in the role of a Greek matron of honor as a godmother. However, extended family celebrations have at times been very superficial; this theme was expressed both in the literature and by my participants.

Sisters compared their identities and considered them important for defining the identities of others. These identities were built partly on facts. Unmarried sisters played a defining role in the family and have had a role that is defined explicitly for them. The notion that sisters could be lost and mourned was universal. In my study, this occurred permanently through the death of a sister and temporarily through a geographic move. For women who emigrated or those who sought refuge from violent regimes, the loss may have been permanent and devastating. These losses were accompanied by guilt, whether from survivors of a holocaust or survivors who were never threatened. In the research about women from other countries and cultures, this description of loss, trauma, violence, and discrimination was a much larger part of the picture.

Other common themes arose related to groupings in families. Groups in a family could form around discrimination and violence, especially if younger sisters were not told about it. This occurred due to sexual assault, but it also occurred in some families because of lesbian identity and the lack of overall family support. In all of these ways, the literature and my research reflected some similarities that universally defined the sister experience.

The missing component during this integration was the element of voice. I did not have the subjective experience of African sisters or of Indonesian sisters, and I did not know what these relationships meant to them as individuals. They may perceive the relationship very differently than it is described by others. In some cases, the differences could be extrapolated, but this would have been done in a very different way than my research itself. Except for the stories of sisters that were gleaned from newspaper accounts and some vignettes, the emotional tone of the material was different as well. It was hard to judge whether those differences would be reflected in sustained interviews with women of different ethnic groups, abilities, sexual orientations, or nationalities. There was a sense that the women were never surprised by what they revealed. The material provided by quantitative research or theoretical summaries did not unintentionally reveal aspects of the sister relationship. Surprises or secrets that would not be shared in the more analytic approach were allowed to emerge from my participants: they actually learned about the relationship as they were telling me the story of sisterhood. Women of many different cultures need to be asked the simple question "Tell me about your relationship with your sister" so that the voices of those women may be more accurately portrayed.

PART THREE

THE ROLE OF SISTERS IN PSYCHOTHERAPY

Introduction to Part III

As a psychologist and psychotherapist, I was very aware that the knowledge generated by my research and by the hermeneutic analysis needed another layer of integration in order for it to be useful to those who practice this craft. I wanted to take the knowledge, the themes, and the experience of sisters into the clinical setting, and this required an analysis of a very different kind. Blending my research with existing theory has been a tricky proposition. First, I had to determine which psychotherapeutic theories to address. Integration of sisters into all existing psychotherapies would be the subject of yet another entire book. Second, I had to make sure the chosen theories were compatible with my phenomenological approach to research. I could have chosen cognitive-behavioral approaches, which have been enjoying much cultural popularity lately, but they have been based on a philosophy of human existence that, I determined, was incompatible with phenomenological views of human nature. Third, I needed to select approaches with which I had a great deal of familiarity.

These three criteria led me to four major approaches. Psychoanalytic and object relations approaches have been created based upon the philosophy of idealism, but those approaches certainly have been consistent with a more subjective and interior view of the self—espoused by phenomenology. The need to bring the view of the interior self into the relationship between the client and others requires dialectic integration with the external world.

This integration creates a bridge between psychoanalytic and object relations theory and phenomenology. The dialectic integration may result in the co-creation of understanding between therapist and clients. This co-creation is a fundamental tenet of phenomenology. The depth of understanding sought by these schools of therapy has considered the early development and family relationships, which created a natural application to developmental understanding between sisters. In addition, I have had some training and familiarity with both of these schools of psychological thought. While not an analyst by any stretch of the imagination, I have been educated and supervised by those who were and have used these ideas in my early practice experiences. Thus, psychoanalysis and object relations approaches met my three criteria for inclusion.

I have also included the psychodynamic derivative from these schools, relational cultural theory. This theory arose originally as a feminist reinterpretation of psychoanalytic and psychodynamic thought, sharing with them a more idealistic approach to human beings. It also seemed to me that the relational-cultural approach was much more closely tied to phenomenology—a position supported by its founders. In contrast to psychoanalytic approaches, the relational-cultural approach has considered the mother–daughter connection in exquisite detail, with a focus on healthy relationships and cultural understandings. It was a natural for inclusion in an understanding of complex sister relationships, yet the primary authors of the theory have done little to consider the sister connection. I have had great familiarity with this approach, as it has been the foundation for my clinical practice for over 25 years and informed a number of other research projects under my supervision. Relational-cultural theory, therefore, met all of my criteria for inclusion.

It would be hard to imagine a text of this nature focused on an important family connection without considering applications to family therapy. Interestingly, family therapy itself has at least a dozen different branches. In searching through them, I settled on the inclusion of narrative approaches, which are closely allied with phenomenological approaches to research, and feminist approaches, which attempt to provide the same re-analysis of family therapy that relational-cultural theory applied to psychodynamic approaches. I have used traditional family therapy approaches in my practice for work with couples and families. Working on this book expanded my knowledge of the feminist and narrative approaches that seemed much closer to my own view of therapeutic application. Therefore, feminist and narrative approaches to family therapy were included in the analysis.

Three chapters cover these applications of my research and the first hermeneutic integration. In each chapter, I have provided an overview of that theoretical approach to sisters and the considerations of the same-gender sibling relationship expressed by major theorists. A second level of hermeneutic analysis has been done; in it, I have integrated the themes from my research and the diversity literature from Part II of this book to create a new set of theoretical applications for psychotherapy. Each of these chapters concludes with considerations for therapists—how they might use the knowledge in this book to deal more effectively with the sequelae of that lifelong connection.

11

Integrating Sisters into Psychoanalytic and Object Relations Therapy

"I feel closer to her on some psychic level than to any friends or lovers; I yearn for a kind of exchange that is not possible without our becoming the same person. The extreme loneliness that results pains me more than I like to admit."

(McNaron, 1985, p. 3)

Many authors have criticized Freud for his misunderstanding of women, and certainly these critiques can be extended to the relationship between sisters. However, closer evaluation of Freudian theory reveals an attempt to understand siblings in some depth and attempts by neo-Freudians to apply some of those concepts to sisters. Object relations theorists also explored the other sex and its influence on same-gender peers. Generally each of the authors considered here— Freud, Klein, Winnicott, Masterson, and others—evaluated the presence of a particular sister in a particular case. Often theoretical development was left unstated. In an attempt to correct some of those omissions, this chapter evaluates psychoanalytic and object relations approaches to therapy with sisters.

Psychoanalysis

The Myths of Oedipus, Elektra, and Antigone

Freudian understanding of family dynamics evaluated the myth of Oedipus as it related primarily to males. The story of the young man who unknowingly murdered his father and married his mother became a symbolic representation of the strivings of male children to supplant their father and marry their mother. Freud was not successful in translating this to female development. Others suggested the myth of Electra might play a similar role in women's development. If the Elektra myth were used as a model for female development, women all want to plot with their brothers to murder their mother. This would need to be done to avenge the philandering and absent father for the affair the mother started in his absence. The daughter and her brother would then be bound together in their desire to welcome the father home after the mother and her lover have been supplanted. If need be, women would be expected to overlook the sacrifice of their sisters and wed themselves to the patriarchy in order to restore its authority. This vision would prevent a woman from having any allegiance to her female relatives, including her mother and sister.

Many authors have suggested an alternative to the Elektra myth as a metaphor for the development of young women, and not even Freud suggested that Elektra was an adequate replacement for Oedipus. Still, the Elektra myth has persisted and is associated with psychoanalytic female psychosexual development. Irigaray (1977/1985) and Kaschak (1992), among others, have suggested that Oedipus' daughter, Antigone, might provide a different, and much less patriarchal, view of women's growth. Antigone had a sister and two brothers, each of whom played a significant part in her narrative; conflicted parents; a stepfather; and difficulty developing her sense of identity. Her ambivalent relationships with all of her family might provide a more adequate approach to understanding women's development. It seems worth retelling the story of Antigone to understand how psychoanalysis might embrace a very different myth for women.

Antigone was a daughter of Jocasta and Oedipus. She was one of four children born to them before they discovered their incestuous mother–son relationship. Upon discovery of this parent–child relationship, Oedipus fled the city after putting out his own eyes. The four siblings survived their father's departure and grew to adulthood. Political differences made enemies of the brothers, and a battle left both sons dead by the other's hand. Antigone, their sister, sought justice for her renegade brother, Creon, who had been left on the battlefield without a proper burial, as dictated by the law. Antigone defied her sister Ismene's advice and advocated for her brother, eventually disobeying the law to bury him. Her punishment at the hands of her uncle, the new ruler of Thebes, was to be buried alive. Antigone alone stood up in support of family relationships and in opposition to the unjust and unfair law of the land. Some have suggested that she represented pure desire arising from the relationship with the masculine elements, in this case her brother and father. Others have said she represents the conscience of the father and, therefore, of us all. Lacan said Antigone was "the turning point of ethics" (Cupelloni, 2000, p. 122), but it seems to me that she is more than that: her lessons are about relationships and context as much as they are about the fairness of the law. She could be a courageous role model who defends relationships and in so doing defines her identity and destiny.

This story may provide early evidence that context is an important part of understanding essential qualities in identity and relationship. Her story might be the first suggestion that context must be considered in the human drama; we cannot all develop in the same ways or be governed by the same laws. Antigone, by her defiance, suggested that legal principles might not be universal principles. She may be an early figure begging us to understand the importance of a family in context and the harbinger for a coming change in the essentialist position.

In defying the law out of love and respect, she became a true representative of the feminine—one who emerged as something quite different from expectations.

The relationship between Antigone and her sister Ismene depicted the conflict between the power of established law, the impotence of women, and the importance of standing up for relationships in the face of insurmountable odds. Ismene, who was at first unable to stand against the law, urged Antigone to give up, but Antigone prevailed. She did not believe that only the strongest and victorious should be honored; instead, she suggested that all persons should be treated with the same honor and dignity. Her humanity convinced her sister, but too late. The fate of Antigone was death for taking such a position. Ismene's fate was left ambiguous.

Together, Ismene and Antigone provide psychoanalysis with mirrored blueprints for the paths of female development. That development created separate, yet related, identities and a continuing dialogue between sisters that led to critical thought, moral growth, and fortitude. It also demonstrated the loss of the connection between different aspects of the feminine when sisters do not support each other in fighting for social justice. The ambiguity of Ismene's fate creates many possibilities for the manner in which one sister's beliefs and fortitude might ultimately influence the development of the other.

Rivalry and Birth Order in Freudian Thought

Despite his failure to find an appropriate myth to represent women's development, Freud contributed a great deal to our understanding about siblings (1905/1962; 1933/1964). He described a number of very important interactions between them, focusing on interactions that involved at least one brother. European and American cultures embraced those understandings, and they can easily be integrated with the findings of the narratives provided by the women in my research project. Freud's view did tend toward the pathological and the pessimistic, while the women in the study had a much more ambivalent yet hopeful view of their sister relationships.

Freud's primary view of sibling relationships was related to birth order and sibling rivalry. He suggested that hostility was the primary narrative underlying the birth of a sibling when a child was young. Sometimes that hostility became murderous, and this was considered common enough that Freud called it *epistemophilia*. He believed that such hostility was gradually suppressed and replaced by affection for the younger brother or sister. According to Freud, one positive outcome of such rivalry was a likely increase in intellectual curiosity and personal ambition. These changes came about because the child attempted to understand all about the younger sibling. How are children born, and what does that mean for the importance of the older child? Why is the younger child suddenly the focus of the parents' attention?

Ambition might emerge in an attempt to compete with the new baby. Houzel (2001) suggested that sibling rivalry was resolved when the internal image of the sibling was split, the hostility was suppressed, and the affection became predominant. Freud suggested that a girl had a different experience of this rivalry due to her identification with her mother. Her way of resolving the dilemma of a new sister or brother included a renunciation of the mother and an attempt to supplant the mother with the father. The rivalry felt by a sister with her brothers and sisters had a different outcome, according to this patriarchal view.

Freud's Themes Integrated

Rivalry

The women's narratives generated many themes consistent with this Freudian view of sibling rivalry. The women described separate and distinct roles related to birth order, with knowledge that the oldest, middle, and youngest sisters had a specific function in the family. Some women described the birth of the next sibling as traumatic. Others suggested that they were old enough to experience the birth as separate from their own role with their mother and father. Disappointment in the birth of a sister, told in retrospect, may support Freud's notion that the hostility of young childhood is forgotten. Yet some sisters acknowledged the desire to annihilate the next sister in infancy, and at least one admitted to trying to kill her sister, wondering if the accidents that happened to her sister were the actual result of her hostility and anger. Some women described the birth of their sister as a time of intense animosity. This trauma and the loss of parental affection were given as justification for physical assault and meanness during childhood. In one instance this was accompanied by homicidal impulses. Questionable accidents with an infant sister were described.

Typically, competition for parental attention was the reason for sister conflict. When one sister's value was touted by parents, another was more likely to become aware of the jealousy she held for her sister. Parental perceptions of the differing abilities between siblings may have led to competition, increased motivation, or resentment of the sister. The mother's role in this was particularly clear: if she valued the sisters in a similar way, cooperative learning replaced competitive strivings. Unmentioned by Freud was the parental role in mediating these conflicts. Many parents of the women in the study actively minimized the elevation of one child over another. They tried not to demonstrate any favoritism toward one and acknowledged the importance of each. Sometimes parental attempts at mediation did result in less conflict between the two girls, but despite these attempts, or in the absence of them, some conflict and rivalry lasted throughout life. Arguments and conflicts were often about unspoken issues of greater concern than the openly-discussed issue. The sisters might have been fighting about two nieces' inappropriate behavior, for instance, when the real issue was the rivalry for their own parents' affection. Such disagreements brought discomfort, and the women tried to justify their own positions. As Freud suggested, sometimes these competitive strivings—when not extreme—were helpful to the women, leading to increased achievement of goals.

During adolescence, rivalry between sisters was sometimes triggered by a 20th- and 21st-century phenomenon. Feminism and women's equality gave sisters as much desire to succeed in the workplace as brothers. Greater independence for women may have triggered less supportive and helpful relationships between sisters. They described moving away from each other to pursue their own interests and careers. For some women, the competition became too much to bear. During Freudian times, such moves would likely occur in the context of a marriage, as they did with Freud's sister Anna. Rarely would he have witnessed the young, unattached female leaving home to achieve independent goals. This phenomenon offers the opportunity for renewed rivalry between sisters. For the women in the research, these rivalries could erupt because of limited financial resources of the parents and perceived unfairness in their distribution; at other times, the rivalry was related to the welcoming of the absent sister home.

Gender Differences

The issue of gender emerged as a theme in the sister relationship. Sometimes the identification with traditional female or expressive traits helped sisters to overcome a conflicted relationship. Some women found that their identification with more traditional male interests (sports were often mentioned) was why they felt less competitive with their sisters. In some of these families, the sister was expected to compensate for the absence of brothers. This role could have been supplanted by the birth of a male child, leaving this sister with a grievance against the mother, a theme that echoed Freud's own explanations. Birth order could dictate the sister relationship in this instance: girls born after the birth of a first and favored male child were not as affected by the conflict-laden feelings apparent in the girl who had filled the son's role in the family.

Triadic Family Relationships

The transition from sibling rivalry to the family complex was an important part of the development of young sisters. The triadic relationship described in the women's narratives suggested that sibling rivalry did have an oedipal feeling, even for girls. Father–daughter–sister rivalry was particularly contentious and angry. Some girls aligned with each other in an attempt to balance a perceived close connection between a third sister and a father or mother. Absence of a father or lack of affection from him was compensated by the sisters' affection for each other. Aligned with one another, they excluded others from their affections. Freud's understanding of the sibling bond suggested that if the sibling or sister bond was too strong, it could trap a child into a perpetual comparison between her siblings and her potential mates.

The pervasiveness of these themes suggests that sisters in the 20th and 21st century describe sibling rivalry, birth order, and the importance of the family complex as themes. Such indirect endorsement of Freud's original ideas was pervasive in the narrative themes of the women in my study. Clearly Freud's contribution to our understanding about rivalry was important, but it did not tell the whole story. In many cases the women's narratives contradicted his ideas, and in some cases they suggested new interpretations or an expansion of Freudian themes.

Themes from the Research and a Reinterpretation of Freud

Rivalry and Conflict Resolution

Women intended to have a close relationship with their sisters and to repair their childhood rivalry. This represented a clear difference between Freud's formulation and the experience described by the women in my study. Maturity and age led to a desire to heal the past and, in many cases, a conscious intention to do so. The rivalry was not repressed. Alternately, the rivalry might have re-emerged into consciousness and action was required to right the wrongs between sisters. The development of insight could have made this process easier; the sustained achievement of one sister could make it more difficult. Maturity led to a sense of patience and humor about the past. Mutuality in the relationship was expected, as was mutual trust. Regret, loss, and awareness of differences were part of the maturity that fueled this quest for insight. Women even tried to heal the breach between two of their sisters. The inability to do so was experienced as a form of female impotence. The loss of a sister to death prior to resolution of conflicts in the relationship led to enhanced attempts to improve other sister relationships in the family. Failure to compensate in this way was a huge disappointment. The sense of self was tied to this mutual trusting relationship, and it continued to define identity throughout life.

Sometimes other individuals tried to assist in this conflict resolution process between sisters. Parents attempted mediation, but many women felt they needed to find their own solutions to the conflicts. Extended family members, friends, and children were often instrumental in helping to ease conflict and rivalry between sisters. On occasion a third party tried to keep the conflict between sisters alive for his or her own benefit. With time, most women felt they had succeeded in easing the rivalry between them and their sisters. Sometimes the resolution led to a closer relationship, sometimes to one that was more detached. Without resolution, the women felt ill at ease, as if they had to travel unknown and emerging paths in the wilderness of the relationship. Recognizing conflict and rivalry, consciously attempting to change it, and grieving for the inability to do so may provide a new application for psychoanalysis. This conscious intention may give analysts a new avenue for exploration and personal development.

Unique Nature of the Female Bond

Freud's recognition of the importance of sibling relationships was clearly grounded in his male role and his Victorian times (see Chapter 1). Women's development was an afterthought or represented only an adjustment in male development. His theory about siblings suffered from the same limitations. His comments were almost universally about the female–male or male–male sibling bond, with little attention to the sister–sister relationship. The narratives of the women in my study stand in clear contrast; for some, the sister held primary importance in their lives, making a unique contribution to personal development and playing a central role in defining the self. Sometimes sisters had difficult attachments based upon their competition for the mother. However, the women also suggested that the triadic relationships between three sisters or two sisters and a mother formed the emotional core of the family. Despite being emotionally intense when it was present, the bonding with the father was clearly secondary to that central female unit. Likewise, the partner or husband–wife relationship could became a corner-stone for increased maturity in the sister bond. New primary relationships gave the sisterly affection a chance to expand and redefine itself and to provide a new foundation for an extended family.

Freud's View of Sexual Orientation and Sister Relationships

Freud's suggestion that the close affection for siblings might impede the develop-ment of heterosexual relationships was also not borne out in this project. He suggested that sibling affection could impede the development of fully mature adult relationships. From today's vantage point, the psychotherapeutic commu-nity has argued that homosexual or lesbian relationships are a normal and healthy attainment of adult sexual love, but Freud felt that male homosexuality repre-sented the inability to give up the affection of siblings for the relationship of an adult non-relative. Freud felt these feelings for siblings re-emerged in adolescence and that they were very powerful forces, leaving little room for attraction or atten-tion to a different primary partner. He made no moral judgments about this but was attempting to define the importance of breaking sibling bonds in later adoles-cent life to make way for a primary partner. These may have reflected his difficulty giving up the centrality of his position in his family of origin and being emotionally present within his marriage.

In some ways Freud's theories reflect the experiences of the women in this study and in other ways they do not. He recognized conflict and rivalry, suggested the importance of the sibling bond as a basis for later adult relationships, and provided some understanding of triadic family connections. These were reflected by the women in the study and may have been in their consciousness, at least partly, because of the cultural adoption of Freud's work. He did not recognize the unique importance of sister relationships, their potential for positive growth between women, and the ability of women to consciously attend to their own conflicts with each other. These themes emerge in psychotherapeutic settings with sisters and the presence of healthy adaptations by sisters might provide a useful focus for psychoanalytic reflection and interpretation.

Klein's Themes Integrated

As discussed in Chapter 1, Melanie Klein had many personal and professional reasons for focusing attention on the developmental integration of sibling relationships. Her work provided many themes that echo the themes of my research. As with Freudian theory, this section will synthesize her major sibling themes with my research findings, comparing and contrasting them. Perhaps the most significant overall difference between those two is Klein's primary focus on pathology and the negative effects of sibling interactions; the women in my study had a more positive view. Of course, her work was also not just specific to sisters, but there were many themes that can be understood in light of the sister relationship.

The Presumed Inferiority of Women

The influence of the oedipal situation on Klein's writings (1975, 1937/1984a, 1957/1984c) led her to a specifically sexualized version of the understanding of the birth of a sister. Her work suggested that very young children understood and witnessed the sexual relationship between the parents and knew that the father's penis was an important part of creating another baby. As she described the reaction to the dynamics between the mother, father, and new baby, several themes emerged. Penis envy formed a cornerstone of her theory; according to Klein, females felt inferior to males because the mother evaluated men and boys more highly. Although this can be found among my research themes, it clearly did not tell the whole story.

The women described gender differences, and some felt undervalued in the family because the parents wanted a son. One woman was treated negatively, according to her sister, because she was "supposed to be a boy"; the father developed a lifelong negativity toward her. In families that had only girls, one daughter was sometimes "treated like a son" and assigned gender-specific responsibilities based upon that role. Once a much–longed-for son was born, the sibling relationships shifted, sometimes resulting in greater alignment among the girls.

In contrast, many women in my study described the female bonding in the family as an important part of the family's emotional core. Brothers and fathers were described as less significant compared to the emotional closeness that they felt toward their mothers and sisters. These female relationships were conflicted and difficult but also emotionally rewarding for many women. The women also described feeling a hormonal kinship with their sisters: they related moods to menstrual cycles and shared the understanding of the birth process. They mentioned their similarities to and differences from both brothers and sisters in terms of physical attributes: some were more genetically like their mother and some were more like their father. So while the difference in gender roles was clearly an issue for some of the women, gender's importance seemed to be mixed. Of course the process that Klein discussed would have been an unconscious process from earliest infancy, one that might have been remembered in interpersonal terms. It is unlikely that the women in the study would have described the penis envy experienced in preschool children, which Klein interpreted from her observation of children in the mid-20th century.

Infantile Aggression

Several of Klein's themes seemed to be unrelated to the stories told by the women about their early childhood experiences with their sisters. None mentioned attacks upon the mother because she was pregnant with another child. There were no suggestions that the women feared becoming like their mothers. This theme certainly has been present in my clinical work with female clients but perhaps did not emerge in the research since mothers were not the primary focus of inquiry. The envy and hatred of the mother's relationship with the father was also not present, perhaps because the youngest participants were already in their teens and had presumably emerged from the oedipal strivings described by Klein. Several women did talk about the rage and envy they felt toward a new baby. One talked about attempts to hurt her new sister and several "accidental" injuries she had caused to the younger girl. This rage toward the sister was not visited upon the mother. Klein's suggestion that the mother's inferiority in the family would lead to a fear of relationships with other women was not corroborated: the women did not suggest a fear of relationships with other women based upon their identification with their mother and her role. The absence of these themes suggest that Klein's view of sisters is greatly outdated or that her focus on the mother–father–child triad produced differing ideas than those found in this project, which focused specifically on sister interaction.

Desire for a Sister

Several other themes of Klein's were reflected in the women's views. Klein recognized that the desire for a sibling had many elements; the women in the study recognized some of these same themes in the desire for a sister. Klein suggested that small children would like to have a child of their own to mother. Many women in my study did function as surrogate mothers for their sisters. Some described the importance of having an older sister who parented and protected them. Frequently, the loss of this sister's presence in the home was a very difficult transition for the younger girl. When a sister moved away, got married, or started college, the younger girl often described feeling abandoned or depressed. Klein also suggested that the young child's desire for the birth of a sibling helped to reassure the young child that she had not harmed the mother with her envy and rage. This theme was not present for the women in the study; again, such processes are presumed to be unconscious in young children and may not have been reflected in the conscious memories of the participants.

Conspiring Against Parents

Klein's statements about sibling importance also conveyed the notion that children wanted siblings so they could form a conspiratorial alliance against the parents. The women in the study gave many examples of such bonding. Many different types of alliances were created. Some felt closely bonded with the sister against an abusive father. Some felt closely bonded with a sister against a controlling mother. Other suggested there were sister pairs who defended against alliances between a third sister and a mother who favored her. There were incidents of childhood pranks in which the sisters conspired to fool the parents. Some adolescents kept their sisters' secrets from the parents. These sister alliances were present throughout life for many of the women; others felt torn between loyalty to their parent and loyalty to a wayward sister. The infantile desire for co-conspirators seemed to have found a healthy place for many women in their lifelong relationship with their sisters.

Diffusing Parental Importance

Klein suggested that siblings helped a young child mature by diffusing the importance of the parents. This was especially present for the women in the study if there were traumatic childhood experiences that required more emotional attunement than the parents could or would provide. One woman talked about the importance of her sister in sheltering her from an alcoholic mother. Another spoke about the way a sister became an important parental figure when her father died during their childhood. During changes in the family structure, such as the formation of a blended family, a sister provided emotional cement for the original sibling group. Another woman suggested that she continued to be parental toward her sister long past the time it was necessary. These parental functions were only one way that the sister's role became important in diffusing the importance of the parent. Young women turned to their sisters for emotional understanding when they felt misunderstood by a parent. Older women planned ways to manage aging parents and how to support each other when parents died. Some described the emotional closeness that unfolded when a parent died. Again, the lifelong relationships of the sisters in the study provided additional support for this theme that went beyond the childhood focus of Klein.

Parents and Sister Rivalry

Klein suggested that additional diffusion might be necessary if the sibling relationships were more conflicted. She felt that cousins or playmates might serve to diminish the parental and sibling relationship angst. Indeed, the women in the study described the importance of some of these relationships. Many felt the extended family network provided them with differing views of their sister relationship. These extended family members included cousins, aunts and uncles, and grandparents. In direct support of Klein's suggestion, the women detailed the importance of these relationships in comparison with the sister role. Some felt closer to the extended family members; others suggested the sister may be closer and they struggled with feelings of jealousy or envy of those relationships. At times female friends took the place of sisters who were estranged or removed by geography; these third parties also made some sisters feel closer to their sisters. Again, the difference between the research themes and those suggested by Klein was related to the valence of feelings. For Klein, others formed the basis for comparison. While that was upheld in my research, the women also expressed the favorable nature of that influence on the growth between sisters.

Development of Pathology

From her clinical work with young children, Klein suggested that sibling relationships contributed to the development of pathology. Her suggestion that fantasized attacks against a sibling in utero might lead to guilt and depression later in life did not seem to be borne out in the narratives of my participants. Although some women in the study experienced depression or had sisters who did, they did not attribute this to early infantile fantasies about the relationship, again perhaps part of the unconscious nature that was maintained about such feelings. Klein suggested that when one sister had a mental problem, the other may fear having it or similar difficulties. The women in the study did describe the sublimation of similar fears by selecting a career that addressed the deficit: one became a mental health profession because of her sister's bouts with depression.

Sexual Orientation

Klein's view of sexual orientation was tied to the pathological understanding of her times. Her sense that lesbian relationships were due to pathology in the mother–daughter or sister–sister connection was described in her clinical applications. In my research some women suggested that their sister relationship was still primary even though they were married or partnered. The women who had developed heterosexual bonds occasionally expressed a preference for their sister over their husband or boyfriend; in other cases, they felt closer to their husband or boyfriend than their sister. One lesbian in the study suggested that she and her sister enjoyed the emotional closeness created by discussing the differences in their sexual orientations. She discussed a unique sense of identity created for each and cited the importance of their connection across these different ways of being in the world. Klein's sense that lesbian attachments represented a lack of full development has become antiquated when compared to the experiences of the women in the study and in relation to theoretical understandings of lesbian development today.

Multigenerational Relationships

The last theme extracted from Klein's work on siblings was a statement about the multigenerational nature of sister relationships. This suggestion was presented as part of a clinical case described by Klein in which the mother was competitive with her teenage daughters in an attempt to rework issues with her sisters. The women in the study recognized this multigenerational dimension, but their descriptions were just as often positive as negative. Many wanted to see a close relationship develop between their nieces or daughters. Some felt they wanted to protect those younger women from the hostility that remained between them and their sisters. None acknowledged a desire to compete with her own daughter or described conflicted interactions with them that may have reflected those sister roles.

Thus, Klein, who leaves a wealth of information about the potential analytic interpretation of sister connections, demonstrated some insights that have remained true to the conscious experience of women today, but many of her ideas were not verified by this project. Some processes were presumed to be unconscious, and this was a study of conscious realization. Nonetheless, many of these women had a great deal of insight. Their awareness of unconscious processes was often explained or questioned during the interviews. Other ideas of Klein's seemed tied to an outmoded context. Still others were partially supported by the feelings and conscious ideas of the women in this project.

The Sister as Object

Turning from more classic analytic formulations to object relations theories, sisters seem again to be in the periphery. Most of the major object relations theorists place sibling relationships in parentheses or footnotes—literally. The clinical cases of each theory have been somewhat more illuminating in providing an understanding of the themes of sisters as important and primary objects for the developing child. According to this approach, children incorporate representations of other people who are initially merged with the sense of self. Over time, the sense of self and the sense of the other are transformed through a series of internal changes. This process is an imagined one, not a physical one. The internal representation of the other, at first merged with the self, becomes divided into good and bad self-objects. To the infant, someone who satisfies her needs represents this good part of her, and that good part is fused with the good part of the object (usually a parent). When the infant or young toddler's needs are not met, that represents the merged bad self-object. Gradually, through the development of skills that enable the child to ambulate, explore, and meet her own needs, she learns ambivalence. All people, including her, have good and bad parts. The self–object is split back into the self and the object, each containing good and bad elements. This signals emotional maturity and the ability to accept ambivalent feelings toward the self and toward the other.

The child learns that sometimes her needs would be met and sometimes not, but this does not signal a failure of love; it is a normal condition. If this ambivalence fails to develop, the child may learn to rely on her own immature resources (as can occur for persons with narcissistic personality disorders); conversely, she may learn to rely too much on others and may be easily disappointed in their failures to meet her every whim (as can occur for persons with borderline personality disorder). The inability to integrate good and bad parts of the self with good and bad parts of the other can result in a defense known as splitting. The trick for parents, and presumably for older sisters, is to provide the right amount of encouragement and support at the right time so that the child can learn to individuate and create a separate emotional identity. People who have navigated that developmental milestone like other people but are not overly dependent upon them. On occasion a girl may help her younger sister to establish stable internal objects that have been integrated with good and bad components and called forth emotional ambivalence, thereby assisting in the separation–individuation process. Sisters may also play a role in the development of personality disorders and the failure of object stability, also referred to as object constancy. Most often themes related to sisters come about due to a parenting role by one sister toward another. Many of the object relations theorists ignore this potential role, so here I have merged their ideas with the evidence from my research that such roles may be played by a sister.

Birth of the Sister

Melanie Klein theorized that one important aspect of wishing for a sibling was the desire to have a child of one's own. Fairbairn (1952) added detail when he described the child's manipulation of an infant sibling as if it were a doll or object. The baby was likely to disappoint the older child when it did not cooperate as an external object that could be manipulated. Klein also discussed the importance of the older child's ability to learn mastery when teaching a younger sibling a task or skill. An infant sibling could become a pretend offspring for a young girl. In these ways, an infant sister may have stimulated an older one to move forward with her mastery of the external world, and this could have had a positive or negative impact on the older sister's object constancy.

My research supported these themes from Fairbairn. There was much evidence that sisters fulfilled the role of a parent substitute. They described the experience of parenting by older sisters. They suggested that baby sisters were longed for and were experienced as important when they arrived. The arrival of an infant sister also stimulated awareness of the loss of the mother's love and affection to the older child; in some cases, the women said so directly. According to object relations theory, the timing of this is very important. If premature, the older sister might have been pushed into an overreliance on herself and may not have established full object constancy. If the infant sister arrived when the older sister had achieved object constancy or was about to (around the age of 3), the effect of the sibling's arrival may have been very positive. The older sister might have been nudged toward an appropriate level of independence while still trusting that the mother was emotionally present. Mothers or fathers who managed this well continued to provide the necessary emotional refueling for their older daughters while attending to the needs of their younger one.

Sister as Primary or Secondary Object

Sisters were likely to become primary or secondary objects for younger sisters who were in the throes of object constancy. Several theorists discussed this possibility and its impact on the developing child. Winnicott and Fairbairn seemed to focus on different polarities in regard to this theme. Fairbairn talked about the potential for developmental difficulty based upon the sister being an unsatisfying and immature object; Winnicott (1977) suggested that the sister's role as a primary or secondary object might enhance the younger girl's development. Women in my research suggested that sisters did sometimes become primary parents. The timing of this may not have directly affected the initial development of object constancy, as the role might have occurred later in childhood. However, the sister's role in repairing the loss of the primary object before full maturity could not be underestimated. This role also had an effect on the older sister, thrusting her prematurely in the role of object, sometimes before she had completed the adolescent separation–individuation process. One woman spoke about her feelings of abandonment when such a sister left the family home to go to college. In another adaptation of this theme, the importance of secondary objects emerged when a young niece was unable to distinguish between her mother and her aunt, as both functioned as primary objects for her.

Some sisters functioned as emotional parents even when the primary parents were present. This was the case with ill mothers or fathers as well as emotionally immature ones. When fathers distanced themselves emotionally, the sisters may have bonded to overcome the sense of emotional loss. The opportunity also occurred in abusive households. The potential for the sister to fill this role depended upon her own emotional constancy and her ability to set aside her own emotional needs or manage them in other ways. Sometimes age spacing made a difference in the ability to fill this role, with much older sisters better able to perform it. The overall outcome of such situations were related the primary parent's ability to help the older daughter through her own object constancy development. A family that experienced good fortune and health when one girl was young sometimes had a less fortunate status when the younger sister was growing up. This circumstance provided object constancy and normal emotional ambivalence for the older daughter, who was then able to fulfill the role of mature object for the younger one. In such cases, the emotional roles shifted at maturity for both girls. They became more equal as each achieved the separation and individuation of adulthood.

Sister as Transitional Object

The term *transitional object* has become a part of the general lexicon. It is most often symbolized by the security blanket to which a young child clings. It is a physical object that serves as a symbol of the parent when the parent is absent. Children who cannot give up their transitional objects may be unable to do so because they fear losing their parents. Bank and Kahn (1982a, 1982b) discussed the importance of the sibling as a transitional object rather than a primary one. The sister who became a transitional object did so for a lifetime. She functioned as a *part object,* according to Kernberg (1980), who linked this role to the development of ego and superego differentiation in children. He discussed the importance that siblings play in this developmental achievement, arguing that they probably fulfill that role through middle childhood. Of course, the women in my study did not use the language of object relations theory, but several referred to such a role for their sister or themselves. One woman described an overwhelming sense of guilt for the way she had treated her sister in childhood—perhaps evidence that her own maturity was tied to that relationship and had not been resolved. Another woman suggested that her sister's presence was especially poignant and important during life-altering events. This also suggested an awareness of the introjected sibling.

Evidence of Mature Ambivalence

Winnicott's case of Gabrielle (see Chapter 1) also provided some important understanding for the development of guilt. As Gabrielle matured in the analysis, she began to consider her sister Susan's feelings. Gabrielle said she felt guilty about having her father's affection and the attention of the analyst when her younger sister did not. Winnicott's work with Gabrielle suggested how important it is to reconcile the ambivalence about the sister, not just the mother. In my research, a close relationship between the mother or father with one sister could create jealousy or distance between sisters. Sometimes this jealousy is resolved; sometimes it is not. Without the benefit of pediatric therapy, as Gabrielle had, some women could not resolve the jealous anger they held toward sisters who had had a more favorable relationship with one parent.

Differentiating the Good and Bad Sister

According to Kernberg (1980) siblings may play a role in the differentiation process. Many themes from my research supported this formulation. The need to integrate the sister may have been restimulated by the research, calling to mind links to the unfinished business of individuation and differentiation. Women recalled the effect of the research on their conscious understanding and commented on how it had changed their perceptions. Most of the women expressed awareness that sisters have passed through developmental stages and those stages have altered the relationship. They expressed the knowledge that the sister remained important throughout these stages. Yet there were many conflicted feelings toward the sister. In the context of a close sister relationship, conflict was understood as inevitable and insignificant to the total fabric of the relationship. As the sisters matured, closeness in their relationship was balanced with an increasing sense of separation and self-definition.

Sibling differentiation has been amplified in recent articles by Vivona (2007), who suggested that lateral differentiation from siblings results in minimizing similarity and maximizing differences. This type of dichotomous identity may restrict both sisters from creating a fully developed internal identity. Balsam (1988) discussed the differentiation from siblings in her explanation of late adolescent clients. Comparison to the sister by women in my research suggested some support for Vivona's and Balsam's theories. The women in the study suggested that their sisters helped them to differentiate into unique identities. These expressions of maturity suggested that object constancy with the sister was obtained and ambivalence was achieved. However, was a price paid for that lateral differentiation? In an attempt to understand the relationship, women often compared themselves to their sisters. It seemed that their identity development depended upon the appropriate balance of conflict and closeness. Yet they discussed at great length the similarities they had with their sisters, physically, emotionally, and experientially. Their shared memories and experiences often formed similar values. Some focused a great deal on the differences, and it may have been those sisters who sacrificed part of their own nature to become different from their sisters.

Persistence of the Sister as Object

Other relationships were compared to the sister relationship in a way that suggested she was internalized or introjected from earliest childhood. In essence, women carried around a sense of their sister that was stable and used it as a basis of comparison for other relationships. Sometimes geographic or emotional distance was necessary for the development of that ambivalence. This distance also created a longing to replace the sister with a substitute object in adulthood. Often she was replaced by a close female friend who was more available. Differences in each sister's maturity were also recognized by the women. Some described the need to reach out to less mature sisters in times of emotional turmoil in the family, thus filling the need of a stable object at a different life stage.

Positive Sister Introjects

The positive influence of sisters is also documented in Bank and Kahn's expansion of the sibling role as object (1982b). According to these authors, partial objects that were introjected as loved and admired in a realistic way could lead to well-being and a sense of emotional depth. Some of the women of the study did talk about the well-being they experienced in their relationship with their sisters. Such experiences occurred throughout the lifespan. According to many, expectations and judgments about the sister's life changed over time. There was also an expression of hopefulness for the sister and for the self. Some attempted to move their relationship to a more mature emotional footing in a deliberate way. Others wanted a more authentic relationship with their sisters. Some felt the need to abandon the family's prescribed roles in order to do this. The mature ego and mutuality of the relationship were clear from such statements and represented a clear sense of potential well-being in the sister relationship. Furthermore, the women suggested that compatibility developed during childhood was often a contributor to a sense of closeness—a direct reference to the emotional connection of early childhood. In their own identity development, the women suggested that the sister helped them to define themselves. Comparison to her helped to differentiate the self. All of these descriptions suggest an awareness of the well-being that Bank and Kahn described.

Pathology due to the Sister as Object

Several theorists have suggested that the immaturity of the sister who fills the role of introjected object can lead to the development of pathology. Fairbairn was the first to suggest such problems. He suggested that inadequate mothering by a sibling may lead to the development of shame in a child. Worse yet, being dependent upon such a relationship as the model for mature development could lead to personality disintegration. Winnicott suggested that sibling birth at the wrong time in development could lead to lifelong depression. If sisters were capable of providing the young child with "good enough" mothering, their departure from the home might have caused abandonment depression for siblings who had still not achieved object constancy (Klein, 1932/75 Masterson, 1988). Bank and Kahn also support this impression.

Only two themes from my research seemed to relate to this potential for pathology. Some women described the lifelong breaches in the sister bond when a third party formed a conflicted triangular relationship. When this third party was the primary parent or mother, pathology could arise from splitting in one, or both, of the sisters. In contrast, the death of a sister produced profound ambivalence in some women and suggested that this developmental milestone had been reached in their relationship prior to death. Such an experience of loss also sparked the desire for more authentic relationships with the remaining sisters.

Sisters who treated each other merely as objects to be manipulated may produce schizoid personality structures in their younger siblings, according to Ralph Klein (1995). He also suggested that sisters who filled the role of primary caregiver may create poor boundaries in a family. Some support for this was present in my research. It came from the description of the oldest sister in a family who was often described as domineering, organized, and, perhaps, exploitive. The exploitive nature of the relationship may have reflected the ability to treat the sister as an object for satisfaction of one's own desires. Clearly, incest between sisters would also document this, but none was present in my research. There was no evidence that directly suggested poor family boundaries were created by this role of sister–parent. Yet some women did describe leaving their parents' home to live with an older sister and her husband prior to maturity. They expressed gratitude about this and some ambivalence, but not the distance and orbiting defenses that schizoid personality structure has suggested.

Multigenerational Themes

In addition to Melanie Klein's suggestions about multigenerational issues, Winnicott's case of Gabrielle provided some illumination. Gabrielle's dis-ease with the birth of her sister was partially a result of her mother's expectations that she would not fare well. This, based upon the mother's own experience of having a sister when she was not yet old enough to give up her mother, suggested that the partial failure of object constancy could have been determined by intergenerational expectations. Gabrielle's relationship with Susan, her younger sister, was traced throughout Winnicott's analysis.

In my sister project, three themes supported this multigenerational expectation about the sister relationship, but the results described by the women were always positive. The next generation of sisters—the daughters of the women— were often considered in their analysis of the relationship. The relationship the interviewee had with her sister was used as a model for the relationship between her daughters. At the birth of one daughter, there was the hope for a sister who might replicate the sister relationship being described by the women. All of these multigenerational themes suggested that the women wanted to have their sister relationship emulated in the next generation.

In 1971, Kohut proposed that siblings could serve several functions in the development of healthy object relationships. He discussed mirroring, twinning, and the desire to merge, and their specific applications to the sibling relationship. Sisters may mirror each other, but they may present the child with clear differences, resulting in the child's developing ability to sacrifice her own needs. For an older sibling this may create frustration but could result in empathy for both herself and the younger child. According to Kohut, the child needs to "feel sufficiently secure to begin taking on the role of the other; and out of this mutual regard for each other a positive relationship unfolds" (Kohut, 1971, p. 39). In the process of twinning, children may become emotionally merged, even though they are physically separate from the other. In the case of sisters, this twinning may be experienced as creating a difference between parent and children—they have learned to think differently than the mother and come to see each other as the more stable object. Such differentiation leads to another stage of anger and frustration, often accompanied by fighting between the sisters that seemed unfounded. Finally, the desire to merge with the sister–object may create a final breaking apart of the relationship, which is both traumatic and full of rage. Sometimes immobility also results from this separation.

Additional Lifespan Themes from the Research

In general, this project offers much support for the understanding of sisters as objects, introjects and transitional objects. In this section I have organized the additional application of those research findings by developmental period—childhood, adolescence, and adult life. I have illustrated some of the themes with examples from the research and some from my clinical practice.

Additional Themes from Childhood

During early childhood, birth of a sister was both expected and traumatic and led to depression or rage at the loss of the parental object. One of the women described her homicidal feelings for her sister. She explained that rage was the expected outcome of the sister relationship. Another woman wanted her sister to emerge and take her place among siblings who were all male. That anticipation was not met when the child who emerged was an infant, not a playmate. The result was the loss of the idealized sister, as well as the loss of the mother, who turned to her infant and away from the child. Similarly, Winnicott's case of Gabrielle presented the advent of depression at the birth of a younger sister when the child was only 21 months old. Thus depression, rage, or more often the cycling of the two emerges at the birth of an expected sister, who takes the primary object away.

The sister may serve as a primary parent to the younger sister, especially if the sister is much older. Of course, the sister's ability to do this depends, in part, on her own maturity. In one clinical case, a 13-year-old girl became a pseudo-parent for her younger sister from birth. The age span between them resulted in the experience of being raised by entirely different families: the parents had managed to free themselves from drug addiction when the older girl was 10, before the birth of the youngest. The older daughter, functioning as a primary parent for her sister, had not had adequate parenting herself. Suffering from a severe case of agoraphobia, which had remained intractable throughout many treatments, it was unclear how she was able to provide a stable object for her sister. The younger girl was ridden with guilt for the older sister's health concerns and was also secretly angry that much of her own young life was being overwhelmed by her older sister's treatment regimens. As the older sister attempted individuation many additional problems arose, resulting in her failed individuation and her retreat into immaturity. This immaturity may have been an attempt to relive her own young childhood and receive the emotional gifts now laden upon her sister. Her younger sister may have suffered the negative effects of lateral differentiation, resulting in a restricted view of herself as "not my sister."

Some sisters who served as the primary objects had to be integrated by the younger sister in order to avoid splitting defenses within the child. When a young girl experienced her sister as loved and hated, the resolution of those disparate feelings could lead to integration of the good and bad objects within the self and a healthy level of confidence in relationships. For example, two African American sisters presented separately for psychotherapy. The older one described her role as important for maintaining the stability of her sisters and brothers. She had been molested by multiple stepfathers; she was uncertain if her sister had been as well. With mixed gender identity, she took on the role of the father object in the family, providing emotional stability through rough and rugged defense of her siblings. She finally emerged as the primary breadwinner for her extended family, providing shelter to siblings and their offspring as necessary throughout life. The next younger sister emerged with a greater ability to form an intimate attachment to another adult. Her emotional issues were manageable with a few psychotherapeutic interventions. It is speculated that her older sister's consistent assumption of a parental role provided her with constancy that the older sister did not experience. That constancy allowed for the development of mature ambivalence in the younger sister. Its development took many years of therapy for the older one. Thus, the maturity of one sister was a consideration in the continuing emotional maturity of each individual and of the relationship between the sisters. The younger sister's stability in this family became a model for the development of the older one in therapy. Their growing connection and trust at midlife helped to create a mature platform for the older sister's growth.

Adolescence

Some separation–individuation themes are unique to adolescence, and these also emerged in the research process. Older sisters may serve as models for the resumption of individuation needs during adolescence. At any age, sisters may help with the differentiation of identity and life or career choices. Some women in the study reported watching their sisters individuate prematurely. One woman's sister married so she would not have to be supported by a family who had fallen on hard economic times. The loss of a primary parent was the trigger for the financial downturn and the eventual premature separation from the family of the older girl. The younger sister described this process and was concerned about its effects on her older sister's life. It was not a model she wanted to emulate, but she was aware of its importance to the family. This differentiation in late adolescence had the effect of giving one sister a definition of being good that was created through the introjection of her sister's sacrifice. Likewise, this definition of the good child within a family provided some sisters with the impetus to pursue their career choices. By watching the struggle of their younger sisters, they developed a career designed to compensate for her losses. These career experiences may have been an attempt to reconcile the individuation of the child who remained dependent upon the family because of physical or mental illness. Their assumption might have been another calamity of differentiation that was restricted by the identity of the sister and the manner in which it was internalized.

In another example of lateral differentiation, a defensive—"I'm not like her"—stance emerged in a younger sister. This fear of being like the sister may have represented an adolescent splitting defense. Two adolescent sisters had literally been split by their parents into the good sister and the bad sister. One had a normal social life and was doing well in school. She was attractive and she was also fair-haired with green eyes and had a lighter skin color than her Latina sister. The other sister—the bad sister—had developed bulimia and was addicted to cocaine. She claimed a bisexual identity, which was barely tolerated by her father. This sister had been in juvenile hall for drug possession and was nearly flunking out of high school. The younger and fair-haired sister worked hard to make up for the pain her older sister had caused her parents. She distanced herself from her sister at school and pretended not to be related to her. These two young women wept for the distance between them when separated from their parents in the therapy room, yet each seemed to agree with the splitting defense of the family when all members were present.

Envy and rage about a sister's life choices seemed to represent a continuing splitting defense on the part of a younger sister. One woman described physically assaulting her sister in adolescence but does not remember why. Another talked about the need to join those criticizing her sister in order to strengthen her own role in the family. Sometimes the person who participated with her was her mother, suggesting another theme from the research related to adolescence.

Adulthood

As sisters entered adulthood and matured through later life, the themes of separation and individuation were often attached to the relationship with the adult partner. Sometimes this included the relationship toward children as well. In mature object relationships, sisters and partners shared relationships that respected the sister as secondary to the primary relationship in adulthood.

Women in my study suggested this outcome as well as the opposite. One woman declared that the relationship with her sister was wonderful but could not replace the husband she had lost. Another sister, the defender of her sister against childhood incest, suggested that her husband knew better than to come between the two sisters. In the second instance, the sister relationship became a metaphor for safety from danger and annihilation, and the husband was tolerated only as long as he supported the relationship between the women. The first woman reporting was a widow, dealing with the death of her husband. The second one was a young adult, still closely tied to her family of origin's themes and traumas. This trajectory suggests a developing maturity for the differentiation and individuation of the sister relationship and its place in the life of women as they grow older.

When a woman had children, they often carried out the narrative of the sister relationship; they benefited from the insight the adult sisters had gained. Appreciation for the generational differences was present, yet women wanted to replicate their sister relationship in their children. Perhaps this was a way of recognizing the sister's role in helping to resolve the separation–individuation crises with the parents. Perhaps they felt their own sisters had been primary objects in their own development. For whatever reason, the desire for sisters in the next generation was often the outcome of positive generativity as women grew older. The sister bond may have become the primary relationship as advancing age brought loss and grief. Healthy sisters participated in each others' healing process and helped each other to care for elderly parents. In this final stage of life, many sisters became each other's caregivers once again. At that stage of life it was often the younger sister who cared for the older one.

Conclusions

There are ways in which this research project provided additional material for the formulation of individual development within the analytic and object relations framework. Sisters experience rivalry and rage at the arrival of a new child. The relationship with the mother and father is often altered when infants are born. Sisters who are mature enough can contribute to the emotional stability and developing relationship skills of younger sisters. They may do this by providing dynamic tension in the triangular relationships with parents. They may also do this by being partial objects that reinforce the parents' constancy. They may also do it by being a primary object themselves and giving the sister more opportunity for refueling as she learns to explore her world.

At different life stages, the younger and older sisters may provide encouragement for individuation or they may limit individuation through rigid individuation. Their mere presence may encourage an older sister to grow or a younger sister to follow. Sometimes sisters diverge in their own identities much more dramatically than they might without a sister in their lives. These theories remain somewhat rooted in a focus on the relationship between men and women, mothers and children, with few insightful ideas about the unique nature of the sister–sister bond.

In providing some support for theorists who have been associated with misogyny and pathology, I have experienced much ambivalence but have tried to remain true to the experiences expressed by my research participants and clients. In the next chapter, I have attempted to take a less pathological and more positive approach to appreciating the sister connection.

12

Relational Cultural Theory and Sisters' Growth in Connection

"Were I a painter able to preserve a day of my life in oils and light, this is the picture I would paint: three thoughtful girls with a broken plate. Each piece telling a part of the story."

Gregory Maguire (1999, p. xi)

In their 1991 book *Women's Growth in Connection*, Jordan and colleagues (Jordan, Kaplan, Miller, & Stiver, 1991) developed a theory that places relational development at center stage (Jordan, 1991a, 1991b, 1991c; Jordan, Surrey, & Kaplan, 1991; Miller, 1991). In their work, they reconsidered and reconstructed psychological understanding of the role that mothers have with daughters. In contrast to many psychological theories, they attempted to emphasize the positive nature of that connection. The authors of this theory, relational cultural theory (RCT), focused on the influence of mothers on daughters—a positive and unique approach to the development of women's identity and relationships. Despite that focus, the role of sisters has been presented only minimally.

This chapter provides an integration of my own research about sister relationships with RCT. To accomplish this I read and reread the works of the primary authors of RCT: Jean Baker Miller, Irene Stiver, Judith Jordan, Janet Surrey, and Alexandra Kaplan, along with works by several other authors affiliated with their group at the Stone Center for Human Development at Wellesley College. I found few themes that directly mention the influence of sisters. I compared those few references to sisters to my research themes. Next, I expanded the major themes from the RCT approach to include the sister relationship and its developmental impact. This integration provided a new step in the understanding of women's relationships and cultural development.

Judith Jordan described the difference between the relational cultural approach and other relational or object-relational approaches. RCT pushed the dynamically oriented therapist to move "from a psychology of 'entities' to a psychology of movement and dialogue" (Miller, Jordan, Kaplan, Stiver, & Surrey, 1997, p.31). This summative statement defines a therapeutic approach that was formed from the professional relationship between half-a-dozen women authors and colleagues.

Their dialogue, lasting over 30 years, created a new understanding of how women's development might be different than men's. The belief that women grow and develop a sense of self through relationships with others is rooted in the mother–daughter relationship. This relationship is different than other parent–child relationships since it does not require the level of separation and individuation necessary for sons that has been described by male-centered theories. In the RCT model, the mother–daughter relationship is primary rather than being an offshoot of the description of male development that has been represented by most psychological approaches.

According to the authors of RCT, young girls and even infants are responsive to the needs of the other—just as they are concerned with their own needs for relationship. This responsiveness may be present at birth for both sexes, but in much of the world it is socially discouraged in boys and encouraged in girls. Miller, Stiver, Jordan, Kaplan, and Surrey described this mutual empathy between mother and daughter as the bedrock of relationship skills. They suggested that the U.S. culture may minimize this skill to serve a patriarchal structure that values external achievement more than relationships. Many other Western countries do the same, although Latin American countries, West Asia, and Hawaii have supported the development of empathy for both sexes. Given RCT's focus on the mother–daughter development and the authors' stance that empathy occurs within relationships, it seems important to expect a sister–sister relationship to enhance relational skills as well. RCT authors have not explored that possibility in depth but have hinted at the importance such a relationship might play.

Sisters in the Writing of Relational-Cultural Theorists

There are few mentions of the sister relationship in the writings of RCT's original authors. Most often, sisters were mentioned in the context of clinical case examples, although there are a few exceptions to this. In Jean Baker Miller's first major work, an edited volume called *Psychoanalysis and Women* (1973a, 1973b), there was no mention of sisters or even much about siblings in the introductory chapter or summative commentaries. Some of the authors in that edited book mentioned brothers of women. Clara Thompson discussed the way that women's depression might be an outcome of differential treatment of male and female children. She described the loss of preadolescent freedoms by girls and the limitations of Victorian adolescence that were not experienced by their brothers (1942/1973). References to sisters were not included; perhaps this was an unconscious intrusion of the sexism in the culture. Miller's edited volume was followed by her association with a strong group of women therapists; their thoughtful analysis of women's psychology became the basis for relational cultural theory.

The RCT authors published their first edited book in 1991. Titled *Women's Growth in Connection* (Jordan, Kaplan, Miller, Stiver, & Surrey, 1991), it contained many articles that had been previously self-published by the Stone Center for Human Development at Wellesley College (the erstwhile home of RCT). This book held some clues to the importance of the sister relationship and some early theoretical formulations by Irene Stiver and Clevonne Turner. Jean Baker Miller's introduction to the book included a sibling case. She again mentioned brothers. Her own adult household of men[1] may have required this focus. In Miller's clinical case the female client described a primary attachment to her father and a difficult relationship with her mother. As the client grew up, her two brothers and father excluded her from their world, contributing to her emotional distance and disconnection from relationships. Miller did not speculate about the potential role a sister may have played in this family interaction.

Janet Surrey (1991b, p. 55) suggested an important role for sisters when she said that the capacity for empathy might have been developed in "important relationships with other significant people in childhood." The mutuality of these relationships was expected to develop throughout adult life. Surrey did not mention sisters, but she did mention sibling relationships as a potent factor in women's development:

> [N]ew learning in current relationships leads to development, whenever possible, in older more long-standing parental or sibling relationships (which are even more challenging to the maintenance of adult self-images). (Surrey, 1991b, p. 65)

Despite this suggestion, Surrey did not provide any real understanding of the sister or sibling role; she did not develop the idea any further.

The mothers of RCT understood that their theory was far from complete and often acknowledged the need for continuing amplification of their ideas. In her chapter *Empathy and Self-Boundaries*, Jordan (1991a) unabashedly denotes that the major:

> flaw in existing theory has been the lack of elaboration of the developmental lines of connection and relationship; there has been a tendency to resort to either the now questionable model of the fused mother–infant pair or heterosexual genital union to conceptualize intimacy or self–other connections ... a vast and rich array of what Stern would call 'self with other' experiences are lost in this model. (Jordan, 1991a, p. 79)

These "other" connections could include the sister relationship, one that has often been a lifelong connection. Miller (1991) made reference to Zella Luria's research (1981). This well-known study evaluated what girls and boys were doing on the playground. Hidden in the girls' seeming inactivity was a tendency to

---

[1] Miller was married to a man and had two sons and no daughters.

evaluate and discuss relationships. This same work might easily be extrapolated to the activities of girls in a family—sisters who spend endless hours discussing the relational consequences and strengths in the family system. Such applications of RCT to sisters required much reading between the lines. Some clinical cases and research findings described in other writings by the relational cultural theorists suggest deeper potential.

In the essay "From Depression to Sadness in Women's Psychotherapy," Stiver and Miller (1997) made three references to the sister relationship; each included a mention of the relationship without much elaboration. First, they described a research study about stillbirths. According to the authors, women became depressed when they were not allowed to express the full strength of their feelings, such as normal sadness; not even sisters allowed women to experience the loss, dismissing it by saying that the woman could conceive another child. Second, the authors described a female alcoholic in recovery who acknowledged that she had been unavailable to her daughters when they were growing up. Her adult children, the sisters, were spending time together when the mother phoned to discuss her role in their development. The authors described the mother's efforts at reconciliation and how they helped to heal and deepen not only the mother–daughter bonds but also the sister–sister bonds. In another vignette, an abusive husband dismissed his wife's sister from their home, demanding she have no future contact with the sister. This sister—the primary emotional support for the woman in the abusive relationship—could no longer fulfill her role. The cowed married sister complied with her husband's demands and the sisters lost contact. The abused woman spiraled into acute depression. Only the relationship with the sister had prevented this from occurring sooner. All three of these examples began to evaluate the importance of the sister relationship in the development of emotional maturity and stability, but they left many unanswered questions.

Wendy Rosen also considered the sister connection in her writing about the relationship between lesbian women and their mothers (1997). With special attention to the sexual differences between heterosexual sisters and lesbian sisters, Rosen recounted the case of a woman who came out to her sister before she was able to do so with her mother. Rosen said that her client came into treatment when her sister was engaged to be married, although she does not pay much attention to this fact in the essay. The therapy centered upon the emotional distance the sister felt from her heterosexual mother and her heterosexual sister, as their relationship with each other was cemented through common interests. The disconnection from the mother–daughter pair began in adolescence. The client came out to her sister first and received a common reaction: the sister was not surprised by this revelation, having deduced it herself. The heterosexual sister felt left out of her lesbian sister's life and did not think she could ask questions about it. When the lesbian client came out to her mother, she was rejected. Rosen concluded, "Mutual empathy, relationship authenticity, and relationship differentiation [were all] . . . derailed" (p. 245) in this mother–daughter relationship. Apparently the same was not true about the sister connection. This example again left many questions about the experience of growth in the relationship between sisters.

Irene Stiver's essay "Beyond the Oedipus Complex: Mothers and Daughters" (1986/1991a) provided greater depth for the sister connection as the author re-evaluated nuclear family relationships in the first 5 years of life. According to this essay, a girl's internal conflicts are created through identification with the mother; at the time of the alleged oedipal complex, the girl has learned that women, including her mother, are devalued in the U.S. cultural frame and within the family. Thus the daughter, by virtue of identification with the mother, is also devalued. Embedded in Stiver's discussion of this loss of self and mother importance was an acknowledgement of the developing girl's awareness of family dynamics. Stiver said that "highly responsive" infants and young preschool girls were well aware of family interactions, including those with siblings. Her description of the rapid growth and cognitive change in the first 5 years of life suggested that children were aware of "rather complicated interactions among family members" (p. 8).

This led Stiver to a discussion of the importance of sibling birth. In many psychological theories, these events were most significant for their effect on the relationship between mother and child. Stiver suggested that the birth of siblings was important because they represented another opportunity for relational connection. This new child offered the developing young girl an "opportunity to enlarge her relational capacities"; to help her move more into "complicated interactions" with others; and to work through internal conflicts about the ways the relationship affected her. During the adjustment to a sibling's presence, the child learned to increase her skill at nurturing complex relationships simultaneously. Stiver suggested that this was due to the girl's:

> identification with her mother in the mothering of the new baby, rage at being displaced, enthusiasm about the opportunity to spend more time with her beloved father which sometimes occurs, and empathic interactions with a mother who often feels quite burdened and torn herself. (p. 12)

When the sibling was female, she, too, experienced a parental expectation of empathy. Each child may have embraced the other with understanding and found a reflective presence there.

At the same time, the mother remembered her own feelings about the birth of siblings. This helped the development of empathy between mother and the older girl. In Stiver's essay she began to understand the mother's complex emotions towards this older child:

> [The experience was] also a reflection of how deeply tied she felt to her daughter, how much she felt what she imagined would be her daughter's pain, and how much she also resented her daughter for interfering with her simultaneous wish to bond with her new baby. (p. 12)

Stiver attempted to clarify the roles of both mother and daughter in the development of mutual empathy. More than any other relational cultural theorist, she examined the same potential in the sister connection.

A similar level of development was given to the understanding of relationships between Black sisters by Clevonne Turner (1997). Part of the second major book by the RCT group, *Women's Growth in Diversity*, Turner's writings lent a unique perspective. She expressed awareness of three different and important themes in the lives of many Black women: (1) their awareness of community in their lives, (2) the androgynous roles for Black women that develop at an early age, and (3) the importance of internalized racism. She dubbed the awareness of internalized racism and the way it is used against other Black women the "seesaw phenomenon" and tied it to the connection between Black sisters. This phenomenon formed the basis for "sibling rivalry" between related and unrelated Black women and referred to competition between those inside of a culture, as well as those in other cultures. This competitive striving aimed to gain favoritism from the majority culture (p. 79). Sisters, both related and unrelated, had the potential to seesaw between empathy for each other and jealousy of the favoritism one received.

Turner also evoked an image of sister relationships when she described a different pathway to relationship differentiation for Black women. In single-parent Black families, young Black girls may be required to assume caretaking roles early in life. Most often this includes care for younger siblings, sometimes sisters. As these young girls grow and develop, they "simultaneously learn to redefine and differentiate their self in relation to their concerns and feelings for significant others (mothers, fathers, siblings, relatives, friends, authority figures, and the Black community-at-large)" (1997, p. 76). This complex set of relationships and the early demands of both mutuality and agency create a strong set of skills for Black women that help to perpetuate resilience against the racism of the U.S. culture. Black women, in Turner's view, develop relational capacity due to the close interconnections of these mutually supportive relationships, including those between related and unrelated sisters.

The relational cultural theorists have been criticized for focusing too much on an optimistic view of mother–daughter relationships. For many years they defended this by citing a need to correct the imbalance created by other theorists who focused more on pathology in the mother–child connection. More recently, two of the primary authors of RCT responded to this criticism, writing about the disconnections that could occur because of relational failure (Miller & Stiver, 1997). It was not surprising that sibling relationship dynamics in that text focused on the problems of *parentification*—the potential for disconnection and emotional distancing that could be caused by using one child in a family to provide for the needs of others. This parentification was viewed quite differently in Turner's cultural framework for Black women, but Miller and Stiver connected it to problems within the dominant culture. Most often parentification occurs when parents are not available. The authors suggested that parental drug abuse, disability, or depression may cause it. Sometimes this process begins at "very early ages" for children (p. 98). The child may believe she could not have mutual relationships and may feel she did not deserve them. In such circumstances, caretaking becomes a large part of her self-definition. However, Stiver and Miller suggested that sometimes the mother–child bond is strengthened during parentification. The interdependency between a young girl and her mother may enhance their growth in the relationship, as well as in other relationships. Positive outcomes are likely if there is a sense of shared caretaking. However, if the responsibility is confusing or conflicted because it is beyond the child's ability—such as a 5-year-old taking a 3-year-old to the playground—the child develops difficulties in mutual exchange. In such cases, Miller and Stiver suggested that the responsibility may lead to "dissonance between how they are perceived by others and how they experience themselves" (1997, p. 100). When this occurs, the capacity for authenticity in relationships diminishes.

But what if two or more sisters are "in it together"? What if the growth takes place between sisters who develop a mutual intersubjectivity as well as a mutual dependence on each other—one who attends to the disciplinary aspects of managing younger children and another who evaluates danger in the environment? Such sisters might share the burden and the authenticity of a struggle, spurring each other to growth in connection that is mutual and resilient. The authors acknowledged resilience could occur when there is "evidence of a close relationship with at least one person and fewer prolonged separations from the primary caregiver during the first years of life" (p. 103). Sisters with well-developed capacities for mutual empathy may have a close relationship. The authors suggested as much when they say:

> [I]n many situations family members—siblings, aunts, uncles—can offer a child some sense of another kind of relationship, one characterized by respect, empathy and encouragement. (p. 103)

Illuminating Thoughts from my Research

There were not many well-developed ideas about sisters in the RCT authors' writings, but some themes were evident. Several ideas related to sisters did emerge from those writings, including gender issues, family roles, the development of mutual relationships outside the mother–daughter dyad, adult changes in relational capacity, a sister's role in defining appropriate sadness, and specific differences created by diversity. Integration of RCT and my research project examined the overlapping themes between them.

Gender Issues

Differences in the upbringing of boys and girls were mentioned by Jean Baker Miller in her case example of the woman with two brothers, an emotionally difficult mother, and a close attachment to her father. In that case, the girl felt excluded from the male world of her brothers and father. Themes from the research echoed these concerns. For some women, the father's assignment of gender identification to his daughters resulted in the loss of emotional closeness between them. Another theme suggested that male–female issues were definitely a part of the changing relationship between sisters as they aged. In the research project the women focused much more on the ways in which the women of a family excluded the males than vice versa. Brothers and fathers may have influenced the alignment within the mother–daughter–sister triad but were not usually a part of its substance. The women also provided evidence that male relatives might have been included or excluded from this mother–daughter–sister connection. Perhaps the focus of the research upon sisters, rather than fathers or brothers, brought out these important distinctions. There did seem to be, however, a sisterhood operating at an emotional level in many of these families, and it was that sisterhood that determined access to the mutually emotional connections within the family. This stands in sharp contrast to the vignette about male exclusion presented by Miller as she wrote the basic text for RCT.

Another gender-based theme was mentioned by Jordan. In evaluating Luria's research (1981) about what girls and boys do on the playground, Jordan provided some ideas about female peer relationships. She did not apply these principles to sisters, but the women in my project did. They described some engendered ways that women related to each other; these differed from the way they related to men. Sisters described a shifting of feelings toward the sister from birth through adulthood that was accompanied by feelings of anticipation, jealousy for parental attention, conflicted interaction with brothers, and honest communication with the sister about these gender issues. However, there was also a theme about emotional preference for men. Some women felt distant from their sisters because of their male identification that was reflected in the preference for emotional ties to men.

Gender identity and family gender issues could also create disconnections for sisters. Sisters with more feminine interests were not considered as close to an athletically gifted woman. In addition, parental desire for a boy at birth could create discrimination within the family. Being born female was sometimes a lasting stigma when parents hoped for a boy. This situation could create a sense of parental favoritism toward the other sister. Sometimes differences in gender identification pushed sisters apart; in other circumstances, some women found greater connection because of their differences.

In trying to find their own balance of gender identities, the women mentioned both instrumental and expressive talents and traits. The relative importance of such traits increased the importance of a particular sister relationship at a given time for some women. During emergencies, when action was required, a sister with greater instrumental skills might have been more highly valued. Likewise, a mutually engaged sister relationship was more important when the focus was upon family disruption; these traits also figured prominently in the caretaking role of aging sisters. Traits and talents that differentiated traditional masculine and feminine roles defined different aspects of the sisters' relationship with each other. Sisters were valued based partly on these abilities.

Discussions of relationships with men and misogyny by people outside the family also created strong bonds between sisters. Sometimes one sister influenced another about these gender discrimination issues. Gender issues were often discussed by the women and created some of the relational dimensions between them. The importance of these identifications seemed to shift as life progressed, underscoring the need to pay attention to the ways that gender, gender discrimination, and gender roles enhanced or changed the relationships between sisters.

Family Roles

Sisters' roles in their nuclear families were also mentioned by relational cultural theorists. Jean Baker Miller and Irene Stiver's description of the parentified child (1997) was an example of these roles. If the parents could not fill certain family responsibilities, they were often adopted by an older child in the family. Miller and Stiver attributed this parentification to drug use, disability, or depression of one parent. Themes from my project reflected this need for an older child to step in and fulfill the role of a parent. One research theme directly supported Miller and Stiver's assertion: parenting by one sister for another may have occurred due to parental unavailability or family disruption. The unavailability was sometimes attributed to work responsibilities and ineffective parents. Some women directly mentioned immaturity or substance abuse by a parent. Another theme attributed this need directly to the mother's inability to fulfill her role or to her absence. In one case, the mother died when the children were still young. In another, she was working several jobs to support a single-parent family. But the women also mentioned fathers and their absence. Some sisters took the father's role in their family, going to work earlier than expected to supplement the family's income. Other girls took over strength-based tasks within the home and completed household repairs, tasks they associated with male-specific roles of the father. A father's absence because of work schedules, divorce, or death created this need. These parentified roles supported the notion of the relational cultural theorists that siblings may take over to help care for younger siblings in a family, producing a positive result for both the older and the younger girl.

Some research themes about parentification expanded the information previously available from RCT. The women in my project acknowledged that older sisters seemed to take over as physical protectors and helped with general parental tasks, but emotional caretaking did not seem to be related to birth order. The emotional or relational needs of the sisters were managed by the sister most capable of managing them. The ability to differentiate relational skills among young sisters suggested an expansion of RCT knowledge. Relational development of girls occurred through the mutual engagement with one sister who was more emotionally proficient. Her skills were recognized and appreciated by even older sisters, who themselves might have managed the family's practical needs or fulfilled a parental function. These experiences suggested a developmental path that defined identity based upon relational capacity and differential relational development. In addition, the women seemed to recognize a lifespan developmental theme: parentification gave way to a more satisfying and mutual relationship as the girls matured.

The consequences of parentification within RCT were described as both positive and negative. Some children were quite capable of taking on parental roles and had developed more mutually satisfying relationships with their mother or father as a result. Other children were required to take on roles beyond their abilities; in these cases a child may have had difficulty creating mutually satisfying relationships as an adult. These potentially negative outcomes did not seem to be addressed directly by the women in the research. Some did mention difficulty seeing a younger sister grow up and acknowledged that they had trouble giving up their own tendency to be a caretaker. This experience was not directly related to parentification, but to a more natural tendency to look out for a younger sister.

Miller and Stiver also acknowledged the important ways in which parentification leads to relational resilience. They suggested that this was especially likely when there was "evidence of a close relationship with at least one person and fewer prolonged separations" of the sister from the mother or father who served as a primary parent (p. 103). Such resilience may develop through the mutual exchange of parental role functions by two sisters of similar age. Although not mentioned explicitly by the relational cultural theorists, it is possible that capacity for authenticity develops between sisters who share parental responsibilities. Sisters who were "in it together," sharing practical and emotional support, may have created the foundation for mutually satisfying friendships in adult life. They may also have provided the relational foundation for lesbian and heterosexual primary relationships. Relational resilience and authenticity that developed in the context of parentification by one or more sister could, therefore, lead to mutually satisfying relationships of many kinds.

While not developed in such detail, other roles were mentioned by Miller and Stiver. They suggested that children in a family used roles such as extrovert, clown, and troublemaker to stay out of connection. The women in my research also described such family roles. There was even a theme suggesting that these other types of roles did not change, perhaps because of their link to identity. The women described diverse roles, including airhead, leader, drunk, playmate, aunt, travel guide, moderator, trophy (fought over by family members), depressed perfectionist, artist, intellect, hub of communications, and adolescent rebel. These roles were created by the expectations of the family members and other persons connected to the girls as they grew up. Sometimes teachers helped to create the expectations; at other times they were established by grandparents who identified the children with different sides of the family. Women in the study also felt their relationships with their sisters were changed by these established roles and expressed regret that they let the roles limit their perceptions of their sisters.

The integration of the RCT literature and the research suggests that two types of roles are created in the family. One kind, created to meet an overarching need for relational or practical support, was less persistent; the other, based perhaps more on personality and identity rather than need, was more persistent. An adolescent rebel may have remained a rebel; a mother substitute may have emerged as a friend. Other components of the integration between the literature and the research findings were also critical, including a look at how the theory and the findings have suggested pathways for the development of other relational cultural skills.

The Development of Empathy

Surrey (1991a, 1991b) and Jordan (1991a) discussed the development of empathy in different chapters of *Women's Growth in Connection*. Each mentioned a potential role for sibling or sister relationships in this development. Likewise, Miller and Stiver (1997) suggested that "in many situations family members—siblings, aunts, uncles—can offer a child some sense of another kind of relationship, one characterized by respect, empathy and encouragement." This notion was clearly reflected in my research themes. The women's collective experience suggested that aunts, cousins, and grandparents were important in their influence on the development of relationships. Their expressions of support for the relationship or their attempts to form divisions within it were significant. The women also described how cousins, in particular, were used as a foil for the relationship—providing a much-needed outlet or creating competitive jealousy within the sister relationship. Sister relationships themselves were important in the development of mutual empathy, a skill that was magnified as the girls matured into women and their life experiences created a sense of common bonding. A sister's plight within the family could also be recognized by her sister-ally, often the only one who really understood and cared deeply about her emotional responses. Such empathy formed the foundation for the development of other relational skills in sisters.

Adult Changes in Relational Capacity

Surrey (1991b) suggested that adult relational capacity created in the context of any relationship can lead to a deepening of that ability in connection with family members, including sisters. According to her, women's growth transcends difficult emotional interactions of the past. The growth learned in one relationship has the potential to enhance other relationships. Sibling relationships embedded in childhood difficulties may make such transfer of skills—from one relationship to another—more difficult. For example, for a woman to view herself as being able to create a deep adult friendship and to move that experience beyond the friend relationship to enhance a primary or work relationship, she may need to overcome a sister's view that she was superficial or self-serving. In my project, the women echoed this theme. While some women documented a growing depth in their sister relationship over time, others noticed the absence of this growth and hoped for it. Their recognition of relationship authenticity suggested the women could understand its presence or absence with the sister. If this authenticity existed between two growing sisters, they were aware of its absence in other sister relationships and felt grateful they shared it. In its absence, they felt envious of others who had such authenticity with their sisters.

Relationship connection, mutuality, and mutual empathy all seemed to be enhanced by similar experiences between sisters. As adults, sisters exposed each other and their families to new opportunities and adventures. As they grew older, the women often pictured their elderly years with their sisters, sharing humor, candor, and support. Many felt the sister relationship would remain when both had outlived other relatives and primary partners. This desire to spend their later years together was reflected in their motivation to create greater growth in connection with their sisters throughout life. The humor, openness, emotional support, and shared life experiences suggested that throughout life the sister relationship grounded the capacity for relationship. This capacity seemed to reflect the mutual empathy, mutual empowerment, mutual respect, mutual growth, and zest of RCT (Miller & Stiver, 1997). The enhancement of such positive relationship capacities may be juxtaposed with the RCT outcome of relational failures and losses that go beyond normal relational resilience.

Depression versus Sadness

Stiver wrote an RCT chapter about the importance of allowing women to grieve and experience sadness so that they do not develop depression. In that work, she mentioned research on the mothers of stillborn children and expressed dismay that not even their adult sisters would allow them to mourn. In contrast, this theme was not reflected in my project. The women mentioned their sisters' childbearing in many respects, but two explicit themes seemed remarkable for the way they contradicted Stiver's suggestions. They wanted to be present to support the sister, pragmatically and emotionally, during times of transition in the family, especially during the birth of children or the loss of a husband or partner. Women also acknowledged the personal significance of a sister's birth process when they said that a sister's experiences giving birth were deeply moving and influenced their own choices about having children. The close identification with the sister's birth experiences suggests that it would be extremely difficult to suppress feelings of empathy connected with a stillbirth. Such reactions would have been defensive or avoidant when they did occur.

Stiver also acknowledged the healing role of the mother–daughter connection and the potential for a sister to play an important role in that healing.

She discussed the case of the alcoholic who reconciled with two daughters. The sisters' bond helped them endure the mother's inability to cope or fill her own maternal roles. The mother's sober acknowledgement of her own failure to be their parent allowed even deeper connection between all three women. This healing role of the mother–daughter–sister triad was clearly reflected in my research interviews. A sister could be an ally or a judge in the difficult relationship with a mother. Such interaction and authenticity in the sister relationship could compensate for shortcomings in the mother's role performance.

In another vignette from the same paper, Stiver suggested that depression could be caused by the loss of the sister connection. She described a man who severed the emotional life-giving bond between his wife and his sister-in-law; this pushed the sad and downtrodden wife into acute depression. The loss of the sister became the trigger for moving from sadness into depression. In a similar way, the women in my project acknowledged the importance of partner compatibility. When compatibility was absent, the women experienced the emotional loss of depth in the sister connection. Sister relationships may have the potential to heal; conversely, the lack of those connections may have the potential for harm. That healing connection might be expected to take different forms in different cultural contexts.

Specific Cultural Contexts for the Sister Connection

Unlike many other theories, RCT explicitly acknowledges diversity issues that may affect the theory's implementation. Two authors, writing about Black women's experience and lesbian women's relationships with their mothers, acknowledged the importance of the sister connection. Relational cultural theorists stated explicitly that Black women should write about the experiences of Black women and lesbian women should write about their own community. In that tradition, several authors have provided a unique cultural perspective about sisters. Clevonne Turner did so, as did Wendy Rosen. In my research project I made no attempt to stratify the sample of participants. Phenomenological methods did not require those sampling techniques. Instead, those methods suggested that the phenomenon of having a sister has an essential core, and the descriptive detail arising from the experience of all women interviewed added to that essence. The implementation of phenomenological saturation suggested that research should be discontinued when no new themes arose in the dialogue with participants. Phenomenology and RCT share the important core understanding that meaning is created in the space shared by people; both embrace the importance of a person's subjective experience as a valid indicator of reality.

Perhaps some themes were overlooked in the saturation process, themes that might have been linked to Turner's and Rosen's suggestions about sisters. Many of those themes were reflected in Chapters 8 and 9. Perhaps the research would have been much richer had I made an attempt to stratify—even though that research strategy belongs in natural science, not as part of the phenomenological approach. Even so, there were a few references by the women in the study to these cultural factors, and they have been illuminated here.

Even though some women of color participated in the research, Turner's seesaw phenomenon and its relationship to sibling rivalry were not mentioned. Sisters did, of course, discuss sibling rivalry and the various levels of support for their achievement by teachers, parents, and extended family members. They did not discuss the larger cultural context of favoritism or ground the seesaw in racism, as Turner did; favored status for Black women has often produced both superiority and guilt. Guilt was present in some of the themes of the research and it was often connected to receiving greater rewards or favored status in the family. The women in the research suggested that the larger community sometimes favored one sister over another; often this favoritism was based upon attractiveness. Yet there is a completely different element of the experience present in Turner's writing—the experience of being on the outside and needing to fit into a culture that is not one's own.

Turner also wrote about relational differentiation in Black families and related the development of this ability to primary relationships with mothers, fathers, and siblings. Sisters were an important part of this formula. Turner recognized what many of the primary relational cultural theorists fail to recognize: she understood that sisters form an integral part of the developing female relational identity. This theme was also reflected in my interviews as the women described the importance of their sister's role in their identity development and relationship skills. There was no specific connection to Black cultural experience.

Turner's ideas about relational cultural identity among Black women also espoused two other ideas; these ideas were reflected in the research findings but were not tied to a specific cultural context. One theme presented in both Turner's writing and the research project was the connection to family as a source of love, strength, and coping. The women of the study clearly described feelings of love and the development of coping skills within the family relationships. They also discussed growth that came from adversity and conflict. The other theme mentioned by both Turner and the women of the study was the notion of early caretaking responsibilities for sisters. In most Black families both parents must work because of low wages based upon discrimination in hiring and pay. In many other Black families, the cultural assault on Black men has created single-parent, women-headed households. The children and extended family members helped to create a safety net for the family's needs. This seemed to create resilience among young Black women rather than reflecting the negative consequences of parentification described by Miller.

Likewise, some of the women in the research project felt the relationship gave them some strengths and maturity that was genuine rather than false. The women I interviewed described the transition to different types of relationships between sisters in adulthood, but this seemed to be less present in Turner's writings. The essential themes about sisters from Turner's descriptions of Black women's identity development were reflected in the essential themes of my research. However, those themes from the research do not often reflect the ethnic or cultural dimension that is explicit in Turner's thought.

Rosen's thoughts about sisters emerged in the context of a paper on lesbian sexuality and the mother–daughter relationship. Describing a client's attempt to come out to her family, Rosen differentiated the reactions of a mother and a sister. Her description provided a unique picture for sister relationships within a hetero-sexual–lesbian dialogue. In Rosen's case vignette, the client came out to her sister first and the sister reacted with acceptance. But when she came out to her mother, she did not accept it and rejected the daughter. Despite their differences, both the mother and the sister had difficulty talking honestly with their lesbian family member about her life and sexuality. In an echo of Rosen's clinical vignette, the lesbian women in the research project said they felt closest to their mothers and sisters, but the closeness was limited by dissimilarity. They expressed a sense that the mother and heterosexual sister's connection was stronger than their own con-nection with either one. Closeness, or the lack of it, was attributed to diverse sources, but one reason for feeling distant was a dissimilarity of life path. The tolerance for difference was also mentioned as a factor. In a clear reflection of Rosen's thought, the women of the study felt that their closeness to family mem-bers was directly related to that person's ability to tolerate the cultural difference between them. One woman did discuss the resilience in the sister relationship, again reflecting Rosen's theme. She said explicitly that the sister relationship was not conditional and was capable of persisting across the differences in sexual ori-entation. Thus, the women of the study closely reflected the cultural experiences described by Rosen in her analysis of the mother–daughter–sister relationship with one lesbian daughter.

As I compared my research themes to existing statements about sisters in RCT, sometimes an angle would catch the bright light of an idea; it would be refracted to add color and enhance the depth of the image. Richer illumination and deeper hues emerged when the themes were allowed to spontaneously reflect, refract, and recreate the relational cultural themes about sisters. The resulting patterns of light and color suggest the promise of deeper hues—shifting bits of color forming new ideas in the understanding of the sister connection.

RCT Themes Applied to Sister Relationships

The authors of RCT made few explicit references to the sister relationship, but many of their concepts can be expanded to encompass the sister–sister interac-tion. Three points of intersection between RCT and my research occurred to me. First I evaluated the major RCT concepts, such as Miller's five good things, relationship differentiation, relationship authenticity, and the developmental goals as they might relate to sister relationships. Then I evaluated several clinical applications, such as the extended understanding of depression in the sister relationship. The examination of potential sister countertransference and transference themes from this represented a third possibility for application, with special consideration for Stiver's evaluation of those topics from an RCT perspective.

Major RCT Concepts Applied to Sister Relationships

In their groundbreaking book *Women's Growth in Connection* (Jordan et al., 1991), the authors discussed the importance of moving from an objectified relationship with the mother—one that saw her as a provider for the child's needs—to an active interchange with the mother. They described a relationship that was mutual from the beginning of its existence. Empathic engagement with the mother allowed for an "encompassing" and "oscillating" sense of self rather than a "bounded" and limited one (Miller, 1991, p. 15). The girl's sense of her own esteem was believed to increase as her ability to be present with another person increased. Both were empowered in the process. The child moved to a more active and "articulated sense of herself" through connection with another (p. 17).

Now, imagine an older sister in this context. The birth of her sister, 5 years younger, provides her with a mirror on the self. She cares for the new infant, not without mixed feelings, but with a clear sense that her empathy is encouraged. According to RCT, the new baby is encouraged to expand her own natural empathy. This encouragement of the empathy in the younger sister, coupled with the natural empathy of the older child, foreshadows mutual engagement. They become acutely aware of each others' feelings. Each grows, rewarded by the parents' gratitude and engagement. A triangular or quadratic relationship develops with the mother in which mutuality is the primary defining characteristic. Later, each sister is encouraged by the reflection of felt emotion in the eyes of the other. Gradually, conflict and rivalry create an interface for the development of relational differentiation. Each comes to believe the potential in the relationship, expressed by statements like "I can be many things in my sister's eyes," "She can be different or the same each time we meet," "My sister changes who she is in our relationship—yet there is a stability that defines who we are in relationship with one another," "Through our relationship we understand and learn to create a complicated explanation of relationship that is not just about rewards and punishments, but about the creation of meaning between sisters," And "This development of relationship and knowledge about the other continues throughout our years of being in relationship with one another." Such awareness and insight are present through many stages of development. Some of these stages have been investigated fully in psychology but others remain unexplored.

The original relational cultural theorists acknowledged a deficit in much of the literature about the development that occurs during latency. They suggested that many interactions between girls have been ignored during this important school-age time. Miller (1991) suggested that a "vast amount of psychological development that occurs within the relationship between girls at this time" is overlooked in psychological theory (p. 19). Consider what sisters are doing during this age. They have begun to take over some of the relational functions of the family. They have learned to communicate about the ways in which family members get along or do not. They have begun to see complexity in their relationships to other siblings, differentiating their own gendered interest from that of boys and other girls. They have become animated on the playground and engaged in discussion; they talk about the ability of one girl to get along with another. Sisters carry these skills from home to school grounds, to athletic fields, to musical stages and back home. Relationship differentiation—an understanding of how the complexity of relating requires adaptation in different contexts—occurs on these fronts. The school-aged girl evaluates her ability to relate with and feel empowered by her sisters, her brothers, and her female friends. This comparative relational development is then brought back into the relationship with the sister, potentially creating stores of memories for future relationship authenticity.

The women in the research project made many references linked to Jordan's definitions of relational differentiation. Surrey defined it as "a process which encompasses increasing levels of complexity, choice, fluidity, and articulation within the context of human development" (1991b, p. 60). Four themes from the sister project seemed especially important in this context. The women described a shifting of feelings toward their sisters from birth through adulthood. These changes were created by feelings of anticipation, jealousy of parental attention, conflicted interaction with brothers, and honest communication with each sister, as an adult, about all of this. It was their honesty that suggested a growing relational differentiation—an oscillation not just between two people in a relationship, but across growing contexts for the relationship with others. That differentiation helped to define the role each sister played in her relationship with each other, but also in her relationship with others in the world. There was so much variety from the research; women described many talks, arguments, and resolutions created by mutuality. Relational skills were developed; the young woman became capable of better engagement with the sister and with others. These relational skills included the tendency of the sister to moderate the effects of others, the attempts of others to intrude in the relationship, and the comparison of sisters' primary relationships. These relational skills moved beyond the sister connection to enhance a multitude of relationships. How authentic did they become?

Is a young girl capable of authenticity with her sister? Authentic relationships are those that meet "the challenge to feel emotionally 'real', connected, vital and clear, and purposeful in relationship" (Surrey, 1991b, p. 60). There is room for anger and other "difficult emotions" (p. 61). Certainly, the women in my research recognized when they had superficial relationships with their sisters. They longed for something deeper, when that was true. They acknowledged conflict and—in a voice for authenticity—suggested that the outcome of such conflict might be a greater understanding of each other. The women also noted their mature understanding of the sister connection. Time had changed it; time made a younger sister/older sister disparity more equal. Some women recognized that the protective role they played with their sisters was a problem, an impediment to growing mutuality; they fought internal instincts to take over when a sister was in trouble, hoping the relationship would grow as a result. So the answer to the question about authenticity is mixed. Some sisters have authentic connections, and it seemed likely that sisters develop the capacity for this continuously throughout life. Perhaps the competition among sisters has too often been the focus in the family, without much emphasis on the positive. Since RCT examines the relationship between mother and daughter in a positive light, an optimistic view of sister relationships might emerge from that theory as well.

The sister relationship may be a testing ground for the development of the five good things detailed in Miller's writings: mutual empathy, mutual empowerment, mutual engagement, mutual growth, and zest. The research suggested some evidence that each of these characteristics of positive connection may appear in the sister relationship—a secondary, or sometimes even primary, training ground for the skills of relational being.

Surrey (1991b) described "increasing capacity for *mutual empathy* [emphasis added], developed in a matrix of emotional connectedness" (p. 56), as a result of presence to the mother's emotional needs. The women in my project described this mutuality within the sister relationship. They were aware when it was present and felt grateful for it; they were aware when it was absent and envied others who had it. They also suggested a developmental arc for such empathy, mentioning the capacity for time to heal and transform the dimensions of the relationship. Sometimes conflict was forgotten; sometimes it was directly addressed and worked through. These changes over time enhanced the capacity for emotional connection and intellectual understanding of the sister's experience.

Mutual empowerment also appeared in the statements of the women and the themes arising from the research. Mutual empowerment seemed to reflect the ability to act based upon a buildup of relational self-confidence. The commitment to take care of the relationship between two people has the potential to lead to more confidence in overall skills and abilities. This has been transferred to other relationships, including that between sisters. The women in the study suggested that the sister relationship was constant throughout life stages, but the relationship was emotionally affected by these changes, sometimes in unexpected ways. There was a sense that each sister should have what she desires most to make her happy, and a wish that the sister's actions would be consistent with movement in that direction. This acknowledgment of empowerment difficulty suggested that the women recognized their own frailties, inabilities as well as abilities, in creating their world as they wish to see it.

Mutual engagement between sisters seemed to be inseparable from the research project. While some women mentioned estrangement in sister relationships, most described an ongoing and lasting connection with frequent engagement. Initiation of contact between geographically separated sisters was also described in significant detail. Many methods were used to maintain contact, but engagement was usually described in the heat of life's crises, difficult discussions, or family conflicts. These descriptions held the exquisite details of the ways sisters engaged with each other. Sometimes the engagement happened in an almost psychic way, as the women described knowing what a sister needed or that she was in the midst of a crisis without direct communication. Other types of engagement occurred in the midst of family celebrations, which were often described as superficial. There was also an engagement with the memories shared throughout a lifetime of family relationships, activities, growth, and loss. The women came to know themselves through the relationship, even talking about the effects of the research itself. The engagement with memories, ideas, and images about the sister brought about new understanding and growth.

Mutual growth was almost required in the context of growing up together. Some women commented upon the lack of connection when there was too much of an age gap between sisters, stating that they did not grow up together or even in the same family. Still, the growth of any siblings in a family has usually occurred naturally. The level of emotional understanding was an important part of that growth. The women in my research project talked a great deal about the changes in the relationship over time; indeed, it was a central cluster in the research structure. The growth in each woman was often defined in the way her sister understood and supported her—or did not. Some women forsook the sister relationship when it did not provide the emotional depth they expected, and they could not stimulate it to greater understanding. Others talked about specific ways in which the experience of the relationship's closeness enhanced them as a person. One woman described in detail the growth each sister experienced when one told the other about her experience of physical abuse by their mother. The acceptance of this subjective experience and the empathy expressed between sisters created a deeper bond between them. Invariably such depth provided the possibility of greater depth in other relationships. Growth between sisters seemed to happen at a natural developmental level, but also rooted them more deeply in connection with themselves and with others.

Zest—how to define such an exuberant term for a relationship? In an attempt to clarify this RCT concept, Christina Robb defined it initially by saying what it was not:

> This is not euphoria, not head-over-heels, not cloud nine, not an "up" with a taste of mania in it. It is a spacious, clear, and clarifying sense of more life, simply turning up the volume . . . [It] can go along with feelings of great sadness or fear, or with joy, courage, anger, or resolution; it

accompanies whatever people feel whenever they can confide in someone they trust, someone who is really listening, and they know for certain, from the response, that their listener "gets it." (2006, pp. 154–155)

It is the experience of being understood at a level that is enlivening. Sisters shared this at a very basic level. The women of my study described knowing their sisters, being able to predict what they might say, and listening to the same story over and over, just because they possessed the ability to understand its importance. These experiences build a trust of energy in the relationship when they are mutual; when they are not, they become a drain on the energy of one sister. Zest appeared among women in the research in many ways. Sisters who laughed until they cried as they told stories about a childhood drama that became funny with time; sisters who experienced a sense of energy after a long phone call across thousands of miles; sisters who danced to a recognized song or burst into song at the sound of a musical score that was a part of their family story; and sisters who look at pictures of one's wedding in which the other played a profound role—all of these experiences enacted this mutual zest. What seemed crucially different for sisters—what defined that relationship as unique—was the way in which there was herstorical recognition and deeply lived knowledge of the other. The zest could emerge from a long-term friendship between women, from heterosexual marriages, and between sisters and brothers, but the connection of deeply lived life experience that was mutual at a physical and herstorical level seemed to have some unique elements. Sister relationships outlast almost any other connection that people have. The depth of time, herstory shared, and the processing of mutuality at so many different levels seems to create a potential for shared mutual space that is not possible in most other connections. Zest is one piece of the evidence for that unique connection.

In the essay by Jordan entitled *The Meaning of Mutuality* (1991c), the author described another outgrowth of women's development—the potential for mutual intersubjectivity. She defined this as the ability to understand the other, while being clear that the frame of reference the other has used is different. When each person in a relationship is able to shift frames in this way, then the mutuality of that intersubjective experience occurs. Embedded in this is knowledge of the other's perspective and respect for it. In my research, this was sometimes experientially based. One woman's advent of motherhood led her to better understand her mother. In the context of sister relationships, such intersubjectivity would have been possible regardless of the similarity of experience. Could a heterosexual sister understand a lesbian sister's loss of heterosexual privilege? Could a lesbian woman understand her sister's difficulty living in a relationship with a man when the culture is inherently sexist? How does the knowledge of that experiential difference create a greater sense of depth in the relationship? Or does the relationship devolve into more superficial conversations? These are the questions raised by intersubjectivity in RCT. The experience of one's difference somehow enhances the potential for mutual empathy and respect if one sister can shift her own lens and become conscious of the one held by her sister. The women of the study talked briefly about some of these intersubjective experiences, particularly when one was favored by a parent or had fewer talents and accomplishments then the other. One woman said the whole family came to appreciate the differences of each by engaging the perspective of one sister, who was more creative, for important solutions to visual and spatial problems. The same family requested the lens of the scientist sister to understand complex medical problems and decipher technical information.

Another touchstone for understanding sister relationship was Jordan's notion of clarity in connection. She defined this clarity as the "capacity to integrate individual and relational goals and to deal with conflict within relationship" (Jordan as quoted in Miller[2], et al., 1997) p. 30). Two themes from the sisters' project were applicable to this concept of clarity in connection. The women suggested that when there was continuing conflict, maturity allowed a woman to free herself from dishonesty and collusion aimed at seeking the peace. In other words, she did not avoid conflict in a relationship, but with maturity she gave it a voice. Such clarity was also present when several women in my research described wanting to heal a breach between two other sisters. Recognizing that a sister could not heal the conflict alone was another sign of clarity in connection. Jordan expanded the concept with this statement that clarity in connection "involves respectfully building a relationship together that both sustains and transcends the individuals engaged in it" (Jordan as quoted in Miller, et al., 1997) p. 32). Themes from the women in the study suggest that they recognized this element of clarity: they expressed gratitude for the length and depth of the connection.

They also recognized the ability of sisters to debrief after a family crisis, getting to the heart of the matter, instead of the flared tempers or irritable frustration expressed by some family members. Together they were able to see the core of the experience for the family, and what such frustration represented—unresolved issues that flared beneath the surface. Recently, I experienced such frustration at the end of a long and difficult week of family interaction when my brother-in-law's emergency hospitalization complicated his daughter's wedding week. Helping my sister through this difficult and challenging time left me exhausted. At a post-wedding gathering with my other sister, I fell and was injured. Frustration and exhaustion spilled over into anger. Both my sister and her daughter, my niece, came to my support and assistance and each asked, "Are you sure this is not about anything else?" Their clarity helped me to think through the other issues that had

---

[2] A review article by Miller, Jordan, Kaplan, Stiver and Surrey contains components penned individually by each author to address some misconceptions about RCT. Quotes from that article are referenced in this manner to give appropriate credit to the individual theorist who wrote each segment.

been stimulated for me that week; growth resulted for the relationship and my own understanding of myself.

In the context of such clarity, communication becomes "interaction and dialogue rather than debate" (p. 62). For the women in the study such communication was represented by a sense of presence in the relationship. It was strengthened by shared traumatic experiences such as being there for the terminal illness of a parent or living through the difficult delivery of a niece. Such presence was anticipated to be available during future times of crisis. Some believed that their sister would have a presence with them even after death. So the developmental outcome of all of these experiences—mutuality, authenticity, empowerment, zest, engagement, clarity, and relational differentiation—was the creation of "relationship and identity [that] develop in synchrony" (p. 65). This was apparent in the enduring quality of the support that women in the study felt emanating from their sisters, whether functional or emotional: a strong sense that the sister would be there when others were not. This outcome also represented an idealistic relational goal for the therapeutic relationship between women who have sisters and their therapists.

Some Specific Clinical Applications of RCT to Sisters

Among the original authors of RCT, Surrey, Miller and Stiver wrote most prolifically about clinical issues. Each author addressed the sister issue or alluded to it on several occasions. Stiver wrote extensively about transference, countertransference, and impasse in psychotherapeutic relationships. Miller talked about the deficiency model of women's psychology in her early works. She suggested that this deficiency led to a conceptualization of women's development in a pathological frame. Because of this, the women authors in the RCT model were initially reluctant to focus on the pathology of women. References to the sister role in such pathology have therefore been slim.

Surrey wrote about the importance of other relationships: "It is probable that, for women at all life stages, relational needs are primary and that healthy, dynamic relationships are the motivating force that propels psychological growth" (1991b, p. 37). The women in my study suggested that painful interactions with sisters might be the impetus for such growth. At times, these difficulties festered and were not easily resolved. Such interactions initiated deep grief for the individual woman and may have required therapeutic intervention. RCT would suggest that the ability to work through difficult interactions with the therapist—dealing directly with conflict in the therapeutic relationship—may help the woman to have a repertoire of skills for healing the sister connection. In addition, the development of such skills in the context of other family relationships or with friends may translate into changing dynamics within the family. A woman who is pained by her sister's response to her may see similar responses in a women's group and learn how she could understand her own contribution to the abyss between her and her sister. Increasing her relational authenticity in that context—where others are also learning authenticity—could enhance the potential for authentic engagement with the sister. Such relational cultural application could provide a way out of the sisters' disconnection, returning them to a more rewarding relationship with each other.

Triangular Relationships: Guilty and Ostracized Sisters

In the same work, Surrey encouraged therapists to explore the capacity for authentic engagement in "broader, more diversified new identifications" (1991b, p. 38). She followed this with a list of potential relationships that might benefit from such new identifications, but she did not include siblings or sisters except by extrapolation. She did mention triangular family relationships, which could include sisters. The women in my study gave many examples of such triangulation with sisters, mothers, fathers, brothers, cousins, and friends. Women felt some guilt if they benefited from such triangular relationships. They may have even diminished their own gifts to increase the self-worth of a sister—an attempt that usually failed. If a woman was too frequently the one ostracized by the triangular relationship, there were many consequences for relationship differentiation and authenticity. Women without sufficient mutuality in their early relationships with their sisters might come to experience other women as rivals or untrustworthy, losing the potential for mutual empathy. If the woman was a lesbian, she might become suspicious of her partner's motives. Some unrealistic fears, bordering on paranoia, could result in isolation from the world of women's mutual relationships.

For women who suffer guilt or fear in their relationships with other women, there are many implicit dangers. Women who feel guilty may attempt to over-compensate—doing too much for others and not receiving enough mutual support themselves. Therapeutic interventions with such a woman might include less self-disclosure on the part of the therapist. The important ways the woman has received authentic caring may be examined. Development of relational differentiation may proceed along the lines of receiving care, disclosing more to others, sharing her weaknesses, and helping to create boundaries for the guilt so that it does not drive her experiences.

If the triangulated sister was ostracized by two sisters, a mother and sister, or some other family combination, it is important to enhance mutuality in the therapeutic relationship. Providing more opportunities for mutual empathy with the therapist and with others, the therapist might examine important aspects of the client's fears and how these reflect painful childhood and adolescent experiences. She might also need to enhance mutual trust. A frank and early discussion about the client's likelihood of "bailing" on therapy when it gets difficult would be very important. Understanding the tendency to move away from connection when conflict arises and the potential for pain that is deep and searing may help the therapist to build more authentic interactions into the relationship.

The therapist may need to exercise caution when searching for examples of mutual or more authentic relationships with the sisters and/or mother, currently and in the past. It seems important to build this mutuality in the individual therapy context before placing it in the context of a women's group. Friendships with other women whose capacity for mutuality is high might need to be encouraged. Depending upon availability, sisters who have not engaged authentically with each other might be engaged in conjoint therapy. In this context, the therapist could examine their ability to build mutual respect and authentic communication with each other. All of these types of intervention would require the authentic involvement of the therapist as an emotional and knowledgeable human being, a role well described by Miller and Stiver (1997).

Depression

Stiver and Miller directly addressed the role of family members in the development of depression. The loss of connection and failure to engage during times of family grief or sadness may result in the development of acute or chronic depressive symptoms. Parents may ignore a child's sadness because they feel accused by it. They may want to avoid a sense of personal failure as a parent. In these cases, the authors did not suggest the role that sisters might have played in the development of sadness that turned to depression. However, the women in my study commented on this in several ways. They described how one sister helped to heal a broken family connection and allowed sadness to emerge. They explained how an unshared traumatic experience had led to greater separation from sisters and greater perception of differences. Shared traumatic experiences, however, led to greater understanding or distancing from sisters, depending on their perception of difference or sameness in reaction. Women who were able to see their sister's perspective about a traumatic event deepened their relationship with her. A woman who was sexually abused by her father was finally able to disclose this information to her sister, and doing so deepened their relationship; fear had kept them apart. The deepening of the relationship resulted because the sister who was not abused was able to be empathic to the sister who was. Likewise, the abused sister understood the other's guilt about being spared this trauma. Therapists may be able to promote this kind of mutual empathy in therapy. Asking a woman to (a) describe how her sister might see the losses both have experienced and (b) evaluate what the differences in perception say about them are ways to enhance mutual growth. Such therapeutic interventions are likely shift the client's perspective, allowing one sister to see the other through her sister's lens.

Therapeutic Interventions with Girls

Intervention with families of young or adolescent girls—when the trauma is fresh—can also create a different potential for authenticity. Helping family members to equally value the contributions of the more emotionally expressive sister; the practical, "take care of business" sister; and the sister leader, who takes charge during a crisis may provide a greater sense of relational differentiation among members of a family. During a crisis, some families value emotion, others value practical response, and some just look for leadership. The therapist might be able to help the sister who holds the less-valued role to teach others about her perspective. Her strengths may provide a different kind of engagement, leading to more authenticity. Recognizing the importance of that engagement to all family members might rescue a woman from depression and help others to develop new relational skills. These types of interventions have the potential to increase family clarity and enhance all sisters' ability to be relational.

Mental Illness and Sisters

The women in the study also mentioned the development of mental illness, including depression and suicidal threats in one woman's sister. Many were unaware of the development of these problems until years later. Once these experiences were brought into the relationship, sisters deepened their connection with one another and helped to transform the depression into sadness that both were able to share. The space between them became the ground for some healing of the emotional breach contained within one. The conjunctive use of sisters in the management of mentally ill clients might provide some movement toward emotional maturity on the part of mentally ill or depressed clients. When coupled with appropriate medical intervention, such support for engagement might enhance self-respect, self-esteem, and assertiveness for the client. In such contexts, the unspoken fears of mental illness might need to be addressed in the healthy sister. Some sisters may choose to remain unaware of the details because they fear developing the illness themselves. Authentic engagement with the therapist and clear understanding of the likelihood of onset in a healthy sister may provide an antidote to such fears. When these fears are addressed, the sister may be a great assistant in the therapeutic management of a mentally ill or chronically depressed sister.

Sister Transference, Countertransference, and Impasse in RCT

The explicit applications by the relational cultural theorists leave room for much more theoretical development. These few examples have provided a beginning way to think about the sister relationship in RCT therapy. Given the psychoanalytic training of the RCT founders, it is not surprising that many of their reflections on sisters were related to the therapeutic management of transference, countertransference, and impasse—those places where the work of the therapy can be sidelined or enhanced by the therapist's awareness and skill.

Transference

Several women in the research project said they had used therapeutic work to help solve issues and concerns in the sister relationship. Their experiences with their sisters—in connection and disconnection—could be transferred to their experiences with the therapist. Stiver (as quoted in Miller, et al., 1997) suggested that the therapeutic stance of RCT therapists provides "fertile ground" for transference in therapeutic relationships based upon empathy and mutuality (p. 38). When the therapist brings more of herself to the relationship with clients—is more emotionally present—she provides the client with greater potential to relate to her as another human being. In a critical analysis of other therapeutic stances, Stiver suggested that this approach is no more likely to create transference than an emotionally distant and objective stance might. In theories such as psychoanalytic or object relations approaches, the prescribed emotional distance of the therapist recreates the client's previous disconnection from others. This disconnection further injures the ability for authentic connection. In general, the relational cultural theorists have suggested that transference is so powerful that it will occur based upon the client's previous relationships, regardless of the experience with the therapist. They cite the unconscious projection that can happen in intimate relationships, as an example. Transference happens; understanding the inherent projections differentiates therapy from much of ordinary life.

RCT offers these approaches for therapists' work with transference (Stiver, 1997). Taking a noncritical and nonjudgmental attitude toward the person who is being transferred to the therapist is essential. In the case of sister transference, the therapist might avoid blaming the sister who disengages, instead helping the client to develop a cognitive and emotional understanding of the sister's own experience—developing mutual empathy and encouraging re-engagement. Therapists who want to help heal these disconnections may need to understand the client's behavior as a way to connect. The client who calls the therapist repeatedly for minor concerns may be trying to create the day-to-day support she felt she did not get from a sister. She may also be repeating a behavior that created distance from the sister, who had her own agenda or preferred the company of friends. In such cases, being a pest engaged the sister during adolescence, even though the engagement was conflicted. Those same behaviors may be a way to try to engage the therapist. Such approaches often have the effect of putting the therapist off. Providing alternative ways to engage outside of the weekly therapeutic hour might be helpful (e.g., scheduled brief phone contacts), especially if the client can initiate them.

Stiver made some more specific suggestions about transference management that may be helpful in working with sister transference. She admonished therapists to consider that interpretations of the transference are often experienced by clients as emotionally distant; instead, the therapist might correct her own inner experience and outer behavior to reflect a different emotional position than the transference source. This means being different in the room instead of providing an intellectual understanding of the transference. Emotional responsiveness to a client's tears does not mean sitting back and providing an analysis while giving the client room to express her sadness. The authenticity of responsiveness requires that the therapist be aware of the client's feelings and may be moved to tears herself. That authentic response may do more than any insight to provide the client with a "corrective emotional experience." According to Stiver, the therapist's reactions need not be contrived but "the therapist needs to become more aware of who she is and how she sincerely does want to relate to the client more constructively than the client experienced in the past" (as quoted in Miller, et al, 1997, p. 40).

Surrey (1991a) discussed the importance of self-disclosure and its effect on transference in this context. She suggested that the timing of self-disclosure by the therapist is important. It may need to rely on the establishment of mutuality between the two. The failure to self-disclose, when appropriate, can lead to emotional distance by the therapist as she manages her own emotional reactions. In considering how this might be related to sisters, it may be important to evaluate how each sister engages. For example, a distancing response by the therapist may replicate an intellectualizing sister's lack of response. The client may feel devalued by the therapist's inability to be authentic. Authentic responses provide the way for the client to differentiate new relational connections from those connections where authenticity remains minimal or impossible—thus increasing her relational repertoire. There may be danger if a client feels burdened by the therapist's disclosure. This, too, may be a sister reaction. The need to be a caretaker in the therapeutic relationship may be a role replicated from childhood sister conversations. Being a caretaker creates the possibility that all relationships become disengaged. Feeling burdened by the needs of others, a woman may not express her authentic individual needs. Helping a client evaluate the establishment of this caretaker role in the early sister connection may help her to be more mutual and engaged with others. As the therapist, most likely a caretaker in her own family, shares her own experiences and provides an appropriate emotional response to the needs of the client, she creates the potential for emotional growth and connection with other women, as well as the sister. Surrey as quoted in Miller, et al., (1997) summarized such potential:

> Clients frequently recall the therapist's risking vulnerability and openness as deepening their sense of themselves as trustable and reliable relational beings and as enhancing their sense of the power and meaning of the therapy relationship. (p. 45)

The women in my project did not explicitly mention transference, but they did talk about a number of insights and emotional expressions that may be helpful to the therapist in understanding sister transference. Some women acknowledged their reluctance to be completely honest with their sisters. They feared that such honesty might create emotional distance and disconnection from a sister. Often they experienced an emotional disconnection throughout the family; their own healing could help to heal the sister connection but often meant they had to reach out to less mature sisters. Alignment in the family was acknowledged, and often the sisters were on opposite sides of those alignments. Helping women to see each others' perspective might then have consequences for the entire family structure.

Sometimes childhood bullying by a sister and her friends was transferred to other relationships, and fear of female friendships was the result. This too might transfer to the therapeutic relationship accompanied by fear of expressing honest emotions. The client might expect ridicule from the therapist for such feelings. Likewise, some sisters developed relational differentiation to maximize their differences with a sister. A woman who is more intuitive and spontaneous in relationships may create that posture to differentiate herself from her sister's more careful and measured stance. This stance may become projected onto the therapist, who is expected to play the sister's part. Growth might come from the therapeutic interpretation of that projection. Such growth was acknowledged by the women in my study as they described greater clarity arising from their part in the sister connection. For some of them, more honesty led to deeper and more trusting relationships.

Countertransference

Surrey (1991a; 1991b) and Stiver (1997) most explicitly addressed counter-transference issues and provide a potential link to the sister relationship. Surrey suggested that the therapist needs a strong community that supports her in her attempt to understand and use countertransference in therapy. Consultation, supervision, and the therapists' own therapy may help to ferret out the important countertransference reactions that might be shared and those that should be managed outside of therapy. The therapist's reactions might be important ones to share if they could help deepen the relationship and increase relational resilience in the client. For example, a therapist who finds that she is often angry with a particular client may be acting out of her own experience and herstory. However, if this reaction is also part of her response to behavior or interactions by the client (persistent lateness to sessions or attempts to engage the therapist past the end of the session), such reactions may help the client understand others' annoyance with her. This is not much different than what occurs in traditional dynamic therapy; the difference lies in the therapist's ability to share normal human reactions to a client's style of relating, resulting in an attempt to understand and adjust her own behavior in light of the client's response. The processing of the therapist's role in all of this does not stop when she shares her emotional response with the client. It becomes an interactive dialogue in which each may share some of the blame and benefit from the growth.

An example might be helpful in applying these countertransference experiences to the sister relationship. Let's assume that the therapist, Jaynthe, has four sisters, each of whom played a different role in her family of origin. Jaynthe's role (as is often the case) was that of family caretaker, second mother, nurturer of the other children when they were in pain. Jaynthe encountered a client, Becky, who reminded her of her next younger sister, Victoria, the one with whom she had the most conflict and rivalry. Victoria played the role of family "wild child," acting out her frustration with the family and hurting many people in the process. Becky, the client, had a history of promiscuity and substance abuse that was very hurtful to members of her family. The therapist found herself wanting to punish Becky, who acted outside of her established commitments by having an affair. Becky, while wanting to understand the affair and her choices, had not experienced any negative consequences for the indiscretion. Jaynthe found herself becoming sharp with the client in session, re-enacting her role in her family, and engaging in a dialogue with Becky about the client's moral compass.

Afterward, Jaynthe asked some colleagues for consultation. Though she initially felt she had done the right thing, this feeling was quickly replaced by thoughts about her reaction and her own family issues. Encouraged to work directly with Becky about these reactions, Jaynthe was able to help Becky evaluate relationship differentiation that might arise from the affair. She helped Becky explore the lack of authenticity in her current marriage. When the therapist acknowledged her own countertransference to Becky, each was able to contribute to the discussion in a manner that highlighted their roles and helped to create a more authentic connection between them. The client was relieved, suggesting that she had many experiences of feeling judged by Jaynthe and felt hopeless to change, based upon similar judgment from her own family members. This example illustrates Stiver's point about the self-disclosing of countertransference by the therapist: "By sharing in carefully timed fashion her own reactions and their meanings, a newer level of connection will emerge" (p. 41).

Surrey (as quoted in Miller et al.,(1997) suggested that both the therapist and the client might become more "spontaneous and open in the relationship over-time" (p. 46) when authentic and honest countertransference processing occurred. Sometimes, this process illuminated and enlarged the relational resilience of the client in the process. That is the hope; but there are also indications that a relationship between client and therapist can be founded upon false premises. When this occurs, impasse can result.

Working Through Impasse with RCT

In her essay about transference and the unconscious (1997), Stiver suggested that the impasse in therapy was usually created by the erroneous assumptions about the relationship held by both the therapist and the client. Perhaps the client assumed a sisterly relationship as a basis for therapy and based her expectations on a positive but unilateral connection. The client acted in accordance with this assumption and that met the needs of the therapist, who wanted to distance herself from emotional connection. The client appeared to be competent and functional as long as these roles were assumed. Once the therapist attempted to explore her own emotional reactions to the client as a method for enhancing relational resilience, however, the client began to deteriorate in her functioning. According to Stiver, this could become the crucial junction, a junction at which the misunderstood roles could become a script for the client–therapist dialogue.

The therapist, scared that she had somehow triggered the client's regression, attempted to be more emotionally removed, and the client began to return to her usual level of functioning. The importance of the client's emotional development became lost and she remained stagnant in her previous role. She continued to be self-focused and out of connection, while superficially going through the motions of treatment. The yearning for connection led to self-destructive acting out, either within or outside of the therapy. Perhaps the client needs to be hospitalized to attempt to reconnect with the brief experience of the therapist's vulnerability— and rewrite her childhood hertory with her sister:

> Thus the downward course of therapy [can develop] out of an interactional dynamic in which both therapist and patient struggle . . . with the expression of yearnings for connection and the fear of such yearnings that led to various modes of distancing and disconnection. (p. 291)

Many women in my project described the longing for a close and connected sister relationship, which they did not experience. Such yearnings would be important to understand as a basis for a potential impasse in the therapeutic relationship.

Stiver acknowledged that impasse may be created by the external life experiences of the client and therapist. This is particularly likely when both are experiencing trauma and those traumas bring up contrasting needs. When a client needs to understand her anger at her sister's betrayal, the client may be at an impasse with a therapist whose beloved sister has just died. Each person in the therapy room is dealing with a different kind of emotion in response to grief (one for the loss of trust, the other for the final disconnection from a close relationship). They may find little common ground for empathy or growth. Sometimes, another therapist is better suited to manage such extreme differences of experience. In most cases of impasse, however, there are steps a therapist can take.

Stiver proposed several steps for ending therapeutic impasse, and they are given here with adaptation for the sister connection. First, the therapist must attend to her own feelings. This means examining the countertransference sources from the relationships with her sister or sisters. Perhaps she had no sisters and has countertransference based upon other female relationships. Maybe she has always longed for a sister and found the client's issues with her sister to be trivial.

In Stiver's second step, the therapist must listen carefully to what the client is saying and try to enact empathy for the client. The intersubjectivity of the therapist has never been more important than in this experience. She must be able to differentiate her own perspective from the lens of the client, understanding their differences and finding a way to cognitively and emotionally relate to her client's experience. The inability to do so requires her to seek consultation or supervision from her supportive collegial community. Stiver's third step in resolving the impasse is the therapist's awareness of the client's need to defend her vulnerabilities. How has the client's sister made her vulnerable? What does she defend? Has she been the strong caretaker for her sister and is now fearful of her own need for care? Has she been the isolated one who now seeks greater family connections? Was she the popular one who has lost her ability to attract male attention, finding a desire for deeper personal relationships out of her reach?

According to Stiver, the therapist has the responsibility to "bring the relationship back into connection from periods of disconnection" (1997, p. 297). In the context of a therapeutic impasse based upon sister relationships, the therapist must work in connection with the client to clarify the transference, admit the countertransference, and distinguish the sister relationship from the client–therapist relationship. It is the therapist's responsibility to take that awareness and increase the likelihood of relational resilience within the therapeutic hour. Ideally, that resilience will translate to a deepening of the connection between the client and her own sisters; it is likely to do so for the therapist and her sisters as well.

Conclusions

RCT might have greater potential to enhance women's lives if its practitioners better integrated an understanding of relationships between sisters and their role in women's development. The foundational relationships that sisters form can enhance mutuality in all other relationships. Failing to understand the importance of the sister connections may cause therapists to ignore strengths within the client. Resilience in relationships and relational differentiation have been foundational in the ability to have satisfying intimate relationships, and nowhere has this resilience or differentiation been strengthened more than in the lifelong connection between sisters. Here the connection runs both deep and wide. It flows from a common source, providing sheltering eddies and refreshing deep pools. With it come snags and boulders, diverting the flow, but also the eventual resurgence of life and the connection to the hidden and unexplored depths of the ocean. Like flowing water, the sister connection holds the promise for new growth, more life, shared resources, and knowledgeable conservation. Much more can be gained if RCT therapists devote themselves to exploring its potential.

13

Sisters in Families: Applications to Family Therapy

"There is no greater agony than bearing an untold story inside of you."

Maya Angelou (n.d.)

Of all therapeutic approaches, the family therapy literature has probably paid the most attention to the importance of siblings. The bonds between those of the same generation in a family are considered very important for the understanding of family construction, interaction, and behavior change. Yet the untold stories of sisters seem to be almost unbearable. The sister–sister connection has often been silenced in this literature, with sibling relationships being treated as genderless.

There have been many therapeutic approaches within the family therapy umbrella; Nichols and Swartz (2008) detail at least eight different schools of thought. Among those schools are approaches that seem most connected to my research. They also seem to offer a connection to sisters and their unique relationships. Family therapists practice theories that are systemic, strategic, feminist, constructivist, and narrative. Each theory has a set of guidelines for intervention. Given these possibilities, it was both necessary and appropriate to limit the number of family theories for this chapter. In the end, I decided to include narrative, feminist, and attachment-based approaches based upon three principles: their applicability to the role of women as sisters, their focus on the meaning of relationship, and their current importance to the field of family therapy. Following the same format as the previous therapy chapters, this chapter draws a little on history, then extracts themes from current thinking, and compares those themes to the findings of my research, ending with an integration of those into recommendations for family therapists.

All of these approaches have applied their concepts to women in general, and some have applied them to sisters in particular. Each has deconstructed previous theories to try to create a new understanding of family structure and roles. For the most part, they are ethnoculturally sensitive and thus more applicable to the families of people from diverse backgrounds and international experiences.

Each of these approaches attempts to shift the hermeneutic from relationship to meaning, creating a new evaluation of the quality of relationships rather than just their structure or function. They have been based upon a different metaphor, one related to the depth and mystery of poststructuralism, rather than the predetermined analysis of mechanical physics. In each there is a collaborative process of discovery between therapist and client. Often a team of therapists provide support and insight into the relationship between client and therapist. Kenneth Gergen (1985) suggested that meaning is constructed in a social context. His deconstruction of family therapy created a bridge that was used by others to found narrative and feminist approaches. As Nichols and Swartz (2008) suggested, "The question for the narrative therapist is not one of truth, but one of determining which points of view are useful and lead to preferred outcomes" (p. 286).

Narrative Approaches

Narrative approaches have shifted the dialogue in family therapy from a behavioral perspective to a relational one. It is not about what people do, but about the stories that they tell themselves. The emphasis is on strength. Narrative approaches have assumed that people are capable and may solve their own problems. People do this through a narrative story told about their lives. These stories are often empowering (Nichols & Swartz, 2008). One of the earliest theorists to espouse a narrative approach was Kaethe Weingarten (1992), who combined her understanding of narrative theory with feminist analysis of the existing family therapy literature. She correctly suggested that the family therapy literature had excluded the woman's narrative. The development of patriarchy-supporting interventions came from the 1950s, a decade in which U.S. women's lives became constricted by the return of veterans from World War II. In that decade, psychological theory was designed to construct and support the traditional nuclear family in the United States. The theories reflected pre-quantum physics, with linear and graphically portrayed diagrams of family structures. The descriptions were all about lines and angles, just like the decade of the 1950s in the United States. After two world wars and a great depression, the 1950s were seen as time to restore order and usher in a new golden age of American life. Women's lives were squeezed back into the narrowly defined roles of mother and housewife. These early structural family therapists focused on the whole constellation of family members but never really succeeded in spreading "blame" for a child's problems beyond the mother.

Narrative practice as it exists now is described by Michael White in his 2007 book *Maps of Narrative Practice*: "When we sit down together I know that we are embarking on a journey to a destination that cannot be precisely specified, and via routes that cannot be predetermined" (p. 4). This approach is closely correlated with a phenomenological understanding I applied when I was interviewing sisters for my research. The use of travel metaphors has been abundant among narrative therapists; *journeys, adventures, exploration,* and *expeditions* have been commonly used terms. When applied to a feminist reanalysis, this metaphor suggests a recognition that women are in the process of discovery, creation, and mapmaking rather than just following blueprints.

Integration of Research Themes with Narrative Approaches

Four primary interventions or guidelines for intervention have been developed for narrative family therapists. The metaphor was different than the metaphor used in other therapeutic approaches, as these interventions were more anthropologic than definitive. These guidelines are *externalizing conversations, re-authoring conversations, re-membering conversations,* and *definitional ceremonies.* Each struck a harmonizing note when I considered the narratives of the women in the research project. The women I interviewed seemed to understand some of these concepts innately. Because their narratives paralleled the narrative therapy described by White and Nichols, I have integrated their narratives with the narrative therapeutic approaches, looking for evidence that this healing process might have benefited these women, and that healing might have occurred naturally.

Historical Context for Narrative Approaches

Prior to the evolution of these narrative approaches, most problems and issues—or even mental illnesses—were assumed to be part of the family structure or the individual's interior. Narrative approaches suggested that understanding the individual's story would allow her to externalize some of the explanation and "re-author" her own life. From the mid-1960s to the early 1970s, and in concert with the civil rights movements in the United States, the exterior landscape was redefined as the source of many difficulties. The overdiagnosis of paranoia in young American Black men and the overuse of borderline personality with women are two examples of how family therapists began to understand the role of social construction in the diagnosis and treatment of individuals. For women, this corresponded with the feminist movement and a cry for solidarity labeled "sisterhood."

Key Concepts and Integration with Research Themes

Narrative family therapists have been admonished to help their clients by encouraging them to evaluate the conversations that internalize pathology or emotional problems and to transform them into externalizing conversations. If the problems can no longer be attributed to the individual interior, they must be embedded in the cultural context. The theory suggests that this makes change and understanding easier and lessens shame, embarrassment, and fear. For instance, a Latina client may discover that her depression emerged not from a disease within but from a disease without—from a culture or family that did not embrace her or provide her with support. Often a metaphor allows the client to revise and reclaim the problem once it is externalized. In the above example, the metaphor of a homeless child might be used.

Attempts to externalize were evident in the research project. Women used metaphors spontaneously when they discussed the acceptance of a sister relationship based upon blood, or when they needed to accept the process of aging. Perhaps too steeped in their own cultural determination, they were not always able to achieve such externalizing conversations without blaming another individual, as when a sister's stress was blamed on her husband rather than the cultural support for his domination. Once the externalizing conversations are discovered and developed, the re-authoring conversation may occur.

Such conversations are helpful in clinical settings and were occasionally mentioned by women in my study. According to Jerome Bruner (1990), they contain two components: the landscape of action and the landscape of consciousness. The process integrates principles from solution-focused therapy with a narrative storyline. The therapist listens for exceptions to the dominant narrative of the person's life and uses those as a metaphor for exploration into previously undiscovered parts of the self. These exceptions provide new opportunities and new ideas about solutions. This step in the narrative approach requires an adventurous and interested spirit on the part of the client and is based upon dramatic oral traditions. These new stories, when well constructed, fill gaps in clients' conscious understanding of themselves, their families, and their role in the larger context.

To illustrate this concept Bruner described one case involving three sisters: Vivienne, Helen, and Adel. Adel committed suicide after 16 years of abuse, during which she protected the younger Vivienne from the same fate. Vivienne constructed a sense of herself as controlled and confined and was diagnosed with agoraphobia and anorexia. The re-authoring conversation connected her with a more rebellious side of herself that had more hope. This re-authoring occurred partly because of the feedback of her older sister, Helen. The vignette suggested that internal states could be redefined through an intentional storytelling between two people—in this case the new story was constructed by Vivienne, Helen, and the therapist.

Re-authoring conversations occurred naturally between sisters in my study, although they did not always have a therapeutic effect. It seems this healing was the natural outcome for sisters who had engaged in intentional efforts to enlarge their conscious experience. Some did so through music, some through therapy, and others through the experience of watching a sister struggle with her own conscious understanding. For example, by talking with each other, sisters were able to re-author their father's alcoholism as it related to their own lives. Sometimes a woman re-authored her own story with the intention of shedding guilt. She was only able to shift the blame to her sister. Martha did this when describing Opal's lack of concern and care for their mother. Sometimes the women did not even attempt re-authoring; for instance, Laurie could not forgive herself for the fight she had with her sister just before she died. Re-authoring may come naturally to some women who sought more depth and intimacy in the sister connection. For others, re-authoring could be learned or modeled in a therapeutic or naturally healing relationship with another person.

After re-authoring, the therapy moves to re-membering conversations. These conversations expand the person's story through the use of other stories and voices. Bruner gave a vignette involving sisters. He introduced a woman who had survived a suicide attempt to a young man who was suicidal. Her suicide attempt was partially based upon her belief that her sister would be a better mother to her children than she was. This belief allowed her to re-member and redefine her suicide attempt as an act of love rather than self-destruction. A new narrative of her life emerged through that process, one that was not dependent upon self-loathing. Introducing the woman to the suicidal man was an attempt to add another story that allowed the young man to expand his associations to his own story. His identity could be revisioned and parts of it discarded—ostensibly the self-destructive part.

Re-membering conversations are sometimes done thorough the suggestion of films, books, or the voice of directors in the theater who bring a different life to the story of an individual—again expanding the frontiers of the person's identity using a metaphorical landscape (much like amplification does in Jungian analysis). Brunner referred to this as a multi- or dual-voiced conception of the self. Some sisters in my research engaged in this process by comparing their relationships with their sisters to the stories of other women, thus bringing in another voice or set of narratives they could draw upon. One woman defined her family by comparing it to the Cleavers from the 1960s television show *Leave it to Beaver*. These re-membering dialogues added members but did not necessarily alter the relationship; they may have altered the narrative about the relationship. In both of these examples, the sisters were able to understand some of their own personality characteristics by re-membering the wish for a family or sister relationship that was more affectionate, close, and emotional.

Definitional ceremonies have been described as formalized and ritualized ways of claiming the re-membered self. This, too, is a dialogue, but it often occurs with an audience, and the audience frequently includes siblings. Isolated from their ethnocultural group, individuals may need to find new rituals. Bruner mentioned this in terms of the transmigration of Jews following the Holocaust. A similar process has been recommended for lesbian women who have become isolated from their families and spiritual traditions or for immigrants whose families or cultures did not survive. Some documentation of the emotional transition apparent in the re-membering seemed necessary—some tangible presence that the transition occurred. Bruner suggested certificates for children, but today a Facebook page or a video on YouTube might be even more appropriate and public. What is important is the way the ritual is constructed by the individual and by those present. Transformation is witnessed. Each of the three stages of the ceremony requires preparation: the initial telling, the audience retelling, and then the retelling of the retelling. These three steps created an important repetition. An example might be the ritual of a lesbian sister's wedding.

Sisters in the research project defined some rituals that were important. They were transformative experiences, and they were witnessed by others. One particularly poignant example was the birth of a sister's child—an experience that transformed the identity of each sister into those of mother and aunt and changed the connections among the sisters and the father of the child. This ritual also demonstrated how women were affected by retelling. Their ways of knowing, including frozen images that appeared like flash photographs, were described as a process of bringing material to consciousness that transformed the sense of self. The way the women's stories came into consciousness through the initial interview, individual reflection, and the second interview created a process similar to this therapeutic one. The researcher was present as the audience as they told their narratives. Particularly noticeable were the ritualized ways in which questions were asked in each interview. Perhaps this was why almost all of the women commented on how the process of the interview itself changed their view or their conscious understanding of the sister connection. The research process was the audience for their definitional ceremony.

All the primary narrative interventions described by Brunner were present in the research themes: sisters externalized, re-authored, re-membered, and ritualized the relationship herstory and its effects upon them. They defined roles and responsibilities this way, but even more importantly they reflected the narratives that narrative family therapists seek by going deeper to a metaphorical understanding. They brought in other individuals and stories to clarify their own experience and their understanding. Sometimes the process of the research was transformative: giving the women a chance to tell their story led to a significant change in their perception of the relationship with the sister. By emulating the pathways provided by the research participants, narrative family approaches could easily be adapted to a therapeutic exploration of sister identity development and interpersonal growth.

Feminist Approaches to Family

Historical Context for Feminist Approaches

Beginning in the 1970s and continuing to the present, feminist writers and therapists in the Western world have attempted to deconstruct the gender discrimination in family therapy. Primary authors who contributed to this effort include Rachel Hare-Mustin (1978); the women of the Women's Project in Family Therapy, including Marianne Walters, Peggy Papp, Olga Silverstein, and Betty Carter (1988);

and Monica McGoldrick, Carol Anderson, and Froma Walsh, whose work has continued to inform feminist dialogues in this new century. Their early criticisms arose from re-evaluations of Bowen's systemic theory (Bowen, 1978; Kerr & Bowen, 1988). I have considered his concepts related to siblings as a way of understanding the feminist divergence from them.

When Bowen discussed siblings, he considered them individually and wrote primarily about each as the third part of a parental triangle. He suggested that sibling rivalry might actually be enhanced by trying to treat each child equally. Based principally on the work of Toman (1961), who described sibling positions in normal families, Bowen constructed those relationships in a more complex way, considering what occurred when a child in a specific position was the focus of a dysfunctional family's projections. Bowen suggested that a therapist could even understand the personalities of long-dead ancestors through an evaluation of sibling relationships. The process of multigenerational transmission was described as the natural tendency of family dynamics to be repeated from one generation to the next. Informed by modeling, genetics, and birth order, the multigenerational transmission of family issues and interactions was believed to be repeated between siblings over time. Bowen also suggested that the relationships between siblings and their parents might help to diagnose the problems in a family's structure, problems they had essentially inherited through an unconscious process of family communication occurring over many generations.

Bowen's assumptions were partially supported by Sulloway's research (2001), which contextualized the birth order issue in the larger cultural and biological context. His findings suggested that the first-born child becomes a regulator of the cultural rules and defends the status quo, while later children are more likely to be rebellious and identify with the underclass. Bowen has been quoted as saying, "Based upon my research and therapy, I believe that no single piece of data is more important than knowing the sibling position of people in the present and past generations" (Bowen, 1978, p. 385).

Despite the importance that Bowen and Sulloway placed on sibling relationships, their understanding seemed to be hampered by a particularly masculine point of view. Older and younger sisters may not adopt the position they hold in the family and culture in the same ways as brothers do. When the disenfranchisement of many of the world's women is considered, the positions of law enforcer and rebel are not the same. Instead, we can see the way patriarchy confined these roles for women, as in the description of Palestinian sisters or Iranian sisters in Chapter 9. Likewise, the specific power invested in elder sisters is different than that invested in elder brothers for many Southeast Asian or West Asian women.

Feminist critics have argued that women's perspective on family relationships is far from universal. The women of Pakistan and the women of Cuba do not have the same sense of relationships within the family, and not all Pakistani women or Cuban women share the same perspective as the other women in their culture. The traditions and gender roles from these countries provide a starting point but can easily deteriorate into assumptions that are based on cultural stereotypes. Excellent theory requires a reformulation and recognition of individual adoption of cultural values and family prescriptions.

Ideas like those put forward by McGoldrick et al. (1989) fit extremely well with the lack of recognition of the sister relationship and its primary role in family emotional life. However, many female theorists have added to the analysis of women's roles within diverse families. Silverstein (2003) traces that history, mentioning the work of Pinderhughes on African American women; Krestan and Bepko's pioneering efforts about lesbian families, and Boyd-Franklin and Garcia-Preto's in-depth look at Latinas. The most recent works by McGoldrick, Giordano, and Garcia-Preto (2005) and McGoldrick and Hardy (2008) evaluate culture at a new level; they examine individual cultures within many national contexts.

Attempted Annihilation of the Sister Connection

McGoldrick, Anderson, and Walsh (1989) gave credit to their predecessors for writing clearly about feminist theory and specifically sister relationships (Downing, 1988; McNaron, 1985). Citing that literature, they suggested several things that make the sister relationship in the family unique. The length of the connection was significant—likely to be the longest of most women's lives if they live a normal lifespan. Many authors recognized the need to return to the sister relationship as a primary partnership at the end of life. The women in my research who were the eldest lived together and had done so as a result of illness or the death of primary partners—returning to the sister bond late in life. All of these authors related the sister relationship to the definition of closeness. They suggested that the defining characteristic of male relationships in a family may be the way they maintain distance. In contrast to this, the women in my research struggled with both closeness and distance. Indeed, it was the central organizing principle of the structure that emerged from the study. The women longed for closeness, defined it, described its metamorphosis over time, and gave great detail about the events, personalities, and family issues that supported or prevented closeness. However, they also defined distance and discussed the ways that sisters kept distance from one another.

The issue of how engendered cultures—and they are all engendered in some way—have created an "annihilation of the role of sister" (McGoldrick et al., 1989, p. 246) is a common theme among feminist approaches in family therapy. McGoldrick and colleagues suggested that this annihilation must be "countered in the clinical work by validating and encouraging the sister bond" (p. 246). The annihilation by other authors served the specific cultural need for heterosexual attachment and unconsciously or consciously provided a method for ensuring that men can control women. The invalidation of woman–woman relationships of all kinds also made women prefer emotionally intimate connections with men, allowing husbands and male partners to take center stage in family life. In a patriarchal culture, that means they take power and control as well.

The women in my study both supported the power of the patriarchy to annihilate sister relationships and also presented some evidence that the annihilation had not occurred. The fact that many compared their sister relationship with their primary relationship says something. Some found the primary relationship with a husband to be more important and significant in the long run. Others suggested that their husband knew better than to interfere with the sister alliance. One cannot help be reminded of the Irving Berlin song "Sisters" from the classic American movie *White Christmas*: "Lord help the mister who comes between me and my sister; and Lord help the sister who comes between me and my man." While quaint, the expression in the song suggests one form of ambivalence portrayed in the film, as the sister relationship was disrupted by the new relationship with prospective husbands.

Sisters as Event Organizers

Another characteristic of the sister relationship suggested in the literature was the sister's role of keeping the family in touch. Usually sisters plan parties and significant events, invite others into their homes for dinner, and maintain the extended family connections. They also are the emotional processors of most families, discussing the family changes, reactions of individual members, and the ways in which each individual is evaluated or judged in the family. Clearly some women in my study had a sister who filled this role, or they provided it themselves. Sometime teams of sisters worked to keep the family in touch with each other. Often this function was taken over by nieces or daughters as the women aged. However, several mentioned nephews who played that role, so it is not completely engendered.

Engendered Roles in the Family

Feminist theorists also suggest specific roles that are different for sisters and brothers. These include the masculine-achieving or instrumental type; the socially gregarious or popular one; the caretaking mother substitute; and the weak, ill, or socially inept sister. Sisters are most often judged on how well they fulfill the caregiving role. This clearly emerged from my research. Some women made derogatory comments about their sisters' lack of presence at the bedside of an ailing mother. Most, however, felt that sisters were present as caregivers, and they had some unique contributions to provide. Often guilt emerged when a woman felt she was not helping the family as much as a sister was, due to geographic distance or the needs of her own immediate family members. Some sisters had the benefits of traveling with their parents and taking them on "adventures," while others were left with the daily task of maintaining care and continuity. These "Disneyland daughters" filled a unique and appreciated family role but sometimes became the focus of anger and frustration. According to the feminist theorists, brothers are much more likely to be judged based upon their achievement or financial success. While this was not explicitly mentioned by the research participants, women did talk about all of the roles that sisters fulfilled in the family. They also evaluated the relative strengths of a sister in her role and how her personality and talents made the role the right one for her. Comparisons of one sister to another occurred. Some women valued their sisters' achievements; others felt overwhelmed by their sisters' competitiveness.

Differing Perceptions of Sisters and Mothers

Like the women in my study who commented spontaneously on how they perceived their sisters and how they came to understand them, McGoldrick and colleagues mentioned the variety of perceptions that can occur. Sisters can be pushed to extremes, becoming polar opposites, if there are only two of them. One of my participants suggested that the daughters' nicknames reflected the role of one as "goody two shoes" and the other as the bad or rebellious sister. Triangles were likely to form with the mother. Feminist family therapists suggest this may be due to cultural limitations on the mother and her own failed achievements being acted out by her daughters. They also suggest that mothers can restrict their daughters' roles differently based upon specific projections for each.

In this instance, my participants added much to the existing literature, giving details about the nature and multiplicity of the triadic relationship between two or more sisters and their mother. While feminist theory suggests the mother had more control, I did not find that to be true. Over the lifespan, women in my research suggested that any of the three women in a family triad may form a bond with the other two, creating a connection that somehow diminished relationships with the third. Sometimes the bond between sisters excluded the mother. Sometimes the relationship between a wife and husband was compared to a sister's relationship with their mother. Sometimes all three women functioned as a team, excluding male family members, or reacted to sexist family rules levied against the girls.

Understanding Sisters Across Generations

The multigenerational transmission of family roles and experiences has been described as the method by which the next generation learns about family issues, secrets, and experiences that persist from grandparent to parent to child. Considering specific multigenerational transmission for sisters stretched the concept. One set of sisters may develop a relationship that becomes the blueprint for generations of unborn sisters, and they fulfill that blueprint without really having it defined explicitly for them. Such relationships may be based on shared survivor guilt, as it is for some Armenian, Jewish, and Cambodian sisters in recent history. Some may be based on the polarization and diminishment of the sister connection. Other transmissions may be restricted based on the upheaval in a country like Afghanistan, Pakistan, or Iran, where women's opportunities to stay connected to sisters in adult life are severely limited by proscriptions to join a husband's family. In my research project this theme was echoed based on the explicitly expressed desire to have daughters emulate a close sister bond between their mother and aunt, so it was intentionally and behaviorally transmitted to the next generation. Some of the women mentioned the relationship between their mother and her sister as a model for a sister relationship that failed to live up to that standard. Multigenerational transmission does seem to have some specific applications to sisters, both theoretically and subjectively.

Herstory and Family History

The position of a sister in the family may hamper attempts to heal rifts in the sister relationship, according to feminist family therapists. It may be easier for a younger sister to reach across the divide than an older one. An older sister who functioned as a parent may have received a lot of parental projection, making it difficult for her to initiate a healing process between them. Among my research themes were descriptions of many different ways that birth order affected the relationship, but the issue of healing was not specifically related to family position; it was the process of healing or the failure of attempts to heal that were commented on much more than the position of the sister in the family or their previous roles. These attempts to heal may occur at any point on the continuum of the sisters' lives together, from childhood through old age.

McGoldrick (1989) traced the lifespan relationships of sisters, suggesting various typical and not-so-typical outcomes over various periods of life. She suggested that sisters could be rivals or caregivers during childhood, become other-identified during adolescent years, and are competitive and focused on other relationships during their young adulthood. At midlife sisters are likely to bond together in the caregiving of older family members, and they become caregivers for each other in later life. Sometimes the crisis of the last parent's death leads to a temporarily intense intimacy that is not maintained. Toward the end of life, generative sisters provide a stimulus for spiritual growth and reconciliation and provide much-needed companionship.

Several issues specific to ethnic cultures in the United States were suggested by McGoldrick. She mentioned the importance of sisters serving brothers in the Latino and Italian cultures, while Irish and Black communities provide much higher expectations and limited protection for daughters. WASP families attempt to provide equal opportunities for sons and daughters. Also, during adolescence, some cultures, most notably those that recognize the strengths of women, expect there to be consistent connection. According to McGoldrick this proscription is common for Black, Scandinavian, Irish, and Jewish sisters.

All of these stages were reflected in my research and were described by women who were remembering them from an earlier time, as well as women who were immersed in them at the moment. Perhaps this added richness to the notion of how the relationships changed. Some of the women were caught in adolescent identity and intimacy development, with a clear desire to differentiate themselves from their sisters. Yet there was great variability in this. Some of the teenagers in the study appreciated and liked their sisters; some fought continuously. One said they never fought until the day she left for college. Older women looked back on earlier years with maturity and may have minimized the difficult interactions of adolescence and childhood, or they may have used these difficulties to explain the lack of closeness throughout life. McGoldrick explained her life stages for the sister relationship as embedded in functionality. The women gave to that functionality depth, breadth, and variety. For example, differences in identity development that were significant, like those for disabled or lesbian sisters, created a different set of narrative possibilities for these lifespan issues.

Gender and Birth Order

The position of the sister in the birth order of a family seemed to interact with the gender composition of the family. Most authors address only two genders, male and female, so the role of transgendered siblings is not well understood in this literature. The first-born daughter is sometimes given the same importance as a first-born son, but for many families, especially those that are patrilineal, this has not been the case. McGoldrick suggested that oldest sisters are likely to be high achievers, but only in families without brothers. In families with both sons and daughters, sisters are likely to have all of the responsibilities of the eldest child but may not receive encouragement for individual achievement. This is a Western construction. Communal cultures sometimes have both achievement and caretaking requirements for an eldest daughter, as all children's accomplishments benefit the family and clan.

Studies from the 1970s suggested that the high-achieving first-born sister is a product of being an only child or being the eldest in a family without sisters. Traditionally middle sisters are defined in the United States as family mediators— the literal go-between. Sometimes they feel excluded, without a sense of special role or responsibility. Youngest children are viewed as special and may be over-indulged by parents who mourn the end of childbearing. In my study, women connected achievement much more frequently to natural gifts and interests rather than to birth order. The position of first child was more likely to be a defining role when there was only one parent. Then the eldest daughter had specific role responsibilities, but these could be either instrumental or relational responsibilities, depending on the role the single parent took and the complementary roles that were unfilled. Some eldest sisters felt the need to "get out of the way" so the family would have fewer people dependent upon limited resources. Others took on the traditional father role in a female-headed home. So the interaction between gender, birth order, and family composition, coupled with circumstances of class, race, ethnicity, and nationality, seems to be just as important in how the eldest daughter's role is defined. Likewise, second daughters, in both my clinical practice and my research, share the parenting roles with elder sisters and sometimes divide them along instrumental and relational lines.

Some interesting effects on gender identity relate to the number of male and female children in a family. The sister–sister bond may be more intense and intimate than the sister–brother or brother–brother bond, which has been described as more competitive. Oldest sisters are more likely to be accepted as authority figures than oldest brothers, perhaps mimicking the actual role of mothers and fathers in those families. When sisters were in a family that had male children, they tended to be more androgynous, while their brothers became more masculine. The presence of male children seemed to stimulate competitive strivings for achievement and influence in the larger world for both genders. So the birth order, gender composition, and sibling pairings give achievement and instrumentality a different focus in different family constellations.

A special relationship is described between twin sisters. The very close nature of the bond and the lifelong sharing of stages, activities, struggles, and identity development may create unrealistic expectations for partners and mates who try to live up to the twin ideal. These specific interplays between gender of siblings and identity seem to form the margins of my research project—because it was focused on sisters, the influence of brothers was not as deeply presented or perhaps reflected upon during the process.

Recommendations from Feminist Family Therapy

McGoldrick suggested that therapists follow specific recommendations in their work with sisters (and indeed with all siblings).

She encouraged family therapists to pay more attention to the role of sisters in the development of identity and family cohesion. Therapists should be aware of the assumption that sisters become automatic caregivers in the family. As seen in her work and in my research, however, sisters do not always fill this role, and in some ways it has been redundant for them to do so. Women in a family might benefit from attention to their judgment about a sister's caregiving and challenged to see different types of contributions made during family crises. In this way, they may more easily share the pragmatic and emotionally supportive roles needed by the family. Many family therapists just need to be reminded to ask about sister relationships in more detail. The richness of the interviews we recorded came in response to one simple question: "Tell me about your relationship with_____." Many times space is not given to the full exploration of these relationships by clients.

McGoldrick also wanted therapists to meet with groups of sisters together to fully understand the dynamics involved. When I used to work with young teens with anorexia—treating them with a family therapy approach—I almost always had some sessions with the sisters alone. This strengthened their relationship, helped to diminish the labels of weak and strong or ill and healthy sister, and gave them a chance to work together to be emotionally present for one another.

Sisters in connection who share a family—defined by a culture, a nation, and a particular set of ancestors—become part of a family garden. In the garden are irises, roses, and flowering plants that must be tended, and when tended they grow to expand the garden in many directions. The feminist family therapist helps that expansion by digging, dividing, and re-planting in different corners of the garden. Each plant blooms in different ways based upon the light, shadow and moisture received. To some extent, the therapist provides equitable access to these necessary and life-sustaining resources. She examines the clumps of bulbs, clearing them of debris so that the interconnections may be examined, divided, and then transplanted. As a result of this work, new theories are created and the sister relationship is more likely to thrive; better soil provides the existing plants with greater capacity for growth as they are tended, separated, and allowed to flourish. Such a garden has influenced the development of this research project and, I hope, the filtered sunlight from my participants' lives has provided some growth for the garden of feminist theory.

Attachment-Based Family Therapy

The psychological literature has buzzed for the past 20 years with the application of long-existing attachment principles to the understanding of early child development. As those attachments have become better understood, it has become clearer that attachment difficulties may be reconciled later in life by having better relationships with individuals who help to create a sense of secure attachment. This understanding of attachment has been integrated into the family therapy literature by Daniel Hughes (2007), among others. The notion that children might have additional and corrective attachment figures as they age created the possibility that sisters may provide primary attachments in each other's lives. Some of the major concepts and themes of attachment form the basis for a family-based attachment theory by Hughes. I have attempted to describe the integration of these concepts as they might apply to the sister relationship and as they are related to my research findings.

Attachment within the family occurs between parents and children and between partners. It creates a secure base through a combination of mutual intersubjectivity and affect regulation. In the process infants learn that the attachment to a primary parental figure provides a secure base from which to explore the world, giving a balance of autonomy and relationship skills. In attachment-based therapy, the therapist reflects the skills of a good parent, regulating affect and allowing individuality to develop. In this way the affect and meaning of the family is co-created with the therapist and parents, leading the way for the child. The child learns to express herself with a cognitive awareness of why the expression is important. Affect for its own sake is abandoned to better integrate the infant into the life of the family and the larger world. The family therapist who uses an attachment-based approach is expected to participate and to be affected by the family's process. It is not a hands-off approach to therapy or one where the therapist is shielded by becoming a blank screen. Each member of the family has a narrative, combining both affect and cognitive understanding. By retelling those narratives, the individual member may become fully integrated into a secure and cohesive family unit.

Hughes outlined some key differences between this approach and other forms of family therapy. The therapist provides safety for a child, and does this actively, if the parent fails to do so. Therapy occurs in the moment—it does not deal with historical events, but is engaged with the current management and regulation of affect in the room. The child is expected to develop regulation skills through engagement with the therapist and the parents. Children participate fully in the family therapy sessions, but the therapist may step in to speak for them if they could not articulate their own feelings and thoughts well. The therapist has an intersubjective experience, being affected by and responding to the affect in the room in a positive way.

Integration of Key Concepts with Research Themes

The two key concepts of attachment-based therapies seemed to have a great deal of applicability to the sister connection. One is the intersubjective nature of attachment, which Hughes defined as a "fundamental interpersonal activity that occurs in all affectional bonds... interwoven to such an extent that when one speaks of their respective influences, one is often describing the same themes twice" (p. 14). This seemed inherent in the narratives of the women in my research. Interwoven influences, mutual activity and support, the building of security with the sister when security existed nowhere else—these were all themes that emerged from the women's voices. When this type of security has been built, it allows for exploration beyond one's comfort zone—the ability to venture out, to explore, and to understand oneself in the exploration. Some sisters adventured together literally, giving each other the opportunity for new growth while providing the back-and-forth exchange of ideas about joint travel. Many paved the way for new explorations for a younger sister—into high school, choosing college classes, finding their way out of domestic violence, coping with rape, or returning to a secure base following a divorce. One sister's personality shifted so drastically when the security of her environment shifted that she was described as a different person each time she was in a new relationship. Most often these connections were with a destructive mate, which led to her own self-destructiveness. At other times, the women described a family that tried to re-establish a sense of safety and security for an adult niece who was being abused. Sometimes aunts provided security in shared values that differed from those of the mother. In all of these ways, women in a family—besides the primary parent—provided the security of attachment for another.

Hughes outlined two other tasks. The attachment of a child requires that a parent, with help from the therapist, co-regulate the child's emotionality. Minor feelings are encouraged and enhanced; loud outbursts, tantrums, and hysterical crying are managed and contained. Similarly, many supportive women or older sisters in a family provide the soothing required to co-regulate this affect. I remember being at a family gathering with a 2-year-old who would not stop crying. Having had little contact with the child, I took him from my sister-in-law and he immediately calmed down. Why? Was there a novelty that assisted with this co-regulation? Many women have had this experience. I have also witnessed on many occasions an older daughter step in to take her sister and distract her with activities that calm and quiet her.

This co-regulation may depend on the primary parent, but it seems that sisters, aunts, cousins, and friends often play an important role. As the child grows, peers help with this co-regulation. Sisters on the soccer field help each other to manage pain, stress, and sadness related to failure. A sister may help another find the right tone for her role in a class play. Each learns about the regulation of these feelings from the other.

Women participants talked about the shared management of grief, anger, sadness, and discrimination and the mutuality of joy, celebration, birth, and friendship. In attachment-based family therapy these emotions help to create new meaning in the lives of all involved. A child is allowed to develop her own identity just as her parent redefines herself in the role of mother. This early and proximal development is clearly influenced by the emotions of sisters and their management of them. This co-creation may be conscious, as in the sister who vowed to make up for another's bad behavior. But most often it is unconscious, as for sisters who take different paths while learning to love active engagement, with one playing volleyball and the other doing jazz dancing. A family that fails to tolerate difference has failed at intersubjective meaning and development of a coherent sense of the self. That sense of self may not develop or may become insecure. Early security may be undermined by a family's rejection of a lesbian or transgendered sister. In those cases, an accepting sister may be able to restore the secure base and the coherent sense of self that is needed. The literature on lesbian sisters suggests this may be one reason that sisters are often told first. The engaged and integrated sense of the self comes from the family and sister balance of intersubjectivity, co-regulation, and co-creation. With these elements in place, the sense of self remains stable and is allowed to enlarge, with new aspects of the self added over time and integrated by those to whom one is most intimately attached.

Explicit Mention of Sisters in Attachment-Based Family Therapy

In most of Hughes' book, the focus is not on the relationship between sisters; that was not his primary focus. Still, at times he suggested a role for sisters in the development of secure attachment. He gave a clinical example of two sisters, Susan and Rachel, who experienced their mother as favoring one of them. In the dialogue reported, the focus was on Susan and her mother, with little room for the perspective and narrative understanding of Rachel's life. In another of Hughes' cases, the mother's family was described in detail. She and her sister suffered abuse at the hands of four brothers, who were chemically dependent. The narrative followed the mother's escape from that home into a destructive marriage, but once again it focused on her children rather than her sister relationship. Hughes did not explore the strength or resilience of the relationship that helped the client survive the abuse. Several mentions were given to sibling affect regulation. Both aggression and shame were mentioned, but not between sisters—only between brothers, or a brother and a sister. All of these vignettes and case illustrations focused on the parent–child interaction in therapy and the improvement of affect regulation in the creation of new meaning for each client. The focus did not shift to a primary emphasis on the sister connection.

Expansion of Attachment-Based Therapy to Sister Relationships

Attachment-based family therapy with an emphasis on this lifelong connection might be expanded to recognize the important role of sisters. How do sisters play a role in creating and maintaining a secure environment for younger sisters, especially in single-parent families? The newspaper story of the bicultural Belgian and Iranian sisters described in Chapter 9 might be an example. As they lived for 6 months in the Belgian embassy in Tehran, waiting to be allowed to return to their mother, what kind of security and safety was provided by the older, Yasmine, for the younger, Sarah? How did the older sister gain enough strength to escape the house of her father and hail a taxi? Was the security—built on the attachment to their mother—embedded in their relationship with each other and forever changed? Another example from my research is provided by the older sister who taught her younger sister about sex and birth control because her mother could not do it. This information helped to create a new sense of identity for the younger sister. This older sister helped to provide her younger sister with a more informed initiation into the rites of adult experience. A sister may intervene when a mother or father was not present for a young child because of their chemical dependency. Safety and the ability to explore the larger world with a low risk of failure may come from the example of a sister who was successfully navigating it. There seems to be an embedded sense of resilience in the ability to repair sister bonds over the course of a lifetime, thus creating an attachment that could be counted on for safety and security, and one that was expected to be mutual.

The regulation of affect between sisters may be accomplished through a sense of matched or dissonant emotional experience. This could lead to a sense that the sister is too emotional or too controlled. Without the maturity of an adult attachment object, the ability to co-regulate may be compromised for both girls. The absence of the secure attachment may result in feelings of shame or lack of personal grounding in their lives. On the other hand, consistent attachment with the same parent may lay the groundwork for sisters to have excellent co-regulation of each others' emotions. This was expressed clearly in the description of the woman whose mother died of cancer when they were teens, and the role the sister played in helping her to understand her father's affect deregulation during the illness. It is most likely present in single-parent Black and Latina families, where the attachment to the parent is culturally strong but supplemented by co-regulation from an older sister. The sisters in my research who moved in together to provide care for an elderly mother and one sister's husband were another example of that kind of co-regulation of affect continuing into later life.

Meaning was clearly constructed between sisters who reported their relationships to me. Likewise, in the development of many women, the attunement of sisters may mean that they create a shared sense of meaning from their common herstory. They may also develop different traits and characteristics related to individualized meanings within the same developmental context. Two sisters' interests diverged into dentistry and music. Memories and meanings were often quite different for sibling pairs. Many experiences may not be shared in abusive families. The in-group and out-group experience described in Chapter 7 may cause sisters to define the meaning of such trauma in very different ways. Also, major life events or changes in the family structure could unsettle the attachment of one while not affecting the attachment of the other—for instance, if parents divorce while one sister is married but another is a teen still living at home. Age gaps often are responsible for the lack of shared meaning and the differential regulation of affect that accompanies it.

A coherent sense of self emerges from these shared meanings and emotions. Identity is stabilized when secure attachment and affect attunement are combined with intersubjective experiences. However, in many cases a young sister may need or want to shift her identity and to be distant from her sister. A woman who is disabled may have a different sense of security in the world than one who is not. The definitions of self that emanate from this difference may create quite different life meanings. On the other hand, traumatic bonding may lead sisters to similar identity elements. Having watched their mother suffer abuse at the hands of a string of male companions, both sisters may develop their own feminist identity elements.

Recommendations for Attachment-Based Family Therapists

How can attachment-based family therapists be more inclusive of the sister relationship in their work? When attending to the secure attachment generated between a parent and child, it is important to notice the differential effect on siblings. Are some sisters better at affect regulation than others? How and why did that occur? As recommended by McGoldrick, it might help to see the sisters alone in order to see the effect on their sense of emotional security. The use of these conjoint sister sessions may provide a space for the bond between them to enlarge and for them to begin to understand their past differences as rooted in the security of their identity within the family.

Hughes recommends the use of playfulness, acceptance, curiousity, and empathy (PACE) in attachment work with families. To translate those constructs into sister work, the therapist may need to help sisters engage in a playful attitude with each other. Storytelling or myth-making may be ways to stimulate this. Each child could be encouraged to finish the story and explain the outcome to each other. Older sisters may be encouraged to imagine being in each other's position. The therapist might ask how they experience life differently and ask them to explain the other sister's perceptions. What would feel more secure and what would be threatened differently from the sister's side of things? Another technique is to stimulate curiosity between sisters, and also to recognize it when it occurs naturally. Giving sisters an opportunity to describe their first day of high school or college might be an engaging activity. The other could be engaged as a videographer of her sister's experience. It may also be helpful to explore the obvious: you share parents, you share gender, you share friends, you have the same skin color, etc.; what does that create for you together?

Therapists should also help create clear communication about positive feelings and should be careful not to replicate the inequities in the family of origin by favoring one sister over another. They might teach sisters the notion that one person's emotions can be matched by another person. This could be done using puppets for young children and correcting overzealous emotion while encouraging direct expression of feelings. The narrative story of each sister related to important events or just their sense of their own development can be done through any of these creative methods or by using toy figures. Special memories and identifying moments may be completely different for one sister than the other. They may be shocked to discover that they remember things differently, or that an event that is so important to one sister cannot even be retrieved by the other. I remember that when we were about 8, my twin sister and I got bows and arrows as a birthday gift from our parents after attending Y camp and falling in love with archery. One of us put an arrow through the plate-glass window of neighbors who were inside having dinner. Each of us still believes we were the one to shoot the arrow. No one else was present, so the truth of the narrative cannot be established. What is clear was who got blamed. Such a difference in narratives might provide a family therapist with excellent information to manage differential treatment of children in a family and the security that that treatment embodied.

Sometimes sisters revise history to take on each other's special talents or activities as if they were their own. These competitive strivings are also an indication of differentially secure attachment in a family and may arise from the provision of security by the sister who had the talents and completed the activities. Her identity may have become confused with the sister's identity. Memories may be contaminated by the provision of security to a sister at a young age. One sister may become confused about whose memory is being discussed.

Hughes recommended that the therapist should support the family's values and work with values that differ between family members. This includes the importance of negotiating differences between sisters. Some may be more traditional, some more avant-garde. Others may be more experienced while a sister remains naïve. One sister may be male-identified and another may be a feminist. Some may be intensely religious and others without faith in any religious system. In a family with several sisters, two may be more adventurous and the other two may be more fearful. These alignments provide information for the therapist about the secure construction of the sister's identity as a base from which she can explore different ideas about herself and about her world.

In the evaluation of a family's attachment potential, the safety for the parents presumably precedes the safety of the children, the theory being that a parent must be secure to provide secure attachment for a child. Siblings are not considered here, but indeed some sisters seem to find security even if it is not presented to them in the form of their parents. They in turn may provide it to others. If this occurs, the emotionally damaging experience may be compensated by a therapist who provides a corrective emotional experience. Sisters need to be evaluated for their ability to do this as well. Can they match affect or attune to each other? Do they exhibit joint attention? Are their intentions congruent? Most often these are exhibited through emotional, not cognitive, interactions. Do they joke with each other? Can one sister laugh at herself when the other pokes fun? Is metaphor or symbolism used between them? All of these qualities may explain secure attachment when it does not seem to be rooted in the parent–child relationship. Even if it is, doesn't the presence of an age- and gender-matched attachment figure add something unique to the equation?

Conclusions

Family therapy, especially when practiced from a narrative, feminist, or attachment-based paradigm, seems to offer many opportunities for the evaluation and engagement of sisters. In the narrative approach, the stories of sisters provide a window into the working of a family and the differential effects of that family over its lifespan. Narrative approaches may be used to help sisters listen to each others' stories in a retelling, re-authoring, and re-membering of the experience. New family rituals may be established that allow each sister to feel supported in redefining how her own story is constructed. Feminist approaches suggest ways that women can understand and deconstruct the family structure. Instead of assuming a heterosexist or specifically gendered outcome, sisters might help each other to see the ways they are restricted, recreating new narratives for their lives. Such efforts may be extremely useful in helping women to bridge the gap between a previous identity and a new one. Attachment-based family therapists are encouraged to use creative ways to help sisters engage with one another's affect regulation. Attunement between sisters may be a powerful tool in re-establishing a secure attachment and providing new options for moving back out into the world after a crisis or loss. In evaluating all of these approaches, I have mentioned the cross-cultural and diversity applications that could be included.

Any artist will tell you that no work is ever truly finished. When it comes to understanding families and sisters around the world, family therapists and this work demonstrate that we have prepped the cloth and readied the oils but have not yet begun to put brush to canvas.

REFERENCES

Abudabbeh, N. (2005a). Arab families: An overview. In M. McGoldrick, J. Giordano, and N. Garcia-Preto (Eds.), *Ethnicity and family therapy* (pp. 423–436). New York: Guilford Press.

Abudabbeh, N. (2005b). Palestinian families. In M. McGoldrick, J. Giordano, and N. Garcia-Preto (Eds.), *Ethnicity and family therapy* (pp. 487–499). New York: Guilford Press.

Almeida, R. (2005). Asian Indian families: An overview. In M. McGoldrick, J. Giordano, and N. Garcia-Preto (Eds.), *Ethnicity and family therapy* (pp. 377–394). New York: Guilford Press.

Angelou, M. (n.d.). BrainyQuote.com. Retrieved October 31, 2010, from BrainyQuote.com Web site: http://www.brainyquote.com/quotes/quotes/m/mayaangelo133956.html.

Anthony, Susan B. (Speech delivered on October 16, 1902). As cited in I. H. Harper (1908). *Life and work of Susan B. Anthony: Including public addresses, her own letters and many from her contemporaries during fifty years, Ida Husted Harper* (Vol. 3). Indianapolis, IN: Bowen-Merrill.

Anzieu, D. (1986). *Freud's self analysis*. New York: International Universities Press.

Apter, T. (2007). *Sister knot: Why we fight why we're jealous and why we'll love each other no matter what*. New York: W. W. Norton and Company, Inc.

Backman, M. (1988, July 7). Keeping women in mind. *Profile*, 9–10.

Balsam, R. H. (1988). On being good: The internalized sibling with examples from late adolescent analyses. *Psychoanalytic Inquirer*, 8, 66–87.

Bank, S. P., and Kahn, M. D. (1982a). Intense sibling loyalties. In M. E. Lamb and B. Sutton-Smith (Eds.), *Sibling relationships: Their nature and significance across the lifespan* (pp. 257–265). Hillsdale, NJ: Lawrence Erlbaum Associates, Inc.

Bank, S. P., and Kahn, M. D. (1982b). *The sibling bond*. New York: Basic Books.

Becerra, R. M. (1998). The Mexican American family. In C. H. Mindel, R. W. Habenstein, and R. Wright Jr. (Eds.), *Ethnic families in America: Patterns and variations* (4th ed.). Upper Saddle River, NJ: Prentice Hall.

British Broadcasting Company. (2003, Dec 3). Belgian girls plead to leave Iran. One-minute world news. Accessed from http://news/bbc.co.uk/2/hi/middle_east/3288757.stm

British Broadcasting Company. (2004, May 6). Belgian sisters return from Iran. One-minute world news. Accessed from http://news/bbc.co.uk/2/hi/europe/3689095.stm

Beeler, J., and DiProva, V. (1999). Family adjustment following disclosure of homosexuality by a member: Themes discerned in narrative accounts. *Journal of Marital & Family Therapy*, 25, 443–459.

Belenky, M. F., Clinchy, B. M., Goldberger, N. R., and Tarule, J. M. (1986). *Women's ways of knowing: The development of self, voice, and mind*. New York: Basic Books.

Bernal, G., and Shapiro, E. (2005). Cuban families. In M. McGoldrick, J. Giordano, and N. Garcia-Preto (Eds.), *Ethnicity and family therapy* (pp. 202–215). New York: Guilford Press.

Berzon, B. (2004). *Permanent partners: Building gay and lesbian relationships that last*. New York: Plume.

Billig, M. (1999). *Freudian repression: Conversation creating the unconscious*. New York: Cambridge University Press.

Bowen, M. (1978). *Family therapy in clinical practice*. New York: Jason Aronson.

Boyd-Franklin, N. (2006). *The Black families in therapy: Understanding the African American experience*. New York: Guilford Press.

Braunbeck, H. G. (1993). "Fly little sister, fly": Sister relationship and identity in three contemporary German stories. In J. S. Mink and J. D. Ward (Eds.), *The significance of sibling relationships in literature*. Bowling Green, OH: Bowling Green State University Popular Press.

Breuer, J., and Freud, S. (1957). Case 5: Fraulein Elisabeth von R. In J. Strachey (Ed. & Trans.), *Studies on hysteria* (pp. 135–181). New York: Basic Books, Inc.

Bruner, J. (1990). *Acts of meaning*. Cambridge, MA: Harvard University Press.

Bryant, A. S., and Demian. (1994). Relationship characteristics of gay and lesbian couples: Findings from a national survey. Journal of Gay and Lesbian Social Services, 1, 101–117.

Burns, T., Hendricks, D., Jones, J., Marinaccio, S. A. II, McEveety, S., Papa, T. J., Segel, D., Shepherd, J., (producers), and Nowrasteh, C. (director) (2009). *The Stoning of Soraya M.* [Motion picture]. USA: Fallen Films.

Chatham, P. M. (1985). *Treatment of the borderline personality*. New York: Jason Aronson, Inc.

Chesler, P. (2001). *Woman's inhumanity to woman*. New York: Thunder's Mouth Press.

Colaizzi, P. F. (1978). Psychological research as the phenomenologist views it. In R. S. Valle and M. King (Eds.), *Existential phenomenological alternatives for psychology* (pp. 48–71). New York: Oxford University Press.

Crosbie-Burnett, M., Foster, T. L., Murray, C. I., and Bowen, G. L. (1996). Gays' and lesbians' families of origin: A social-cognitive-behavioral model of adjustment. *Family Relations*, 45, 397–403.

Cross, W. E. Jr. (1971). Negro-to-Black conversion experience. Toward a psychology of Black liberation. *Black World*,20(9), 13–27.

Cupelloni, P. (2000). Anna and her father. *Journal of European Psychoanalysis*, 10–11, 111–133.

Delaney, F. (2008). *Ireland: A novel*. New York: Harper Paperbacks.

De Master, C., and Giordano, M. D. (2005). Dutch families. In M. McGoldrick, J. Giordano, and N. Garcia-Preto (Eds.), *Ethnicity and family therapy* (pp. 534–544). New York: Guilford Press.

Department of Homeland Security, Office of Immigration Statistics (2008). *Yearbook of immigration statistics, 2007*. National Technical Information Service, Washington, DC.

de Saint-Exupéry, A. (2000). *The little prince* (R. Howard, Trans.). New York: Houghton, Mifflin, Harcourt. (Original work published in 1943.).

Downing, C. (1988). Psyche's sisters: Reimagining the meaning of sisterhood. San Francisco, CA: Harper and Row.

English, M. (1996). Transgenerational homophobia in the family: A personal narrative. In P. Cupelloni (2000), Anna and her father. *Journal of European Psychoanalysis*,10–11, 111–133.

Eriksen, S., and Gerstel, N. (2002). A labor of love or labor itself: Care work among adult brothers and sisters. *Journal of Family Issues*, 23, 836–856.

Faderman, L., with Xiong, G. (1999). *I begin my life all over: The Hmong and the American immigrant experience*. Boston: Beacon Press.

Fairbairn, W. R. D. (1952). *Psychoanalytic studies of the personality*. New York: Routledge.

First, E. (2000). Freud's sisters: A fantasia on a photograph. *Studies in Gender and Sexuality*, 1, 309–324.

Fischer, R. (1989). Psychotherapy of the narcissistic personality disorder. In J. F. Masterson and R. Klein (Eds.), *Disorders of the self. New therapeutic horizons: The Masterson approach* (pp. 69–89). Philadelphia, PA: Brunner/Mazel, Inc.

Fishel, E. (1979). *Sisters: Love and rivalry inside the family and beyond*. New York: Morrow Publishing.

Freud, S. (1962). *Three essays on the theory of sexuality* (J. Strachey, Ed. & Trans.). New York: Basic Books. (Original work published in 1905.)

Freud, S. (1964). *New introductory lectures on psycho-analysis* (The College Edition; J. Strachey, Ed. & Trans.). New York: W. W. Norton & Company, Inc. (Original work published in 1933.)

Freud, S. (1975). *Two case histories* (The Standard Edition of the Complete Psychological Works of Sigmund Freud, vol. 10, J. Strachey, Ed. & Trans., in collaboration with A. Freud, assisted by A. Strachey & A. Tyson). London: The Hogarth Press and the Institute of Psycho-analysis. (Original work published in 1909.)

Freud, S. (1977). *New introductory lectures on psycho-analysis* (The Pelican Freud Library Edition of the Complete Psychological Works of Sigmund Freud, vol. 1, J. Strachey, Ed. & Trans.). New York: W. W. Norton & Company, Inc. (Original work published in 1933.).

Freundlich, M., and Lieberthal, J. K. (2000) The gathering of the first generation of adult Korean adoptees: Adoptees' perceptions of international adoption. From http://www.adoptioninstitute.org/proed/korfindings.html (accessed 6/23/09).

Friedan, B. (1974). *The feminine mystique*. New York: Dell Publishing Co. (Original work published in 1963.)

Garcia-Preto, N. (2003). Latino families: An overview. In M. McGoldrick, J. Giordano, and N. Garcia-Preto (Eds.), *Ethnicity and family therapy* (pp. 153–165). New York: Guilford Press.

Gartrell, N., Hamilton, J., Banks, A., Mosbacher, D., Reed, N., Sparks, C. H., and Bishop, H. (1996). The national lesbian family study: 1. Interviews with prospective mothers. *American Journal of Orthopsychiatry, 66,* 272–281.

Gergen, K. J. (1985). *The social construction of the person* (edited with K. E. Davis). New York: Springer-Verlag.

Gibran, K. (1994). *The Vision: Reflections on the way of the soul* (J. R. I. Cole, trans.) London: Penguin Books. (Original work published in 1961.)

Gilligan, C. (1993). *In a different voice: Psychological theory and women's development* (6th edition). Cambridge, MA: Harvard University Press. (Originally published in 1982.)

Ginsburg, L. M. (2003). An unexamined post-script to the demise of Sigmund Freud's seduction theory: A spurious reification or prescient second thoughts? *International Forum of Psychoanalysis,12,* 265–272.

Giordano, J., McGoldrick, M., and Klages, J. G. (2005). Italian families. In M. McGoldrick, J. Giordano, and N. Garcia-Preto (Eds.), *Ethnicity and family therapy* (pp. 616–628). New York: Guilford Press.

Giorgi, A. (1985). *Phenomenology and psychological research*. Pittsburgh: Duquesne University Press.

Graybill, E. (1985, Feb. 28). Memories of the 1915 massacre are still vivid for two Bloomington Armenian survivors. *The Daily Pantagraph.* Accessed from http://www.chgs.umn.edu/Histories/turkishArmenian/memories.html

Green, R. (2000). Lesbians, gay men, and their parents: A critique of LaSala and the prevailing clinical "wisdom." *Family Process, 39,* 257–266.

Greenberg, J. S., Seltzer, M. M., Orsmond, G. L., and Krauss, M. W. (1999). Siblings of adults with mental illness or mental retardation: Current involvement and expectation of future caregiving. *Psychiatric Services, 50,* 1214–1219.

Grubb, D. (1989). Three bipolar women: the boundary between bipolar disorders and disorders of the self. In J. F. Masterson and R. Klein (Eds.), *Disorders of the self. New therapeutic horizons: The Masterson approach* (pp. 411–426). Philadelphia: Brunner/Mazel, Inc.

Hancock, K. A. (1995). Psychotherapy with lesbians and gay men. In A. R. D'Augelli and C. J. Patterson (Eds.), *Lesbian, gay, and bisexual identities over the lifespan* (pp. 398–432). New York: Oxford University Press, Inc.

Hare, B. R. (1985). Stability and change in self-perception and achievement among Black adolescents: A longitudinal study. *Journal of Black Psychology,* 11(2), 29–42.

Hare-Mustin, R. T. (1978). A feminist approach to family therapy. *Family Process,* 17 (2), 181–194.

Helms, J. E. (1995). An update of Helms' White and people of color racial identity models. In J. G. Ponterotto, J. M. Casas, L. A. Suzuki, and C. M. Alexander (Eds.), *Handbook of multicultural counseling* (pp. 181–198). Thousand Oaks, CA: Sage.

Hines, P. M., and Boyd-Franklin, N. (2003). African American families. In M. McGoldrick, J. Giordano, and N. Garcia-Preto (Eds.), *Ethnicity and family therapy* (pp. 87–101). New York: Guilford Press.

Houzel, D. (2001). The "nest of babies" fantasy. *Journal of Child Psychotherapy, 27,* 125–138.

Hughes, D. (2007). Attachment focused family therapy. New York: W.W. Norton.

Hughes, J. M. (1989). *Reshaping the psychoanalytic domain: The work of Melanie Klein, W.R.D. Fairbairn, and D.W. Winnicott.* Berkeley: University of California Press, Ltd.

Irigaray, L. (1985). *The sex that is not one* (C. Porter & C. Burke, Trans.). Ithaca, NY: Cornell University Press. (Original work published in 1977.)

Jalali, B. (2005). Iranian families. In M. McGoldrick, J. Giordano, and N Garcia-Preto (Eds.), *Ethnicity and family therapy* (pp. 451–467). New York: Guilford Press.

Jones, C., and Shorter-Gooden, K. (2003). *Shifting: The double lives of black women in America.* New York: HarperCollins Publishers.

Jordan, J. V. (1991a). Empathy and self-boundaries. In J. V. Jordan, A. G. Kaplan, J. B. Miller, and I. P. Stiver (Eds.), *Women's growth in connection: Writings from the Stone Center* (pp. 67–80). New York: Guilford Press.

Jordan, J. V. (1991b). Empathy, mutuality, and therapeutic change: Clinical implications of a relational model. In J. V. Jordan, A. G. Kaplan, J. B. Miller, and I. P. Stiver (Eds.), *Women's growth in connection: Writings from the Stone Center* (pp. 283–290). New York: Guilford Press.

Jordan, J. V. (1991c). The meaning of mutuality. In J. V. Jordan, A. G. Kaplan, J. B. Miller, and I. P. Stiver (Eds.), *Women's growth in connection: Writings from the Stone Center* (pp. 81–96). New York: Guilford Press.

Jordan, J. V. (1997a). Clarity in connection: Empathic knowing, desire, and sexuality. In J. V. Jordan (Ed.), *Women's growth in diversity: More writings from the Stone Center* (pp. 50–73). New York: Guilford Press.

Jordan, J. V. (1997b). A relational perspective for understanding women's development. In J. V. Jordan (Ed.), *Women's growth in diversity: More writings from the Stone Center* (pp. 9–24). New York: Guilford Press.

Jordan, J. V., Kaplan, A. G., Miller, J. B., and Stiver, I. P. (1991). *Women's growth in connection: Writings from the Stone Center.* New York: Guilford Press.

Jordan, J. V., Surrey, J. L., and Kaplan, A. G. (1991). Women and empathy: Implications for psychological development and psychotherapy. In J. V. Jordan, A. G. Kaplan, J. B. Miller, and I. P. Stiver (Eds.), *Women's growth in connection: Writings from the Stone Center.* (pp. 27–50). New York: Guilford Press.

Joseph, S. (1994). Brother/sister relationships: Connectivity, love, and power in the reproduction of patriarchy. *American Ethnologist, 21,* 50–73.

Kamya, H. (2003). African immigrant families. In M. McGoldrick, J. Giordano, and N. Garcia-Preto (Eds.), *Ethnicity and family therapy* (pp. 101–116). New York: Guilford Press.

Kanuha, V. K. (2005). Na Ohana: Native Hawaiian families. In M. McGoldrick, J. Giordano, and N, Garcia-Preto (Eds.), *Ethnicity and family therapy* (pp. 64–77). New York: Guilford Press.

Kaschak, E. (1992). *Engendered lives.* New York: Basic Books.

Kernberg, O. F. (1976). *Object-relations theory and clinical psychoanalysis.* New York: Jason Aronson.

Kernberg, O. F. (1980). *Internal world and external reality: Object relations theory applied.* New York: Jason Aronson.

Kerr, M. E., and Bowen, M. (1988). *Family evaluation: An approach based on Bowen theory.* New York: W. W. Norton.

Killian, K. D., and Agathangelou, A. M. (2005). Greek families. In M. McGoldrick, J. Giordano, and N. Garcia-Preto (Eds.), *Ethnicity and family therapy* (pp. 573–585). New York: Guilford Press.

Kim, B. C., and Ryu, E. (2005). Korean families. In M. McGoldrick, J. Giordano, and N. Garcia-Preto (Eds.), *Ethnicity and family therapy* (pp. 349–362). New York: Guilford Press.

Kim, Y. (2006). Current perspectives on clinical studies of PTSD in Japan. In N. Kato, M. Kawata, and R. K. Pitman (Eds.), *PTSD: Brain mechanisms and clinical implications.* Tokyo: Springer Japan.

King, M. L., Jr. (June 6, 1961). Commencement address at Lincoln University of the Commonwealth of Pennsylvania.

Klein, M. (1969). The psychoanalysis of children. New York: Humanities Press.

Klein, M. (1975). *The psycho-analysis of children: Writings of Melanie Klein* (The Works of Melanie Klein, vol. 1). New York: Delacorte Press/Random House. (Original work published in 1932.)

Klein, M. (1984a). Love, guilt and reparation. In R. E. Money-Kyrle (Ed.), *The writings of Melanie Klein (Vol. 1): Love, guilt, and reparation, and other works, 1921–1945* (pp. 306–343). New York: The Free Press. (Original work published in 1937.)

Klein, M. (1984b). Mourning and its relation to manic-depressive states. In R. E. Money-Kyrle (Ed.), *The writings of Melanie Klein (Vol. 1): Love, guilt, and reparation, and other works 1921–1945* (pp. 344–369). New York: The Free Press. (Original work published in 1940.).

Klein, M. (1984c). Envy and gratitude. In R. E. Money-Kyrle (Ed.), *The writings of Melanie Klein (Vol. 3): Envy and gratitude and other works, 1946–1963* (pp. 176–235). New York: The Free Press. (Original work published in 1957.).

Klein, R. (1995). Intrapsychic structures. In J. F. Masterson and R. Klein (Eds.), *Disorders of the self. New therapeutic horizons: The Masterson approach* (pp. 45–68). Philadelphia: Brunner/Mazel, Inc.

Kohut, H. (1971). *The analysis of the self: A systematic approach to the psychoanalytic treatment of narcissistic personality disorders* (The Psychoanalytic Study of the Child Monograph No. 4). Madison, CT: International Universities Press.

Krull, M. (1986). *Freud and his father.* New York: Norton.

Kusnir, D. (2005). Salvadoran families. In M. McGoldrick, J. Giordano, and N. Garcia-Preto (Eds.), *Ethnicity and family therapy* (pp. 256–268). New York: Guilford Press.

Laird, J. (1996). Invisible ties: Lesbians and their families of origin. In J. Laird and R. J. Green (Eds.), *Lesbians and gays in couples and families: A handbook for psychotherapy* (pp. 89–122). San Francisco: Jossey-Bass Publishers, Inc.

Laird, J., and Green, R. J. (Eds.) (1996). *Lesbians and gays in couples and families: A handbook for psychotherapy* (pp. 15–27). San Francisco: Jossey-Bass Publishers, Inc.

Laszloffy, T. A. (2005). Hungarian families. In M. McGoldrick, J. Giordano, and N. Garcia-Preto (Eds.), *Ethnicity and family therapy* (pp. 586–594). New York: Guilford Press.

Lee, E., and Mock, M. R. (2005). Chinese families. In M. McGoldrick, J. Giordano, and N. Garcia-Preto (Eds.), *Ethnicity and family therapy* (pp. 302–318). New York: Guilford Press.

Leung, P. K., and Boehnlein, J. K. (2005). Vietnamese families. In M. McGoldrick, J. Giordano, and N. Garcia-Preto (Eds.), *Ethnicity and family therapy* (pp. 363–375). New York: Guilford Press.

Lothane, Z. (2007). Sigmund Freud and Minna Bernays: Primal curiosity, primal scenes, primal fantasies-and prevarication. *Psychoanalytic Psychology, 24,* 487–495.

Luria, Z. (1981, October). Presentation at the Dedication Conference, Stone Center, Wellesley College, Wellesley, MA.

Maguire, G. (1999). *Confessions of an ugly step-sister: A novel.* New York: William Morrow.

Mandelbaum, A. (1980). Family Characteristics of Patients with borderline and narcissistic personality disorder. *Bulletin of the Menninger Clinic, 44*(2) 201–211.

Masterson, J. F. (1988). *The search for the real self.* New York: The Free Press.

Masterson, J. F., and Klein, R. (1989). *Psychotherapy of the disordered self: The Masterson approach.* Philadelphia: Brunner/Mazel, Inc.

Matsumoto, V. (1984). Japanese American women during World War II. *Frontiers: A Journal of Women's Studies, 8,* 6–14.

McGill, D. W., and Pearce, J. K. (2005). American families and English ancestors from the colonial era: Anglo Americans. In M. McGoldrick, J. Giordano, and N. Garcia-Preto (Eds.), *Ethnicity and family therapy* (pp. 520–533). New York: Guilford Press.

McGoldrick, M. (1989). Sisters. In M. McGoldrick, C. M. Anderson, and F. Walsh (Eds.), *Women in families: A framework for family therapy* (pp. 244–266). New York: W. W. Norton & Company, Inc.

McGoldrick, M. (2005). Irish families. In M. McGoldrick, J. Giordano, and N. Garcia-Preto (Eds.), *Ethnicity and family therapy* (pp. 595–615). New York: Guilford Press.

McGoldrick, M., Anderson, C. M., and Walsh, F. (Eds.) (1989). *Women in families: A framework for family therapy* (pp. 244–266). New York: W. W. Norton & Company, Inc.

McGoldrick, M., Giordano, J., and Garcia-Preto, N. (Eds.). (2005). *Ethnicity and family therapy.* New York: Guilford Press.

McGoldrick, M. and Hardy, K. V. (Eds.) (2008) *Re-Visioning Family Therapy, (Second Edition): Race, Culture, and Gender in Clinical Practice.* New York: Guilford Press.

McGraw, L., and Walker, A. J. (2007). Meanings of sisterhood and developmental disability: Narratives from White nondisabled sisters. *Journal of Family Issues, 28,* 474–500.

McHale, S. M., and Pawletko, T. M. (1992). Differential treatment of siblings in two family contexts. *Child Development, 63,* 68–81.

McHale, S. M., Sloan, J., and Simeonsson, R. J. (1986). Sibling relationships of children with autistic, mentally retarded, and non-handicapped brothers and sisters. *Journal of Autism and Developmental Disorders, 16,* 399–413.

McKenzie-Pollock, L. (2005). Cambodian families. In M. McGoldrick, J. Giordano, and N. Garcia-Preto (Eds.), *Ethnicity and family therapy* (pp. 290–301). New York: Guilford Press.

McNaron, T. A. H. (1985). *The sister bond: A feminist view of a timeless connection* (The Athene Series). New York: Pergamon Press.

Miller, J. B. (1973a). Introduction. In J. B. Miller (Ed.), *Psychoanalysis and women* (pp. xi–xxv). Maryland: Penguin Books Ltd.

Miller, J. B. (1973b). Conclusion. In J. B. Miller (Ed.), *Psychoanalysis and women* (pp. 375–406). Maryland: Penguin Books Ltd.

Miller, J. B. (1991). The development of women's sense of self. In J. V. Jordan, A. G. Kaplan, J. B. Miller, and I. P. Stiver (Eds.), *Women's growth in connection: Writings from the Stone Center.* (pp. 11–26). New York: Guilford Press.

Miller, J. B., Jordan, J. V., Kaplan, A. G., Stiver, I. P., and Surrey, J. L. (1997). Some misconceptions and reconceptions of a relational approach. In J. V. Jordan (Ed.), *Women's growth in diversity: More writings from the Stone Center* (pp. 25–49). New York: Guilford Press.

Miller, J. B., and Stiver, I. P. (1997). *The healing connection: How women form relationships in therapy and in life.* Boston: Beacon Press.

Minces, J., and Pallis, M. (1982). *The house of obedience: Women in Arab society.* New York: Palgrave Macmillan.

Mindel, C., Habenstein, R., and Wright, R. (1998). *Ethnic families in America: Patterns and variations.* Upper Saddle River, NJ: Prentice-Hall.

Miner, V. (1988). *All good women.* New York: Crown Publishing Inc.

Mize, L., and Pinjala, A. (2002). Sisterhood narratives: Opportunities in connections. *Journal of Feminist Family Therapy, 14,* 21–51.

Mize, L. K., Turell, S. and Meier, J. (2004). Sexual orientation and the sister relationship: Conversations and opportunities. *Journal of Feminist Family Therapy, 16,* 1–19.

Moon, S. (1998) Begetting the nation: The androcentric discourse of national history and tradition in South Korea. In E. H. Kim and C. Chungmoo (Eds.), *Dangerous women: Gender and Korean nationalism.* New York: Routledge.

Moore, B. L. (2003). *Serving our country: Japanese-American women in the military during World War II.* New Jersey: Rutgers University Press.

Moustakas, C. E. (1994). *Phenomenological research methods.* Thousand Oaks, CA: SAGE Publications, Inc.

Murray, N. (2008). Review: Palestine: peace not apartheid by Jimmy Carter, and The Ethnic cleansing of Palestine by Ilan Pappe. *Race and Class, 49,* 97.

Nath, S. (2005). Pakistani families. In M. McGoldrick, J. Giordano, and N. Garcia-Preto (Eds.), *Ethnicity and family therapy* (pp. 407–421). New York: Guilford Press.

New York Times (2008, Feb.). Pakistan again arrests Musharraf opponent. Accessed from http://www.nytimes.com/2008/02/03/world/asia/03iht-pakistan.1.9695008.html

Nichols, M. P., and Schwartz, R. C. (2008). *Family therapy: Concepts and methods* (8ᵗʰ ed.). Boston: Allyn & Bacon.

Noor, M. J. (2004). Daughters of Eve: Violence against women in Pakistan. Unpublished Master's Thesis. Massachusetts Institute of Technology. Accessed from: http://dspace.mit.edu/handle/1721.1/7582

Okri, B. (1999) *Mental fight: An anti-spell for the 21st century.* London: Phoenix House.

Orsmond, G. I., and Seltzer, M. M. (2000). Brothers and sisters of adults with mental retardation: Gendered nature of the relationship. *American Journal on Mental Retardation, 105,* 486–507.

Oswald, R. F. (2000). Family and friendship relationships after young women come out as bisexual or lesbian. *Journal of Homosexuality*, *38*, 65–83.

Oswald, R. F. (2002). Resilience within the family networks of lesbians and gay men: Intentionality and redefinition. *Journal of Marriage and Family* ,*64*, 374–383.

Overseas Adopted Koreans (2010). *Statistics on Overseas Koreans*. Accessed on March 29, 2010 from http://oaks.korean.net/n_stastics/StatsProg.jsp?bID=13004.

Patterson, C. J., Hurt, S., and Mason, C. D. (1998). Families of the lesbian baby boom: Children's contact with grandparents and other adults. *American Journal of Orthopsychiatry*, *68*, 390–399.

Piercy, F. P., Soekandar, A., Limansubroto, C. D. M., and Davis, S. D. (2005). Indonesian families. In M. McGoldrick, J. Giordano, & N. Garcia-Preto (Eds.), *Ethnicity and family therapy* (pp. 332–338). New York: Guilford Press.

Pilisuk, M., and Hillier Parks, S. (1986). *The healing web: Social networks and human survival*. Boston: University Press of New England.

Pruchno, R. A., Patrick, J. H., and Burant, C. J. (1996). Aging women and their children with chronic disabilities: Perceptions of sibling involvement and effects on well-being. *Family Relations*, *45*, 318–326.

Quindlen, A. (1994). *One true thing*. New York: Random House.

Ramu, G. N. (2006). *Brothers and sisters in India: A study of urban adult siblings*. Toronto: University of Toronto Press.

Raphael, S. M., and Meyer, M. K. (2000). Family support patterns for midlife lesbians: Recollections of a lesbian couple 1971–1997. *Journal of Gay & Lesbian Social Services*, *11*, 139–151.

Ricci, J. (2005 August 7,). "Day of remembrance" brings prayers of peace. *Los Angeles Times*.

Ricoeur, P. (1995). Reflections on a new ethos for Europe. *Philosophy and Social Criticism*, *21* (5–6), 3–13.

Robb, C. (2006). *This changes everything: The relational revolution in psychology*. New York: Farrar, Straus, & Giroux.

Root, M. P. P. (2005). Filipino families. In M. McGoldrick, J. Giordano, and N. Garcia-Preto (Eds.), *Ethnicity and family therapy* (pp. 319–331). New York: Guilford Press.

Rosen, W. B. (1997). The integration of sexuality: Lesbians and their mothers. In J. V. Jordan (Ed.), *Women's growth in diversity: More writings from the Stone Center* (pp. 239–259). New York: Guilford Press.

Rostosky, S., Korfhage, B., Duhigg, J., Stern, A., Bennett, L., and Riggle, E. (2004). Same-sex couple perceptions of family support: A consensual qualitative study. *Family Process*, *43*, 43–58.

Sánchez-Ayéndez, M. (1998) The Puerto Rican family. In C. Mindel, R. Habenstein, and R. Wright (Eds.), *Ethnic families in America: Patterns and variations*. Upper Saddle River, NJ: Prentice-Hall.

Scarf-Merrell, S. (1997). *The Accidental bond: How siblings influence adult relationships*. New York, NY: Ballantine Books.

Senapati, R., and Hayes, A. (1988). Sibling relationships of handicapped children: A review of conceptual and methodological issues. *International Journal of Behavioral Development*, *11*, 89–115.

Sherwin-White, S. (2007). Freud on brothers and sisters: A neglected topic. *Journal of Child Psychotherapy*, *33*, 4–20.

Shibusawa, T. (2005). Japanese families. In M. McGoldrick, J. Giordano, and N. Garcia-Preto (Eds.), *Ethnicity and family therapy* (pp. 339–348). New York: Guilford Press.

Silverstein, L.B. (2003). Classic texts and early critiques. In L.B. Silverstein and T.J. Goodrich (Eds.), *Feminist family therapy: Empowerment in social context*. Washington, DC: American Psychological Association Books.

Stalker, K., and Connors, C. (2003). Children's perceptions of their disabled siblings: "She's different but it's normal for us." *Children & Society*, *18*, 218–230.

Stark, V. (2007). *My sister, my self*. New York: McGraw-Hill.

Stevens, E. P. (1973). Marianismo: The other side of machismo in Latin America. In A. Pescatello (Ed.), *Female and male in Latin America: Essays*. Pittsburgh: University of Pittsburgh Press.

Stiver, I. P. (1991a). Beyond the Oedipus complex: Mothers and daughters. In J. V. Jordan, A. G. Kaplan, J. B. Miller, and I. P. Stiver (Eds.), *Women's growth in connection: Writings from the Stone Center*. New York: Guilford Press. (Original published in 1986.).

Stiver, I. P. (1991b). The meaning of care. In J. V. Jordan, A. G. Kaplan, J. B. Miller, and I. P. Stiver (Eds.), *Women's growth in connection: Writings from the Stone Center*. (pp. 250–267). New York: Guilford Press.

Stiver, I. P. (1997). A relational approach to therapeutic impasses. In J. V. Jordan (Ed.), *Women's growth in diversity: More writings from the Stone Center* (pp. 288–310). New York: Guilford Press.

Stiver, I. P., and Miller, J. B. (1997). From depression to sadness in women's psychotherapy. In J. V. Jordan (Ed.), *Women's growth in diversity: More writings from the Stone Center* (pp. 217–238). New York: Guilford Press.

Straka, R. (2003, Feb.). The violence of Hmong gangs and the crime of rape. *FBI Law Enforcement Bulletin*. Retrieved from http://findarticles.com/p/articles/mi_m2194/is_2_72/ai_98253655/pg_2/

Suárez, Z. (1998) The Cuban-American family. In C. Mindel, R. Habenstein, and R. Wright (Eds.), *Ethnic families in America: Patterns and variations*. Upper Saddle River, NJ: Prentice-Hall.

Sulloway, F. J. (2001). Birth order, sibling competition and human behavior. In H. R. Holcomb III (Ed.), *Conceptual challenges in evolutionary psychology: Innovative research strategies*. Dordrect & Boston: Kluwer Academic Publisher.

Surrey, J. L. (1991a). Relationship and empowerment. In J. V. Jordan, A. G. Kaplan, J. B. Miller, and I. P. Stiver (Eds.), *Women's growth in connection: Writings from the Stone Center* (pp. 152–180). New York: Guilford Press.

Surrey, J. L. (1991b). The self-in-relation: A theory of women's development. In J. V. Jordan, A. G. Kaplan, J. B. Miller, & I. P. Stiver (Eds.), *Women's growth in connection: Writings from the Stone Center* (pp. 51–66). New York: Guilford Press.

Tharp, M. (2009, June 6). Five Hmong sisters get five degrees. *Merced SunStar*. Retrieved from http://mercedsunstar.com/115/story/886066.html.

Thompson, C. (1973). Cultural pressures in the psychology of women. In J. B. Miller (Ed.), *Psychoanalysis and women*. New York: Brunner-Mazel and Penguin Books. (Original work published in 1942.)

Thoreau, H. D. (1906). *The journal of Henry D. Thoreau, Vol. 1*. Princeton, NJ: Princeton University Press.

Toman, W. (1961). *Family constellation*. New York: Springer Publishing Company.

Turner, C. W. (1997). Clinical applications of the Stone Center theoretical approach to minority women. In J. V. Jordan (Ed.), *Women's growth in diversity: More writings from the Stone Center* (pp. 74–90). New York: Guilford Press.

Ugarriza, D. N. (2006). Social support unique to African American mothers. *Journal of African American Studies, 10*, 19–31.

Ung, L. (2005). *Lucky child: A daughter of Cambodia reunites with the sister she left behind*. New York: HarperCollins Publishers Inc.

Vang, C. T. (2004). Hmong-American K-12 students and the academic skills needed for a college education: A review of the existing literature. *Hmong Studies Journal,5*, 2–31.

Vivona, J. M. (2007). Sibling differentiation, identity development, and the lateral dimension of psychic life. *Journal of the American Psychoanalytic Association,55*, 1191–1215.

Voorpostel, M., van der Lippe,T., Dykstra, P. A., and Flap H. (2007). Similar or different? The importance of similarities and differences for support between siblings. *Journal of Family Issues, 28*, 1026–1053.

Waters, M., Carter, B., Papp, P., Silverstein, S. (1988) *The invisible web: Gender patterns in family relations*. New York, NY: Guilford.

Weingarten, K. (1992). A consideration of intimate and non-intimate interactions in therapy. *Family Process., 31(1)*, 45–59.

Wei Xing Zhu, L. L., and Hesketh, T. (2009) China's excess males, sex selective abortion, and one child policy: Analysis of data from 2005 national inter-census survey. *British Medical Journal*, (338), 920–923.

White, M. (2007). *Maps of narrative practice*. New York: W. W. Norton & Company, Inc.

Winawer, H., and Wetzel, N. A. (2005). German families. In M. McGoldrick, J. Giordano, & N. Garcia-Preto (Eds.), *Ethnicity and family therapy* (pp. 555–572). New York: Guilford Press.

Winnicott, D. W. (1977). *The Piggle: An account of the psychoanalytic treatment of a little girl*. Maryland: Penguin Books Ltd.

Winnicott, D. W. (1987). *Babies and their mothers*. Massachusetts: Addison-Wesley Publishing Company, Inc.

Woo, E. (2006, August 4). Jean Baker Miller, 78; Changed psychological views of women. *The Los Angeles Times* [online newspaper] B8. Available at: http://articles.latimes.com/2006/aug/04/local/me-miller4

INDEX

ability, xvi, 94–95, 97. *See also* talents
abortion, 54, 108
  in China, 240
  Cuban Americans and, 234
abuse
  age difference and, 186
  depression and, 341
  mother-daughter-sister interaction and, 72, 82
  Pakistanis and, 255–56
  protectiveness and, 138
abusive relationships, 104
academic achievement, 190
  Chinese Americans and, 239
  self-sister comparisons and, 200
achievement
  Chinese Americans and, 239
  family, 94–95
  Japanese Americans and, 242
activities, 207
adaptations
  ethnic identity and, 278–79
  family, 95–96
admiration, 44, 131–34
adolescence
  Black sisterhood and, 227
  communication in, 125
  disclosure of sexual orientation and, 218
  guilt, 162
  lifespan themes from, 314–15
  pregnancy in, 227
  protectiveness in, 38
  role models in, 225–26
adoption
  within Black community, 229–30
  of Chinese females, 240
  informal, 229–30
  in-groups and, 282
  Korean, 243
  by lesbians, 288

separation and, 286
adultery, stoning and, 260–61
adulthood
  lifespan themes from, 315–16
  relational capacity changes in, 328–29
advice, 114
  mutual influence and, 138–39
affection, 134
  age spacing and, 186
  sibling bonds and, 12
affect regulation, 362–63, 366
affirmations, 45
African Americans. *See also* Black sisterhood
  caregiving among, 278
  differentiation in, 331
  parenting diffusion among, 283
  prejudice against, 225
  racism and, 227–28
  role models, 284
African ancestry, 224–30
age
  caregiving between sisters and, 216
  closeness and, 78–79
  identity and, 52
  spacing, 183–86
age difference, 50–51
  admiration and, 133–34
  brothers and, 92–93
  communication and, 43, 123
  conflict avoidance and, 150
  among Cuban Americans, 235
  effects of, 183–86
  family structure and, 91
  identity and, 179
  Korean Americans and, 243
  lack of mutuality and, 130
  object relations theory and, 308
  protectiveness and, 136–37
  role models and, 51, 185

Cambodian Americans, 247–48
care, mutual, 128
career choice
  contexts and, 196
  identity and, 52
  influence of illness on, 172
  self-sister comparisons and, 203–4
  sibling rivalry and, 149–50
career stressors, 45
caregiving
  Black sisterhood and, 229–30
  sisters with disabilities and, 215
  Irish Americans and, 265
  roles, 223
  between sisters, 216
  with sisters of difference, 277–78
caretaking, 74–78, 223
  by brothers, 215
  in crises, 104
  family roles and, 196
  geographic distance and, 76–78
  mother-daughter-sister interaction and, 76–78
  mutual, 129–30
  protectiveness and, 135–36
  serious illness and, 166–67
  sharing of, 174–75
Carter, Betty, 354–55
Castro, Fidel, 234
categories, xiv
Catholicism, 263
  Cuban Americans and, 234
  Irish, 264
  Roman, 269–70
celebrations, 100
  reactions to, 116–17
Central Americans, 237–38
character traits
  differences in, 190–91
  personality type and, 189
  self-sister comparisons and, 205
  shared, 188
  unshared, 189
Chatham, Patricia M., 24–25
Chesler, Phyllis, 13
childbirth, 39, 45, 117–18. *See also* birth
childcare, by sisters, 101–2
childhood
  conflicts, 141–42
  death in family in, 175
  disability, 212
  gender issues in, 191–92
  guilt, 162
  illness, 169
  infantile aggression in, 303
  lifespan themes from, 313–14
  pain, 88–89
  protectiveness in, 135
  sibling rivalry in, 150

childish antics, 153–54
childlessness, 115–16
child-mother-father dynamic, 5
children
  comparing, 118–19
  co-regulating, 364
  favorite, 197
  of lesbian parents, 222
  middle, 181
  number of, 113
  only, 19
  parentified, 225
  sister relationship and, 316
  therapy, 14
  as topic of communication, 124
  youngest, 181–82
Chinese Americans, 238–40
chores, 92
Christians, 207–8
  Arab, 257
Civil War, 286–87
clitoral stimulation, 11–12
closeness, 40–41, 42–43
  in the absence of
    partners, 103
  age difference and, 185
  age spacing and, 51
  anticipation and, 121
  artificial, 122
  bias affecting, 285–88
  changing perceptions and, 89
  family, 89
  geographic distance and, 164
  lack of, 89–90, 332
  measuring, 120–23
  to mothers, 78–79
  physical presence and, 120–21
  reaction to interviews and, 61–62
  to sisters, 78–79
  sustained, by cultural
    traditions, 287
  between twins, 122–23
clusters, xiv
cognitive-behavior therapy, 291
colonization, 251
comadre roles, 234
commonality, 201–2
communication, 43–44, 123–27, 339
  conflict resolution and, 146–47
  lack of, 124–25
  methods of, 124
  mutuality and, 129
  nonverbal, 44, 124
  open, 130
  patterns, within families, 126
  of positive feeling, 367
  sibling rivalry and, 153
  topics of, 124

healing, 47–50, 120
  loss and, 163–78
  mother-daughter-sister relationship and, 330
  self, 176–78
  of sister relationship, 176–78
  after sister's death, 176
  after trauma, 170–71
The Healing Connection (Miller & Stiver), 27
health
  care, 165–68
  contexts and, 196
  identity and, 52
  issues, 48
hembrismo, 236
hermeneutic analysis, 211, 271, 293
heroine worship, 184
herstory, 36–42, 65
  family history and, 359–60
  identity and, 52
  oral, 34, 58–59
  self-sister comparisons and, 202
Hindus, 252–55
history. *See* herstory
Hmong Americans, 249–50
  gangs of, 273
  gender roles of, 284
holidays, 161–62
homesickness, 164–65
homework, 115
homicidal impulses, 46, 313
homophobia, 218, 220
homosexuality. *See also* sexual orientation
  Klein, Melanie, and, 17
  in Netherlands, 266
  self-sister comparisons and, 202
  among siblings, 10
  stigma management and, 219
honesty, 66, 123, 125
  lack of, 153
honor killing, 261
ho'oponopono, 251
hormones
  fluctuation, 206
  kinship from, 302–3
  physiology and, 53
hospitalizations, 168
Hughes, Daniel, 362
Hungary, 269
hurtful behavior, 68–70
husbands, 101–2. *See also* partners
  conflict with, 113
  death of, 174
  gender bias and, 193
  sisters-in-law and, 39
  support from, 173
hymen reconstruction, 261

idealism, 291
identity, 179. *See also* ethnic identity

Antigone and, 296
co-creation of, 364
comparison of, 290
derived from differences, 278–79
development, 361
dichotomous, 310
disabilities and, 214
disparity of, 211–12
diverse sisters' lives and, 272–75
factual information and, 52–53, 207–8
Fairbairn and, 19
family roles and, 198
female relational, 331
gender, 51, 325
gender issues and, 191–93
intimacy v., xv–xvi
national, loss of, 225
positive introjects and, 311
self-sister comparisons and, 200–205
separate talents and, 193–94
separation of, 187–88
shared, 195, 272
time and, 50–52
illness. *See also* mental illness
  childhood, 169
  influence of, on career choice, 172
  protectiveness and, 135–36
  serious, 166–67
immersion/emersion, 228
immigration
  African, 225
  Arab, 257
  Asian Indian, 254
  Cambodian, 247–48
  Central American, 237–38
  Chinese, 238–39
  Cuban, 233–34
  effects of, 289–90
  family dissolution and, 245
  family role changes and, 285
  Filipino, 251–52
  government limitations on, 239, 241
  Hmong, 249
  Korean, 243
  Mexican, 231
  Pakistani, 256
  Palestinian, 262
  Puerto Rican, 235
  reform, 242
  separation caused by, 286
  Vietnamese, 246
impasse, 346–48
incest, 7–8
  confronting, 171–72
  Klein, Melanie, and, 16
  protectiveness and, 137–38
independence
  disabilities, 215
  of Greek American sisters, 268